CORPORATIONS AND THE PRIVILEGE AGAINST SELF-INCRIMINATION

This book asks whether the well-established privilege against self-incrimination applies to corporations, whether it should, and if so, to what extent. It provides research and theory on fair trial rights of corporations as defendants that is currently lacking from existing research. The research is conducted along two lines: firstly, the book analyses the origin, ratio and scope of the privilege against self-incrimination from a European perspective as well as from the perspectives of three selected national systems (Belgium, England and Wales and the United States of America). It covers the established CJEU case law in competition cases, the rulings in *DB v Consob* and *Adler Real Estate* and addresses Directive (EU) 2016/343. Secondly, it encompasses both theoretical and practical considerations, such as the relevance of privilege in relation to pre-existing documents, internal investigations and the applicability of the privilege against self-incrimination in different types of cases. It will appeal to scholars of EU criminal law, but also to white-collar and competition practitioners.

Volume 18 in the series Hart Studies in European Criminal Law

Hart Studies in European Criminal Law

Series Editors: Professor Katalin Ligeti, University of Luxembourg;
Professor Valsamis Mitsilegas, Queen Mary University of London;
Professor Anne Weyembergh, Brussels Free University

Since the Lisbon Treaty, European criminal law has become an increasingly important field of research and debate. Working with the European Criminal Law Academic Network (ECLAN), the series will publish works of the highest intellectual rigour and cutting edge scholarship which will be required reading for all European criminal lawyers.

The series is happy to consider both edited and single authored titles. The series defines 'European' and 'criminal law' in the broadest sense, so books on European criminal law, justice and policy will be considered. The series also welcomes books which offer different methodological approaches.

Volume 1: *EU Criminal Law after Lisbon: Rights, Trust and the Transformation of Justice in Europe*
Valsamis Mitsilegas

Volume 2: *Challenges in the Field of Economic and Financial Crime in Europe and the US*
Edited by Vanessa Franssen and Katalin Ligeti

Volume 3: *Chasing Criminal Money: Challenges and Perspectives On Asset Recovery in the EU*
Edited by Katalin Ligeti and Michele Simonato

Volume 4: *Limits to EU Powers: A Case Study of EU Regulatory Criminal Law*
Jacob Öberg

Volume 5: *The Needed Balances in EU Criminal Law: Past, Present and Future*
Edited by Chloé Brière and Anne Weyembergh

Volume 6: *Redefining Organised Crime: A Challenge for the European Union?*
Edited by Stefania Carnevale, Serena Forlati and Orsetta Giolo

Volume 7: *White Collar Crime: A Comparative Perspective*
Edited by Katalin Ligeti and Stanislaw Tosza

Volume 8: *Criminal Liability of Managers in Europe: Punishing Excessive Risk*
Stanisław Tosza

Volume 9: *The European Union and Deprivation of Liberty: A Legislative and Judicial Analysis from the Perspective of the Individual*
Leandro Mancano

Volume 10: *The Legitimacy of EU Criminal Law*
Irene Wieczorek

Volume 11: *The Fight Against Impunity in EU Law*
Edited by Luisa Marin and Stefano Montaldo

Volume 12: *Controlling Immigration Through Criminal Law: European and Comparative Perspectives on 'Crimmigration'*
Edited by Gian Luigi Gatta, Valsamis Mitsilegas, and Stefano Zirulia

Volume 13: *The Principle of Mutual Trust in EU Criminal Law*
Auke Willems

Volume 14: *Surveillance and Privacy in the Digital Age: European, Transatlantic and Global Perspectives*
Edited by Valsamis Mitsilegas and Niovi Vavoula

Volume 15: *The External Dimension of the EU's Policy against Trafficking in Human Beings*
Chloé Brière

Volume 16: *Criminal and Quasi-criminal Enforcement Mechanisms in Europe: Origins, Concepts, Future*
Edited by Vanessa Franssen and Christopher Harding

Volume 17: *Data protection, Migration and Border Control: The GDPR, the Law Enforcement Directive and Beyond*
Teresa Quintel

Volume 18: *Corporations and the Privilege against Self-Incrimination*
Stijn Lamberigts

Corporations and the Privilege against Self-Incrimination

Stijn Lamberigts

•HART•
OXFORD • LONDON • NEW YORK • NEW DELHI • SYDNEY

HART PUBLISHING

Bloomsbury Publishing Plc

Kemp House, Chawley Park, Cumnor Hill, Oxford, OX2 9PH, UK

1385 Broadway, New York, NY 10018, USA

29 Earlsfort Terrace, Dublin 2, Ireland

HART PUBLISHING, the Hart/Stag logo, BLOOMSBURY and the Diana logo are trademarks of Bloomsbury Publishing Plc

First published in Great Britain 2022

A catalogue record for this book is available from the British Library.

A catalogue record for this book is available from the Library of Congress.

Library of Congress Control Number: 2022944908

ISBN: HB: 978-1-50995-331-8
ePDF: 978-1-50995-333-2
ePub: 978-1-50995-332-5

Typeset by Compuscript Ltd, Shannon

To find out more about our authors and books visit www.hartpublishing.co.uk. Here you will find extracts, author information, details of forthcoming events and the option to sign up for our newsletters.

ACKNOWLEDGEMENTS

This book has been in the making for several years. During this process, I have benefited from the support, feedback and guidance of many, to whom I would like to express my deepest gratitude.

First and foremost, I would like to thank Professor Katalin Ligeti and Professor Frank Verbruggen. Professor Ligeti encouraged me to write my PhD thesis, which has resulted in this book. I remain forever indebted for her support and constructive advice, and the countless opportunities that furthered my academic and personal development. I have very much appreciated Professor Verbruggen's insightful feedback and his warm welcome at the KU Leuven's Institute of Criminal Law.

My work has greatly benefited from Professor Vanessa Franssen's committed guidance during the writing of my thesis.

I express my gratitude to Professor Koen Lenaerts, Professor John AE Vervaele and Professor Jörg Gerkrath for their valuable feedback.

I have greatly appreciated the opportunities and facilities provided to me by the University of Luxembourg – in particular, by the Faculty of Law, Economics and Finance and the Doctoral School of Law – as well as by the KU Leuven.

I would like to acknowledge the help and advice of all the academic experts and practitioners. I particularly recognise the invaluable assistance of Professor Sarah Sun Beale, Professor Samuel W Buell and Professor John R Spencer during my research stays at Duke University and the University of Cambridge.

I would like to thank Hart Publishing and the different individuals involved for the assistance provided to me.

I am deeply grateful for the support of my friends and of my current and former colleagues during the writing process of this book.

I cannot begin to express my thanks to my family, in particular to my parents and grandparents. I dedicate this book to them.

CONTENTS

LIST OF ABBREVIATIONS

AG	advocate general
AHR	ad hoc representative
CC	Belgian Criminal Code
CCL	corporate criminal liability
CCP	Belgian Code of Criminal Procedure
CCVSL	Belgian Criminal Code for Violations of Social Law
CEA	Civil Evidence Act 1968
CED	Collective Entity Doctrine
CEL	Belgian Code of Economic Law
CEO	chief executive officer
CFR	Charter of Fundamental Rights of the European Union
CFTC	Commodity Futures Trading Commission
CJ	Court of Justice
CJA	Criminal Justice Act 1987
CJEU	Court of Justice of the European Union
CJPOA	Criminal Justice and Public Order Act 1994
CMCHA	Corporate Manslaughter and Corporate Homicide Act 2007
CoA	Court of Appeal
CoC	Belgian Court of Cassation
CoE	Council of Europe
ConsC	Belgian Constitutional Court
CPS	Crown Prosecution Service
DB	Deutsche Bank
DOJ	Department of Justice

DPA	Deferred Prosecution Agreement
DTI	Department of Trade and Industry
EC	European Commission
ECHR	European Convention on Human Rights
ECtHR	European Court of Human Rights
EP	European Parliament
EPA	Environmental Protection Act 1990
EPPO	European Public Prosecutor's Office
E&W	England and Wales
FBI	Federal Bureau of Investigation
FiC	First instance Court
FSMA	Belgian Financial Services and Markets Authority
GC	General Court
GCEA	General Customs and Excise Act
IP	intellectual property
ISP	internet service provider
ITC	Income Tax Code 1992
JM	Justice Manual (previously the United States Attorneys' Manual)
LLP	Limited Liability Partnership
MS	Member State
NPA	Non-Prosecution Agreement
OLAF	European Anti-Fraud Office
PA	personal assistant
PACE	Police and Criminal Evidence Act 1984
POI	presumption of innocence
POI Directive	Directive (EU) 2016/343 of the European Parliament and of the Council of 9 March 2016 on the strengthening of certain aspects of the POI and of the right to be present at trial in criminal proceedings

PSI, privilege	privilege against self-incrimination
PT	Preliminary Title
RIPA	Regulation of Investigatory Powers Act 2000
RRD	Required Records Doctrine
SEC	Securities and Exchange Commission
SCOTUS	The Supreme Court of the United States of America
SOCPA	Serious Organised Crime and Police Act 2005
SFO	Serious Fraud Office
TFEU	Treaty on the Functioning of the European Union
TEU	Treaty on European Union
UKHL	UK House of Lords
UKSC	UK Supreme Court

TABLE OF CASES

European Union

Court of Justice

General Court

Opinions

Council of Europe

European Court of Human Rights

European Commission of Human Rights

Belgian Case Law[1]

[1] Case law of the CoC can be consulted at https://juportal.be/zoekmachine/zoekformulier and https://justitie.belgium.be/nl/rechterlijke_orde/hoven_en_rechtbanken/hof_van_cassatie/documenten/arresten_van_cassatie. Case law of the ConsC can be consulted at www.const-court.be/nl/search/judgment.

English Case Law

US Case Law

TABLE OF LEGISLATION

European Union

Treaties and EU Charter

Secondary Legislation

Regulations

Directives

Other Documents

Council of Europe

Conventions and Protocols

International Conventions

National Legislation

Belgium

Legislation

Other Documents

E&W

Legislation

Other Documents

USA

Legislation

Other Documents

Other Sources

1

Introduction

I. Corporate Offenders and Procedural Safeguards

In the aftermath of the collapse of Lehman Brothers, Belgian consumers complained to the Economic Inspection Service, because of the sale of structured products of Lehman Brothers by Citibank Belgium. That service and later also the Belgian prosecution service required Citibank Belgium and the head of its legal service to provide internal documents under threat of a *sensu stricto* criminal sanction. This case raises several questions: is the individual involved entitled to invoke the PSI to refuse the production of the documents sought? Does it matter whether these documents belong to the corporation or not? Can the corporation refuse to produce the internal documents? If so, who should express the corporation's wish to exercise the PSI? In the end, a CoA ruled that requiring the handing over of these documents under threat of a criminal sanction infringed both the individual's and the bank's PSI.[1]

Corporations play an important role in modern society. Correspondingly (and unsurprisingly), CCL has been introduced in many countries to combat corporate wrongdoing.[2] The extensive research and theory on the substantive criteria of such liability are, however, not paralleled by commensurate research into the fair trial rights of corporations as criminal defendants.[3]

Corporations in general, and multinational corporations in particular, have acquired substantial significance to the economy and socio-economic power. At the same time, they frequently engage hazardously with their staff, for instance at a construction site, and the general public.[4] The impact and the transnational

[1] CoA Brussels 21 May 2012, [2012] Dr pén entr 143. The CoC confirmed the relevant part of the CoA ruling: CoC 19 June 2013, P.12.1150.F. It has meanwhile confirmed that a suspect cannot be compelled to provide evidence that proves the charges made against him and he can thus not be punished for not communicating information which will expose him: CoC 20 November 2018, P.18.0688.N. In another ruling the Court found that a suspect cannot be punished for his failure to participate in the investigation: CoC 31 May 2017, P.17.0388.N.

[2] According to Vermeulen et al, only five EU MSs had not introduced CCL: G Vermeulen et al, *Liability of Legal Persons for Offences in the EU* (Maklu, 2012) 31.

[3] On this topic, M Pieth and R Ivory, 'Emergence and Convergence: Corporate Criminal Liability Principles in Overview' in M Pieth and R Ivory (eds), *Corporate Criminal Liability – Emergence, Convergence, and Risk* (Springer, 2011) 38–48.

[4] A Pinto and M Evans, *Corporate Criminal Liability*, 4th edn (Sweet & Maxwell, 2021) 4.

nature of corporate activities often confront states with the limits of their ability to regulate and control them within traditional state boundaries. This weakness becomes even more obvious when states deal with large multinationals, conglomerates or groups of multiple legal entities operating in different countries worldwide, which can restructure or relocate activities to other countries. At the same time, having corporate operations in multiple jurisdictions is challenging for the corporation too: for example, it may have a PSI in one country, whereas in another jurisdiction it may have a compelled cooperation duty in relation to the same information. Similarly, a corporation may, in addition to the numerous questions that pop up due to any takeover, face additional challenging questions when it takes over a corporation abroad that is under investigation: can it claim any PSI in relation to those activities?

Corporations, regardless of their size and structure, can and do commit different types of offences. Often these offences are covered by economic or financial criminal law, but the range of potential offences is much broader. Faced with this reality, the call for and use of CCL have increased over the past few decades, leading in continental Europe to the gradual supplementing or even superseding of the initial approach based on (punitive) administrative law.[5] CCL has raised many questions, from both a theoretical and a practical point of view. To what extent can corporations be held criminally liable for offences requiring *mens rea*? How should one conduct criminal proceedings against corporations? To what extent do corporations benefit from procedural safeguards that were historically conceived for human beings? States worldwide have adopted different approaches to such questions. Some systems base CCL on a model of vicarious liability, whereas others favour an anthropomorphic model.[6] Some states accepted the very idea of CCL quite early on, while others only did so a few years ago.[7] Yet others are still reluctant to accept it. The debate on CCL usually centres on the questions of how criminal liability can be attributed to a corporation and which sanctions can be imposed upon it. Procedural questions, such as how corporations should be tried and what specific measures can be taken during such trials, are often given less attention.

The applicability of fair trial rights, such as the PSI, to corporations is not self-evident because of their specific features. Several states have extended fair trial rights to corporations without a fundamental debate. Taking into account the

[5] This increased attention for CCL is equally matched by a growing literature on the topic: S Adam, N Colette-Basecqz and M Nihoul, *La responsabilité pénale des personnes morales en Europe* (die Keure, 2008); D Brodowski et al (eds), *Regulating Corporate Criminal Liability* (Springer, 2014); J Gobert and AM Pascal, *European Developments in Corporate Criminal Liability* (Routledge, 2011); Pieth and Ivory, *Corporate Criminal Liability* (n 3); Pinto and Evans (n 4); D Stoitchkova, *Towards Corporate Liability in International Criminal Law* (Intersentia, 2010); Vermeulen et al (n 2).

[6] Anthropomorphic in the sense that corporations are to the largest extent possible treated like individuals.

[7] D Roef, 'Corporate Criminal Liability' in J Keiler and D Roef (eds), *Comparative Concepts of Criminal Law*, 3rd edn (Intersentia, 2019) 334–35. For example, in Luxembourg CCL was only introduced in 2010 by an Act of Parliament of 3 March 2010.

specific characteristics of corporations, one may nevertheless wonder whether corporations should be granted fair trial rights in the same way as individuals.[8]

So far, the ECtHR has unambiguously accepted the overall applicability of the right to a fair trial to corporations,[9] albeit without always paying close attention to the differences between corporations and individuals.[10] However, the Court has not yet,[11] in relation to corporations, dealt in depth with each specific right such as the PSI. Whereas certain other fair trial rights, such as access to a court,[12] can be applied to corporations in a rather similar way as to individuals, this seems, at first sight, less obvious for the PSI, which is often connected to the protection of *human beings* against physical and psychological coercion. The CJEU, too, has already ruled that certain provisions of the CFR[13] are applicable to corporations.[14] Nonetheless, a great deal of its case law on fair trial rights of corporations has been generated by the field of EU competition law.[15] In this field, there are indeed various cases where the CJEU has explicitly ruled on the question of fair trial

[8] On the principle of equality, see s III below.

[9] *Dombo Beheer BV v the Netherlands* App no 14448/88 (ECtHR, 27 October 1993) para 35; *Produkcija Plus Storitveno Podjetje DOO v Slovenia* App no 47072/15 (ECtHR, 23 October 2018) para 60; *SA-Capital Oy v Finland* App no 5556/10 (ECtHR, 14 February 2019); B Tilleman and N Van Damme, *Proceshandelingen van en tegen rechtspersonen* (die Keure, 2020) 351. The Slovenian case addressed a fine for obstruction of inspection. In proceedings regarding an administrative fine for obstruction of an inspection, the corporation challenged the finding that such an obstruction had taken place. No hearing had taken place, nor were witnesses heard. The ECtHR found a violation of the rights of the corporation under Art 6 §1 ECHR. The ECtHR awarded €52,500 in compensation (50% of the obstruction fine). The ECtHR has also accepted other fundamental rights' applicability to legal persons, eg *Atima Limited v Ukraine* App no 56714/11 (ECtHR, 20 May 2021) (Art 1, Protocol no 1).

[10] *Dupuis and Others v France* App no 1914/02 (ECtHR, 7 June 2007); *Paykar Yev Haghtanak Ltd v Armenia* App no 21638/03 (ECtHR, 20 September 2007); *Baroul Partner-A v Moldova* App no 39815/07 (ECtHR, 16 July 2009). See also P Gilliaux, *Droit(s) européen(s) à un procès équitable* (Bruylant, 2012) 73; PHPHMC van Kempen, 'The Recognition of Legal Persons in International Human Rights Instruments: Protection Against, and Through, Criminal Justice?' in Pieth and Ivory, *Corporate Criminal Liability* (n 3) 373.

[11] The European Commission of Human Rights has accepted that corporations can rely on the POI: *Zegwaard and Segwaard BV v The Netherlands* App no 26493/95 (ECHR, 9 September 1998). The ECtHR, too, has accepted that entitlement: *Aannemersbedrijf Gebroeders Van Leeuwen BV* App no 32602/96 (ECtHR, 25 January 2000) para 1; *Vastberga Taxi Aktiebolag and Vulic v Sweden* App no 36985/97 (ECtHR, 23 July 2002) para 122. The Court's finding in *SA-Capital Oy* (n 9) that the complaint under Art 6(2) ECHR was inadmissible was unrelated to the fact that the applicant was a corporation: paras 106–10.

[12] *Julius Kloiber Schlachthof GmbH and Others v Austria* App nos 21565/07, 21575/07 and 21580/07 (ECtHR, 4 April 2013) para 33.

[13] Since the entry into force of the Lisbon Treaty on 1 December 2009, the Charter has according to Art 6(1) TEU the same legal value as the treaties.

[14] Case C-279/09 *DEB v Bundesrepublik Deutschland* ECLI:EU:C:2010:811; Case C-418/11 *Texdata Software GmbH* ECLI:EU:C:2013:588, paras 72 and 73; Case C-74/14 *'Eturas' UAB and Others v Lietuvos Republikos Konkurencijos taryba* ECLI:EU:C:2016:42, para 38. See also P Oliver, 'Case C-279/09, DEB v Germany, Judgment of the European Court of Justice (Second Chamber) of 22 December 2010' (2011) 48 *CML Rev* 2023.

[15] Case C-301/04 P *Commission v SGL Carbon AG* ECLI:EU:C:2006:432; Case C-466/19 P *Qualcomm and Qualcomm v Commission* ECLI:EU:C:2021:76; Case T-112/98 *Mannesmannröhren-Werke AG v Commission* ECLI:EU:T:2001:61. On that topic, see T Bombois, *La protection des droits fondamentaux des enterprises en droit européen répressif de la concurrence* (Larcier, 2012).

rights of undertakings.[16] As far as the PSI is concerned, those cases go back to the 1980s.[17] Therefore, even though the CJEU has regularly refused to recognise EU competition law fines as criminal in nature,[18] this case law offers an interesting source of information regarding the privilege of corporations. The 2016 POI Directive addresses the PSI, yet legal persons are excluded from its scope.

II. Corporations, Punitive Cases and the Privilege against Self-Incrimination

The notion of 'corporation', for the purpose of this book, refers to entities exercising economic activities and having a separate legal personality that sets them apart from their shareholders.[19] Legal personality implies the existence of separate assets and liabilities.[20] This notion is to be preferred over other terms such as 'undertaking',[21] as the existence of a separate legal identity is in principle the defining criterion for the attribution of rights. Preference is given to the term 'corporation' instead of 'legal person' as the latter concept is particularly broad. For example, it would also include public legal persons, such as (regional) governments, which were or are immune from punitive liability. Non-profit associations also fulfil the requirement of a separate legal identity.[22] Admittedly, non-profit associations do not aim to make profit and many of them do not exercise economic activities in the same way as corporations. At the same time, issues such as who can represent the legal entity also arise when police officers seek to interview a non-profit association. Therefore, the findings of this book will often be relevant for those entities as well.

[16] With regard to the POI: Case C-199/92 P *Hüls AG v Commission* ECLI:EU:C:1999:358, paras 149–50; Case C-89/11 P *E.ON Energie AG v Commission* ECLI:EU:C:2012:738, para 73; *'Eturas'* (n 14) para 38; L Ortiz Blanco and K Jörgens, 'The institutional Framework' in L Ortiz Blanco (ed), *EU Competition Procedure*, 4th edn (Oxford University Press, 2022) 33.

[17] Recently the CJEU has addressed the PSI in relation to a natural person: Case C-481/19 *DB v Consob* ECLI:EU:C:2021:84; Case C-546/18 *FN and Others v Übernahmekommission* ECLI:EU:C:2021:711.

[18] A Kalintiri, *Evidence Standards in EU Competition Enforcement – The EU Approach* (Hart Publishing, 2019) 26–28. The CJEU, in its ruling in Case C-501/11 P *Schindler Holding Ltd and Others v Commission* ECLI:EU:C:2013:522, para 33, has taken note of the *Menarini* ruling of the ECtHR.

[19] On this topic, see V Franssen, 'European Sentencing Principles for Corporations' (DPhil Thesis, KU Leuven, 2013) 1–3.

[20] H Braeckmans and R Houben, *Handboek vennootschapsrecht* (Intersentia, 2020) 22.

[21] This concept is commonly used in the field of EU competition law: A Jones and B Sufrin, *EU Competition Law*, 6th edn (Oxford University Press, 2016) 116–37.

[22] Prior to legislative changes in 2018 regarding the criminal liability of legal persons, a wide range of public legal persons were exempt from Belgian criminal liability. On that topic, see E de Formanoir, 'La nouvelle loi sur la responsabilité pénale des personnes morales' in C De Valkeneer and HD Bosly (eds), *Actualités en droit pénal 2019* (Larcier, 2019) 67–82; MJ Horseele and F Verbruggen, 'Zelfkastijding met een slapstick. Strafrechtelijke aansprakelijkheid van politieke publiekrechtelijke rechtspersonen met eenvoudige schuldigverklaring als enige straf' [2019] *Nullum Crimen* 195; A Werding, 'La responsabilité des personnes morales: au revoir décumul, bienvenue responsabilité pénale de l'état?' in V Franssen and A Masset (eds), *Actualités de droit pénal et de procédure pénale* (Anthemis, 2019) 81–125.

In this book, the concept 'PSI' encompasses the following three elements: (i) the right of suspects not to answer questions during interviews with the police or equivalent officers,[23] during punitive pre-trial hearings and at the punitive trial; (ii) the right not to be compelled to provide evidence, including oral statements, or to facilitate access to evidence if doing so would tend to incriminate the person providing it; and (iii) the right not to have negative inferences drawn from the choice to remain silent.[24] My decision to refer throughout this book to the PSI rather than to the right to silence is based upon the following considerations: although the right to silence and the PSI are often used interchangeably,[25] they are not identical, and the latter better encompasses the subject of our research than the former. Whereas the former focuses on oral communication and the issue of adverse inferences from a person's choice to remain silent, the latter is broader in the sense that it also encompasses issues such as compulsion to hand over self-incriminating documents, or compelled cooperation duties.[26] At the same time, the right to silence is broader in certain respects as it covers not only self-incriminating oral statements, but any statement as such.[27] The notion 'privilege' more clearly emphasises the special status of the PSI *sensu stricto*:[28] it allows one to deviate from the duty citizens have to cooperate when their assistance is sought in the gathering of evidence where following it would tend to lead to self-incrimination. In this sense, the notion 'privilege' clearly points to favourable treatment.[29] Admittedly, this distinction between what constitutes a privilege and what constitutes a right is not always clear in this context, as the two are at times used interchangeably.

My choice to focus on the PSI, and not on another procedural safeguard, can be explained by its specificities and the challenges in applying it to corporations. Its specificities relate to its underlying rationales and to the way in which it can be exercised.

The privilege is often associated with the protection of individuals against improper (physical or psychological) compulsion or even with human dignity.[30] If these were the sole rationales for the privilege, it might be difficult to accept that corporations can invoke it. As they do not have a mind and a body in the same sense as individuals, corporations cannot be directly compelled physically

[23] For example, in certain cases, investigating acts are carried out by customs officers rather than by classic police officers.

[24] Element (iii) essentially deals with situations where the fact that a suspect chooses not to answer questions or refuses to make statements at trial can be used as evidence of his/her guilt.

[25] I de la Serna, 'Discours prononcé par Monsieur le Procureur général I de la Serna – Le droit au silence', 2, www.om-mp.be/om_mp/files/en-savoir-plus/mercuriales/parquets%20generaux/Mons/PG%20Mons%20mercuriale%202014.pdf; I Dennis, *The Law of Evidence*, 5th edn (Sweet & Maxwell, 2013) 152; H Quirk, *The Rise and Fall of the Right of Silence* (Routledge, 2017) 8.

[26] Dennis, *The Law of Evidence* (n 25) 151.

[27] S Treschel, *Human Rights in Criminal Proceedings* (Oxford University Press, 2006) 342.

[28] In a strict sense, the privilege would principally correspond with element (ii).

[29] Quirk (n 25) 8.

[30] ALT Choo, *The Privilege against Self-Incrimination and Criminal Justice* (Hart Publishing, 2013) 6.

or mentally to answer a question the way a person of flesh and bone can be.[31] Another rationale is, however, also invoked to justify the privilege: it protects the will of the accused to remain silent.[32] This rationale also raises questions when one considers corporations. Who is capable of exercising the will of a corporation to remain silent? The different models of CCL often struggle with the question how one can decide whether a corporation can have a guilty mind. This demonstrates that establishing the will of a corporation is particularly difficult.

Furthermore, the decision to exercise the privilege or not to exercise it always has to be made by individual(s). As a corporation does not live and breathe like individuals do, one could conclude that it is not capable of exercising it: it must rely on individual(s) to exercise the privilege on its behalf.[33] There are inherent tensions between the corporation's PSI and that of the individual. For example, individuals might be inclined to put the blame on the corporation, especially if they can avoid incurring punitive liability themselves by doing so. Another question is who can exercise the corporation's privilege. For example, in a hypothetical scenario, both the CEO and the CEO's PA are questioned in the course of punitive proceedings against the corporation. Both of them are aware of certain incriminating elements. If only the corporation's official representatives, such as the CEO, are entitled to invoke the corporation's privilege during questioning, this could have far-reaching consequences for the corporation's liability, as the PA could be forced to incriminate the corporation, unless he or she could rely on a personal PSI.[34]

Similarly problematic is the question whether the use in a punitive case of documentary evidence, either in paper or electronic form, obtained under compulsion is compatible with the PSI of corporate defendants. This issue is contentious, and it has been answered differently across legal systems. Since corporations are fictitious entities possibly employing hundreds or even thousands of employees, the use of documents as evidence is very relevant for the purpose of corporate prosecutions. Corporate activities can leave a long paper or electronic trail and therefore it is crucial for corporations to know whether the PSI offers protection against the use of incriminating documents obtained under compulsion.

In addition to the aforementioned elements, I focus on the privilege because of the links it has to several other fair trial rights, in particular the POI, but also the right of access to a lawyer. The connection with the POI lies in the fact that extensive restrictions of the privilege impact on the POI, which essentially obliges prosecutors to prove the defendant's guilt. The privilege equally has links with the

[31] However, it cannot be excluded that individuals working for the corporations could be exposed to such compulsion.

[32] *Jalloh v Germany* App no 54810/00 (ECtHR, 11 July 2006) para 100.

[33] The fact that corporations always act through individuals also plays a role when it comes to establishing CCL. To some extent, this physical dependence is intertwined with the question whether corporations are really capable of having their 'own will'.

[34] Even if the PA could rely on a personal privilege, it might in certain legal systems be set aside by granting immunity to the PA.

right of access to a lawyer. Not only can the help of a lawyer be needed at trial: it may also help to prevent excessive compulsion during interviews or help to navigate production orders and help a suspect set up his defence strategy early on.

To the two key concepts included in the book's title, corporations and the PSI, a third one – punitive cases – is to be added, as the book's scope does not consider only criminal proceedings *sensu stricto*.

The applicability of the PSI to different types of cases is a central issue throughout this book: does the privilege only apply to criminal cases *sensu stricto*? Does it have any relevance in administrative investigations that may result in punitive sanctions? Can one claim its applicability in a civil case between private parties? Throughout this book, I will mainly focus on the applicability of the privilege in punitive cases. Therefore, its scope is not limited to cases labelled as criminal by (national) law, but it includes other punitive procedures covered by Article 6 ECHR.

To determine what constitutes a 'punitive' case, I rely on the ECtHR's jurisprudence. The Court developed a set of criteria to assess whether a case is considered 'criminal' for the purposes of the application of rights laid down in the ECHR.[35] According to the Court, the following non-cumulative[36] criteria spelled out in *Engel* determine whether a criminal charge is at stake: the classification of the offence under domestic law,[37] the offence's nature, and the nature and degree of severity of a penalty.[38] The last two criteria ensure, in particular, that procedural safeguards implicitly or explicitly guaranteed by Article 6 ECHR, such as the PSI or the *ne bis in idem* principle, included in the Seventh Protocol to the ECHR, apply even in cases which are labelled as administrative or disciplinary under (supra)national law.[39] The 'nature of the offence' refers mainly to its purpose, which, in order to qualify as criminal for the purpose of the ECHR, must be deterrent and punitive,[40] rather than compensatory.[41] In assessing the offence's nature, attention should also be paid to the scope *ratione personae* of an offence: in principle, it is

[35] DJ Harris et al, *Law of the European Convention on Human Rights*, 3rd edn (Oxford University Press, 2014) 373–76; C Van den Wyngaert, S Vandromme and P Traest, *Strafrecht en strafprocesrecht in hoofdlijnen*, 11th edn (Gompel & Svacina, 2019) 714–16.

[36] Where necessary, the two latter criteria can be applied cumulatively if they are individually not conclusive: *Ezeh and Connors v United Kingdom* App nos 39665/98 and 40086/98 (ECtHR, 9 October 2003) para 86.

[37] That criterion is considered as a starting point: *Gestur Jonsson and Ragnar Halldor Hall v Iceland* App nos 68273/14 and 68271/14 (ECtHR, 22 December 2020) para 85.

[38] *Engel and Others v the Netherlands* App nos 5100–5102/71, 5354/71 and 5370/72 (ECtHR, 8 June 1976) paras 30 et seq; *A and B v Norway* App nos 24130/11 and 29758/11 (ECtHR, 15 November 2016) para 105; *Produkcija Plus* (n 9) para 39; *Carrefour France v France* App no 37858/14 (ECtHR, 1 October 2019) para 40; *Gestur Jonsson* (n 37) paras 75 and 77; S Benzidi and F Lefèvre, *Gros plan sur la FSMA: Chronique de jurisprudence depuis la création de la Commission des sanctions à nos jours* (Larcier, 2022) 174–75.

[39] Van den Wyngaert et al (n 35) 692.

[40] *Ezeh and Connors* (n 36) para 102.

[41] *Grande Stevens and others v Italy* App no 18640/10 (ECtHR, 4 March 2014) para 96; Harris et al (n 35) 374.

to apply to the population at large, or at least to a larger group, such as taxpayers, in order for Article 6 ECHR to apply.[42] At the same time, the ECtHR has held that the scope *ratione personae* is merely one of the relevant indicators.[43] A requirement of guilt under national law in order to impose a penalty tends to indicate that the offence is criminal in nature,[44] and its classification in other states can be relevant for determining the nature of an offence.[45] When assessing the severity of the penalty, one needs to consider the penalty that could be imposed, rather than the one that is eventually imposed.[46] The fact that an offence is not punishable by imprisonment is by itself not decisive in excluding the applicability of the criminal limb of Article 6 ECHR.[47]

In light of the rather general nature of the *Engel* criteria, it comes as no surprise that their application can be difficult in practice and that different courts may reach different conclusions when applying them. The *Engel* criteria leave broad discretion to (supra)national courts.[48] For example, the ECtHR has held that competition proceedings, which under national law did not qualify as criminal, could be labelled as criminal,[49] whereas the CJEU, which has adopted the *Engel* criteria in several cases,[50] has regularly refused to label EU competition law fines as criminal in nature.[51] This has not precluded the CJEU from applying numerous

[42] Harris et al (n 35) 374. On that issue also, see *Gestur Jonsson* (n 37) paras 86–91.

[43] *Ezeh and Connors* (n 36) para 103.

[44] For an application of this criterion by the ECtHR, see *Produkcija Plus* (n 9) para 42. With regard to supervisory proceedings which did not result in a fine, but in a declaratory decision, the Court decided that they did not have a criminal character. In the same case, the ECtHR concluded that a fine of €105,000, which was considered an administrative fine under national law, imposed on a corporation came within the criminal limb of Art 6 ECHR. The fine was imposed for the obstruction of an inspection.

[45] WA Schabas, *The European Convention on Human Rights – A Commentary* (Oxford University Press, 2015) 277.

[46] *Grande Stevens* (n 41) para 98.

[47] *Gestur Jonsson* (n 37) para 78; *Vegotex International SA v Belgium* App no 49812/09 (ECtHR, 3 November 2022) para 67. The Court decided that the criminal limb was not applicable in that case. The absence of imprisonment or conversion of fines into deprivation of liberty played a role in the Court's decision in *Gestur Jonsson*: paras 94–97.

[48] N Joncheray, 'De l'usage de l'article 6 CEDH face aux autorités administratives indépendantes dotées d'un pouvoir de sanction' in L Fromont and A Van Waeyenberge (eds), *Actualités de la protection juridictionnelle dans et par l'Union européenne* (Larcier, 2017) 241; A Weyembergh and N Joncheray, 'Punitive Administrative Sanctions and Procedural Safeguards – a Blurred Picture that Needs to Be Addressed' (2016) 7 *New Journal of European Criminal Law* 190, 197.

[49] *A Menarini Diagnostics SRL v Italy* App no 43509/08 (ECtHR, 27 September 2011).

[50] Case C-489/10 *Łukasz Marcin Bonda* ECLI:EU:C:2012:319, paras 36–37; Case C-617/10 *Åklagaren v Hans Åkerberg Fransson* ECLI:EU:C:2013:280, para 35; Case C-537/16 *Garlsson Real Estate SA and Others v Consob* ECLI:EU:C:2018:193, para 28; Case C-524/15 *Luca Menci* ECLI:EU:C:2018:197, para 26; *DB v Consob* (n 17) para 42.

[51] The fact that Art 23(5) of Council Regulation (EC) No 1/2003 of 16 December 2002 on the implementation of the rules on competition laid down in Articles 81 and 82 of the Treaty holds that decisions imposing fines are not of a criminal law nature would as such not be conclusive in light of the *Engel* criteria. See similarly A Bailleux, 'The Fiftieth Shade of Grey Competition Law, "Criministrative Law" and "Fairly Fair Trials"' in F Galli and A Weyembergh (eds), *Do Labels Still Matter?* (Editions de l'Université de Bruxelles, 2014) 139. In Case C-117/20 *bpost SA v Autorité belge de la concurrence* ECLI:EU:C:2022:202, the CJ did consider that: 'In the present case, however, it is sufficient to note, as the referring court makes clear, that the two sets of proceedings referred to in the main action

procedural safeguards to such proceedings,[52] while at the same time it pays attention to the impact of procedural safeguards on the effectiveness of EU competition law.[53]

National courts, as well as the CJEU and the ECtHR, have included a wide variety of cases and penalties within the scope of the *Engel* criteria. These cases have included tax surcharges,[54] fines imposed by an authority that protects investors and oversees the financial markets[55] or proceedings conducted by a competition authority.[56] The ECtHR itself has recognised this evolution as including an ever-wider range of cases that are not labelled as criminal by national law. In its case law it distinguishes between the so-called hard core of criminal law and less stigmatising offences.[57] The Court has used this distinction in some cases to justify a less strict application of some of the ECHR's fair trial rights where less stigmatising offences are involved.[58] That line of case law can be understood as an attempt by the Court to refine its generous approach by distinguishing the hard core of offences from peripheral offences. The approach to refine or even limit the scope of protection is not unsurprising: by recognising that a broad range of penalties come within the scope of the right to a fair trial or within the scope of the *ne bis in idem* principle, procedural rights are now being invoked in situations that were not necessarily anticipated by (supra)national authorities. In the context of the PSI, one can refer to the issue of its applicability in administrative proceedings during which one is regularly under an obligation to provide information.[59] In relation to *ne bis in idem*, one can refer to the issue of different types of penalties for the same behaviour.[60] As Weyembergh and Joncheray have pointed out, the *Jussila* case law has increased the confusion, and one may wonder whether its result is the creation of a third category, namely quasi-criminal measures.[61] Throughout this book I will use the traditional *Engel* criteria.

In sum, throughout the book I will rely on the notion of 'punitive' cases and the content of that notion as defined by the *Engel* criteria. A central issue in this context will be to determine at what stage of a punitive case the privilege applies.

are proceedings for the imposition of administrative penalties of a criminal nature, meaning that the criminal classification of those proceedings, in the light of the criteria referred to in paragraph 25 of the present judgment, is not in question.'

[52] On this issue, see Jones and Sufrin (n 21) 895 et seq; Weyembergh and Joncheray (n 48) 199.

[53] On this issue, see Bailleux (n 51) 141 and 147–50.

[54] *Jussila v Finland* App no 73053/01 (ECtHR, 23 November 2006).

[55] *Grande Stevens* (n 41).

[56] *Menarini* (n 49).

[57] *Jussila* (n 54) para 43; *Grande Stevens* (n 41) para 120; *Özmurat İnşaat Elektrik Nakliyat Temizlik San ve Tic Ltd Şti v Turkey* App no 48657/06 (ECtHR 28 November 2017) para 28; *De Legé v Netherlands* App no 58342/15 (ECtHR, 4 October 2022); *Vegotex* (n 47) paras 76 and 122. In *Özmurat*, the Court found that Art 6 §1 ECHR was violated as no hearing had taken place, which was necessary because the credibility of the inspection report was challenged by the corporation.

[58] *Menarini* (n 49) para 62; *SA-Capital Oy* (n 9) para 71.

[59] AG Pikamäe handed down an interesting Opinion in relation to administrative proceedings in Italy in *DB v Consob* (n 17): Case C-481/19 *DB v Consob* ECLI:EU:C:2020:861.

[60] *Jóhanneson and others v Iceland* App no 22007/11 (ECtHR, 18 May 2017).

[61] Weyembergh and Joncheray (n 48) 191 and 196.

III. Structure and Methodology

The main research question that is answered in this book is: Does the PSI apply to corporations, should it apply to corporations and, if so, to what extent? Throughout the book I shall use the following hypothesis, which I will also put to the test: 'The model of CCL has an impact on whether and to what extent the privilege applies to corporations, for instance, because it indicates whether a corporation is capable of having its own will.'

In order to answer the main research question, several additional questions require an answer.

First, I examine the roots and historical rationale(s) of the PSI (chapter two). That analysis is necessary as an understanding of the privilege's long history and its development in relation to individuals is helpful for the purpose of research. The privilege was initially designed for individuals, and to understand its rationale(s) it is instructive to start by analysing those historical origins. Concretely, I trace the roots of the privilege to the medieval *ius commune* and its development therefrom. There is a wealth of sources on the privilege's history, often emphasising different elements to explain the evolution of the privilege. Self-evidently, the chapter includes a review of the relevance of the historical rationales of the privilege in relation to corporations.

In chapter three, I examine how different corporations and natural persons are for the purpose of the PSI, by considering certain corporate specificities. After considering the specificity of corporate personhood, I focus on the following three specific corporate features:

- the (im)possibility of exerting physical or psychological pressure on corporations to compel them to provide self-incriminating evidence;
- the importance of documentary evidence for the purpose of corporate prosecutions; and
- the impossibility for the corporation to exercise the privilege independently.

That analysis, which determines whether corporations and natural persons are comparable categories of persons for the purpose of the PSI, is merely the first step of the principle of equality test carried out in chapter three. The principle of equality requires, on the one hand, that comparable situations should not be treated differently, unless such treatment is objectively and reasonably justified, and on the other hand, that different situations should not be treated equally, subject to the same proviso.[62] I answer the following five questions in turn: (i) are corporations

[62] Case C-127/07 *Société Arcelor Atlantique et Lorraine and Others v Premier ministre and Others* ECLI:EU:C:2008:728, para 23; Case C-31/13 P *Hungary v Commission* ECLI:EU:C:2014:70, para 73; A Alen and K Muylle, *Handboek van het Belgisch Staatsrecht* (Kluwer, 2011) 501; D Edward and R Lane, *Edward and Lane on European Union Law* (Edward Elgar, 2013) 390; K Lenaerts and P Van Nuffel, *EU Constitutional Law* (Oxford University Press, 2021) 116; S Sottiaux, 'Het gelijkheidsbeginsel: langs oude paden en nieuwe wegen' [2008–09] *Rechtskundig Weekblad* 690, 692.

and individuals comparable categories[63] for the purpose of the privilege? If this is not the case, corporations should not be entitled to the privilege, unless this can be objectively and reasonably justified; (ii) provided they constitute comparable categories, the next question is does treating them differently serve a legitimate aim?[64] Such a legitimate aim could be ensuring effective access to evidence of criminal misconduct by corporations, their officials and employees; (iii) thirdly, is the criterion of distinction an objective one?[65] This step is unlikely to raise particular concerns;[66] (iv) next, are the different treatments suitable and necessary[67] to achieve the legitimate aim?[68] Where less restrictive alternatives can help achieve the legitimate aim, or where the treatment is not suitable to achieve the legitimate aim, this fourth step can be difficult to take; and (v) lastly, is the differentiated treatment of corporations *sensu stricto* proportionate?[69] To that end, I consider whether the means employed are in balance with a legitimate aim. This assessment also needs to take stock of the effects of that measure.[70] National and European Courts do not always apply these criteria according to the step-by-step approach that I suggest here. For example, questions (iv) and (v) are at times considered under the heading 'proportionality'.

Chapters four to nine address specific elements of the PSI: the contemporary rationales of the privilege, self-incrimination, compulsion, evidence protected by the privilege, applicability of the privilege *ratione temporis* and waiver of the privilege.

The topics of these chapters are studied at both the national and supranational levels. For the supranational systems, I include the approaches taken by both the CoE and the EU. For the CoE, the focus is on the ECtHR's landmark judgments that have significantly impacted on the evolution of the Court's case law, some of which were handed down in the 1990s, without, however, overlooking recent developments in relation to the privilege. For the EU, I focus on the cases of the

[63] Alen and Muylle (n 62) 504–05; Harris et al (n 35) 788–90; S Haverkort-Speekenbrink, *European Non-Discrimination Law – A Comparison of EU Law and the ECHR in the Field of Non-Discrimination and Freedom of Religion in Public Employment with an Emphasis on the Islamic Headscarf Issue* (Intersentia, 2012) 99–100; K Lenaerts, 'The Principle of Equal Treatment and the European Court of Justice' [2013] *Il Diritto dell'Unione Europea* 461, 481–82; S Sottiaux, *Grondwettelijk recht*, 2nd edn (Intersentia, 2021) 430–31.

[64] Alen and Muylle (n 62) 503.

[65] ibid.

[66] The ConsC accepted legal persons as opposed to individuals as an objective criterion: ConsC 8 March 1994, 22/94; ConsC 10 May 2007, 75/2007; ConsC 18 April 2013, 52/2013. It addressed a difference in treatment of individuals and legal persons in relation to criminal fines due to the fine conversion mechanism applicable in Belgium. That mechanism was introduced as legal persons cannot face imprisonment fines. It considered that a reasonable justification was available: ConsC 18 January 2018, 148/2017.

[67] Here, 'necessary' refers to the requirement to check whether less intrusive measures could have been taken.

[68] Haverkort-Speekenbrink (n 63) 105; Sottiaux, *Grondwettelijk recht* (n 63) 433.

[69] Sottiaux, *Grondwettelijk recht* (n 63) 433.

[70] Alen and Muylle (n 62) 506.

CJ and the GC that have impacted their view on the privilege in the long term, supplemented with recent cases and the POI Directive.

On the national level, I consider the approaches taken by Belgium, E&W and the US federal legal system. I focus on the case law of the selected countries, as well as on relevant statutory provisions and doctrine. In relation to the USA, the focus is on the federal level. Moreover, as the privilege essentially requires examining the Fifth Amendment to the Federal Constitution, the focus on federal law is warranted, particularly since that case law applies to the different states too.[71]

These specific legal systems have been chosen, inter alia, on the basis of the various models of CCL that they apply. Whereas the USA relies on the model of vicarious liability for attributing criminal liability to corporations, E&W classically use the identification doctrine.[72] Belgium applies an anthropomorphic model for attributing criminal liability. The use of legal systems with different models of CCL is warranted in light of my aforementioned hypothesis. In addition to their respective models of CCL, the above countries are also interesting as they have accepted CCL at different points in time and E&W and the USA have thus had more time to develop their case law on the entitlement of corporations to the PSI. In addition, they represent inquisitorial and adversarial systems. Furthermore, the selection of national systems comprises countries that adhere to the ECHR and one that does not, just like it includes an EU MS and non-EU MSs. In that sense, it allows us to assess the impact of the ECHR, the ECtHR's case law and EU law on the national systems. My choice of national systems was, moreover, influenced by my choice to use sources in languages I understand.

In chapter ten, I analyse the models of CCL in the different (supra)national systems and their approach towards the corporate PSI, and I examine whether the model of CCL adopted by the selected (supra)national legal orders has indeed impacted on their (un)willingness to accept a corporate PSI. The final part of the chapter considers incentives adopted by the national legal orders to encourage corporations to cooperate when they are implicated in misconduct. These incentives can include non-prosecution agreements and other types of negotiated justice, which may be made dependent on the full cooperation of corporate defendants. Corporations may thus have to help identify culpable individuals within the corporation. The national approaches towards such investigations are considered.

In chapter eleven, a proposal is made for a balanced corporate PSI. The chapter draws from the findings made in the other chapters and provides an answer to the main research question.

The final chapter, chapter twelve, concludes.

[71] *Malloy v Hogan* 378 US 1, 8 (1964).

[72] Specific acts rely on more specific models of liability, eg s 7 of the Bribery Act 2010.

2

The Roots and Historical Rationale(s) of the Privilege against Self-Incrimination

Several national, international and supranational legal instruments include a provision on the PSI.[73] In the past that was not always so self-evident. The privilege's history is intertwined with struggles against coercive practices, such as torturing suspects or questioning them while under oath to obtain (self-incriminating) evidence. Throughout history,[74] compulsion has often played a role in the discovery of the truth.

In this chapter, I unpack and examine the historical roots of the privilege to shed light on its shifting rationale(s). This furthers my analysis on whether extending the PSI to corporations is justified. A wealth of scholarship on the broader history of the privilege already exists. With this in mind, the ensuing analysis mainly draws on those secondary sources, which specifically help to explain the privilege's rationales.

The privilege nowadays does not have the same exact scope in all countries and is continuously developing. It is thus no surprise that historically it did not develop at the same pace in all legal systems. Nevertheless, regardless of national origin, those advocating and those criticising the privilege often used similar arguments. Therefore, I do not split my analysis into different geographical chapters. Instead, I focus on those common elements that have played an essential role in the privilege's history. Where relevant, I point out national differences that explain why the privilege developed at a different pace in specific countries.

Before addressing two particular types of compulsion that played a role in the privilege's history, I consider the PSI's roots in the *ius commune*. In later sections of the chapter, I focus, respectively, on the consolidation of the privilege and the role of attorneys in its early development, and the relevance of the historical rationales of the privilege for corporations.

[73] eg Fifth Amendment to the US Constitution; Art 14(3)g ICCPR; Art 7 POI Directive.

[74] The idea that compulsion, or threats of using it, can be useful to unveil the truth is, sadly, still alive: *Gäfgen v Germany* App no 22978/05 (ECtHR, 1 June 2010).

I. *Nemo Tenetur Prodere Seipsum*

The PSI is often associated with the principle *nemo tenetur prodere seipsum*. Levy has translated this as 'no man is bound to accuse himself',[75] whereas Helmholz translated it as 'no one is bound to betray oneself'.[76]

The principle has its roots in the *ius commune*,[77] which consisted of general principles inspired by Roman or canon law.[78] The rediscovery of important sources of Roman law, such as the *Corpus Iuris Civilis*, furthered its development from the twelfth century onwards. As universities developed, they began to teach this body of principles to students from different European countries.[79] European secular courts and ecclesiastical courts often relied on the principles of the *ius commune* when dealing with cases. Nevertheless, the *ius commune* did not have the same impact in all European countries. For example, in E&W there was a clear distinction between the procedure applied in secular courts and that in ecclesiastical courts, with only the latter strongly relying on the *ius commune*. One of the *ius commune*'s principal weaknesses was that the general rules found in it were often subject to exceptions and complications,[80] meaning that the result in practice often differed from the general rule.[81]

The *nemo tenetur* principle was included in the thirteenth-century glossaries to the decretals of Pope Gregory IX and endorsed by other influential authors.[82] Manuals on criminal and civil procedure similarly referred to it,[83] just like (ecclesiastical) courts throughout Europe.[84] In the early days of the *nemo tenetur* principle, the Christian doctrine on confession and the duty of self-preservation played a fundamental role.[85] According to Helmholz Durantis, a prominent writer on the

[75] LW Levy, *Origins of the Fifth Amendment* (Oxford University Press, 1968) 3 and 94.

[76] RH Helmholz, 'Origins of the Privilege against Self-Incrimination: The Role of the European Ius Commune' (1990) 65 *New York University Law Review* 962, 962. The difference in translation reflects the broad list of translations of the verb 'prodere'.

[77] RH Helmholz, 'The Privilege and the Ius Commune: The Middle Ages to the Seventeenth Century' in RH Helmholz et al, *The Privilege against Self-Incrimination* (University of Chicago Press, 1997) 17.

[78] MH Eichbauer, 'Medieval Inquisitorial Procedure: Procedural Rights and the Question of Due Process in the 13th Century' (2014) 12 *History Compass* 72, 73.

[79] RC Van Caenegem, *European Law in the Past and Future* (Cambridge University Press, 2002) 13.

[80] Helmholz, 'Origins of the Privilege against Self-Incrimination' (n 76) 974; A Zeeman, *Dulden of meewerken? – een onderzoek naar de toepassing van het nemo tenetur-beginsel bij de sfeerovergang van controle naar opsporing* (Gompel & Svacina, 2019) 256.

[81] Helmholz, 'Origins of the Privilege against Self-Incrimination' (n 76) 974.

[82] W Barnes, 'Hadley v Baxendale and Other Common Law Borrowings from the Civil Law' (2005) 11 *Texas Wesleyan Law Review* 627, 644; Helmholz, 'Origins of the Privilege against Self-Incrimination' (n 76) 967. Saint John Chrysostom may have been the first to formulate the principle: PJ Roles, *The Privilege Against Self-Incrimination* (Lambert Academic Publishing, 2010) 15.

[83] Helmholz, 'Origins of the Privilege against Self-Incrimination' (n 76) 967; H Silving, 'The Oath: I' (1959) 68 *Yale Law Journal* 1329, 1346.

[84] In those cases, references were regularly made to leading continental lawyers; Helmholz, 'Origins of the Privilege against Self-Incrimination' (n 76) 970–71.

[85] MRT Macnair, 'The Early Development of the Privilege against Self-Incrimination' (1990) 10 *OJLS* 66, 71; Zeeman (n 80) 256.

ius commune, supported by other authors, including Panormitanus, relied on a longer wording of the principle to argue that no one is to testify against himself because no one is bound to reveal his own shame.[86] To make this argument, the authors relied on a commentary of a letter of Saint Paul to which they gave the following meaning: 'men and women should confess their sins to God, but they should not be compelled to make their crimes known to anyone else'.[87] The duty of self-preservation further supported the principle:[88] that duty did not cease because someone might have committed a crime. By making a self-incriminatory statement, one might contribute to one's own 'destruction' by exposing oneself to a harsh punishment.

The arguments in favour of the *nemo tenetur* principle help us understand its underlying justifications as well as those of the PSI. The reference to the duty of self-preservation suggests that authors in those days considered that requiring a person to provide information that could be used to their detriment runs counter to any person's instincts. Moreover, the doctrine on confession shows that an early privacy argument was associated with the principle,[89] as persons only had to share their crime with God – and not with the authorities. In other words, the principle should ensure that a person could largely keep his knowledge to himself.

Although important scholars, members of clergy and ecclesiastical courts referred to the principle, its limits and exceptions severely affected its role in practice.

II. The Oath *Ex Officio*

A. General Principles

One of the main restrictions to the *nemo tenetur* principle was the oath *ex officio*, also known as the oath *de veritate dicenda* or inquisitorial oath (throughout this chapter, 'the oath').[90] It obliged the person who had taken it to answer questions

[86] *Nemo tenetur prodere seipsum, qua nemo tenetur detegere turpitudinem suam*; Helmholz, 'Origins of the Privilege against Self-Incrimination' (n 76) 981.

[87] Helmholz, 'Origins of the Privilege against Self-Incrimination' (n 76) 982. See also J Langbein, *The Origins of Adversary Criminal Trial* (Oxford University Press, 2003) 277–78.

[88] Macnair (n 85) 71.

[89] Zeeman (n 80) 255.

[90] When it came into use in the 13th century, European societies were well acquainted with the use of oaths in criminal procedure. Another oath had been widely used: the oath of purgation, taken by a suspect to clear himself of all suspicion. The underlying idea behind that oath was that the oath-taker and his helpers would not endanger their souls by falsely swearing. The oath of purgation was of Germanic origin and initially it was the wrath of the secret forces of nature that the oath-taker accepted in case he was lying. The essential difference between it and the oath *ex officio* is that the purgating oath was a tool to be acquitted, whereas the *ex officio* oath was a tool to extract incriminating evidence. See Levy, *Origins of the Fifth Amendment* (n 75) 5; Silving (n 83) 1340; RC Van Caenegem, *Geschiedenis van het Strafprocesrecht in Vlaanderen van de XIe tot de XIVe Eeuw* (Koninklijke Vlaamse Academie voor Wetenschappen, Letteren en Schone Kunsten van België, 1956) 148.

put to him truthfully and it amounted to psychological compulsion, which often resulted in self-incrimination. Once a person took the oath, he faced a difficult trilemma: if he spoke the truth, he could be contributing to his own conviction;[91] if he lied, he would expose himself to perjury; and not saying anything at all could result in him being considered guilty[92] or being punished. The fear of perjury in those days had an even stronger impact than today: perjury amounted to dishonouring God's name. Its presumed strength was that, given the importance of religion in the societies of those days, one would not lie after having taken the oath.[93] According to its critics, requiring someone to take it would amount to enticing someone to commit perjury, which would amount to committing a sin.[94]

The oath, introduced under Pope Innocent III in the thirteenth century,[95] was part of the wider reform of the procedure used by the ecclesiastical courts.[96] The new procedure was inquisitorial and initially used for prosecuting misconduct by members of the clergy.[97] Shortly thereafter, it was also used in the fight against heresy,[98] a serious concern to the Catholic Church throughout Europe.[99] Proving heresy was difficult, as a person's intimate convictions often remain invisible, especially if one knows that they may result in prosecution.

Reconciling the oath with the *nemo tenetur* principle is challenging. That principle is at odds with taking an oath and providing self-incriminating statements. Levy has attempted to overcome this tension by arguing that the text of the *nemo tenetur prodere seipsum* principle was longer. According to him, the full text of the principle was: 'No one is bound to produce against himself, but when exposed by common report he is bound to show whether he can show his innocence and is permitted to purge himself'.[100] According to this longer version, a person had to provide evidence once he was properly brought before a court or where reasonable suspicion was shown.[101] Macnair has challenged this view and argued that

[91] Provided that he had committed a wrongful act.

[92] Zeeman (n 80) 247. Joan of Arc's case is a concrete example: HA Kelly, *Inquisitions and Other Trial Procedures in the Medieval West* (Ashgate, 2001) 1016.

[93] E Moglen, 'The Privilege in British North America: The Colonial Period to the Fifth Amendment' in Helmholz et al (n 77) 119.

[94] Zeeman (n 80) 256.

[95] JH Wigmore, *A Treatise on the System of Evidence in Trials at Common Law Including the Statutes and Decisions of All Jurisdictions of the United States* (Little, Brown & Co, 1905) 3073.

[96] The ecclesiastical courts originally had a more limited jurisdiction than secular courts. Their jurisdiction included cases involving clergy and several specific matters such as marriage, church properties and the offences against religion: Levy, *Origins of the Fifth Amendment* (n 75) 43–44.

[97] ibid.

[98] The offence's principal characteristic is that one adheres to a religion or set of ideas that do not correspond with the established religion or set of ideas.

[99] Pope Innocent III described it as high treason against God: Levy, *Origins of the Fifth Amendment* (n 75) 21.

[100] *Licet nemo tenetur seipsum prodere; tamen proditus per famam, tenetur seipsum ostendere, utrum possit suam innocentiam ostendere, et seipsum purgare.* Levy, *Origins of the Fifth Amendment* (n 75) 96.

[101] Macnair (n 85) 71.

this longer version was a thirteenth-century exception to the shorter version of the principle, designed to deal with heresy.[102] In an era when religion and political power were strongly connected,[103] heresy was considered to warrant the use of exceptional procedures.[104] Macnair rightly stresses that even if one adheres to the longer wording of the principle, a prima facie case against the person was in principle needed, as the risk of fishing expeditions was otherwise very real.[105]

Helmholz has also stressed the contested status of the oath. The oath's opponents argued, relying on another *ius commune* rule, that a judge could not impose the oath, as there was no specific accuser.[106] Since the oath was typically used in cases where proceedings had been launched *ex officio*, this was a first way of attacking the oath. According to this rule, a judge could not start proceedings against a person by his own decision: there had to be prima facie indications of guilt, or a person with a legitimate interest in having the suspect convicted had to make an accusation.[107] Those who defended the oath would rely on exceptions to this rule, such as that there was public knowledge (*fama publica*). Where *fama publica*, an early version of probable cause, against a person was shown, they considered that a judge could himself launch the proceedings. Opponents and supporters of the oath disagreed on how high the standard of *fama publica* had to be.[108] In this context, opponents of the oath argued that the specific charges were often not communicated before the oath had to be taken. Moreover, they referred to the aforementioned argument that no one is bound to testify against oneself because no one is bound to reveal his own shame and because of the cruel trilemma. Unsurprisingly, the oath's supporters relied on a *ius commune* exception to that rule. They argued that it does not apply when it was publicly known that an offence had been committed, there were reasonable grounds to believe that the suspect had committed that offence and the public had an interest in punishing the offence.[109]

The *nemo tenetur* principle was not absolute, and where a prima facie case was shown, it could be set aside according to its critics. The lower the bar of that prima facie case was set, the more limited the protection of the *nemo tenetur* principle became.

[102] ibid 71.

[103] Zeeman (n 80) 247.

[104] Eichbauer (n 78) 75; Zeeman (n 80) 256.

[105] Macnair (n 85) 72; J Meese, 'The Sound of Silence. Het zwijgrecht en het nemo tenetur-beginsel in strafzaken. Een historisch en rechtsgevergelijkend overzicht' in A Van Oevelen, S Rutten and J Rozie (eds), *Zwijgrecht versus spreekplicht* (Intersentia, 2013) 50.

[106] Referred to as *nemo punitur sine accusatore*. Helmholz, 'Origins of the Privilege against Self-Incrimination' (n 76) 975.

[107] There were both religious and procedural reasons. ibid 975.

[108] ibid 977–78.

[109] ibid 983; Zeeman (n 80) 256–57. Continental authors like Damhouder considered that a defendant was not allowed to refuse to answer specific questions about the offence of which they were suspected.

B. Regional Differences

Although the struggle against the contested oath played a role in the history of the development of the PSI, there are important regional differences between E&W and several continental states. An understanding of the differences in criminal procedures and standards of proof can help explain these differences.

In England, Henry II put in place a grand jury in 1166, through a legislative act, the Assize of Clarendon. This jury had to appear before the royal judges when they visited the different parts of the country and had to inform them of any person accused or suspected of robbery, murder, theft or hiding the perpetrator of any of those crimes. As they were members of the local community, they were in a good position to inform the royal judges.[110] In the thirteenth century a second type of jury, the trial or petty jury, received the responsibility to decide on the question whether a suspect was guilty or not.[111] The standard of proof required in order to find someone guilty was persuasion.[112] The introduction of the trial jury is strongly linked to the demise of the ordeals. Ordeals were an irrational practice with Germanic roots that Christianity had picked up. It was essentially an appeal to God to find out whether someone was innocent or guilty.[113] The ordeals faced harsh criticism in those days for their questionable truthfulness,[114] their arbitrary character, the fact that hardened criminals managed to pass them and because they forced God to perform miracles.[115] As of the Fourth Lateran Council (1215), priests could no longer assist in ordeals by performing rituals and the ordeals thereby lost their moral force.[116] The use of the aforementioned oath of purgation was turning into a sort of farce and there was a need for improvement.[117]

[110] Assize of Clarendon 1, http://avalon.law.yale.edu/medieval/assizecl.asp; JR Spencer, *La procédure pénale anglaise* (PUF, 1998) 5.

[111] M Mulholland, 'Introduction' in M Mulholland and B Pullan (eds), *Judicial Tribunals in England and Europe, 1200–1700* (Manchester University Press, 2003) 8; JR Spencer, 'Introduction' in M Delmas-Marty and JR Spencer (eds), *European Criminal Procedures* (Cambridge University Press, 2002) 7.

[112] JH Langbein, *Torture and the Law of Proof – Europe and England in the Ancien Régime* (University of Chicago Press, 1977) 80; MR Santucci, 'L'exception anglaise' in B Durand (ed), *La torture judiciaire – approches historiques et juridiques* (Centre d'histoire judiciaire éditeur, 2002) 214.

[113] For example, the practice of throwing a suspect in water, while hands and feet were tied. Those who were guilty would float, as the water, which had been blessed by a priest, rejected them.

[114] Zeeman (n 80) 246–47.

[115] B Durand, 'Réflexion préliminaire: Une histoire juridique de la torture est-elle possible?' in Durand, *La torture judiciaire* (n 112) 21; Levy, *Origins of the Fifth Amendment* (n 75) 6; H Pihlajamäki, 'Swimming the Witch, Pricking for the Devil's Mark: Ordeals in the Early Modern Witchcraft Trials' (2000) 21 *Journal of Legal History* 35, 36; Spencer, 'Introduction' (n 111) 8 and 9; RC Van Caenegem, 'Reflexions on Rational and Irrational Modes of Proof in Medieval Europe' (1990) 58 *Legal History Review* 263, 264.

[116] AL Lowell, 'The Judicial Use of Torture' (1897) 11 *Harvard Law Review* 220, 223; Meese, 'The Sound of Silence' (n 105) 48; Zeeman (n 80) 246–47. Ordeals did not stop from one day to the next. In practice, other legal instruments such as local charters in Flanders and the *Decretum Gratiani* had already influenced the thinking and practice on ordeals: Van Caenegem, *Geschiedenis van het Strafprocesrecht* (n 90) 234.

[117] Wigmore (n 95) 3073. For the oath of purgation, see n 90.

The demise of ordeals also required continental countries to look for new solutions. Although criticised, many had considered ordeals as a reliable tool, and thus the new law of evidence needed to be at least as secure as the old one.[118] This led to the adoption in several continental countries of the aforementioned inquisitorial model in secular courts.[119] In these inquisitorial proceedings, defendants were the object of the investigation and extensive effort was invested in obtaining a confession.[120] The oath was considered indispensable to achieving a conviction.[121] The distinction between the criminal procedure in use for common law offences and that used for canon law offences (such as heresy) was significantly smaller in several continental countries than in E&W.[122] One of the particular characteristics of this inquisitorial model was its strictly regulated law of evidence, commonly referred to by its French name: *la preuve légale*.[123] This specific law of evidence had to guarantee the correctness of judgments[124] – some would say more for the judge's moral comfort than for the factual correctness of the judgments.[125] In order to achieve this goal, strict rules regulated the probative value of different types of evidence and the level of punishment that they warranted.[126] The standard of proof in this new model was in principle much stricter than the standard required for the English jury.

The inquisitorial model, adopted by the Catholic Church for its ecclesiastical courts, not only played an important role in those courts and in secular courts in several continental countries, but impacted on E&W too – first, because ecclesiastical courts used it there too, often to fight heresy. Later on, several prerogative courts[127] adopted some of these inquisitorial traits, and particularly the oath. This led to a struggle in E&W between the common law courts, in which the oath was not in use and in which juries played a role, and the ecclesiastical and prerogative courts.[128]

[118] Langbein, *Torture and the Law of Proof* (n 112) 6–7; Spencer, 'Introduction' (n 111) 9. Or, as Langbein worded it: 'it (the judgment) was to rest upon standards of proof so high that no one would be concerned that God was no longer being asked to resolve the doubts.'

[119] On that topic, see Wigmore (n 95) 3074.

[120] Zeeman (n 80) 247.

[121] LW Levy, 'Origins of the Fifth Amendment and Its Critics' (1997) 19 *Cardozo Law Review* 821, 822.

[122] The inclusion of the oath in general criminal procedure instruments such as the *Styl Crimineel* or in the *Ordonnance Criminelle* attests to that.

[123] On this topic, see E Esmein, *History of Continental Criminal Procedure* (Little, Brown & Co, 1913) 251–71.

[124] JM Carbasse, 'Les origines de la torture judiciaire en France du XIIe au début du XIV siècle' in Durand, *La torture judiciaire* (n 112) 383; Spencer, 'Introduction' (n 111) 9.

[125] Judges needed the moral comfort of knowing that they had not sinned by convicting an innocent person: de la Serna (n 25) 4; JQ Whitman, 'The Transition to Modernity' in MD Hubber and T Hörnle (eds), *The Oxford Handbook of Criminal Law* (Oxford University Press, 2014) 92–93.

[126] In order to impose the death sentence or heavy corporal punishment on a defendant, in principle either a defendant needed to voluntarily confess or two reliable eyewitnesses had to testify: J Monballyu, *Zes eeuwen strafrecht: de geschiedenis van het Belgische strafrecht (1400–2000)* (Acco, 2010) 65; Langbein, *The Origins of Adversary Criminal Trial* (n 87) 339. For lighter offences, the judge's subjective persuasion sufficed: Langbein, *Torture and the Law of Proof* (n 112) 10.

[127] Such as the King's Council, the Court of Star Chamber and the High Commission: Levy, *Origins of the Fifth Amendment* (n 75) 100–01.

[128] Extensively on that struggle, see Levy, *Origins of the Fifth Amendment* (n 75).

C. The Abolition of the Oath

As I have highlighted, critics of the oath could rely on several arguments based on the *ius commune*, such as that one should only confess to God, and on the duty of self-preservation.[129] Taking the oath and disclosing self-incriminating information threatened the life of the person taking the oath as he could face execution. Sir Edward Coke[130] referred to the oath as a great form of oppression, as an 'invention of the devil to send the soul of sinners to hell' and as an illegal instrument that caused miscarriages of justice.[131] In France, Guillaume de Lamoignon similarly criticised it, as it could lead to perjury by the suspect.[132] In Flanders, like in E&W and France, the oath was criticised for the risk of perjury that it created.[133] In E&W, opponents of the oath challenged it, referring to the Magna Carta to argue that it violated common law.[134]

Supporters of the oath, including some English Members of Parliament, stressed its importance as it was efficient at finding suspects guilty and it was common to claim that without the oath the country would be flooded with blasphemous people.[135] This belief in the oath led to its incorporation in the procedure of a new prerogative court, the Court of High Commission, established in 1557.[136] Some French lawyers also defended it as a psychological form of torture that was required in order to obtain sufficient proof to impose the heaviest penalties.[137]

In E&W, the long struggle against the oath led to its abolition in 1641, when King Charles I had to accept the abolition of two courts that used the oath, the Court of High Commission and the Star Chamber.[138] One should consider the abolition in the context of the Civil War and the waning power of Charles I, who had to call a meeting of Parliament for the first time in a decade.

The abolition of the oath took longer in other European countries. As the oath was often part of the criminal procedure of secular courts, this is understandable. There was no similar struggle between secular and ecclesiastical courts on the use of the oath. For example, the order of King Philip II of 9 July 1570 (*Styl Crimineel*)[139] regulated multiple aspects of criminal procedure for secular courts and it applied in several parts of what is now Belgium.[140] Art 6 of this Order imposed the oath

[129] ibid 3, 78, 94 and 235.

[130] He became chief justice of one of the leading common law courts, the Court of Common Pleas, at the beginning of the 17th century: Levy, *Origins of the Fifth Amendment* (n 75) 246.

[131] ibid 231 and 233.

[132] Silving (n 83) 1350.

[133] J Monballyu, 'De Raad van Vlaanderen en de hervorming van het Strafrecht (1756–1787)' (1996) 64 *Legal History Review* 48, 60.

[134] References were often also made to 14th century statutes to claim that the oath violated them: Levy, *Origins of the Fifth Amendment* (n 75) 148, 158, 171, 194, 235 and 236.

[135] ibid 255.

[136] ibid 76, 77 and 126. The Court of High Commission was competent to investigate, for instance, heresy.

[137] Silving (n 83) 1350.

[138] Levy, *Origins of the Fifth Amendment* (n 75) 281; Zeeman (n 80) 262.

[139] Order on the criminal procedure of 9 July 1570.

[140] Monballyu, *Zes eeuwen strafrecht* (n 126) 38.

upon the suspect. Even in 1670, at a time when E&W had abolished the oath, the French *Ordonnance Criminelle* that regulated criminal procedure included the oath.

Ironically, the Catholic Church, largely responsible for the oath's widespread use, played an important role in its abolition in continental Europe countries. As discussions on the use of the oath grew stronger towards the end of the seventeenth century, Pope Innocent XII asked Francis Memmius in 1698 to provide a study on the oath.[141] In the aftermath of that study and due to external pressure, the oath was abolished in 1725 in criminal cases heard under canon law. Memmius concluded that the oath was unjust and cruel:[142] he found that it amounted to the most serious torture, even more cruel than physical torture as it tortures the soul by inducing the fear that one would dishonour God's name (by committing perjury).[143] According to him, a person committing perjury under oath could not be blamed as it is a quasi-automatism induced by the idea of self-preservation and therefore the oath is unjust.

His study was a catalyst for the debate on the abolition of the oath on the Continent.[144] His ideas easily found support in the Age of Enlightenment, with its focus on reason, the individual and human dignity.[145] Those who proposed reform often referred to England.[146] For example, Voltaire referred to England as a model of how things should be done.[147] The individual now was the bearer of rights,[148] which led to particular focus on procedural safeguards for suspects.[149] The argument that the oath was not acceptable in light of the idea of self-preservation gained additional force in the context of the focus on reason and human nature.[150] Beccaria attacked the oath and considered it irrational. He found it difficult to understand why an individual had to face the dilemma of either offending God (through perjury) or aiding in his own destruction.[151] Beccaria found it difficult to comprehend how an individual could be made to take an oath to speak the truth if the contrary was in his greatest interest.[152] He considered it ineffective.[153] Bentham equally opposed it and considered it a form of tyranny that inclined people to perjure themselves.[154]

[141] G Bechor, *God in the Courtroom: The Transformation of Courtroom Oath and Perjury between Islamic and Franco-Egyptian Law* (Brill, 2012) 154; Silving (n 83) 1346.
[142] Bechor (n 141) 154.
[143] ibid.
[144] Bechor (n 141) 154.
[145] Similarly on the importance of the context of the Age of Enlightment, see Zeeman (n 80) 266–67.
[146] Esmein (n 123) 359.
[147] ibid.
[148] Bechor (n 141) 155; M Böse, 'Die verfassungsrechtlichen Grundlagen des Satzes "Nemo tenetur se ipsum accusare"' [2002] *Goltdammer's Archiv fur Strafrecht* 98, 114.
[149] Esmein (n 123) 368.
[150] ibid 359.
[151] C Beccaria, *An Essay on Crimes and Punishments (translation)* (Little & Co, 1872) 72.
[152] ibid 71.
[153] ibid 72.
[154] Though he was not particularly favourable of the privilege: see 52 and 60 below.

In France, changed views led to the oath's abolition in 1789 and 1791. The different classes in French society[155] had expressed their grievances against the oath, namely that it ran counter to the sentiment of self-preservation and caused perjury. The focus had to be on the voluntary declarations of suspects, as this better fitted the new system, where evidence was evaluated freely.[156] In Germany, there was also a strong emphasis on the voluntariness of the suspect's statements.[157] The two concepts – the free evaluation of evidence and the prohibition on forcing suspects to take the oath – were spread widely following the conquest of large parts of Europe by France, including Belgium and the Netherlands.[158] The free evaluation of evidence was not entirely new, as the inquisitorial model already used it for lighter offences and in those cases where partial evidence was present, in the absence of a confession or two eyewitnesses.[159] Langbein links this to the availability of other sanctions, which became more widely used in the sixteenth and seventeenth centuries (such as imprisonment and forced labour).[160] The free evaluation of evidence avoided situations of impunity in the absence of a confession or two eyewitnesses.

III. Torture

A. General Principles

I have highlighted the impact of the demise of ordeals on the standard of proof and the different models of criminal proceedings. In E&W, trial juries developed. They required persuasion to find someone guilty. The inquisitorial model, used in ecclesiastical courts throughout Europe and in secular courts in several continental countries, relied on a strictly regulated law of evidence. Judicial torture was a second tool with which to obtain confessions. The result of the different standards of proof was that torture played a more important role in the history of several continental states than in E&W.[161]

[155] In 1789, the three groups in society – the clergy, the nobility and the common people – presented their grievances in the so-called *cahiers de doléances*. These reports incorporated the views and wishes in the field of matters that should be reformed: Esmein (n 123) 397.

[156] Silving (n 83) 1352.

[157] M Pieck, 'The Accused's Privilege against Self-Incrimination in the Civil Law' (1962) 11 *American Journal of Comparative Law* 585, 589.

[158] Silving (n 83) 1352.

[159] Langbein, *Torture and the Law of Proof* (n 112) 47.

[160] ibid 48. See also Art 2 of Title XIX of the *Ordonnance Criminelle*, http://ledroitcriminel.fr/la_legislation_criminelle/anciens_textes/ordonnance_criminelle_de_1670.htm; Art 34 of the *Constitutio Criminalis Theresiana* of 1769.

[161] Langbein, *Torture and the Law of Proof* (n 112) 73 and 139; Santucci (n 112) 219.

The rationale behind torture was that a person could not focus on telling lies due to the pain and would tell the truth.[162] Clearly, the acceptance of torture as an evidence-gathering technique is an explicit denial of the principle that one cannot be forced to accuse oneself. In cases of prosecution for heresy or for witchcraft, there was an additional argument in favour of torture: the physical pain should liberate the person from the demon that was inside him.[163] It was a common practice to first threaten the suspect with torture, before the actual torture would take place.[164] That often sufficed to make people talk. This practice, known in Flanders and the Netherlands as *anxten*,[165] highlights the status of torture as a measure of last resort, not to be used if the mere threat of it sufficed. It also sets the background against which torture should be seen: the suspect should be scared and the process of getting a confession relied on, in addition to physical compulsion, psychological compulsion.

In principle, some safeguards existed to prevent excesses. Torture was limited to offences punishable by death or heavy corporal punishment,[166] and it required a judicial decision.[167] Moreover, substantial indications of guilt were needed.[168] These indications could, for example, consist of the testimony of an eyewitness or circumstantial evidence of sufficient gravity.[169] To guarantee the reliability of confessions made during torture, a strict, cynical rule applied: confessions made during torture were not enough.[170] The confession was only useful if the suspect confirmed it outside the torture chamber several hours after the torture had stopped.[171] He was free to withdraw his confession, in which case he could be tortured again, up to three times.[172] In practice, these safeguards were not always respected, and torture was used in cases where insufficient evidence to justify it was available.[173]

[162] Durand, 'Réflexion préliminaire' (n 115) 31–32; E Hubert, *La torture aux Pays-Bas autrichiens pendant le XVIIIe siècle* (Office de publicité J Lebège et Cie, 1897) 13; Monballyu, *Zes eeuwen strafrecht* (n 126) 360.

[163] OF Dubuis and M Ostorero, 'La torture en Suisse occidentale (XIVe–XVIIIe siècles)' in Durand, *La torture judiciaire* (n 112) 562.

[164] GM De Meyer and EWF Van Den Elzen, 'Tortura incognita – Het pijnlijk verhoor in de Zuidelijke en Noordelijke Nederlanden tijdens de middeleeuwen' (1986) 54 *Legal History Review* 307, 317; Langbein, *Torture and the Law of Proof* (n 112) 15.

[165] To frighten.

[166] S Dauchy, 'La torture judiciaire dans les anciens Pays-Bas' in Durand, *La torture judiciaire* (n 112) 517; Hubert (n 162) 36–37.

[167] Dauchy (n 166) 517; T Le Marc'hadour, 'La question préparatoire dans les Pays-Bas français (1679–1790)' in Durand, *La torture judiciaire* (n 112) 753.

[168] Dauchy (n 166).

[169] Langbein, *Torture and the Law of Proof* (n 112) 5.

[170] Monballyu, *Zes eeuwen strafrecht* (n 126) 360–61; Esmein (n 123) 113–14.

[171] Hubert (n 162) 54. Practice differed throughout Europe on this point: whereas in Belgium the confession could only be confirmed several hours after the torture had ceased, practice in France was to confirm the confession immediately after torture had stopped.

[172] Esmein (n 123) 114.

[173] M Polaschek, 'The History of Torture in Austria' in Durand, *La torture judiciaire* (n 112) 605–06.

Two elements facilitated the spread of use of torture. As the power of states[174] grew notably in the thirteenth century, they became increasingly involved in the administration of criminal justice and displayed a growing eagerness to prosecute crime.[175] Secondly, the Church's struggle against heretics added to the vulgarisation of torture.[176] The Church's view, which was traditionally not particularly favourable towards the use of torture,[177] evolved and in 1252 Pope Innocent IV adopted the *Bulla ad extirpanda*, which allowed torture to be used against heretics.[178] By the sixteenth century, torture, like the oath, was firmly established in some of the leading continental legislative instruments on criminal procedure.[179]

B. The Abolition of Torture

The abolition of torture took place in most states of continental Europe in the eighteenth century.[180] Two elements contributed to this evolution: the changing views on torture in society[181] and the loosening of the rules on the law of evidence. These elements largely correspond to the factors that I previously analysed in relation to the abolition of the oath.[182] The abolition of torture shook the balance in favour of physical integrity and the interests of the suspect, whereas previously the effective prosecution of crime and state security weighed heavier.[183]

[174] States in a sense which also refers to counties, controlled by earls, or a duchy. In addition to these two elements, reference can also be made to more general changes in society, such as increases in traffic between different communities and the growth of cities, making it difficult to find witnesses: Durand, 'Réflexion préliminaire' (n 115) 26.

[175] Van Caenegem, *Geschiedenis van het Strafprocesrecht* (n 90) 222.

[176] ibid.

[177] For example, Pope Saint Nicolas I expressed doubts on the results of torture in 866 in a letter to the Bulgarians: Durand, 'Réflexion préliminaire' (n 115) 18. Saint Augustine seems to be more moderate: he limited himself to stressing that torture should be used in a moderate manner and expressed some scepticism: M Schmoeckel, 'La survivance de la torture après la chute de l'Empire romain' in Durand, *La torture judiciaire* (n 112) 321–22. Others understand his work as strongly opposed to torture: D Foyer, 'Régards théologiques sur la torture (période scolastique)' in Durand, *La torture judiciaire* (n 112) 362.

[178] English version consulted at www.documentacatholicaomnia.eu/01p/1252-05-15,_SS_Innocentius_IV,_Bulla_%27Ad_Extirpanda%27,_EN.pdf. Law 25 also stipulates that torture should not lead to death or cause limbs to break.

[179] In most of Belgium, the applicable provisions could be found in the Ordinance of 9 July 1570 on criminal procedure adopted by Philip II, which still applied in the 18th century in Belgium. Provisions on torture were equally included in the German *Constitutio Criminalis Carolina* of 1532 (excerpts available at https://pages.uoregon.edu/dluebke/Witches442/ConstitutioCriminalis.html), as well as the *Ordonnance Criminelle*: Dauchy (n 166) 522.

[180] Torture was abolished in 1752–54 in Prussia, in 1780 in France and in 1787 in Belgium (and, after its continued use, again in 1794 by the French). Langbein, *Torture and the Law of Proof* (n 112) 10.

[181] Spencer, 'Introduction' (n 111) 9.

[182] See 20–22 above.

[183] Schmoeckel (n 177) 884.

The evolution towards the free evaluation of evidence reduced the importance of a confession and thus indirectly the use of torture to obtain one.[184] This allowed for the criticisms on torture to gain strength in practice.[185]

Similarly to the criticisms against the oath, abolitionists had criticised torture for several centuries. Already in the sixteenth century medical practitioners and Christians – both Protestants and Catholics – had argued against it, initially without much success.[186] Juan Luis Vives and Michel de Montaigne[187] opposed it. Vives considered torturing to be a contradiction of humanity and considered it anti-Christian.[188] Confessions obtained with the help of torture were not reliable and were thus useless.[189] Montaigne was inspired by Vives's ideas, which he further developed, and he tried to discredit torture by comparing it to cannibalism.[190] The opposition against torture grew stronger in the seventeenth century and amongst its opponents were now also members of high judicial authorities.[191] Torture was considered to be a demonstration of the inhumanity of the absolutist states of the *Ancien Régime*.[192] The critics started to be successful in their struggle against torture during the Age of Enlightenment.[193] Individuals such as Thomasius, Voltaire and Beccaria, as well as the enlightened absolutists they influenced, furthered its abolition.[194] Several arguments supported their call for abolition. Beccaria opposed torture as he considered it to be a punishment, not to be applied to a person who had not been found guilty by a judge.[195] He added that a person who is subjected to torture cannot speak freely,[196] and considered it the best way to guarantee that hardened criminals would be released and innocent people convicted.[197] Furthermore, he explicitly referred to England in arguing for the abolition of torture.[198] Sonnenfels and von Martini considered torture useless, save for one exception: after he had confessed, a suspect could be tortured in order to reveal his accomplices.[199] Frederic II of Prussia (1712–86), influenced by the ideas of the Age of Enlightenment, also played an important role. Shortly after taking up office in 1740, he strongly restricted the use of torture by means of a

[184] Le Marc'hadour (n 167) 768.
[185] Langbein, *Torture and the Law of Proof* (n 112) 60.
[186] Durand, 'Réflexion préliminaire' (n 115) 33–34.
[187] Vives, 1493–1540; Montaigne, 1533–92.
[188] Schmoeckel (n 177) 886.
[189] ibid.
[190] ibid.
[191] Durand, 'Réflexion préliminaire' (n 115) 35.
[192] Schmoeckel (n 177) 888.
[193] ibid 884.
[194] Durand, 'Réflexion préliminaire' (n 115) 36.
[195] C Beccaria, *Traité des délits et des peines- traduction française*, (Edition Cujas, 1966) 82.
[196] de la Serna (n 25) 4.
[197] Beccaria, *Traité des délits et des peines* (n 195) 82.
[198] ibid 87.
[199] Polaschek (n 173) 610.

secret order.[200] After concluding that the criminal justice system had not suffered because of this reform, he formally abolished torture in 1754.[201]

Nevertheless, even in the eighteenth century certain members of the judiciary, for instance in what is now Belgium and Austria,[202] as well as legal experts opposed abolition.[203] They thought that torture helped preserve order within the state and facilitated proving offences.[204] They explained judgments, which led to the sentencing of innocent people, as cases where the judge wrongfully used torture.[205] Saint Alphonsus Maria de' Liguori, a member of the clergy, did not contest the legitimacy of torture in the eighteenth century but nevertheless highlighted that torture should only be used after less intrusive means had been used and that it should not be used when it was fully proven that the offence was committed by the suspect.[206] They could not, however, prevent other scholars and heads of state from eventually picking up on the abolition of torture by Frederic II, even though they were able to keep it secret for a while.[207]

IV. Consolidation of the Privilege against Self-Incrimination

I situated the abolition of the oath and torture in an era when the individual became more important due to the ideas of the Age of Enlightenment and in light of several centuries of criticism of such forms of compulsion, as well as changes in the law of evidence in several continental states.

The next step in the evolution of the *nemo tenetur* principle towards the PSI was the consolidation, often in statutory provisions, of the freedom not to be compelled to incriminate oneself. This evolution did not always lead to an explicit provision that stipulates that a person cannot be required to incriminate himself, as the statutory provisions can be more subtle. The French Code d'instruction criminelle (1808) abolished the obligation for suspects to take the oath.[208] Like in France, Dutch defendants, under the Dutch Code of Criminal Procedure of 1838, were still considered to bear a moral duty to answer questions of judges, yet no formal sanction applied in case of a refusal to do so.[209] In E&W, the privilege was

[200] Schmoeckel (n 177) 888.
[201] Langbein, *Torture and the Law of Proof* (n 112) 62.
[202] Polaschek (n 173) 611.
[203] Schmoeckel (n 177) 885.
[204] Dauchy (n 166) 531; Schmoeckel (n 177) 885; Zeeman (n 80) 267.
[205] Schmoeckel (n 177) 888.
[206] Foyer (n 177) 364.
[207] Schmoeckel (n 177) 889.
[208] Art 75 of the Code limits the oath to witnesses. For the original text of the Code, see http://ledroitcriminel.fr/la_legislation_criminelle/anciens_textes/code_instruction_criminelle_1808/code_instruction_criminelle_1.htm. At the same time, suspects had a moral duty to answer questions of a judge: Zeeman (n 80) 268.
[209] Meese, 'The Sound of Silence' (n 105) 59; Zeeman (n 80) 269–70.

recognised in case law,[210] as well as in several legislative provisions. Section 18 of the Indictable Offences Act 1848 explicitly required that the accused person be informed that he could not be compelled to say anything.[211] Authors have accepted that from 1830 onwards the PSI was available in Belgium.[212] In the USA, the PSI was explicitly enshrined in the Constitution, together with other safeguards.[213] Moglen has argued that this constitutionalisation of the privilege was part of the process of Americans separating themselves from British imperial rule.[214] In this process, the PSI, along with other rules, became a constitutional right.[215] The constitutionalisation of the privilege and other safeguards was aimed at preventing tyrannical practices.[216] Levy understands the constitutionalisation as a 'ritualistic gesture', expressing the broader idea that the citizen is the master of the government and not the other way around.[217]

V. The Missing Piece of the Puzzle?

In the previous sections, I have suggested that the privilege has roots going back to the *nemo tenetur* principle. The principle's exact scope was not, however, clear, and disagreement existed on when it could be set aside. Throughout history, different types of coercive practices restricted the *nemo tenetur* principle. Once the latter practices were abolished, several states recognised, principally in the eighteenth and nineteenth centuries, implicitly or explicitly, that a person cannot be compelled to incriminate himself. Yet, one may wonder whether that suffices to ensure an effective PSI.

Langbein convincingly argues that it does not.[218] He connects the privilege's effectiveness to access to a lawyer at the trial stage, the POI and the obligation on the prosecution to discharge the burden of proof.[219] This evolution took place thanks to the shift in the eighteenth and nineteenth centuries[220] from a trial

[210] *Regina v Robert Mea an Attorney* (1703) 2 Lord Raymond 927, 92 ER 119; *Dominus Rex v Cornelius et al* (1743) 2 Strange 1210, 93 ER 1133.

[211] Similarly, see J Langbein, 'The Historical Origin of the Privilege against Self-Incrimination at Common Law' (1994) 92 *Michigan Law Review* 1047, 1061; Levy, 'Origins of the Fifth Amendment and Its Critics' (n 121) 846; Wigmore (n 95) 3085.

[212] de la Serna (n 25) 5–6. On the early case law of the CoC, see n 427 below.

[213] On its wording and implications, see Levy, *Origins of the Fifth Amendment* (n 75) 422–24.

[214] Moglen (n 93) 144.

[215] Levy, *Origins of the Fifth Amendment* (n 75) 405; Moglen (n 93) 138.

[216] Moglen (n 93) 138.

[217] Levy, *Origins of the Fifth Amendment* (n 75) 430 and 431.

[218] Langbein, 'The Historical Origin' (n 211) 1081. Critically on Langbein's views, see Levy, 'Origins of the Fifth Amendment and Its Critics' (n 121) 843–49.

[219] Langbein, 'The Historical Origin' (n 211) 1048.

[220] This timing seems at first sight at odds with Wigmore's. Wigmore considered that in the aftermath of the abolition of the Court of Star Chamber and the Court of High Commission in 1641, a broad PSI started to be claimed in common law courts. In his view, the tensions between the common law courts and the prerogative courts focused on the lack of proper proceeding or accusation, rather than

model, where the accused was supposed to reply to the charges against him,[221] to a model where he could test the strength of the prosecution's case, with the help of a lawyer.[222] Under the old model, different obstacles, such as restriction of access to a lawyer at trial[223] or the ineffectiveness of the POI,[224] were in place that hindered exercising the privilege. That held true also in the common law trial courts, where at least in E&W torture and the oath did not play an important role. From 1500 to 1620, at trial, defendants were, however, according to Wigmore, urged, pressed and bullied to answer.[225] In the new model, where the strength of the prosecution case was being tested and where the beyond reasonable doubt standard of proof was formulated,[226] the suspect could take a more passive role. Although Langbein focuses mainly on the developments in E&W, Moglen has shown that this reasoning similarly played an important role in the USA.[227] Langbein's argument is also relevant for continental countries. There, too, the POI received more attention in the eighteenth century and it was, for example, included in Article 9 of the French *Déclaration des droits de l'homme et du citoyen* (1789).[228] Moreover, Langbein's arguments that connect the PSI to other defence rights such as access to a lawyer are also relevant for such countries.

VI. Applying the Historical Rationales to Corporations

Historically, the PSI had several justifications. They did not benefit from unanimous acceptance, and exceptions to the privilege often greatly reduced the privilege's applicability in practice. One needs to consider these rationales in their historical context, where the focus was on natural persons and where CCL had yet to develop. The focus in the early days of corporations was on civil liability for damages.[229]

on the question whether a suspect can as such refuse to answer incriminating questions. That nuance was in his view lost after the aforementioned abolition, and claims were made that no man is bound to incriminate himself, regardless of the way in which proceedings were launched. Wigmore does, however, concede that the old habit of questioning and urging the accused only disappeared at the beginning of the next century: Wigmore (n 95) 3088 and 3090.

[221] Langbein, 'The Historical Origin' (n 211) 1047. He refers to this model as 'the accused speaks'. Similarly, in relation to the situation in what is now Belgium, see Monballyu, *Zes eeuwen strafrecht* (n 126) 358.

[222] Langbein, 'The Historical Origin' (n 211) 1048.

[223] ibid 1047–49.

[224] Zeeman (n 80) 265.

[225] Wigmore (n 95) 3085.

[226] Langbein, 'The Historical Origin' (n 211) 1070.

[227] Moglen (n 93) 114.

[228] D Chalus, 'La dialectique "aveu-droit au silence" dans la manifestation de la vérité judiciaire en droit pénal compare' (2009) 43 *La Revue Juridique Themis* 321, 342.

[229] TJ Bernard, 'The Historical Development of Corporate Criminal Liability' (1984) 22 Criminology 3, 4–5.

The privilege had close ties with the notion of self-preservation. It would run counter to a person's instincts to provide information that could lead to his own punishment, including the death penalty. This duty of self-preservation did not cease to apply once one became a suspect. This justification was invoked to challenge torture and the oath as evidence-gathering tools, such practices being particularly cruel in light of the concept of self-preservation. In my view, this justification has a role to play in the context of the PSI of corporations: several states have introduced provisions that require the production of pre-existing documents, as well as statements. Failure to comply with them can result in sanctions.[230] One could consider them to be a modern threat to self-preservation: failure to comply could lead to sanctions and so could providing wrongful information,[231] and cooperating could facilitate a conviction (unless cooperation were part of a settlement or a limited use rule applied).[232] Furthermore, eighteenth-century English case law accepted the applicability of the PSI to documents, reasoning that courts would not compel a person to produce evidence against himself.[233] This case law shows that the privilege was not limited to oral statements, although the oath and torture were primarily used to obtain that type of evidence. In the next chapter, I will further examine whether corporations can for this purpose be assimilated to individuals.

The second historical justification of the privilege was an early privacy rationale: persons did not have to disclose their offences to authorities. They only had to disclose their offences to God. This rationale focuses particularly on individuals, but one should not be too quick to dismiss a privacy rationale in relation to corporations.[234]

Thirdly, the need to protect against miscarriages of justice justified the privilege. Practices such as the oath and torture led to perjury and to unreliable evidence. This rationale may be hard to transpose to corporations, as it does not warrant the applicability of the privilege to pre-existing documents. Excessive compulsion cannot as such change the content of documents that already exist. At the same time, excessive compulsion can have an impact on the ability and willingness of individuals to exercise the PSI.

Lastly, Langbein has correctly pointed out that the privilege is warranted by the changing views in the eighteenth and nineteenth centuries that allowed suspects to take a more passive role, as it is for the prosecution to show their guilt.

[230] eg the *Citibank* case.

[231] Such provisions typically sanction providing wrongful information.

[232] By providing the (damaging) information one has.

[233] *Regina* (n 210); *Dominus Rex* (n 210); *Rex v Dr Purnell, Vice-Chancellor of Oxford* (1748) 1 Wilson, KB 239, 95 ER 595; DM Horowitz and SK Wirth, 'The Dead and Resurrection of the Required-Records Doctrine' (2017) 86 *Mississippi Law Journal* 513, 518.

[234] In contrast, see J Dine, 'Criminal Law and the Privilege Against Self-Incrimination' in S Peers and A Ward (eds), *The European Union Charter of Fundamental Rights* (Hart Publishing, 2004) 280. For a more nuanced approach, see D Feldman, 'Corporate Rights and the Privilege Against Self-Incrimination' in D Feldman and F Meisel (eds), *Corporate and Commercial Law* (LLP, 1996) 368–69.

In this sense, the PSI has strong links with the POI and the prosecution's obligation to carry the burden of proof.[235] In that sense, the privilege helps ensure a suspect's liberty to define his defence strategy without being required to contribute to his own conviction.[236] Corporate defendants too should be free to set up their defence strategy.

[235] P Oliver, 'Companies and their Fundamental Rights: A Comparative Perspective' (2015) 64 *ICLQ* 661, 668.

[236] Zeeman (n 80) 279 and 723.

3

How Different Are Corporations for the Purpose of the Privilege against Self-Incrimination?

The previous chapter highlighted the PSI's strong ties to anthropological aspects, such as protection against torture or the oath. At first sight, these ties may justify, in light of the principle of equality, a different treatment of corporations when it comes to the PSI.[237] Specific features of the corporation, such as the impossibility of exercising the privilege independently, further seem to suggest such differentiated treatment.

Nevertheless, a deeper analysis of these features may show that some of the privilege's historical rationales are indeed relevant for corporations.[238] For example, requiring a corporation to provide self-incriminating evidence can be at odds with its self-preservation, understood as the natural inclination to preserve itself from harm or destruction:[239] it can face significant fines, reputational damage due to a prosecution,[240] prejudice to its stock price, shareholder lawsuits,[241] dissolution or debarment from contracting with the government.

This chapter focuses on the prima facie differences between individuals and corporations that are relevant to the PSI. The analysis does not focus on the impact of the law of individual countries on these specificities, but rather on specificities that are generally relevant. It will help to clarify whether corporations and individuals are comparable categories of persons for the purpose of the PSI. In order for them to be comparable for the purpose of the privilege, their situations do not need to be identical.[242] The presence of some discrepancies between individuals

[237] See above 10–11.

[238] Moreover, the privilege may have at present additional justifications that can apply to corporations too.

[239] www.merriam-webster.com/dictionary/self-preservation.

[240] AD Lowell and CD Man, 'Federalizing Corporate Internal Investigations and The Erosion of Employees' Fifth Amendment Rights' (2011) 40 *Georgetown Law Journal Annual Review of Criminal Procedure* iii, vi.

[241] R Kloeber, '"Between the Rock and the Whirlpool": Corporate Cooperation Credit and Issues of Compelled Self-Incrimination' (2018) 32 *Notre Dame Journal of Law, Ethics and Public Policy* 635, 638.

[242] Alen and Muylle (n 62) 505–06.

and corporations does not as such imply that they are incomparable. Next, I apply the other steps of the principle of equality test.

Although I attempt to include the largest possible range of types of corporations, some of the differences may be less relevant for certain types. The importance of documentary evidence can be more limited in a small corporation than in a multinational with hundreds of local branches. This is not surprising: as more individuals become involved, power is delegated internally and larger trails of internal communication develop. Most corporations can be found between these two extremes.[243] For my research, the corporate structure is more relevant than its turnover. Corporate structure is understood as the internal division of responsibilities, competences and tasks, as well as the external relations with other corporations. For example, if a corporation is a wholly owned subsidiary of a larger group, does that affect the way in which its procedural rights are exercised?[244] Nevertheless, several elements raised in this chapter may be equally relevant for corporations run by a single individual.

When corporations are under investigation or prosecuted, many procedural challenges arise.[245] The law on procedural safeguards focused historically on individuals, as CCL is still relatively new in many countries.[246] Nijboer has claimed that it is therefore unsuited for corporate prosecutions.[247] According to Gobert and Punch, the development of a criminal procedure *sensu stricto* adapted to corporations has been hindered by the practice in some jurisdictions of equating corporations and individuals for the purpose of criminal procedures.[248] Although they accept that prosecutions of both corporations and individuals should be just and fair, they argue that those concepts do not necessarily imply the same thing for both categories.[249] Stephens has suggested that corporations should not benefit from protection designed for those who live and breathe.[250] In my view, one should

[243] http://ec.europa.eu/eurostat/statistics-explained/index.php/Archive:Business_economy_-_size_class_analysis.

[244] Case C-268/14 P *Italmobiliare SpA v Commission* ECLI:EU:C:2015:697, para 40.

[245] For example, a corporation that is trying to avoid criminal liability through a winding up or merger. On a civil fine which qualified as criminal according to the ECtHR imposed after a merger by absorption, see *Carrefour France* (n 38).

[246] On its history, see Bernard (n 229). In several countries, the codes of criminal procedure were drafted before such liability existed.

[247] JF Nijboer, 'A Plea for a Systematic Approach in Developing Criminal Procedural Law Concerning the Investigation, Prosecution and Adjudication of Corporate Entities' in A Esser et al (eds), *Criminal Responsibility of Legal and Collective Entities* (MPI, 1999) 303 and 307. The USA is far more familiar with issues such as the PSI of corporations, and relevant case law dates back to the beginning of the 20th century, when CCL was underdeveloped in continental Europe: *Hale v Henkel* 201 US 43 (1906); *Wilson v United States* 221 US 361 (1911). Corporate prosecutions in this chapter should be understood as prosecutions where the corporation itself is suspected of having committed an offence, potentially together with one or more individuals.

[248] J Gobert and M Punch, *Rethinking Corporate Crime* (Cambridge University Press, 2003) 179.

[249] ibid 180–81.

[250] She recognises that many disagree with that approach and she argues in favour of a consistent approach towards corporate rights and obligations. B Stephens, 'Are Corporations People? Corporate Personhood under the Constitution and International Law' (2013) 44 *Rutgers Law Journal* 1, 38.

not assume that corporations cannot be the victim of the violation of fair trial standards. The *Yukos* case has made this painfully clear.[251] The collateral damage of a corporate indictment,[252] let alone a conviction, even if overturned in the end, can be severe.[253] Nevertheless, I agree that the concrete application of procedural safeguards to corporations requires an in-depth analysis.[254]

Before I turn to the comparability question, I briefly consider the main theories of corporate personhood as some of these theories have played a role in the debate on the applicability of the PSI and other safeguards to corporations.

I. Corporate Personhood

Corporations are legal persons, yet does this mean that they can be assimilated to natural persons? Or does the word 'legal' indicate that corporations are fictitious persons who owe their existence to the law, entirely differently to human beings?[255]

Under the fiction theory, corporations could not be punished or held accountable for offences or sins due to their lack of soul, will and body.[256] This theory relies on St Thomas Aquinas' argument that real persons have a rational individuated substance.[257] The main benefit of this theory for corporations is that they cannot face criminal liability. At the same time, the lack of individuated substance, referred to as subjectivity in German philosophy, makes it similarly difficult to attribute rights to them.[258] When the corporation is considered as a fictional entity, considering it as a holder of 'human rights' is unlikely.[259]

The concession theory has influenced the debate on corporations and the PSI. This theory developed in the context of the rise of states towards the later Middle Ages.[260] States attempted to centralise power and did not look favourably upon

[251] Yukos received an astronomically high tax bill and its procedural rights under Art 6 ECHR were violated, as it did not have sufficient time to study the case file: *Oao Neftyanaya Kompaniya Yukos v Russia* App no 14902/04 (ECtHR, 20 September 2011) para 551.

[252] Kloeber (n 241) 638–39; Lowell and Man (n 240) iii and vi.

[253] Arthur Andersen faced obstruction of justice charges in relation to the shredding of documents linked to Enron's accounting. At that time, it was a direct competitor of the Big Four. It was convicted, leading to the loss of employment for tens of thousands of its employees. In 2005 SCOTUS overturned its conviction, but the damage was already done: *Arthur Andersen LLP v United States* 544 US 696 (2006).

[254] eg *Bernh Larsen Holding AS and others v Norway* App no 24117/08 (ECtHR, 14 March 2013).

[255] On this issue, see Franssen, 'European Sentencing' (n 19) 229–32; Pinto and Evans (n 4) 5–13.

[256] Franssen, 'European Sentencing' (n 19) 230.

[257] ibid 230.

[258] J Dewey, 'The Historic Background of Corporate Legal Personality' (1926) 35 *Yale Law Journal* 655, 659–60.

[259] SG Wood and BG Scharffs, 'Applicability of Human Rights Standards to Private Corporations: An American Perspective' (2002) 50 *American Journal of Comparative Law* Suppl 531, 541–42. According to them, SCOTUS's refusal in *Hale* to grant corporations access to the PSI can be linked to the consideration of corporations as fictional entities.

[260] Dewey (n 258) 666–67.

the powers of bodies such as congregations and guilds. The powers of such bodies were thus removed and were only returned if explicitly granted to them by the state.[261] This theory is particularly relevant when one considers corporations up to the start of the second half of the nineteenth century, a period when they were still rare.[262] From the mid-nineteenth century onwards, establishing a corporation became more common thanks to general incorporation laws.[263] Originally, establishing a corporation required a charter granted by the sovereign.[264] This meant that the state had considerable control over the corporation.

Beyond these two traditional theories, new ones have developed. According to the aggregate entity doctrine, the corporation is the combination of its members and shareholders.[265] Several authors consider the real entity theory as the predominant one, but that view is challenged.[266] Although this theory considers corporations as fictitious persons without body or soul, it recognises them as real socio-economic actors with significant power;[267] it treats the corporation as distinct from its members.[268] The theory similarly accepts that corporations have the potential to cause significant harm.[269]

II. (Im)possibility of Exerting Physical or Psychological Pressure on Corporations

Chapter two stressed the privilege's strong link with the protection against physical and psychological compulsion. Opponents of a corporate PSI readily refer to the impossibility of exercising physical or psychological pressure on a corporation to argue against such a privilege.[270] A corporation does not as such have limbs

[261] Franssen, 'European Sentencing' (n 19) 230.
[262] Stephens (n 250) 8.
[263] Pinto and Evans (n 4) 8–13.
[264] SA Trainor, 'A Comparative Analysis of a Corporation's Right Against Self-Incrimination' (1994) 18 *Fordham International Law Journal* 2139, 2163–66. Charters contained their purpose, powers and structure: Stephens (n 250) 8.
[265] Oliver, 'Companies and their Fundamental Rights' (n 235) 663.
[266] Franssen, 'European Sentencing' (n 19) 231; Stephens (n 250) 12. In contrast, see Wood and Scharffs (n 259) 543. According to the latter, the aggregate entity theory is dominant at least among US scholars.
[267] Franssen, 'European Sentencing' (n 19) 231.
[268] BL Garrett, 'The Constitutional Standing of Corporations' (2014) 163 *University of Pennsylvania Law Review* 95, 108.
[269] SS Beale, 'A Response to the Critics of Corporate Criminal Liability' (2009) 46 *American Criminal Law Review* 1481, 1482–83.
[270] VS Khanna, 'Corporate Defendants and the Protections of Criminal Procedure: An Economic Analysis' (2004) Law & Economics Working Papers No 04-015, 12–13 and 47, http://repository.law.umich.edu/cgi/viewcontent.cgi?article=1029&context=law_econ_archive; Oliver, 'Companies and their Fundamental Rights' (n 235) 667.

that can be twisted or kicked;[271] nor can it face imprisonment.[272] It cannot face psychological stress during police questioning or the fear of pre-trial detention or post-conviction imprisonment.[273] One can hardly imagine a corporation making an involuntary confession due to psychological compulsion.[274] A corporation can at first sight not face the cruel trilemma mentioned in chapter two.[275] Some of the aforementioned theories can further support the opponents of a corporate PSI: the fiction theory stresses the lack of corporate body or will. Although the concession theory focuses on the limitations of the powers and rights of corporations rather than on their fictional character, one can rely on it to defend a more restrictive approach in relation to corporate procedural safeguards.[276]

In other words, at first glance, one of the principal justifications of the PSI does not apply fully to corporations. Nevertheless, several reasons advocate for a more nuanced view.

First, some of the other historical rationales or alternative justifications warrant the privilege's applicability.[277]

Secondly, corporations can indirectly face physical and psychological compulsion to provide evidence: just as corporations rely on individuals to act on their behalf, they may be compelled through them. For example, corporate employees or officials can face arrest and detention, which may induce the corporation to cooperate with the authorities.[278] For the purpose of my analysis, I distinguish a scenario where the corporation and its personnel or officials meet the conditions to invoke the PSI, as well as a scenario where only the corporation meets the conditions but its personnel or officials do not.

[271] JC Coffee, '"No Soul to Damn: No Body to Kick": An Unscandalized Inquiry into the Problem of Corporate Punishment' (1980–81) 79 *Michigan Law Review* 386, 459; Feldman (n 234) 366 and 370; M Tushnet, 'Do For-Profit Corporations Have Rights of Religious Conscience?' (2013) 99 *Cornell Law Review* 70, 73.

[272] JE Fisch, 'Criminalization of Corporate Law: the Impact on Shareholders and Other Constituents' (2007) 2 *Journal of Business and Technology Law* 91, 91; Franssen, 'European Sentencing' (n 19) 234 and 236.

[273] On the issue of moral and social pressure, see JD Jackson and SJ Summers, *The Internalisation of Criminal Evidence* (Cambridge University Press, 2012) 272; P Roberts and A Zuckerman, *Criminal Evidence*, 2nd edn (Oxford University Press, 2010) 512–16 and 543. At the same time, individuals can also rely on the PSI in connection to charges that can only result in a fine, in which case the difference between individuals and corporations is less significant.

[274] Khanna (n 270) 4 and 47. Instead, Khanna argues that the only limit on the power of the prosecution to gather evidence from corporations should be avoidance of excessive interference with business and the costs of complying with unlimited requests for information.

[275] Tushnet (n 271) 73.

[276] Dine (n 234) 280; Feldman (n 234) 374.

[277] G Stessens, *De nationale en internationale bestrijding van het witwassen* (Intersentia, 1997) 310.

[278] In Brazil, the authorities sought Facebook's cooperation to access information related to an organised crime case. In light of its non-compliance, the authorities arrested the vice-president for Latin America until the next day: www.theguardian.com/technology/2016/mar/01/brazil-police-arrest-facebook-latin-america-vice-president-diego-dzodan.

In the former scenario, the individuals can in principle rely on their own PSI.[279] To the extent that these individuals choose to do so, the corporation can indirectly benefit from protection against incrimination: evidence which the individual conceals might not only be self-incriminating; it might also incriminate the corporation. For example, a manager responsible for environmental issues cuts back on the maintenance of water purification systems, knowing that this can result in hazardous water leaking into a nearby river. This information would not only tend to incriminate the manager personally, it may also (help) establish CCL. If the manager invokes his privilege, this can be beneficial for the corporation.[280] Even in this scenario, the protection offered to the corporation is precarious: there is no guarantee that the corporate officials or employees will exercise their own privilege. They may prefer to cooperate with the authorities or they may be unable to rely on their privilege.[281]

The corporation faces an even less favourable situation in the second scenario.[282] The individuals cannot invoke their own PSI because the conditions to do so are not met and they can thus be compelled to provide incriminating evidence against the corporation. Hence, it is particularly important both for the individuals involved and for the corporation that a clear indication is given to the individuals as to the capacity in which they are being interviewed: as a representative of the corporation, as a witness or as a suspect.

One may argue that corporate officials and employees at times face compulsion during a government investigation into corporate wrongdoing in their role as corporate pawns, rather than in their individual capacity.[283] This pressure is unsettling:[284] whilst refusing to cooperate with the prosecuting authorities can expose the individuals and possibly the corporation to punitive sanctions,[285] choosing to cooperate with the investigation can result in the disclosure of evidence that incriminates the corporation, and if the employees provide false information they can face perjury charges. In other words, the situation amounts to a sort of

[279] Alternatively, they should typically receive guarantees that the evidence given under compulsion would not be used against them personally, eg through a grant of immunity.

[280] On the other hand, at times, the corporation's defence can be harmed if employees conceal this sort of information. In certain jurisdictions, corporations will often seek to cooperate with the prosecuting authorities as there are particular incentives for them do so.

[281] This can be the case, for example, where these individuals were granted immunity in relation to their statements, or there can be a rule under national law that evidence obtained under compelled questioning provisions cannot be used against them personally.

[282] The second scenario can turn into the first one.

[283] Where they are themselves suspects, they can face the compulsion both in a personal capacity and as a corporate pawn.

[284] In cases of major alleged corporate wrongdoing, it is not hard to imagine that the corporation's employees or officials, in light of the extensive media coverage, will be aware of the potential outcome for the corporation and their personal employment.

[285] In those situations where they are themselves not (yet) entitled to their own privilege. In the absence of a corporate PSI, the corporation may face charges for obstructing the investigation, either under a general obstruction provision or under a sector-specific provision, or contempt charges.

cruel trilemma to which the corporation is exposed through the individuals on which it relies. The argument that corporations face compulsion through their officials and employees finds support in the way many states[286] treat corporations under substantive criminal law: they accept that corporations can commit criminal offences through the individuals on which they rely.[287] Admittedly, the attribution of criminal liability to corporations has been challenged,[288] often due to the difficulty associated with attributing guilt[289] to an entity 'without a soul'.[290] Nevertheless, if one manages to accept that a corporation can have a guilty mind through attribution, one can argue that it can also have a will that can be compelled[291] and that it should thus be able to rely on the privilege.

There is another reason to suggest that corporations too can face compulsion. Although a corporation itself cannot feel ashamed,[292] the reputational damage it suffers by a conviction or even by merely being under investigation in a punitive case[293] can put significant pressure on it. Reputational damage can take different forms: the stock value of a publicly traded company can take a hit once the corporation is under investigation, current trade partners and customers[294] may wish to dissociate themselves from it, and potential customers and trade partners may prefer a competitor. Moreover, the corporation can suffer collateral damage, such as the suspension of projects due to the uncertainty of the outcome of the punitive investigation.[295] Franssen argues that stigmatising effects are most likely to be present where the offence affects the quality of the principal activities of the corporation.[296] Prosecutors can use the risk of reputational damage, as they can use it to further force corporations to provide evidence.

The corporation may face strong pressure not only from the threat of reputational damage and collateral damage: it may face further pressure when the model of CCL sets a low threshold in order for the corporation to be found guilty. In other words, the threat of criminal prosecution may be particularly serious

[286] On different models of CCL, see Roef (n 7) 333–73.

[287] F Deruyck, 'De rechten van verdediging van de rechtspersoon in de Belgische strafprocedure: van verre evident, maar verre van evident' [2016] *Nullum Crimen* 17, 35.

[288] AW Alschuler, 'Two Ways to Think about the Punishment of Corporations' (2009) 46 *American Criminal Law Review* 1359.

[289] On the issue of attributing guilt to corporations, see M Böse, 'Corporate Criminal Liability in Germany' in Pieth and Ivory, *Corporate Criminal Liability* (n 3) 228 and 230–31; PH Bucy, 'Why Punish? Trends in Corporate Criminal Prosecutions' (2007) 44 *American Criminal Law Review* 1287, 1288; Franssen, 'European Sentencing' (n 19) 238–42.

[290] On this issue, see Roef (n 7) 335.

[291] See also Feldman (n 234) 370.

[292] Franssen, 'European Sentencing' (n 19) 246.

[293] Coffee (n 271) 428.

[294] Franssen, 'European Sentencing' (n 19) 250.

[295] Bucy (n 289) 1289. For example, instead of investing in a new factory or product, budgets may need to be saved for covering penalties and legal fees.

[296] Franssen, 'European Sentencing' (n 19) 247 and 248. A tax evasion conviction of a major car manufacturer may not have the same stigmatising effect as its conviction connected to faulty car safety features.

where a very broad vicarious liability system is in use.[297] Admittedly, even if a corporation has access to the PSI, it may decide to forsake certain procedural safeguards and accept an out-of-court settlement in order to avoid harsher penalties in a classic trial.[298]

Moreover, if one considers corporations in light of the real entity doctrine, rather than under the fiction theory, one can more readily accept that corporations, as real socio-economic actors, can face compulsion. Admittedly, even under that theory, one needs to be willing to consider compulsion with a certain level of flexibility to accept my argument that corporations may, albeit indirectly, be compelled to provide incriminating evidence.

I consider that corporations can face compulsion,[299] albeit not in exactly the same way as individuals. I conclude that, in relation to the concept of 'compulsion', individuals and corporations constitute comparable categories.

III. Importance of Documentary Evidence

A second, possibly relevant specificity is the role documentary evidence plays in corporate prosecutions. Case law and the literature stress the crucial importance of documentary evidence[300] for corporate prosecutions[301] and the detrimental impact on such prosecutions of a corporate PSI that covers documents.[302] Even though this might disregard the relevance of other elements, such as testimony by current or former employees or officials[303] who can act as whistleblowers, it is definitely true that in corporations documentary evidence can play a role and gathering all relevant documents can be burdensome, particularly in larger corporations.[304] In order to understand the documentary evidence and maximise its evidentiary value, explanations given by knowledgeable individuals are key.[305] The bigger the

[297] P Bharara, 'Corporations Cry Uncle and Their Employees Cry Foul: Rethinking Prosecutorial Pressure on Corporate Defendants' (2007) 44 *American Criminal Law Review* 53, 74.

[298] K Ligeti and S Tosza, 'Challenges and Trends in Enforcing Economic and Financial Crime: Criminal Law and Alternatives in Europe and the US' in K Ligeti and S Tosza (eds), *White Collar Crime – A Comparative Perspective* (Hart Publishing, 2019) 24.

[299] Similarly, in the context of EU competition law, see Joined Cases C-238/99 P, C-244/99 P, C-245/99 P, C-247/99 P, C-250/99 P to C-252/99 P and C-254/99 P *Limburgse Vinyl Maatschappij and Others v Commission* ECLI:EU:C:2002:582, paras 273–75 (*LVM*).

[300] Documentary evidence comprises classic documents, such as board minutes, its articles of association and its bookkeeping, but also 'digital documents' such as the chatlogs between employees using an internal instant messaging platform on the corporation's network, or emails.

[301] *Braswell v United States*, 487 US 99, 115 (1988); Khanna (n 270) 46.

[302] *Hale* (n 247).

[303] BL Garrett, 'Corporate Confessions' (2008) 30 *Cardozo Law Review* 917, 927. Garrett nevertheless admits that such prosecutions still rely to a great extent on documents.

[304] AG Wahl (n 244) paras 44, 70, 100 and 111. The list of documents seems to be endless: *Braswell* (n 301) 101, fn 1.

[305] J Arlen and SW Buell, 'The Law of Corporate Investigations and the Global Expansion of Corporate Criminal Enforcement' (2020) 93 *Southern California Law Review* 697, 715.

corporation becomes in terms of employees, branches and subsidiaries, the greater the amount of documentary evidence generated. These documents can vary widely in nature and depend on the field in which the corporation operates.[306] It should also be noted that several countries have tended to restrict the scope of the PSI in relation to documentary evidence over the last decades.[307] It is unlikely that states would accept that corporations could rely on the privilege in order to refuse to hand over self-incriminating documents where individuals are not allowed to do so. At the same time, in those countries where the privilege offers little protection to documentary evidence, one can hardly criticise a corporate PSI by referring to the importance of documentary evidence in corporate wrongdoing cases if such evidence is not protected by the privilege.

Documentary evidence can play an important role in the application of the different models of CCL.[308] As corporations do not act in the same way as individuals, establishing their *mens rea* and *actus reus* can be challenging. In jurisdictions relying on the identification doctrine, it is crucial to determine who the directing mind of the corporation is. In order to understand whether a person has a sufficiently important position in the corporation, a close examination of the company's articles of association, its constitution and the contracts with its management is necessary.[309] A comparable, yet more limited, analysis will have to be made in jurisdictions relying on a vicarious model for CCL.[310] In such systems, the prosecution needs to check whether or not the employee purportedly triggering the corporation's liability was on a 'private mission'. This entails looking at the employee's employment contract, job description and corporate guidelines. In countries that apply a model of CCL that focuses on organisational fault, the role of documentary evidence is particularly relevant.[311] Board minutes can be helpful in understanding what the directors did or did not do in order to prevent the type of offence that took place, just as corporate policy documents, guidelines and other documents can help shed light on possible corporate wrongdoing.

At the same time, documentary evidence can play a central role in the prosecution of individuals too, often, but not exclusively,[312] in cases involving white-collar crime. In such cases, documentary evidence can help disentangle the often-complex processes that have taken place. As corporate wrongdoing is regularly situated in the field of white-collar crime, one may wonder whether it is not the type of offence rather than the natural person–corporation distinction that determines the importance of documentary evidence.

[306] For example, the instant messaging logs between traders involved in the Libor scandal.
[307] Feldman (n 234) 384 et seq. So has the fourth section of the ECtHR: *De Legé* (n 57).
[308] Gobert and Punch (n 248) 189–90.
[309] ibid.
[310] ibid.
[311] ibid.
[312] For example, the exchange of encrypted messages may be crucial in a terrorism case.

One can also imagine corporate crime cases where there are little or no documents, for example because there were only a few individuals involved and they left (or tried to leave) no paper trail.

Admittedly, there are indications of a particular importance in corporate prosecutions: first of all, cumbersome models of CCL add to the difficulty of adducing sufficient evidence for a conviction. Furthermore, as corporations are not persons of flesh and blood, documentary evidence can be a useful additional type of evidence in assessing *actus reus* and *mens rea*. Particularly in large-scale corporations, it can help put together the complex puzzle of the extent and seriousness of the involvement of different individuals in the commission of the wrongdoing. Lastly, corporations often operate in highly regulated business fields, and in such fields a number of documents typically need to be created and maintained in the regular course of business.

Nevertheless, I consider that focusing on the importance of one type of self-incriminating evidence – documents – to consider individuals and corporations as different categories is erroneous for the reasons I have outlined. To the extent that the positions of individuals and corporations would not be identical in relation to documents, one should recall that the two categories need to be comparable, not necessarily identical.

IV. Impossibility of Exercising the Privilege against Self-Incrimination Independently

Corporations are unable to exercise the PSI without the intervention of one or more individuals.[313] This is not surprising and corresponds to my finding that corporations will typically face compulsion indirectly. The impossibility of exercising the privilege independently is a key difference between corporations and individuals.[314] Unlike individuals, who can weigh their interest in exercising or refraining from exercising the privilege on their own, corporations cannot exercise it independently. In practice, one or more individuals will have to decide whether they exercise the corporation's PSI, provided it is available to corporations.

A. Exercising the Privilege

The PSI is often considered as a personal privilege. It offers protection to the holder of the privilege against compelled self-incrimination. This personal character

[313] Nor any other fair trial right. See P Waeterinckx, *De strafrechtelijke verantwoordelijkheid van de rechtspersoon en zijn leidinggevenden* (Intersentia, 2015) 120 and 124. They are also generally unable to act without their agents' help. See *Wilson* (n 247) 377.

[314] Admittedly, some categories of individuals too may have difficulty exercising it; one can think of mentally ill persons and infants.

is used by the opponents of a corporate PSI to challenge it.[315] They consider it incompatible with the personal character of the privilege to allow individuals to refuse cooperation by arguing that this would tend to incriminate someone else (the corporation) rather than themselves.

Provided that one looks beyond that argument and accepts that individuals can exercise the corporation's privilege, the question nevertheless remains which individual or individuals are entitled to do so. Several models can be envisaged for such a corporate privilege.

According to a very restrictive approach to the corporate PSI, only one specific person would be allowed to exercise it. This person is then the contact point for the authorities when they wish to interview the corporation or when they seek documents of the corporation. This person would oversee the choosing of a lawyer for the corporation, and would decide whether to exercise the corporate PSI or instead opt for a more cooperative approach. To guarantee that the corporation can freely define its defence strategy, choosing this individual should in principle be left to the corporation. Nevertheless, one must limit the risk of appointing a person with a conflict of interest. Therefore, this model should be equipped with a mechanism to limit that risk. Such a mechanism could consist in allowing the legal representatives, including individual board members, as well as shareholders and the prosecutor to seize a court when they can show that there is a prima facie conflict of interest between the protection of the defence of the corporation and the person who has been appointed to exercise the corporation's defence rights. One can wonder whether it is preferable for the court competent to handle the case to decide on the matter or rather another court. When such a conflict arises before a pre-trial or trial court is handling the case, an FiC should be competent to address the perceived conflict of interest. Admittedly, this can be a delicate matter, as one will not necessarily want to disclose damaging information. Such a model seems more suited than a system whereby a court mandatorily appoints a representative once a legal representative of the corporation is himself suspected of the crime. There will not necessarily be a conflict of interest between them, eg because they have a similar defence strategy.

A second, broader model allows legal representatives who,[316] individually or jointly, can represent the corporation in invoking the corporation's privilege. Whether this model significantly increases the number of individuals depends on the type of corporation. In a one-person corporation, this will not be the case.[317]

Still broader is the model according to which not only the legal representatives can invoke the corporation's privilege, but also the leading individuals.[318] Leading

[315] Feldman (n 234) 373. He would nevertheless accept such a privilege where this would protect an officer or shareholder of the corporation.

[316] On this model's disadvantages: P Waeterinckx, 'De (afgeleide) rechten van verdediging van de rechtspersoon. Heeft een rechtspersoon het recht te zwijgen, eventueel met of zonder bijstand van een raadsman?' [2015] *Nullum Crimen* 73, 86.

[317] Also on this model, see below 220–21.

[318] Waeterinckx, 'De (afgeleide) rechten van verdediging' (n 316) 86–87. Also on this model, see below 197–98 and 221.

individuals in this sense are those individuals who were in charge of an activity or operation of the corporation. For example, the person in charge of a specific building site for a construction company could qualify as a leading individual. In the context of the prosecution of a car manufacturer for a mechanical failure, the individual in charge of the engineering of the affected car models could qualify as a leading individual.

Finally, one could consider adopting a corporation-wide PSI.[319] Such a model would allow any corporate employee or official to refuse to provide evidence where this would tend to incriminate the corporation. Applied to the aforementioned example of the CEO and the PA, this would entail that the PA too can rely on the corporation's privilege. One could render this model even broader, relying on the autonomy of criminal law, by including those individuals that are as such not directly employed by the corporation[320] but work indirectly for the corporation, such as security guards or external consultants.

B. Conflicts of Interest in the Context of the Corporation's Privilege

Conflicts of interest are common in any field of law. Two murder suspects can have conflicting interests, as each of them may want to try to put the blame on the other in order to avoid a conviction or at least to get as light a sentence as possible.[321] In the context of the corporate PSI, there is a high chance that such conflicts will occur.[322] All employees and officials are part of the corporation and they are the actors through whom the corporation can act. They are the physical components that externalise the corporation.

A first set of conflicts of interest arises when a suspected corporate official or employee faces questioning by the authorities about an offence, while the corporation too is a suspect. If the individual discloses specific information that exculpates the corporation,[323] he might at the same time incriminate himself. In this scenario, there is a clear tension between the individual's PSI and the corporation's defence.

[319] Deruyck, 'De rechten van verdediging' (n 287) 36. On this model, see below 196–97 and 221–22.

[320] In the sense that under labour law they have no employment contract with the corporation.

[321] Buell argues that the dynamics between a corporation and the individuals it employs differ from the situation of two murder suspects. Corporations are more likely to disclose criminal offences before the prosecuting authorities are aware of them, whereas individuals hoping for a better outcome for themselves by disclosing information on their accomplices or co-conspirators will ordinarily seek to cooperate only after the prosecuting authorities have become aware of the offence. One should be careful when considering this argument outside the US context: the US dynamics provide for particular incentives for corporations to disclose information. S Buell, 'Is the White Collar Offender Privileged?' (2014) 63 *Duke Law Journal* 823, 870–71.

[322] See AG Bobek's Opinion in Case C-546/18, para 57.

[323] For example, he admits that he fraudulently bypassed the internal control systems and acted for purely personal gain.

Similarly, an individual who provides information that is exculpatory for himself might be incriminating the corporation.

Even in the hypothesis that the corporation is the only suspect or where the evidence is not incriminating for the individual, he may still face a hard choice, in the absence of a corporate PSI:[324] he could harm the corporation by talking and harm his personal interests by not talking.[325] At the same time, disclosing evidence might also harm the corporation and the individual indirectly. A manager who discloses information to the prosecution that contributes to the corporation being sanctioned may feel an impact on his bonus,[326] on the value of the corporate stock he holds or, in major cases, on his employment as such due to the impact of the punitive case on the corporation.[327]

Two particular elements may compound the conflict of interests between the individuals and the corporation: the possible use of economic power by the corporation and the corporation's inability to 'talk' without the intervention of an individual and the associated risk of 'scapegoating'.

The corporation wields economic power over its employees and officials;[328] it may use this power to settle the conflict of interest. Once it is under investigation for its possible involvement in an offence, its choice to adopt a cooperative attitude instead of refusing any cooperation can affect the prosecution's decision to prosecute the corporation. Several national criminal justice systems have introduced mechanisms such as NPAs and DPAs to induce corporations to adopt the former attitude. The use of the corporation's economic power can include promises to pay fines and legal fees if the individual cooperates with the investigation, along with threats that refusal to cooperate will be considered unfavourably. The economic power can also come into play during non-official investigations,[329] such as internal investigations,[330] ordered and paid for by the corporation. During such investigations, traditional safeguards such as the PSI typically do not apply in the same way as in an official investigation.[331]

[324] Either because no such privilege exists in that jurisdiction or because the individual is not within the circle of individuals who can exercise the corporation's privilege.

[325] As he can hide behind neither his own nor the corporation's privilege, he can face a variety of charges, such as contempt and failure to cooperate under a sector-specific compelled questioning provision.

[326] In light of a large settlement with the authorities in a money laundering case in 2018, ING lowered staff bonuses: www.rtlz.nl/beurs/bedrijven/artikel/4579186/ing-bank-schrapt-bonussen-schikking-witwasaffaire-om-nederland.

[327] See also Feldman (n 234) 366–67.

[328] Garrett, 'Corporate Confessions' (n 303) 920.

[329] In the sense that these investigations are not conducted by judicial authorities or agents of an enforcement agency.

[330] Internal investigations can unveil the scope of allegations of criminal offences conducted in the corporate context, as well as other troubles. They can be conducted before or after an official investigation has been launched, or run in parallel with an investigation by the authorities. On the early stages of private and public investigation after detection of a possible offence, see Arlen and Buell (n 305) 714.

[331] Buell, 'Is the White Collar Offender Privileged?' (n 321) 870. Although employees may not be beaten or detained by those conducting the internal investigation, their situation remains precarious: they will not necessarily have access to a lawyer during such an investigation. Moreover, they have no

Nevertheless, the corporation will not necessarily rely on economic power to the detriment of individuals. Continental countries do not always follow the US approach, where corporations are subjected to a compelled cooperation model. Moreover, in small corporations, the interests of the corporation and the individuals will often advocate in favour of a common defence strategy.[332] There are also situations where the corporation may have lost (some) of its economic power over the individual: for example, when the person has left the corporation in the meantime.

Although corporations wield economic power over individuals, they suffer from a structural disadvantage. They lack the ability to speak without the intervention of individuals and they thus risk that individuals could use them as scapegoats. If corporate officials, or other (high-)ranked employees, are under investigation, they may try to put the blame on the corporation to downplay their own role in the wrongdoing.[333] For example, a junior employee working in a port died while dismantling a potentially dangerous object, due to a lack of training and information on how to handle the device.[334] The authorities can target a long list of potential suspects: the corporation, its management, the safety advisor and the employee working with the victim. One can imagine that the employee working with the victim will try to blame the accident on the lack of a corporate safety plan and a general corporate culture of negligence towards risk, and that he will stress understaffing and other deficiencies in the corporate organisation. The safety advisor could stress that even though he drafted the necessary safety protocols, the corporation decided not to execute them or to implement them only to a certain extent in order to save money. In such a scenario, the corporation might become a victim of its officials or other employees, as it cannot defend itself independently. Moreover, just like certain mechanisms encourage corporate cooperation, other mechanisms, such as whistleblower legislation or grants of immunity, can encourage employees or officials to come forward and provide information detrimental to the corporation.

V. Comparable Categories

In the introduction, I suggested that the strong focus on anthropological aspects of the historical rationales of the PSI, combined with some specific features of corporations, may warrant a differentiated treatment of corporations. My analysis

guarantees that statements made during such an investigation will not be handed over to the prosecution. See CoC 20 April 2015 P.13.0874.N and the Opinion of AG Timperman; CJ Carpenter, 'Federal Prosecution of Business Organizations: The Thompson Memorandum and Its Aftermath' (2007) 59 *Alabama Law Review* 207, 221–22; Garrett, 'Corporate Confessions' (n 303) 918.

[332] Small and medium-sized enterprises still make up the vast majority of corporations: http://ec.europa.eu/eurostat/statistics-explained/index.php/Archive:Business_economy_-_size_class_analysis.

[333] Waeterinckx, *De strafrechtelijke verantwoordelijkheid van de rechtspersoon en zijn leidinggevenden* (n 313) 120.

[334] www.standaard.be/cnt/dmf20150527_01700596.

suggests that the two categories of persons, natural persons and corporations, are in the end more comparable than one might have expected.

As I have already said, corporations have no limbs that can be twisted or kicked, nor can they face imprisonment. Similarly, a corporation that directly suffers from psychological compulsion or the classic cruel trilemma of self-incrimination, contempt or perjury is hard to imagine. Nevertheless, my analysis has shown that corporations can suffer indirectly from both physical as well as psychological compulsion. Its employees and officials can face this hardship in their capacity as corporate pawns. To the extent that these individuals can invoke their personal PSI, it may similarly protect the corporation. Yet, where this is not the case, the corporation's officials and employees face a trilemma: by refusing to provide evidence, they may land themselves and possibly the corporation in trouble in the form of obstruction or equivalent charges. Providing false statements is similarly dangerous as perjury charges can be brought. The third option, providing evidence against the corporation, harms both the corporation and indirectly also the individuals themselves. The risk of reputational damage is a further type of compulsion that can force the corporation into providing evidence, particularly in states where the threshold of the model of CCL is low. In other words, although the corporation cannot face a medieval torture instrument such as the rack, it can face other types of intense pressure.

In relation to the importance of documentary evidence in corporate prosecutions, I concede that it can be highly relevant for the purpose of corporate prosecutions. Whereas documents can similarly be very relevant in the prosecution of individuals, I have highlighted several elements that confirm the importance of such evidence for corporate prosecutions, for example in the application of cumbersome models of CCL. Nevertheless, in my view, it does not warrant the position that corporations and individuals are not comparable categories.

The third specific feature of corporations, the impossibility of exercising the privilege independently, sets them somehow apart from individuals. In my view, that impossibility does not imply that corporations and individuals are two incomparable categories. Instead, it means that unless there is an objective justification not to grant the PSI to corporations, one needs to consider which individuals can exercise it, taking into account the possible conflicts of interest. Overcoming this difference can be done through different models of a corporate PSI. As the corporation relies on individuals to exercise its privilege, conflicts of interests are a serious threat and the corporation risks being scapegoated. At the same time, its economic power and policies that reward corporate cooperation can put the corporation's employees and officials in a precarious position.

In sum, specific corporate features point out that corporations may not be identical to individuals. Yet, the discrepancies between them do not, in my view, support the conclusion that they do not constitute comparable categories for the purpose of the first step of the principle of equality test. Instead of focusing on their particularities, one should take into account that compelled self-incrimination will lead to a similar result for corporations and individuals: it will increase the likelihood that a punitive case is successfully brought against them.

VI. Legitimate Aim

I now turn to the next steps of the principle of equality test.[335]

The mere conclusion that corporations and individuals are comparable categories for the PSI's purpose does not preclude a different treatment, provided it is objectively and reasonably justified. The requirement of a legitimate aim is typically not hard to meet. The principal aim of such a difference in treatment is ensuring effective access to evidence to combat corporate wrongdoing. This aim is legitimate and the criterion is thus met. This finding does not imply that the measure of excluding corporations is adequate to achieve this aim. Nor does it imply that there are no less restrictive means to do so.

VII. Objective Criterion of Distinction

The criterion of distinction should be objective in the sense that it has to be based on facts or elements that do not rely on a subjective appreciation.[336] Like the requirement of a legitimate aim, this condition is usually not difficult to meet. Individuals and corporations can easily be distinguished, on the basis of the following criterion: corporations have a legal personality that is not linked to a specific single human body and thus is somewhat artificial. This criterion can be determined in a way that does not rely on any subjective preferences and thus amounts to an objective criterion. National case law[337] has accepted the criterion of being a legal person as an objective criterion, whilst the ECtHR[338] and the CJEU[339] have accepted distinctions that took into account the for-profit or non-profit character of legal persons in cases of differences in treatment.

VIII. Suitability and Necessity[340]

In order for the exclusion of corporations to be suitable to achieve the legitimate aim, the distinction needs to be able to contribute to achieving that aim. The fact that other measures may contribute more to the legitimate aim does not imply that the measure is not suitable. By excluding corporations from the privilege's scope, it can indeed be easier to gain access to evidence incriminating the corporation,

[335] Considered at 10–11.

[336] Objective criteria are, for example, having a specific business licence or having passed an exam.

[337] ConsC 10 May 2007 (n 66) B.6; ConsC 18 April 2013 (n 66) B.5.3.

[338] *VP Diffusion Sarl v France* App no 14565/04 (ECtHR, 26 August 2008) para 2.

[339] *DEB* (n 14) paras 50, 52 and 62.

[340] As I indicated in the introduction, suitability and necessity are not always treated as a separate step, but rather are treated under the broader heading 'proportionality', together with what I treat as proportionality *sensu stricto*.

its officials and employees. With no privilege to exercise, corporate officials and employees will not be able to refuse to provide documents that tend to incriminate the corporation. Nor can they refuse to provide oral statements that would tend to incriminate the corporation. At the same time, the concrete contribution to achieving the aforementioned legitimate aim depends on how the exclusion of corporations is crafted: if it solely implies that officials and employees cannot refuse to provide evidence that would exclusively incriminate the corporation, the contribution to the legitimate aim may be limited. In such a case, they would still be allowed to refuse to cooperate where they would also risk incriminating themselves personally. Yet, if the exclusion of corporations implies that its employees or officials cannot refuse to provide oral statements or documentary evidence that incriminates the corporation, not even where this would personally incriminate them, the contribution to the legitimate aim would be far greater. In sum, in both cases the exclusion of corporations from the scope of the privilege is suitable to achieve the legitimate aim, but in the latter case it is more suitable and entails a more severe impact on the individuals' personal defence.

In order to assess the necessity of the differentiated treatment of corporations, one needs to analyse whether less restrictive tools could be used to achieve the legitimate aim.[341] In my view, several measures are less far-reaching than a full exclusion of corporations from the privilege's scope.

A. Cooperation Credit

A less restrictive tool is the use of cooperation credit, which rewards corporations instead of excluding them from the privilege. Corporations could then choose to rely on the PSI, but they would have strong incentives not to do so. The cooperation credit rewards corporations when they disclose wrongdoing and cooperate with the authorities. It can take different forms, resulting in a decision not to charge the corporation or to offer it an NPA, a DPA or another type of settlement. Compared to the option of excluding corporations from the privilege altogether, this solution is clearly less restrictive on corporations. Although they have an incentive to cooperate, they can refuse to do so and thus rely on the privilege. Corporations will often prefer to cooperate: not only can this be the best tool to limit the risk of reputational damage, but it can also help to put an end to the insecurity more quickly. At the same time, the cooperation credit approach ensures that authorities can obtain access to highly relevant evidence.[342] It will often give them access not only to evidence that they could also have obtained if corporations were as such excluded from the privilege, but also to evidence that they may otherwise

[341] K Lenaerts, 'How the ECJ Thinks: A Study on Judicial Legitimacy' (2013) 36 *Fordham International Law Journal* 1302, 1348.

[342] Kloeber (n 241) 646.

not have access to: corporations, particularly the larger ones, can and often do conduct internal investigations.[343] As these are typically conducted by outside counsel, the findings can, under certain conditions, benefit from the protection of the attorney–client privilege. Unless the corporation decides to share them,[344] the findings of these internal investigations would thus not necessarily be accessible to the authorities. The right amount of cooperation credit may make them so.[345]

B. A Limited Corporate Privilege against Self-Incrimination

Another less restrictive tool is a limited corporate PSI. The previously discussed models[346] range from a corporate privilege that allowed only one specifically designated person to exercise the privilege to a model under which all corporate officials and employees could refuse to incriminate the corporation. Nevertheless, opting for one of the narrow models of a corporate PSI may reduce its effectiveness for the corporation, or even reduce it to an empty shell. Similarly, one could envisage restricting the corporate privilege *ratione materiae*. For example, one could exclude (certain) categories of pre-existing documents from the scope of the corporation's PSI.

C. Immunity or Limited Use Provisions

Two tools can help the authorities in gathering evidence without forcing the person who provides it to incriminate himself: grants of immunity and limited use provisions. By using these tools to obtain evidence from key individuals, corporate prosecutions would remain possible even if the corporations are granted access to the PSI. These techniques do not leave any discretionary power to the person: where immunity is provided or where a limited use provision applies, the person can indeed be required to provide evidence, even if he would prefer not to. Immunity requested by the prosecutor and granted by a court gives the immunised person the guarantee that his immunised evidence will not be used against him in a punitive case. Prosecutors can thus use immunity to gather evidence from key persons within the corporation to successfully build a case against the corporation

[343] ibid 638.

[344] If the authorities are not aware of the wrongdoing, deciding whether to come forward with the findings or to instead try to resolve the matter internally is a critical question that the corporation needs to consider. On that issue, see Arlen and Buell (n 305) 714.

[345] Gathering evidence that can be leveraged with authorities is not the only reason to conduct such investigations. A thorough internal investigation in itself can sometimes help a corporation to avoid liability as such as part of affirmative defence. See, in a workplace harassment case, *Burlington Industries, Inc v Ellerth*, 524 US 742 (1998), 765; KJ Smith and LR Colvin Stone, 'Conducting Effective Internal Investigations' (2017) 44 *Employment Relations* 91, 92.

[346] See also ch 11, s I.

itself and other individuals. Moreover, it can still build a punitive case against the immunised person, provided that it finds independent[347] evidence against him. Under limited use provisions, a person is typically required to provide oral statements or documents, which may be self-incriminating, yet at the same time the statute often provides that that evidence cannot be used in a criminal case *sensu stricto* against the compelled person. Limited use provisions do not preclude the use of the compelled evidence against persons other than the person that has given it. In other words, the compelled evidence can still play a role in the prosecution of the corporation or other individuals. Admittedly, this may lead to a situation where the protection is undercut: if everyone's compelled evidence can be used against everyone except for the person providing it, then it is possible that the protection of the limited use provision is circumvented. This is very true for the corporation's privilege: if all key persons within the corporation can be compelled to provide evidence that would incriminate them personally and possibly also the corporation, that evidence, according to a classic limited use provision, could still be used against the corporation.

D. Evidence Gathering through Searches or Cooperation of Third Parties?

Lastly, I consider the possibility of gathering evidence through searches and seizures, as well as the possibility of gathering evidence of corporate wrongdoing from third parties. Where the authorities gather evidence themselves, without the compelled active cooperation of the person concerned, the privilege does not in my view come into play.[348] If the authorities execute a search at the premises of the corporation or at the house of some of its officials or employees, no active self-incrimination is required; the persons need only to undergo the search. To the extent that a statutory instrument would impose a duty to produce evidence during such a search, the privilege can again be relevant.

In addition to searches and seizures, the authorities may also seek evidence from third parties.[349] A competitor may provide incriminating evidence against the corporation to avoid incurring punitive liability himself. Some third parties, such as telecom operators and banks, will often have specific cooperation duties, and failure to comply will typically expose them to significant sanctions.

Both of these measures are at first sight less intrusive than compelled self-incrimination by the corporation: neither require active cooperation of the corporation or its officials and employees. Nevertheless, searches can be very intrusive in terms of the right to respect for the home. Moreover, one can hardly

[347] Independent in the sense that it is not derived from the immunised evidence that he has provided.
[348] eg FiC Brussels 9 February 2021, [2021] Dr pén entr 255.
[349] A current or former employee who becomes a whistleblower can also provide highly relevant information.

deny that seizing the server of a corporation to find some specific documents may have a far greater impact than requiring the corporation to hand over a specific document. Similarly, where the authorities seek the incriminating information from the ISP of the corporation, this raises questions in relation to the privacy of the corporation and the individuals behind it. Thus, searches and even compelled cooperation of third parties that handle sensitive private data may be restrictive in relation to rights other than the privilege. Whereas the measures examined in sections VIIIA–C above constitute less restrictive alternatives than the complete exclusion of corporations from the privilege, I am hesitant to come to the same conclusion here.

IX. Proportionality *Sensu Stricto*

The final step is the assessment of the proportionality *sensu stricto*. To that end, one must consider whether the means employed – the exclusion of the corporation from the PSI – are in balance with the legitimate aim of ensuring effective access to evidence to combat corporate misconduct. This assessment also needs to take stock of the measure's effects.[350] The PSI is an important safeguard. Therefore, entirely excluding corporations from its scope is particularly far-reaching. This policy harms the possibility of corporations freely setting up their defence and it also restricts other fair trial rights of corporations, such as the POI. That justification is similarly relevant for corporations, as it is a justification that is not specifically aimed at natural persons. In addition, if the exclusion of corporations is crafted in such a way that it also prevents corporate officials and employees from exercising their personal privilege, it is even more far-reaching.

In light of the possibility of using less restrictive measures, the impact on the corporation's ability to define its defence strategy and on other fundamental safeguards such as the POI, I conclude that the principle of proportionality is not respected. In other words, in my view, a general exclusion of corporations from the scope of the PSI is not justified in light of the principle of equality.

[350] Alen and Muylle (n 62) 506.

4

Contemporary Rationales of the Privilege against Self-Incrimination

A clear understanding of the privilege's contemporary rationales helps one to understand what the privilege seeks to protect. Grasping those rationale(s) is relevant for specific issues, such as the applicability of the privilege to documentary evidence or the tension between the privilege and the compelled production of passwords or encryption keys. The analysed systems have a common feature: they all rely on multiple rationales to ground the privilege. Yet the manifold justifications have not resulted in one or more unchallenged rationale(s).[351] This lack of a generally accepted justification can make it easier to restrict the privilege. Hereafter, I consider the privilege's main contemporary rationales.

I. Protection from Cruel Choices

According to this rationale, the privilege protects a person from exposure to a cruel choice.[352]

The idea that requiring someone to incriminate oneself is cruel or hard has received consideration in E&W.[353] The argument goes that the privilege protects against ill-treatment and the cruel choice[354] of being forced to speak the truth and thereby incriminate oneself or to commit perjury to evade punishment.[355] This justification shows clear links to the use in the past of the *ex officio* oath[356] and other abusive practices.[357] Some of these abuses could still occur in the absence of the

[351] Dennis, *The Law of Evidence* (n 25) 196; M Redmayne, 'Rethinking the Privilege Against Self-Incrimination' (2006) 27 *OJLS* 209, 218; Roberts and Zuckerman (n 273) 548.

[352] *R v Director of Serious Fraud Office, Ex parte Smith* [1993] AC 1, 32; CoC 21 February 1882, [1882] Pas 74, 74–75; *Pennsylvania v Muniz* 496 US 582, 596 (1990).

[353] A Zuckerman, 'The Privilege against Self-Incrimination May Not Confer a Right to Refuse Disclosure of Incriminating Documents that Came into Existence Independently of the Disclosure Order' [2007] *Civil Justice Quarterly* 395, 395.

[354] *R v Director of Serious Fraud Office* (n 352) 32.

[355] Critically on this issue, see Jackson and Summers (n 273) 268; Roberts and Zuckerman (n 273) 549. This dilemma can turn into a trilemma where one would face contempt for failure to speak.

[356] FMW Billing, *The Right to Silence in Transnational Criminal Proceedings* (Springer, 2016) 161.

[357] *R v Director of Serious Fraud Office* (n 352) 31.

privilege.[358] For example, where statutory provisions criminalise failure to provide evidence,[359] suspects are confronted with a cruel choice:[360] failing to answer could amount to an offence; providing evidence may lead to self-incriminating testimony; and providing false statements can similarly give rise to sanctions.[361] This justification has been challenged on several grounds.[362] It presupposes that the person is guilty.[363] This, in turn, leads to Bentham's criticism that it is an 'old woman's reason' to justify the privilege by arguing that it is harsh or cruel to require self-incrimination.[364] The harshness has been challenged as perjury charges are rarely brought against accused persons in E&W.[365] Moreover, the idea of damnation that was once connected to telling lies has lost much of its relevance.[366] Redmayne argues that the privilege can indeed help create distance between a punitive case and the person who is interviewed. In this sense, the privilege would allow someone not to answer questions when doing so would conflict with deeply held commitments.[367]

In the USA, SCOTUS has also connected the privilege to the protection against the cruel trilemma.[368] The protection against the cruel trilemma[369] justification shows the influence of the privilege's history on the US system.[370] Similarly to E&W, American authors have pointed out that this rationale fails to consider that criminal law often confronts individuals with cruel choices,[371] against which no protection is available.[372] These critics fail to see why one needs particular protection from this cruel choice and not from others. Unsurprisingly, US doctrine also criticises this as it presupposes that the person invoking it is necessarily guilty,[373]

[358] *Lam Chi-Ming and Other Appellants v The Queen Respondent* [1991] 2 AC 212, 222.

[359] For example, in the context of economic crime.

[360] At least to the extent that there is no rule excluding such evidence from a punitive case.

[361] See also Billing (n 356) 161.

[362] It has even been argued that the current E&W system, which entitles a defendant to testify or not at trial, creates a dilemma: testify and expose oneself to cross-examination or stay silent and risk an adverse inference: S Sedley, 'Wringing Out the Fault: Self-Incrimination in the 21st Century' (2001) 52 *Northern Ireland Legal Quarterly* 107, 118.

[363] Dennis, *The Law of Evidence* (n 25) 205.

[364] ibid 206.

[365] Redmayne (n 351) 227.

[366] Roberts and Zuckerman (n 273) 550.

[367] Which could also imply refusing to testify where it would harm someone close to the interviewee: Redmayne (n 351) 225.

[368] *Murphy v Waterfront Commission of New York Harbor*, 378 US 52, 55 (1964). See also *Pennsylvania v Muniz* (n 352) 596.

[369] Self-accusation (by answering the questions), perjury (for lying under oath) or contempt (for refusing to answer questions).

[370] I Comisky, L Feld and S Harris, *Tax Fraud and Evasion: Offenses, Trials, Civil Penalties* (Thomson Reuters, 2022) 15.02, 1. The preference for an accusatorial system instead of an inquisitorial one is also to be considered in light of the negative connotation of the inquisitorial systems used by ecclesiastical courts and prerogative courts: M Berger, *Taking the Fifth* (Lexington Books, 1980) 37.

[371] SW Buell, 'Criminal Procedure Within the Firm' (2007) 59 *Stanford Law Review* 1613, 1636.

[372] For example, where a mother, as a witness, has to provide incriminating testimony against her child: AR Amar and RB Lettow, 'Fifth Amendment First Principles: The Self-Incrimination Clause' (1994–95) 93 *Michigan Law Review* 857, 890. Similarly, choosing between accepting a guilty plea in order to obtain a lesser punishment or trying to fight the case can also be hard.

[373] Amar and Lettow (n 372) 890.

since innocent people do not face the trilemma: they can provide evidence without facing the risk of self-incrimination. It is tricky to generalise the idea that innocent suspects will give a statement, as there can be a number of reasons why innocent suspects may prefer to stay silent.[374] They might, for instance, not be guilty of the offences on which they are questioned but guilty of other offences which are not under investigation, or they might be scared.

Connected to the cruel trilemma is the argument that the privilege protects against abuses and inhumane methods of self-incrimination. This justification, which relies on the protection of human dignity, may indeed preclude statutory provisions that would allow for the use of techniques similar to torture. Yet, it faces criticism on different levels: not only does the privilege in itself not suffice to offer that protection,[375] other provisions of the Bill of Rights can provide protection against such abuses.[376] Whether this rationale provides support for the application of the privilege to corporations depends on the extent to which one is willing to accept that corporations can indirectly be confronted with the aforementioned types of hardship.[377]

The ECtHR has also linked the privilege to the protection against improper compulsion,[378] which is meanwhile reconfirmed by the EU legislator in the preamble to the POI Directive.[379] In *Murray*, the ECtHR held that the privilege provides protection against improper state compulsion, which contributes to the avoidance of miscarriages of justice and to the safeguarding of the aims of Article 6 ECHR.[380] In *DB v Consob*, the CJEU referred to the reasoning adopted in *Murray*.[381] It linked the privilege to protection against coercion.[382] This is also the view taken by the EC in its 2019 Manual of Procedures in the context of competition law infringements.[383] Nevertheless, the CJEU has so far paid less attention to the privilege's rationale than the ECtHR. The privilege thus does not protect against all compulsion[384] and some coercive measures could be acceptable, provided they

[374] Meese, 'The Sound of Silence' (n 105) 70.

[375] Berger, *Taking the Fifth* (n 370) 34.

[376] On this issue, see J Dressler and AC Michaels, *Criminal Procedure – Investigation* (Lexis Nexis, 2013) 419.

[377] See ch 3.

[378] *Ibrahim and Others v United Kingdom* App nos 50541/08, 50571/08, 50573/08 and 40351/09 (ECtHR, 13 September 2016) para 266; *Wanner v Germany* App no 26892/12 (ECtHR, 23 October 2018) para 23; *De Legé* (n 57) para 63.

[379] recitals 25 and 27.

[380] *John Murray v UK* App no 18731/91 (ECtHR, 8 February 1996) para 45; *Lutsenko v Ukraine* App no 30663/04 (ECtHR, 18 December 2008) para 49, in which the Court linked the privilege to the evidence's reliability. For a case where the privilege was connected to Art 10 ECHR by the European Commission of Human Rights, see *K v Austria* App no 16002/90 (ECHR, 13 October 1992).

[381] *DB v Consob* (n 17) para 38.

[382] Joined Cases C-293/13 P and C-294/13 P *Fresh Del Monte Produce Inc v European Commission and European Commission v Fresh Del Monte Produce Inc* (CJ, 24 June 2015) paras 193–98; *LVM* (n 299) para 275; *DB v Consob* (n 17) para 39.

[383] Antitrust Manual of Procedures, pp 11–12 of the section on requests for information, https://ec.europa.eu/competition/antitrust/antitrust_manproc_11_2019_en.pdf.

[384] Harris et al (n 35) 422; SJ Summers, *Fair Trials – The European Criminal Procedural Tradition and the European Court of Human Rights* (Hart Publishing, 2007) 157–58.

do not destroy its very essence.[385] That justification does not lead to an absolute[386] or unlimited privilege. Indeed, the ECtHR subjects the privilege to a balancing test. It takes into consideration the nature and degree of compulsion, the importance for the public interest of investigating and punishing the offence concerned,[387] the availability of relevant safeguards in the procedure and the use made of the evidence.[388] For example, the ECtHR recognised that in cases that clearly call for an explanation from the accused, the accused's silence could, under certain conditions, be taken into account when assessing whether the person is guilty.[389] Moreover, defending the privilege based on the argument that it protects against miscarriages of justice is risky. It is often waived and by itself does not necessarily provide sufficient protection against wrongful convictions.[390] Since a waiver is possible, some consider it unlikely that suspects, particularly vulnerable ones,[391] will truly rely on their privilege, especially in the absence of other safeguards, such as access to a lawyer.[392]

In *Saunders*, the ECtHR further elaborated on its reference to improper compulsion and held that the privilege protects a person against compulsion that would defy his will.[393] Defying a person's will is understood broadly, eg in a case where the suspect is informed about his privilege while he is similarly informed that he can face punitive liability for refusing to testify[394] or when the police closely collaborate and coach an informant placed in the cell of the suspect.[395] The focus

[385] *Quinn v Ireland* App no 36887/97 (ECtHR, 21 December 2000) para 59; *Marttinen v Finland* App no 19235/03 (ECtHR, 21 April 2009) para 73; *De Legé* (n 57) para 68.

[386] M Berger, 'Self-Incrimination and the European Court of Human Rights: procedural issues in the enforcement of the privilege' [2007] *European Human Rights Law Review* 514, 517; M Veenbrink, *Criminal Law Principles and the Enforcement of EU and National Competition Law: A Silent Takeover?* (Kluwer Law International, 2019) 19.

[387] This criterion is not systematically listed in subsequent case law alongside the other criteria (*Pavlenko v Russia* App no 42371/02 (ECtHR, 1 April 2010) para 100; *Niculescu v Romania* App no 25333/03 (ECtHR, 25 June 2013) para 111; *Kalneniene v Belgium* App no 40233/07 (ECtHR, 31 January 2017) para 47); *De Legé* (n 57) para 68. It nevertheless remains relevant: *Marttinen* (n 385) paras 74 and 75; *Prade v Germany* App no 7215/10 (ECtHR, 3 March 2016) paras 35 and 41.

[388] *Jalloh* (n 32) paras 97, 101 and 117; Veenbrink, *Criminal Law Principles* (n 386) 20. These criteria are also listed in the longer list of criteria that should be considered when assessing the overall fairness of criminal proceedings, summarised in *Ibrahim* (n 378) para 274; *Simeonovi v Bulgaria* App no 21980/04 (ECtHR, 12 May 2017) para 120. The ECtHR has applied them with regard to an alleged violation of the PSI in *Radzevil v Ukraine* App no 36600/09 (ECtHR, 10 December 2019) paras 68–74.

[389] *Murray* (n 380) para 47.

[390] I Dennis, 'Instrumental Protection, Human Right or Functional Necessity? Reassessing the Privilege against Self-Incrimination' (1995) 54 *CLJ* 342, 349–50; Roberts and Zuckerman (n 273) 560.

[391] Dennis, 'Instrumental Protection' (n 390) 350.

[392] *Averill v UK*, App no 36408/97 (ECtHR, 6 June 2000) paras 59–61; *Magee v UK* App no 28135/95 (ECtHR, 6 June 2000) para 39 et seq; *Zachar and Cierny v Slovakia* App nos 29376/12 and 29384/12 (ECtHR, 21 July 2015) para 59; Access to a lawyer can be particularly helpful where adverse inferences can be drawn from silence.

[393] *Saunders v UK* App no 19187/91 (ECtHR, 17 December 1996) para 68.

[394] *Shabelnik v Ukraine* App no 16404/03 (ECtHR, 19 February 2009) para 59. Other elements, such as the retraction of his statements and allegations by another person of coercion by the investigator, similarly played a role in the court's reasoning.

[395] *Allan v United Kingdom* App no 48539/99 (ECtHR, 5 November 2002) para 52. This does depend on the circumstances of such cooperation: *Bykov v Russia* App no 4378/02 (ECtHR, 10 March 2009)

on the will of the person has impacted on the privilege's scope in terms of evidence that is covered.[396] According to the ECtHR, the privilege does not, in principle, apply to material which may be obtained through the use of compulsory powers, but which has an existence independent of the will of the suspect, such as DNA, urine samples and documents obtained pursuant to a warrant.[397] The reasoning behind the distinction is that in relation to evidence that has an existence independent of the will of the accused person, compulsion cannot taint the reliability of the evidence – it merely allows for its discovery.[398]

The cruel choice argument's role in Belgium is limited for several reasons.[399] It has strong ties with the use of the *ex officio* oath by special courts such as the Star Chamber and the opposition against it under common law.[400] As the procedure in use in Belgium at the time of the English Star Chamber was more uniform in the sense that ecclesiastical courts and regular criminal courts relied on a similar procedure, all courts were familiar with the oath and thus the cruel choice argument is evoked less often. The fact that suspects are, at present, not interviewed under oath also explains the rareness of references to the cruel choice argument.[401] Moreover, contempt plays a far more limited role in Belgium.[402] In light of recent case law of the ConsC and the CoC, the argument has become more relevant, specifically with regard to orders of investigating judges to provide access to, for instance, smartphones.[403] Suspects can now be confronted with the choice of facing criminal prosecution for failure to provide access or cooperating and thus providing access to evidence that can be used against them. The connected argument that the privilege protects against improper compulsion has received more attention in Belgium,[404] as the privilege is often said to protect against miscarriages of justice and against improper compulsion and the obtaining of evidence in defiance of the will of the accused.[405]

para 102; A Ashworth, 'Self-Incrimination in European Human Rights Law – a Pregnant Pragmatism?' (2008) 30 *Cardozo Law Review* 751, 761–62.

[396] *Jalloh* (n 32) para 102; *Marttinen* (n 385) para 69. The ConsC applied that criterion in its ruling on a compelled decryption order: ConsC 20 February 2020, 28/2020.

[397] *Saunders* (n 393) para 69; *De Legé* (n 57) paras 67 and 75.

[398] A Macculloch, 'The Privilege against Self-Incrimination in Competition Investigations: Theoretical Foundations and Practical Implications' (2006) 26 *Legal Studies* 211, 230.

[399] CoC 21 February 1882 (n 352) 74.

[400] Billing (n 356) 161.

[401] Except where a suspect is wrongfully labelled as a witness, as witnesses do take the oath when interviewed by an investigative judge or at a criminal trial *sensu stricto*.

[402] Art 80 CCP.

[403] See ch 7, s III.

[404] Art 16 of the Act of 20 July 1990 on pre-trial detention precludes the use of such detention as immediate punishment or as a tool to exercise coercion. The CoC has ruled that this is a consequence of the PSI. Pre-trial detention warrants cannot justify the detention on the basis of a clear lack of cooperation: CoC 10 February 2021, P.21.0163.F.

[405] CoC 13 May 1986, [1985–86] ArrCass 1230, 1233; ConsC 12 October 2017, 116/2017, B.14.4; Opinion of AG Vandermeersch in CoC 19 June 2013, P.12.1150.F, [2013] RDPC 1021, 1023; MA Beernaert, HD Bosly and D Vandermeersch, *Droit de la procedure pénale*, 9th edn (Die Keure, 2021) 31; J Huysmans, *Legitieme verdediging* (Intersentia, 2017) 804; O Michiels and G Falque, *Principes de*

The protection from cruel choices rationale should not be considered too readily to be an outdated relic from the past. The use of compelled cooperation duties, combined with the criminalisation of non-compliance, can indeed lead to the trilemma,[406] and in this sense is relevant for several countries. Admittedly, particularly in E&W, this argument is often undercut by provisions that exclude the use of compelled evidence in a punitive case against the person who provided it in order to protect the essence of the privilege. Yet corporations may face painful consequences: even if evidence could not be used against a specific individual, use against third parties such as the corporation is likely not excluded. Therefore, the cruel trilemma, albeit in a modified form, can also be relevant in relation to the corporate PSI.[407]

II. The Protection of the Innocent

The privilege has been justified as it protects the innocent. It should help avoid wrongful convictions. Notably, the ECtHR has, unsurprisingly, often stressed its importance in order to avoid miscarriages of justice.[408] The Court regularly justified the privilege by reference to improper compulsion, and such compulsion does indeed pose a threat, even to innocent persons.[409] The privilege is not an absolute right[410] and it does not protect against all compulsion.[411] That the privilege may make it harder to convict the guilty is the reverse side of the coin. It may at first sight seem odd that innocent persons would benefit from the privilege, as speaking out seems to be the best option for them.

That rationale has faced severe criticism in E&W,[412] not only because speaking out seems an innocent person's best defence. One can hardly argue that the privilege by itself suffices to protect vulnerable interviewees, as they can waive it.[413] Other mechanisms, such as access to a lawyer and the recording of interviews, are important accompanying measures. The rationale fails to explain why self-incriminating documents are protected by the privilege in certain jurisdictions. The risk that innocent people would talk themselves into trouble does not arise in relation to documentary evidence.[414]

procédure pénale (Larcier, 2019) 412; R Verstraeten, *Handboek strafvordering*, 5th edn (Maklu, 2012) 855. Compare with *Kalneniene* (n 387) para 47.

[406] Self-incrimination by cooperating, punishment for non-compliance or punishment for providing wrongful information.

[407] See 36–37.

[408] *Murray* (n 380) para 45; *Kalneniene* (n 387) para 47; *De Legé* (n 57) para 63.

[409] See ch 4, s I.

[410] *Savic v Austria* App nos 10487/16 and 10502/16 (ECtHR, 15 September 2020) para 20.

[411] ibid.

[412] Critically, see Dennis, *The Law of Evidence* (n 25) 197.

[413] *AT & T Istel Ltd and Another Appellants v Tully and Another Respondents* [1993] AC 45, 53; Quirk (n 25) 21.

[414] Dennis, *The Law of Evidence* (n 25) 197.

The argument that only guilty people benefit from the privilege should not be accepted too easily: one may have good reasons to remain silent. In my view, some innocent persons would benefit from the privilege: a personality that is not appreciated by the jury, past criminal activity and vulnerability are all elements that could play against an innocent person. Moreover, one may not be able to give meaningful answers at that moment,[415] or one may be bewildered or be trying to protect family members.[416] This has clearly been recognised by SCOTUS, as it referred to timidity and nervousness in arguing that not everyone is particularly fit to give testimony and that in such cases, rather than nullifying any suspicion against them, individuals run the risk of heightening suspicion merely by testifying.[417] To that one may add the case of persons who are unfit in the sense that they come across as being dangerous.[418] SCOTUS has held that although there may be cases where the privilege protects the guilty, it often also protects the innocent.[419]

At the same time, the rationale has been criticised in the USA too. The privilege by itself does not suffice to fully exclude that unreliable evidence is given under compulsion.[420] Berger and others have suggested that the number of cases where the privilege really serves the aim of protecting the innocent is low and that in this light the privilege is too wide as it covers a lot of cases where this justification is not relevant.[421] SCOTUS itself has held that the privilege's aim is not to protect the innocent from conviction, but rather to preserve the integrity of a judicial system in which even the guilty are not to be convicted unless the prosecution shoulders the burden of proof.[422] SCOTUS also refuted the idea that the privilege helps promote the truth,[423] saying rather that the privilege protects a person's privacy and that it is connected to the prosecution's obligation to carry the burden of proof.[424] Some authors have connected the privilege to the idea that it will lead to more reliable evidence,[425] as the privilege allows guilty persons to remain silent, instead of forcing them to tell lies. Therefore, distinguishing the guilty from the innocent should become easier. Given the low percentage of persons that rely on

[415] Corporations may need to investigate internally what went wrong before their representatives can meaningfully answer certain questions.

[416] Quirk (n 25) 18–19.

[417] *Wilson v United States* 149 US 60, 66 (1893).

[418] Dressler and Michaels, *Criminal Procedure* (n 376) 419.

[419] *Murphy* (n 368) 55; *Quinn v United States* 349 US 155, 162 (1955).

[420] Berger, *Taking the Fifth* (n 370) 29.

[421] ibid.

[422] *Tehan v Shott* 382 US 406, 415 (1966).

[423] Justifying a privilege that allows one not to disclose evidence on the basis that this furthers the truth may at first sound confusing. The underlying ideas behind this justification are that compulsion leads to unreliable evidence and persons may prefer perjury instead of self-incrimination. See Berger, *Taking the Fifth* (n 370) 30.

[424] *Tehan* (n 422) 415 and 416.

[425] Quirk (n 25) 19; DJ Seidmann and A Stein, 'The Privilege Helps the Innocent: A Game-Theoretic Analysis of the Fifth Amendment Privilege' (2000) 114 *Harvard Law Review* 430, 433. For a reply to their critics, see A Stein, 'The Privilege Helps the Innocent: A Response to Critics' (2008) 30 *Cardozo Law Review* 101.

the privilege, one may wonder whether this aim is really achieved. This rationale does not, in my view, provide a strong foundation for a corporate PSI.

In Belgium, the POI is often mentioned together with the need to offer protection against improper compulsion.[426] These references are typically influenced by the ECtHR's case law. Admittedly, the CoC had already connected the privilege to the need to ensure truthful testimony.[427] In a recent, criticised ruling, the CoC ruled that the PSI first and foremost serves to protect the right to a fair trial by excluding incorrect compelled statements.[428]

Although it might not seem self-evident to connect the protection of the innocent rationale of the privilege to corporations, one can argue that this rationale is relevant for them too. For example, when a corporation faces an investigation that could result in its punitive liability, it may want to gather more information before making a statement to the investigating authorities. If the corporation communicates information to the authorities prematurely which turns out to be incomplete or incorrect, possibly because its internal investigation is still ongoing, the corporation can face harmful consequences.

III. The Privilege against Self-Incrimination and the Presumption of Innocence

The privilege's roots show that in the past it has been linked to the POI. At present, several legal orders still show strong links between the privilege and the POI. Both E&W and the USA consider the privilege to be a distinguishing feature of their adversarial model.[429]

The ECtHR has repeatedly connected the privilege to the POI,[430] just like the European legislator in the preamble to the POI Directive.[431]

[426] Opinion of AG Vandermeersch in CoC 19 June 2013, P.12.1150.F; Beernaert et al (n 405) 33; Verstraeten, *Handboek strafvordering* (n 405) 855. Compare with: *Kalneniene* (n 387) para 47.

[427] In 1882, the CoC recognised a limited privilege for witnesses questioned under oath: CoC 21 February 1882 (n 352) 74. It explicitly justified this finding on the basis of the liberty to set up one's defence, the rejection of physical or moral compulsion and the need to assure truthful testimony. In contrast, see CoC 10 July 1916, [1917] Pas 195, 196.

[428] CoC 4 February 2020, P.19.1086.N.

[429] Roberts and Zuckerman (n 273) 552–53. Yet see the same authors critically on this argument at 553.

[430] *Saunders* (n 393) para 68; *Krumpholz v Austria* App no 13201/05 (ECtHR, 18 March 2010) para 30; *Allen v United Kingdom* App no 25424/09 (ECtHR, 12 July 2013) para 93; *Vella v Malta* App no 69122/10 (ECtHR, 11 February 2014) para 38; *Corbet and Others v France* App no 7989/11 (ECtHR, 19 March 2015) para 32; *Kapetanios and Others v Greece* App nos 3453/12, 42941/12 and 9028/13 (ECtHR, 30 April 2015) para 82; C Conings and R De Keersmaecker, 'To Save but Not Too Safe: Hoogste Belgische rechters zien geen graten in het decryptiebevel voor de verdachte' [2020] *Tijdschrift voor Strafrecht* 163, 169; G Lasagni, *Banking Supervision and Criminal Investigation – Comparing the EU and US Experiences* (G Giappichelli Editore/Springer, 2019) 246; Treschel (n 27) 348.

[431] Recitals 24–25; J Rozie, M Vanderhallen and P Tersago, 'Het zwijgrecht als tweesnijdend zwaard: een fundamenteel recht van verdediging of een katalysator voor schuldigverklaring?' [2021] *Nullum Crimen* 461, 461.

This connection to the POI, at least in its sense of the state's obligation to bear the burden of proof beyond reasonable doubt, has been questioned, as requiring a suspect to self-incriminate does not change the level of proof required.[432] It is self-evident that requiring a suspect to self-incriminate makes it easier to discharge that burden of proof.[433] One should, rather, understand the reference to the POI in the sense that it would not amount to much protection if a government could compel any accused person to provide evidence against himself. This is the meaning intended by the ECtHR: the government should do the work of providing the evidence against the person,[434] instead of defying his will by compelling it from him.[435] The prosecution should itself discharge the burden of proof, without compelling the suspect to contribute to this effort.[436] The privilege thus protects a suspect from being downgraded to a source of information.[437]

Similar arguments can be found in the CJEU's case law, which has, in turn, referred to the ECtHR's case law.[438] The CJEU justified the privilege also by connecting it to the rights of defence.[439] According to the CJEU, the rights of defence would be infringed where an undertaking would be required to answer questions which would entail an admission of an infringement of EU competition law.[440] More precisely, it connected the privilege to the obligation on the EC to bear the burden of proof.[441] The privilege thus shows ties with the more general right to a fair trial.[442]

[432] Redmayne (n 351) 218 and 219.

[433] Similarly, see Roberts and Zuckerman (n 273) 554. Alldridge and Swart strongly criticise the link between the privilege and the POI. They argue that there is nothing inconsistent in stating that the burden of proof is on the prosecution while allowing inferences to be drawn from the accused's silence: P Alldridge and B Swart, 'The Privilege against Self-Incrimination in Proactive Policing' in S Field and C Pelser (eds), *Invading the Private – State Accountability and New Investigative Methods in Europe* (Routledge, 1998) 255.

[434] See Harris et al (n 35) 422.

[435] *Saunders* (n 393) para 69; *Balitskiy v Ukraine* App no 12793/03 (ECtHR, 3 November 2011) para 38; *Kalneniene* (n 387) para 47; *Wanner* (n 378) para 23; *De Legé* (n 57) para 66. S Greer, 'The Privilege, Defence Disclosure, and Confession Evidence' (1994) 21 *Journal of Law & Society* 102, 109; C Van de Heyning, 'Het zwijgrecht in digitale tijden: de strijd om decryptiesleutels naar het Grondwettelijk Hof' [2019] *Tijdschrift voor Strafrecht* 307, 309.

[436] Greer (n 435) 109; S Royer and W Yperman, 'Wankele argumenten van hoogste Belgische hoven in uitspraken over decryptiebevel' [2020] *Nullum Crimen* 441, 442.

[437] J Meese, 'Recht om te zwijgen maar toch verplicht om te spreken?' [2019–20] *Rechtskundig Weekblad* 1322, 1322; Van den Wyngaert et al (n 35) 750.

[438] *DB v Consob* (n 17) para 39. In the judgment, the right to silence was used to refer to the right to remain silent and to avoid self-incrimination.

[439] To the limited extent that it is recognised in competition proceedings: Case 27/88 *Solvay & Cie v Commission* ECLI:EU:C:1989:388; Case 374/87 *Orkem v Commission* ECLI:EU:C:1989:387, para 34; *LVM* (n 299) para 273. The link with the rights of defence has been made in Belgium too: CoC 6 May 1993, [1993] ArrCass 455, 478; ConsC 25 January 2001, 4/2001, B.5.5; CoC 10 February 2021 (n 404); R Declercq, 'Le droit au silence' in Centre interuniversitaire de droit comparé, *Rapports belges au IXe Congrès de l'Académie internationale de droit comparé* (CIDC, 1974) 618; F Kuty, 'L'étendue du droit au silence en procédure pénale' [2000] *Revue de droit pénal et de criminologie* 309, 321.

[440] Case C-411/15 P *Timab Industries and CFPR v Commission* ECLI:EU:C:2017:11, para 83.

[441] *Orkem* (n 439) para 35; Joined Cases T-236/01, T-239/01, T-244/01 to T-246/01, T-251/01 and T-252/01 *Tokai Carbon Co Ltd and Others* ECLI:EU:T:2004:118, para 402; Case T-297/11 *Buzzi Unicem SpA v Commission* ECLI:EU:T:2014:122, para 60.

[442] CoC 11 March 1992, [1992] ArrCass, 658; CoC 19 June 2013 (n 1).

In Belgium, too, the privilege is often connected to the POI,[443] including the prosecution's obligation to carry the burden of proof.[444]

In *Tehan*[445] and other rulings,[446] SCOTUS has connected the privilege to the state's obligation to discharge the burden of proof. Berger has linked this to the reference in *Murphy*[447] to a fair state–individual balance.[448]

The privilege and the POI are considered to help maintain a balance as the state generally has more power and resources than private parties during punitive proceedings.[449] Quite rightly, Berger has stressed the wide ambit of the state's powers when conducting an investigation and prosecution against someone.[450] If the privilege were to be removed, the balance would be distorted. Yet critics in E&W consider this argument analogous to fox hunting, according to which the fox needs to have a fair chance of staying alive,[451] in that it denies access to useful evidence.[452] Instead of dismissing this argument by referring to Bentham's argument that this is a foxhunter's justification, I agree that the privilege has quite some value as it allows suspects to determine which attitude they want to adopt in relation to the accusations against them and thus freely set up their defence.[453] Amar and Lettow criticise this argument since the beyond reasonable doubt standard of proof as such already imposes a heavy burden to discharge on the prosecution.[454] Moreover, they rely on the argument that the *nemo tenetur* principle is not absolute: they adhere to one of the interpretations of the principle according to which once a prima facie case was shown, the person had to show his innocence.[455] The interpretation on which they rely is not generally shared and, as I highlighted, that principle's precise scope and its exceptions remain a point of discussion among historians, just as it was back in the days when the principle was first developed.[456]

Do the POI and thus the obligation of the state to carry the burden of proof as such not suffice to maintain such a fair balance between the individual and the state? In my view, the added value of the privilege is that it explicitly lays down a limitation on the sources that the prosecution may use to discharge that burden: the suspect himself cannot be required to be such a source of evidence. Nevertheless, critics may not find this rationale convincing and may argue that

[443] CoC 10 February 2021 (n 404); Declercq, 'Le droit au silence' (n 439) 623; Huysmans, *Legitieme verdediging* (n 405) 804; Van den Wyngaert et al (n 35) 750.

[444] CoC 9 January 2002, P.00.1531.F and P.01.0671.F, [2002] ArrCass 2002 65.

[445] *Tehan* (n 422) 415.

[446] *Miranda v Arizona* 384 US 436, 460 (1966); *Murphy* (n 368) 55; *Quinn v United States* (n 419) 162.

[447] *Murphy* (n 368) 55.

[448] Berger, *Taking the Fifth* (n 370) 39.

[449] ibid.

[450] Including searches and seizures, subpoenas for evidence or the suspect's arrest.

[451] Roberts and Zuckerman (n 273) 553.

[452] Dennis, 'Instrumental Protection' (n 390) 354; Dennis, *The Law of Evidence* (n 25) 201.

[453] Meese, 'The Sound of Silence' (n 105) 72.

[454] Amar and Lettow (n 372) 894.

[455] ibid 896.

[456] See ch 2.

this notion of the PSI imposes a high price on a criminal justice system that is already overloaded.[457]

In this sense, the privilege also ensures that a person can freely set up his defence strategy and decide on his attitude towards the accusations made against him.[458] Should a person be compelled to provide evidence that helps the authorities to build a case against him, that freedom would be strongly limited. The privilege has been connected to personal autonomy,[459] human dignity[460] and the liberty of the person.[461]

The connection to the POI focuses on the obligation of the authorities to gather the evidence themselves, and in this light the privilege does not preclude the use of practices such as searches and seizures of evidence, as long as they do not require the person to actively participate in the evidence-gathering process.[462] Such measures give the authorities another way of gaining access to pre-existing documents that a person would refuse to hand over.

One may add that connecting the privilege to the POI further suggests that it does not offer absolute protection. The ECtHR has accepted that the presumption, which has an explicit legal basis in the ECHR, can face restrictions, for example, in the context of using rebuttable presumptions, if they stay within reasonable limits.[463]

The POI as a rationale of the PSI is, in my view, also highly relevant for corporations. They too can face the powers of the criminal justice system, including searches and seizures at their premises, and their officials and employees can be questioned and put in pre-trial detention. Moreover, corporate convictions can have far-reaching consequences for the corporation and its stakeholders. In this sense, requiring that the state carries the burden of proof, without enlisting the corporation in the process through compulsion, seems justified. Nevertheless, I concede that courts focus very much on the individual in their rulings.

[457] Berger himself is aware of this criticism: Berger, *Taking the Fifth* (n 370) 40–41.

[458] CoC 21 February 1882 (n 352); Beernaert et al (n 405) 31; de la Serna (n 25) 3; Meese, 'The Sound of Silence' (n 105) 72; Van de Heyning, 'Het zwijgrecht in digitale tijden' (n 435) 317; C Van de Heyning and P Tersago, 'Onderzoeksrechter kan code smartphone afdwingen van verdachte' [2020] *Juristenkrant* 1, 7.

[459] Choo (n 30) 8; Sedley (n 362) 125. Sedley argues that where cogent reasons are present, the privilege can be set aside. He thereby strongly relies on a proportionality test.

[460] K Spagnoli, 'De ongewenste getuige en het zwijgrecht' [1999] *Tijdschrift voor Fiscaal Recht* 64.

[461] T Werquin, 'Droit pénal social: le droit de ne pas contribuer à sa propre incrimination, le droit au silence et l'obstacle à la surveillance' [2000] *Journal des Tribunaux* 82.

[462] Ashworth (n 395) 768. According to the CoC, the necessary interaction between police officers and a person whose house is searched does not require the suspect's active cooperation: CoC 14 March 2017, P.14.1001.N. It found that the suspect did not have to be informed of the PSI, nor did it take issue with the fact that he did not have the opportunity to consult his counsel by phone. Tersago pointed out that the room for questioning in such cases is limited to questions necessary for the carrying out of the search. Questions on the facts which the person might have committed are only to be asked after the procedural safeguards included in Art 47*bis* CCP have been complied with: P Tersago, 'De voorlichting van verdachten over hun procedurele rechten als fundamentele waarborg voor het recht op een eerlijk proces' [2018] *Politie & Recht* 183, 184.

[463] Harris et al (n 35) 462.

Furthermore, corporations often have more economic power to fight a case and one could thus argue that the balance between the corporation and the state is not to be considered in the same way as that between the individual and the state. Although big corporations will often have vast financial resources to fight a case, this counter-argument is in need of nuancing: not all corporations are multinationals with extensive financial resources.[464] Moreover, even vast financial resources do not necessarily exempt bigger corporations from the state's powers, although the financial resources admittedly facilitate the mounting of a defence.[465] The role the privilege plays in ensuring that defendants are free to set up their defence is, in my view, very relevant to corporations too. If one accepts that they can face punitive liability, accepting their freedom to choose their defence strategy is nothing but the reverse side of the coin.

IV. Privacy Protection

In the USA, and E&W, the privilege has also been justified on privacy grounds. In this sense, it guarantees a private enclave.[466] The privilege ensures a person is left alone when information is sought from him under compulsion.

The privacy rationale[467] has faced criticism. According to this justification, the privilege would ensure that one can keep one's knowledge as well as one's private thoughts to oneself.[468] This justification is not unanimously accepted.[469] One of the arguments that is referred to is that community interests will often be of greater importance than the privacy interest, particularly once there are significant indications against the person.[470] If privacy is the privilege's justification, one may wonder why persons can be required to answer self-incriminating questions, provided that they are not used in a punitive case, or why they can be required to give blood or DNA samples.

Whereas it played an important role in some of SCOTUS's rulings, for example on documentary evidence, this rationale seems to have lost importance. The relative weight of the different justifications and competing interests depends on the different approaches taken by SCOTUS justices to criminal justice. Some focus more on a crime control model, others on a due process model.[471] In *Fischer*,

[464] A O'Neill, 'The Privilege and the Company' (2004) 39 *Irish Jurist (New Series)* 111, 135.

[465] One can hardly deny that Arthur Andersen had vast resources to fight the charges against it.

[466] *Miranda* (n 446) 460.

[467] Billing (n 356) 160.

[468] Opinion of Lord Mustill in *R v Director of Serious Fraud Office* (n 352) 31 and 40. Mustill adds that this justification does not preclude some curtailment where this is indispensable for the stability of society. He adds that statutory interference with the right is almost as old as the right itself. See also Quirk (n 25) 10.

[469] *AT & T* (n 413) 52.

[470] ibid 52; Roberts and Zuckerman (n 273) 552.

[471] Dressler and Michaels, *Criminal Procedure* (n 376) 386.

SCOTUS found that the Fifth Amendment privilege was not intended as a general protection of privacy and it suggested that the Fourth Amendment addresses the issue of personal privacy.[472] The Fifth Amendment indeed only protects against one type of disclosure: the compelled disclosure of self-incriminating information. The privilege does not protect against the disclosure of information as such – merely against the compulsion to disclose it personally. Gerstein has stressed, at least in serious criminal cases, the importance of the public admission linked to self-condemnation.[473] In practice, in the USA, the privacy argument is easily overridden by the use of grants of immunity.[474] In E&W, too several statutory provisions require compelled cooperation. These practices restrict a person's choice to keep his information to himself and they only guarantee him that he cannot be confronted with the compelled information in (certain) punitive cases. Thus, whereas such provisions can be defendable considering other rationales of the privilege, they seem to be at odds with the privacy rationale.

Unlike in the USA and E&W, the privacy justification of the privilege has received little attention in Belgium. This is unsurprising: the Belgian debate on the privilege strongly relies on the rationales used by the ECtHR. Those rationales pay limited attention to the PSI's privacy rationale. One may argue that it is implicitly playing a role in relation to the 'improper compulsion' and the 'defying of the will' argument, but the ECtHR has not addressed it as explicitly as E&W and American courts.

I admit that my analysis of the privacy rationale of the privilege has not provided strong arguments in favour of a corporate PSI. Instead, arguments in E&W, as well as in the USA, are very closely linked to individuals.

In sum, the privilege protects a patchwork of different interests, some of which are relevant to corporations. Whereas certain restrictions may be defendable in light of one or more rationales, such restrictions can be at odds with other rationales. None of the (supra)national systems have provided for an incontestable rationale.

[472] *Fischer v United States* 425 US 391, 400 (1976). On the interaction between these two Amendments, see BH Choi, 'For Whom the Data Trolls: A Reunified Theory of Fourth and Fifth Amendment Jurisprudence' (2015–16) 37 *Cardozo Law Review* 185.

[473] RS Gerstein, 'Privacy and Self-Incrimination' (1970) 80 *Ethics* 87, 91.

[474] *United States v Balsys* 524 US 666, 692 (1998); Amar and Lettow (n 372) 891; Buell, 'Criminal Procedure Within the Firm' (n 371) 1637. Granting immunity to a person allows for the self-incriminating information to be disclosed while its discloser gets a guarantee that this information will not be used against him.

5

Self-Incrimination

The analysed (supra)national systems all pay attention to compelled cooperation that would expose one to self-incrimination and thus expose one to punitive sanctions. Self-incrimination is a trigger to determine the applicability of the PSI. At the same time, the systems are all familiar with a right to silence for suspects, who can, for instance, choose to remain silent during police and equivalent interviews, thus not only when there is a risk of self-incrimination by answering specific questions. In this chapter, I consider the notion of (transnational) self-incrimination.

The ECtHR considers that one can invoke the privilege as of the moment that one faces a sufficiently concrete risk of self-incrimination.[475] It should be recalled that the ECtHR uses an autonomous notion of what amounts to a criminal case based on the *Engel* criteria,[476] the same criteria I use to determine what constitutes a punitive case. If a person can claim that there is a risk of self-incrimination, even though he does not yet face self-incrimination under national law,[477] this criterion is met. The ECtHR does not limit the applicability of the privilege to the most serious type of punitive cases.[478]

In order for the risk of self-incrimination to be sufficiently concrete, the evidence that the person is required to give does not need to be directly incriminating;[479] it suffices that it can indirectly incriminate him.

The ECtHR has repeatedly addressed the question of when such a threat is sufficiently concrete. First, this will be the case when someone is charged with a criminal offence,[480] within the autonomous ECHR meaning.[481] Moreover, even in

[475] The ECtHR too recognises a right to silence for suspects during questioning by police or equivalent services, in which case the requirement of a risk of self-incrimination is not required.

[476] See 7–9.

[477] Understood as the risk of incurring a criminal sanction *sensu stricto*.

[478] *Aleksandr Zaichenko v Russia* App no 39660/02 (ECtHR, 18 February 2010) para 39; *De Legé* (n 57) para 47. It applies even in cases involving traffic offences, although the Court has at times taken a more permissive attitude in several of these cases.

[479] *Saunders* (n 393) para 71; *Ibrahim* (n 378) para 268. It stressed that the privilege is not limited to actual confessions or to directly incriminating statements. For statements to be self-incriminating, it suffices that they substantially affect the accused person's situation: *Schmid-Laffer v Switzerland* App no 41269/08 (ECtHR, 16 June 2015) para 37; *Beuze v Belgium* App no 71409/10 (ECtHR, 9 November 2018) para 178.

[480] *Funke v France* App no 10828/84 (ECtHR, 25 February 1993) para 44; A Gray, 'The Privilege: Using American and European Law to Protect a Fundamental Right' (2013) 16 *New Criminal Law Review* 527, 546; Jackson and Summers (n 273) 250. The ECtHR has stressed the importance of notifying a suspect of his PSI. In principle, there can be no justification for failure to notify a suspect of that right. Yet, even

the absence of pending proceedings,[482] the privilege can come into play if compulsion is used to obtain evidence from the person.[483] Nevertheless, a combined reading with *Weh* indicates that the privilege typically comes into play where there are pending or anticipated punitive proceedings.[484] The privilege is also relevant when compelled evidence is later used in a criminal case.[485] Furthermore, witnesses can also face a sufficiently concrete risk,[486] for example, when they face questions by an investigating judge that would steer them in the direction of self-incrimination.[487]

Admittedly, determining the concreteness of the risk is difficult, and this assessment is case-specific. In *Weh*,[488] the ECtHR found that such a link did not exist where the registered car owner had to disclose who had been driving it at a specific time.[489] It did not accept the applicant's argument that this requirement amounted to forced self-incrimination. It found that no proceedings for speeding were pending against him, nor anticipated.[490] In the context of compulsory requests

in the absence of such a notification, the Court checks whether the proceedings as a whole were fair. The lack of a notification might be remedied by immediate access to a lawyer: *Beuze* (n 479) para 130.

[481] In order for someone to be charged with a punitive offence, an official notification that he is alleged to have committed a criminal offence is required, or another act which indicates such an allegation and which similarly substantially impacts the suspect's position: *Beuze* (n 479) para 119; Harris et al (n 35) 376 et seq. No formal charge is required: Zeeman (n 80) 321. One can be substantially affected when there are plausible reasons to suspect that the person is involved in a punitive case: *Bandaletov v Ukraine* App no 23180/06 (ECtHR, 31 October 2013) para 56. When someone has already been convicted for his involvement in a criminal offence, the ECtHR at times admits that he can be required to be interviewed as a witness to identify other individuals involved: *Wanner* (n 378) paras 29–31.

[482] The fact that in the end no use is made (for instance, because the case is time-barred) in criminal proceedings of allegedly incriminating evidence obtained under compulsion does not preclude the PSI's applicability: *Shannon v UK* App no 6563/03 (ECtHR, 4 October 2005) para 34.

[483] *O'Halloran and Francis v UK* App nos 15809/02 and 25624/02 (ECtHR, 29 June 2007) para 35.

[484] *Weh v Austria* App no 38544/97 (ECtHR, 8 April 2004) para 42; *Wanner* (n 378) para 24; *De Legé* (n 57) para 65. In *Beghal* the Court considered that the PSI of a woman questioned at the airport in order to establish if she might be 'a person concerned in the commission, preparation or instigation of acts of terrorism', while she was told that she was not arrested and not suspected of being a terrorist, was not engaged. Failing to provide answers at questioning was a punishable offence. The woman was never charged and no later prosecution for a terrorism offence was launched: *Beghal v United Kingdom* App no 4755/16 (ECtHR, 28 February 2019) paras 114–23.

[485] *Saunders* (n 393) para 67; *Weh* (n 484) para 43; Veenbrink, *Criminal Law Principles* (n 386) 19.

[486] The Court has recognised the risk that someone may be called to testify as a witness whereas he in fact is a suspect: *Lutsenko* (n 380) paras 50–51. In *Brusco*, it also showed willingness to look at the concrete circumstances to determine one's status (witness/suspect). Being required to take the oath, in combination with the penalty for perjury, amounted to pressure in this specific case. Moreover, the person had not had access to a lawyer, nor had he been informed of his privilege: *Brusco v France* App no 1466/07 (ECtHR, 14 October 2010) paras 47, 50, 52 and 54.

[487] *Serves v France* App no 20225/92 (ECtHR, 20 October 1997) para 47. According to AG Pikamäe (n 59) para 87, the privilege does not exempt one from attending a supervisory authority's hearing or to delay it as such. He added that the authority can assess whether and to what extent the refusal to appear may be warranted by a failure to guarantee that the privilege would be respected. The ECtHR ruled that it is as such problematic if a person cannot invoke the privilege at a hearing by a parliamentary committee to the extent that he would be called to answer questions that could incriminate him: *Corbet* (n 430) para 32.

[488] *Weh* (n 484) para 42.

[489] In contrast, see *O'Halloran* (n 483) para 35.

[490] *Weh* (n 484) para 53. In contrast, see *Krumpholz* (n 430) para 42.

to hand over documents relating to accounts at foreign banks, the Court reached a different finding. The court repeatedly found that a person cannot rule out the possibility that he would be charged with tax evasion if documents related to his bank accounts or investment in companies showed that he had gained untaxed additional income, and thus concluded that the privilege applied.[491] Moreover, it found the fact that such a case was only launched four years later unconvincing.[492] Yet, in other cases linked to taxation and income declaration, it found that no punitive proceedings were anticipated, even though the person involved had been read a 'warning' which contained the government policy in cases of fraud.[493]

Where no sufficiently concrete risk of self-incrimination is present, the person cannot invoke the privilege to refuse to provide evidence according to the ECtHR.[494] In *Savic*, the Court addressed whether a fine for non-compliance with a cooperation duty under gambling legislation, imposed for refusal to provide information to the police, violated the PSI.[495] It found that the person was not suspected of any offence. The individual was not substantially affected and a refusal to provide information was thus punishable.[496] Nevertheless, the privilege can still become relevant at a later stage of the case: where a person gives evidence under the threat of sanctions at a point when the risk of self-incrimination is too low, he can rely on the PSI when such evidence is later used against him in a punitive case.[497]

Compared to the ECtHR, the CJEU, in competition cases,[498] interprets self-incrimination strictly. It recognised a limited privilege as a general principle of (at that time) Community law.[499] The CJEU found that an undertaking could be required to provide the EC with information and documents. That information can be used to establish the existence of an infringement by the undertaking or by another undertaking.[500] Yet the EC may not go so far that it would, by means of a decision calling for information, undermine the undertaking's rights of defence.[501]

[491] *JB v Switzerland* App no 31827/96 (ECtHR, 3 May 2001) para 66; *Chambaz v Switzerland* App no 11663/04 (ECtHR, 5 April 2012) para 54.

[492] *Chambaz* (n 491) para 55.

[493] In *Weh*, the Court gave some insights on its analysis of *Allen*: *Weh* (n 484) para 45. It referred to the lack of pending or anticipated punitive proceedings.

[494] *Savic* (n 410) paras 25 and 26. But see n 475.

[495] The employee had handed over the keys to the money deposit box of the machines, but refused to provide information. Later on, she referred to her employer's instructions prohibiting her to give information to the authorities on the company's operating procedures.

[496] The Court indicated that the individual could have relied on the privilege if questions had been asked that suggested a suspicion against her.

[497] *Saunders* (n 393) para 67; *De Legé* (n 57) para 65.

[498] *Orkem* (n 439); *Qualcomm* (2021) (n 15) paras 140–47. On the reconfirmation of the privilege as a general principle, see *LVM* (n 299) para 273.

[499] Similarly, see Joined Cases C-125/07 P, C-133/07 P, C-135/07 P and C-137/07 P *Erste Group Bank AG and Others v Commission* ECLI:EU:C:2009:576, para 270.

[500] ibid para 271; Case T-34/93 *Société Générale v Commission* ECLI:EU:T:1995:46, para 74; *Mannesmannröhren-Werke* (n 15) para 65; Case T-446/05 *Amann & Söhne GmbH & Co KG and Cousin Filterie SAS v Commission* ECLI:EU:T:2010:165, para 327; Case T-371/17 *Qualcomm and Qualcomm v Commission* ECLI:EU:T:2019:232, para 179; Lasagni, *Banking Supervision* (n 430) 255.

[501] *Orkem* (n 439) para 34; *Timab* (n 440) para 83; Lasagni, *Banking Supervision* (n 430) 254; L Wissink, *Effective Legal Protection in Banking Supervision* (European Law Publishing, 2021) 90.

The Court then held that compelling an undertaking to provide answers that might involve an admission of the existence of a competition law infringement on its part could not be accepted,[502] as the EC needs to carry the burden of proof.[503] In other words, a very narrow privilege was recognised in competition cases[504] that the Court did not label as criminal. In the CJEU's view, the privilege does not allow an undertaking to refuse to hand over real evidence, such as pre-existing documents,[505] or to refuse to answer (most factual questions).[506] By requiring undertakings to answer factual questions, the CJEU's case law is less protective than the ECtHR, which has accepted that an indirect risk of self-incrimination is sufficient to trigger the privilege.

Beyond the field of competition law, EU law offers additional sources that provide for a PSI. The CFR does not contain an explicit provision on the privilege,[507] and thus consolidates the ECHR tradition of the privilege as an implicitly guaranteed safeguard. Prior to the CJEU's ruling in *DB v Consob*,[508] scholars had already pointed to Article 47 CFR as a second source for the privilege in the EU legal order.[509] As such, it is also connected to Article 48 CFR, which enshrines the POI.[510] Article 47, paragraph 2 CFR is the EU law reflection of Article 6(1) ECHR,[511] with both a broader and a smaller scope of application. Its scope is broader as it is not restricted to the 'determination of civil rights and obligation or of any criminal charge'.[512] Yet, its scope is more limited as it applies to the MSs only

[502] *Qualcomm* (2021) (n 15) para 143; Ortiz Blanco and Jörgens (n 16) 37; T Ward et al, '13. Enforcement and Procedure' in D Bailey and LE John, *Bellamy & Child European Union Law of Competition*, 8th edn (Oxford University Press, 2019) 1148.

[503] *Orkem* (n 439) para 35; *Amann* (n 500) para 325; *Qualcomm* (2019) (n 500) para 180; H Andersson, *Dawn Raids under Challenge: Due Process Aspects on the European Commission's Dawn Raid Practices* (Hart Publishing, 2018) 167.

[504] The narrow privilege also covers admissions of actions which the EC can consider as an aggravating factor: *SGL Carbon* (n 15) para 69; Veenbrink, *Criminal Law Principles* (n 386) 155. Also during inspections carried out under Art 20(4) of Regulation 1/2003 undertakings cannot be required to admit infringements of competition law: Joined Cases T-289/11, T-290/11 and T-521/11 *Deutsche Bahn AG and Others v Commission* ECLI:EU:T:2013:404, para 82; Veenbrink, *Criminal Law Principles* (n 386) 149.

[505] *Amann* (n 500) para 328; Veenbrink, *Criminal Law Principles* (n 386) 146 and 147. In *Qualcomm* (2019) (n 500) para 192, the GC stated that an undertaking cannot claim a violation of its privilege in case it has to compile information into a document in response to questions considered as factual by the GC. The CJ also did not find that the privilege was infringed, as the undertakings did not have to admit that they committed an infringement of competition law: *Qualcomm* (2021) (n 15) para 147.

[506] For example, in *Qualcomm* (2019) (n 500) paras 188–94, the GC found that undertakings could be required to provide internal figures that allow the EC to reconstruct the facts and run its own calculations, as well as explanations with regard to factual discrepancies revealed by materials the EC had in its possession and internal documents that confirm the undertakings' claim that they considered relevant EU law guidance when making pricing decisions.

[507] According to Art 6(3) TEU, fundamental rights guaranteed by the ECHR (and by MSs' constitutional traditions) constitute general principles of EU law.

[508] *DB v Consob* (n 17).

[509] D Sayers et al, 'Right to an Effective Remedy and to a Fair Trial' in S Peers et al (eds), *The EU Charter of Fundamental Rights: A Commentary* (Hart Publishing, 2014) 1262.

[510] D Sayers, 'Presumption of Innocence and Right of Defence (Criminal Law)' in Peers et al (n 509) 1323.

[511] *DEB* (n 14) para 32; L. Pech et al, 'Right to an Effective Remedy and to a Fair Trial' in Peers et al (n 509) 1250. Also on this issue, see Jones and Sufrin (n 21) 895.

[512] Sayers et al (n 509) 1258.

when they are implementing EU law.[513] Although this notion has been interpreted broadly,[514] it remains narrower than the ECHR, which applies even in purely internal cases that have no connection to EU law. In this context, Article 52(3) CFR is of particular importance.[515]

In *DB v Consob*,[516] the CJEU confirmed that the safeguards afforded by Article 47, paragraph 2 and Article 48 CFR include a right to silence for individuals charged within the sense of Article 48 CFR.[517] Individuals cannot face punishment for failure to provide answers which might establish their liability in a punitive case or their *sensu stricto* criminal liability. The Court expressly distinguished the setting in *DB v Consob*[518] from EU competition proceedings. It found that the privilege applies in proceedings which can lead to the imposition of an administrative sanction of a criminal nature.[519] It also ruled that even in cases where no such penalty can be imposed, the need for a supervisory authority to respect the privilege throughout its investigation could also stem from the fact that evidence may later be used in criminal proceedings in order to prove a criminal offence.[520] Like the ECtHR, the CJEU confirmed that the privilege is not confined to directly incriminating evidence,[521] but also covers information on factual questions which can later be used to support the prosecution and which are thus relevant towards a conviction or a penalty.[522]

Thirdly, the privilege is also guaranteed by the POI Directive,[523] which is clearly inspired by the ECtHR's case law. The privilege, guaranteed by Article 7 of the

[513] Art 51(1) CFR. In addition to applying to the MSs, the CFR applies as such to EU institutions, bodies, offices and agencies.

[514] *Texdata* (n 14) para 73; *Åkerberg Fransson* (n 50) paras 20–21.

[515] Its scope and meaning should be the same as the privilege guaranteed by the ECHR and the ECtHR's case law. Yet, the former provision stresses that EU law can go beyond the minimum protection offered by the ECHR. See Case C-420/20 *HH* ECLI:EU:C:2022:679, para 54.

[516] In his Opinion in *DB v Consob* (n 59), AG Pikamäe advised the Court to decide that several provisions of EU secondary legislation can be interpreted in such a manner that they are consistent with the PSI as derived from Arts 47 and 48 CFR. The Court agreed with the AG. Both the Directive and the Regulation provided for very extensive investigatory powers, coupled with an obligation for MSs to provide sanctions in case of non-cooperation. The Court concluded that the provisions at issue do not explicitly require that sanctions are imposed upon a natural person who refuses to give answers that might prove his liability for offences punishable by administrative sanctions of a criminal nature, or *sensu stricto* criminal liability.

[517] *DB v Consob* (n 17) para 45; *FN* (n 17) 44.

[518] Consob had imposed two financial penalties, of €200,000 (insider dealing) and €100,000 (unlawful disclosure of inside information) on an individual. In addition, a €50,000 penalty was imposed for an administrative offence because he had asked for the hearing, at which he was to be heard in his capacity of a person aware of the facts, to be postponed and when he had appeared he had refused to answer questions.

[519] Which falls within the scope of my definition of punitive cases.

[520] *DB v Consob* (n 17) para 44.

[521] Admissions of wrongdoing or directly incriminating remarks.

[522] *DB v Consob* (n 17) para 40. The Court then went on to stress that the privilege cannot justify every failure to cooperate, eg by refusing to appear, or the use of delaying tactics designed to postpone a hearing.

[523] On the Directive, see S Cras and A. Erbežnik, 'The Directive on the Presumption of Innocence and the Right to Be Present at Trial' [2016] issue 1 *Eucrim* 25. The PSI is also enshrined in Arts 3(8) and 9(2) Regulation (EU, Euratom) No 883/2013 of the European Parliament and of the Council of 11 September 2013 concerning investigations conducted by the European Anti-Fraud Office (OLAF) and

Directive, is available to suspects and accused natural persons from the moment the person is suspected or accused of having committed a criminal offence, and it continues to apply until a final decision is taken.[524] This broad approach shows that the Directive is intended to apply from the very early stages of a criminal case, as is the case under the ECHR as well.[525] In any case, the Directive needs to respect the non-regression clause enshrined in its Article 13.

Although the privilege's codification in the POI Directive is to be welcomed, that instrument raises questions as to its applicability to situations where the risk of self-incrimination appears in cases that are not *sensu stricto* criminal cases or where compelled evidence was obtained in such cases and is later introduced in a *sensu stricto* criminal case (the *Saunders* scenario).[526] The Directive's scope is limited to 'criminal proceedings'.[527] Suggestions to adopt a broader scope,[528] reflecting the *Engel* criteria, did not make it into Article 2 of the Directive. Such a broad interpretation of 'criminal' would give the EU legislator a very broad competence under Article 82(2)b TFEU. Nevertheless, the first sentence of recital 11 suggests that the scope of the Directive could be broader than proceedings that are formally qualified as criminal by the legislator.[529] The second sentence of recital 11, however, stipulates that:

> This Directive should not apply to civil proceedings or to administrative proceedings, including where the latter can lead to sanctions, such as proceedings relating to competition, trade, financial services, road traffic, tax or tax surcharges, and investigations by administrative authorities in relation to such proceedings.

Read together, the two sentences of recital 11 are confusing, particularly in light of the CJEU case law, which has in several cases adopted the *Engel* criteria.[530] In any event, in cases where Articles 47 and 48 CFR apply, the broad PSI accepted by the CJEU in *DB v Consob* can be invoked. The legal status of testimony and other evidence obtained under compulsion in non-punitive proceedings – proceedings in principle not covered by the Directive – raises a particular question. Considering *Saunders*, one needs to be attentive to prevent fair trial violations[531] due to the

repealing Regulation (EC) No 1073/1999 of the European Parliament and of the Council and Council Regulation (Euratom) No 1074/1999, as well as in Art 41 of the Council Regulation (EU) 2017/1939 of 12 October 2017 implementing enhanced cooperation on the establishment of the European Public Prosecutor's Office.

[524] POI Directive, Art 2.

[525] See similarly para 25 of the Proposal.

[526] The ECtHR only considered the compelled statements' use in a criminal trial, not the question whether the privilege was already applicable at the time of the interviews by the civil servants.

[527] Arts 1 and 2, as well as recital 11.

[528] Amendments 6 and 39 of EP Document of 20 April 2015, A8-0133/2015, www.europarl.europa.eu/sides/getDoc.do?pubRef=-//EP//NONSGML+REPORT+A8-2015-0133+0+DOC+PDF+V0//EN.

[529] Lasagni considers that the *Engel* criteria are brought back on the field: Lasagni, *Banking Supervision* (n 430) 247.

[530] *Bonda* (n 50) paras 36–37; *Åkerberg Fransson* (n 50) para 35.

[531] Joint position paper of Fair Trials and the Legal Experts Advisory Panel on the proposed Directive on the strengthening of certain aspects of the presumption of innocence and of the right to be present at trial in criminal proceedings of 11 November 2014, 9, www.fairtrials.org/wp-content/uploads/Presumption-of-Innocence-Position-Paper2.pdf.

admission in criminal proceedings of evidence obtained in non-punitive proceedings by the use of compulsion.[532] Assuming that the legislator wanted to limit the application of the Directive to criminal cases *sensu stricto*, which is defendable in light of Article 82(2)b TFEU, I consider that the use of compelled evidence at a criminal trial still comes within the scope of the POI Directive.

As a general rule, the privilege in E&W provided protection against compulsion to provide self-incriminating testimony, as well as against compulsion to provide self-incriminating documents.[533] The general formulation of the privilege can be found in *Blunt v Park Lane Hotel*.[534] The privilege can be invoked both in civil[535] and in punitive proceedings.[536] In that sense, E&W common law seems more generous than the POI Directive,[537] which the legislator seemingly intended to limit to *sensu stricto* criminal cases. The broad formulation shows that not only suspects but also witnesses can rely on it.[538] Suspects that have been cautioned or defendants in a criminal trial *sensu stricto* have access to a broader privilege as they can plainly choose to remain silent and thus refuse to reply not only where their answers would be self-incriminating. The privilege could be relied upon to oppose search orders.[539]

In assessing whether a reply would tend to expose someone to a penalty or criminal charge *sensu stricto*, a wide discretion is left to the person relying on the privilege.[540] The risk must be real and appreciable,[541] and not imaginary.[542]

[532] For example, by requiring the person involved to answer questions under the threat of sanctions.

[533] *Beghal v Director of Public Prosecutions (Secretary of State for the Home Department and others intervening)* [2015] UKSC 49, [2015] 3 WLR 344, 366; *AT & T* (n 413) 49; Dennis, *The Law of Evidence* (n 25) 153–54.

[534] [1942] 2 KB 253, 257.

[535] L Macgregor, C Peacey and G Ridsdale, *Civil Litigation 2020–2021* (Oxford University Press, 2020) 325. In civil cases, one can also rely on the privilege when the evidence would incriminate one's spouse or civil partner. With regard to criminal cases, see A Keane and P McKeown, *The Modern Law of Evidence*, 13th edn (Oxford University Press, 2020) 717; P Matthews and HM Malek, *Disclosure*, 4th edn (Sweet & Maxwell, 2012) 396.

[536] Keane and McKeown (n 535) 715. Yet in civil proceedings, one can no longer rely on the threat of forfeiture to refuse to reply in civil proceedings. See s 16(1)a CEA; R Glover, *Murphy on Evidence*, 14th edn (Oxford University Press, 2015) 528.

[537] Prior to Brexit, the UK had decided, in accordance with its specific status under EU law, not to participate in the adoption of the Directive.

[538] Keane and McKeown (n 535) 714.

[539] The latter possibility has been restricted in relation to specific matters: s 72 Senior Courts Act 1981. On that matter, see Keane and McKeown (n 535) 714 and 723–24. Although the Act restricts the privilege, at the same time it provides limitations on the use of so obtained material in a *sensu stricto* criminal case.

[540] Glover (n 536) 529; D Ormerod and D Perry (eds), *Blackstone Criminal Practice 2021* (Oxford University Press, 2020) 2799.

[541] *Coogan v News Group Newspapers Ltd and another, Philips v Same* [2012] WLR 848, 856–57; C Allen et al, *Practical Guide to Evidence*, 5th edn (Routledge, 2016) 418; Ormerod and Perry (n 540) 2799; S Sime, *A Practical Approach to Civil Procedure*, 23rd edn (Oxford University Press, 2020) 347. A questionable interpretation was given in *Beghal v DPP* (n 533). The risk of prosecution was held to be low because of the likelihood that the evidence would be excluded at trial because of s 78 PACE. Regardless of the possibility that the evidence would be excluded, it could lead the prosecution to other evidence that would not be excluded. It thus had the potential of increasing the risk for the suspect:

This includes the risk of prosecution, but also the possibility that the prosecution would use that information when deciding whether or not to prosecute the person.[543] This is the case where the answers could provide a stepping stone in the chain of evidence required for prosecution.[544] In this sense, E&W adheres to the broad approach taken by the ECtHR in assessing the required concreteness of the risk of self-incrimination.[545]

Yet, this general principle has come under pressure. First, the privilege has been restricted on several occasions by statute. These restrictions may be admitted by E&W law, but they may be at odds with the ECtHR's case law.[546]

In Belgium, the privilege typically comes into play when someone is charged in a punitive case or such proceedings are anticipated,[547] or when evidence has been obtained under compulsion outside the context of punitive proceedings and is later introduced in punitive proceedings.[548] Unsurprisingly, these scenarios correspond to my finding in relation to the ECtHR's case law, as well as in other national systems.

Once someone can be considered as charged in a punitive case, they can benefit from the privilege, which includes the right not to cooperate with one's own incrimination.[549] Whether someone has acquired this status depends on the facts of the case.[550] A person that has been accused of an offence by others involved in the case can have the status of suspect.[551] This has been considered by the CoC in the context of an investigation into cattle fodder contamination, where the Court

Dissenting Opinion of Lord Kerr in *Beghal*; J Doak, C McGourlay and M Thomas, *Evidence: Law and Context*, 5th edn (Routledge, 2018) 180.

[542] *Den Norske Bank ASA v Antonatos and Another* [1999] QB 271, 288–89.

[543] High Court of Justice Queen's Bench Division Commercial Court, 13 July 2007, *Kensington International Limited v The Republic of the Congo (formerly the People's Republic of the Congo) v Vitol Services Limited, Vitol Broking Limited, Gilles Chautard, Shlomo (SAM) Lambroza*, official transcript, para 32; Macgregor et al (n 535) 325; Sime (n 541) 347.

[544] *Sociedade Nacional de Combustiveis de Angola UEE and Others v Lundqvist and Others* [1991] 2 QB 310, 331; Glover (n 536) 528.

[545] If the evidence against a person is already so strong that proceedings will be launched regardless of the evidence he would give, one cannot successfully claim the privilege: Keane and McKeown (n 535) 716. These authors rightly point out that even if there is already some evidence against the person, providing additional evidence may increase the risk that proceedings are brought.

[546] The ECHR was incorporated through the Human Rights Act 1998. On the interaction between national law and the ECHR and the ECtHR's case law, see Billing (n 356) 154–56. According to s 2 of that Act, E&W courts are to take into account ECtHR case law.

[547] CoC 20 November 2018 (n 1). It is possible that a *sensu stricto* criminal case is being built while a not purely criminal investigation is ongoing, eg by the tax administration.

[548] R Verstraeten and P Traest, 'Het recht van verdediging in de onderzoeksfase' [2008] *Nullum Crimen* 85, 98.

[549] FiC Dendermonde 17 November 2014, 2016/18, [2016] TStrafr 255, 257; CoC 19 June 2013 (n 1); Beernaert et al (n 405) 31; R Declercq, *Beginselen van strafrechtspleging*, 6th edn (Kluwer, 2014) 833; F Koning, 'Reconnaissance du droit du citoyen de refuser de donner accès à un système informatique nonobstant l'ordre de la loi, et reconnaissance d'un droit de recours contre un refus du parquet de laisser consulter son dossier d'information' [2016] *Revue de Jurisprudence de Liège, Mons et Bruxelles* 733, 734.

[550] CoC 29 November 2011, P.11.0113.N, 28.

[551] CoC 16 September 1998, A.94.0001.F, [1998] JLMB 1340, 1352.

reasoned as follows:[552] the aim of the check was to avoid further contamination; such a check can take place regardless of any suspicion of an offence; at the time of the check there was no indication that the individuals concerned had committed an offence; and the two individuals concerned were questioned together.[553] Thus, the aim of the investigation matters to the CoC when it examines whether a punitive charge was pending.[554] In a 2018 case, the CoC approved the analysis made by the CoA with regard to checks carried out by customs officials.[555] The privilege was not considered to apply (as the person was not charged within the meaning of Article 6 ECHR)[556] at the time the suspect was under an obligation to cooperate. The proceedings as a whole were considered to comply with Article 6 ECHR and no evidence had to be excluded according to the CoC.[557] According to the ConsC, a punitive case is pending once elements available to the police officers or judicial authorities can justify a suspicion that this person might have participated in an offence that they are investigating.[558] With regards to an on-site inspection by the tax authorities, the ConsC, relying on the ECtHR's decision in *Van Weerelt*, found that to the extent that such an inspection only seeks to establish correct taxation, the taxpayer cannot rely on the privilege.[559]

Until the so-called Salduz Act of 13 August 2011,[560] suspects were not systematically informed of their privilege.[561] Article 47*bis*(1)d CCP has provided since

[552] Civil servants of the agriculture ministry investigated problems with animals on several farms as they were trying to determine the contaminated cattle fodder's origin to prevent further contamination. In this context, they checked the common cattle-fodder supplier of several farms.

[553] CoC 29 November 2011 (n 550) 29.

[554] Similarly, see *Saunders* (n 393) para 67; CoA Ghent 26 November 2008, [2008] TStrafr 48, 52; FiC Bruges 27 April 2009, [2010] TFR 17, 19; CoC 20 November 2018 (n 1). See also H Berkmoes, 'Verhoor-Regelgeving-Consultatie en bijstand door een advocaat- Proces-verbaal- Rechten arrestanten (Salduz-wet)' in C Postal, *Postal Memorialis. Lexicon strafrecht, strafvordering en bijzondere wetten* (Kluwer, 2014) V112/23.

[555] CoC 20 November 2018 (n 1). Customs had learned from police information that a widescale gasoline fraud was ongoing. Customs then checked several trucks of the defendant and indeed noticed use of the wrong type of fuel. It then carried out checks of the bookkeeping. The person was considered as a suspect only a few months later. The CoA had considered that the privilege did not apply at the time of the records check by Customs. On the PSI in relation to customs authorities, see AL Claes and M Horseele, 'Finding Nemo (tenetur)? Een stand van zaken en de toepassing in het douanerecht' [2021] *Nullum Crimen* 384.

[556] Even if a person is not considered as charged at the time of the compelled cooperation, the privilege can still be relevant if the evidence is later used in a punitive case against him.

[557] The Court took into account the elements considered by the CoA, such as the claim by Customs that the requested documents had to be kept under bookkeeping requirements, as well as that it was not shown that Customs threatened with fines or sanctions for non-compliance.

[558] ConsC 14 February 2013, 7/2013, B.28.1.

[559] ConsC 12 October 2017 (n 405) B.14.4.

[560] Act modifying the Code of Criminal Procedure and the Act of 20 July 1990 on provisional detention, to grant rights to anyone who is questioned and anyone who is deprived of liberty, including the right to consult a lawyer and to be assisted by him. On this Act, see M Minnaert, 'De Salduz-wet' [2011] *Nullum Crimen* 273–309.

[561] Art 47*bis* CCP did foresee that interviewees, regardless of their status, had to be informed that their statements could be used as evidence. In *Beuze*, the ECtHR considered that, given the absence of access to an attorney, this information was insufficiently clear to guarantee the PSI's effective use: *Beuze* (n 479) para 181. Similarly on the importance of the notification of the privilege and the right of access to a lawyer, see J Huysmans, 'Het recht op bijstand van een advocaat bij het verhoor: een ruim maar relatief recht' [2020] *Politie & Recht* 40, 42.

then that, regardless of the interviewed person's status,[562] a warning has to be given at the beginning of the interview that the interviewee cannot be required to incriminate himself;[563] this is the so-called light privilege.[564] For those who could be charged with criminal offences *sensu stricto*, Article 47*bis*(2)2° added that they also have to be informed that, once they have identified themselves, suspects can choose to answer the questions asked of them or stay silent;[565] this is the so-called full version of the privilege.[566] Similar protection needs to be provided to persons that do not have the status of suspect but turn out to be suspects[567] in the course of the interrogation. Meanwhile, Article 47*bis* CCP has been amended by the Act of 21 November 2016 on certain rights of persons that are being questioned.[568] The Belgian legislator sought to implement the EU Directive on Access to a Lawyer[569] in Belgian law through this Act.

Although the large majority of criminal investigations *sensu stricto* are being conducted by the public prosecutor, a minority of investigations are, at the time of writing, led by an investigating judge. During interrogations by such a judge, the safeguards of Article 47*bis* CCP apply.[570] Witnesses are in principle only required to take the oath during judicial investigations.[571] Suspects, on the other hand, do not take the oath; they cannot take it[572] even if they are to ask to do so,[573] and they are not required to tell the truth.[574] Moreover, they can choose to invoke their privilege selectively by answering certain questions and staying silent with regard

[562] According to the CoC, an interview within the meaning of that provision is a conducted questioning on offences which may be charged to a person referred to in that Article, conducted by a competent official, written down in a report as part of a criminal investigation or judicial enquiry with the aim of discovering the truth: CoC 6 November 2018, P.18.0299.N. It does not cover spontaneous statements or indications given by a person who is addressed by a competent official in relation to his behaviour or situation, the sole purpose of whose interpellation is to obtain a true and fair view of the facts established in order to be able subsequently to take an appropriate decision: CoC 5 November 2019, P.19.0384.N.

[563] Currently Art 47*bis* (1)1° CCP. The CoC had previously held that where someone is being questioned as a witness, while he is a suspect in a case that is closely connected to the case in which he is about to be questioned as a witness, he should be informed about his right not to be forced to incriminate himself: CoC 16 February 1996, A.94.00002, [1996] ArrCass 198, 199.

[564] Berkmoes (n 554) V112/31.

[565] Currently Art 47*bis* (2)2° CCP.

[566] Berkmoes (n 554) V112/34. On the implementation during interviews of the notification of the right to remain silent in Belgium, see Rozie et al, 'Het zwijgrecht als tweesnijdend zwaard' (n 431) 465–66; C Van de Heyning, 'Presumption of Innocence: Procedural Rights in Criminal Proceedings – Social Fieldwork Research (FRANET)', 40, https://fra.europa.eu/sites/default/files/fra_uploads/belgium-2021-country-research-presumption-innocence_en.pdf.

[567] Currently Art 47*bis* (6)5° CCP.

[568] Act on certain rights of interviewed persons.

[569] Directive 2013/48/EU of the European Parliament and of the Council of 22 October 2013 on the right of access to a lawyer in criminal proceedings and in European arrest warrant proceedings and on the right to have a third party informed upon deprivation of liberty and to communicate with third persons and with consular authorities while deprived of liberty.

[570] Art 70*bis* CCP.

[571] Art 75 CCP. Art 155 CCP stipulates that they also take the oath at trial.

[572] P Tersago, *Verklaringen van verdachten in het strafproces* (Intersentia, 2020) 96.

[573] CoC 20 June 2000, AR P.98.0965.N, [2002–03] RW 1095, 1095; Verstraeten and Traest (n 548) 98.

[574] Tersago, *Verklaringen van verdachten* (n 572) 95; R Verstraeten and F Verbruggen, *Strafrecht en strafprocesrecht voor bachelors*, 13th edn (Intersentia, 2020) 180. Yet they cannot go as far as to create false documents, as this would amount to a new offence: A Vandeplas, 'Over het verhoor' [2002–03] *Rechtskundig Weekblad* 1095, 1096.

to other questions.[575] If suspects were to take the oath, this would amount to a violation of the right of defence.[576] Witnesses, however, are required to take the oath, yet failure to do so does not lead to the nullity of the interrogation.[577] Failure to take the oath, or to answer the questions, can result in a fine.[578] Nevertheless, if a witness would expose himself to prosecution by answering the questions asked, he has the right not to answer them.[579] If a witness tells lies to the investigative judge, this does not necessarily qualify as perjury; one can only be convicted for perjury if one sticks to those lies until the closing of the hearings in the trial stage.[580]

Thus, like other national systems, Belgium recognises a broader protection for suspects in a *sensu stricto* criminal case, as they do not have to refer to a risk of self-incrimination. Others cannot just choose to remain silent, yet they can claim the privilege where they would run the risk of incriminating themselves.

The use, in a *sensu stricto* criminal case, of compelled[581] evidence obtained in a different investigation either before that criminal case was launched or while it was ongoing has been considered several times by the CoC and extensively debated in practice.[582] This debate was, unsurprisingly, strongly influenced by the aforementioned case law of the ECtHR. Often in investigations that may be punitive, even though they are not necessarily criminal investigations *sensu stricto*, persons are under an obligation to provide information, and failure to do so can typically be sanctioned. Unlike in E&W, Belgian legislation typically does not include a provision that precludes the use of such compelled evidence in a criminal case against that person. Therefore, it is not surprising that there is significant case law on it. Even in light of the POI Directive, Belgium has not notified the EU of any changes to the provisions, present in various areas of law, that include compelled cooperation duties.[583]

In my opinion, the practice of merely asking someone, without reference to penalties for non-compliance, for information or documents during such an investigation and subsequent admission of them as evidence in a punitive case is not necessarily problematic.[584] As the privilege protects against compelled cooperation, nothing prevents the use of voluntarily disclosed evidence.[585]

[575] Verstraeten and Traest (n 548) 98; Vandeplas (n 574) 1095. The fact that they choose to rely on their right to silence does not preclude police officers from asking further questions: CoC 2 February 2021, P.20.1067.N.

[576] CoC 16 September 1998 (n 551) 1352; Verstraeten and Verbruggen, *Strafrecht en strafprocesrecht* (n 574) 180.

[577] Verstraeten and Verbruggen, *Strafrecht en strafprocesrecht* (n 574) 182.

[578] Art 80 CCP.

[579] CoC 21 February 1882 (n 352); Beernaert et al (n 405) 34; Kuty, 'L'étendue du droit au silence' (n 439) 329. In contrast, see CoC 10 July 1916 (n 427) 196.

[580] Verstraeten and Verbruggen, *Strafrecht en strafprocesrecht* (n 574) 183.

[581] By the authorities.

[582] See 84–86.

[583] https://eur-lex.europa.eu/legal-content/EN/NIM/?uri=CELEX:32016L0343.

[584] Similarly, see L Huybrechts, 'Het niet meewerken aan zijn eigen beschuldiging in belastingzaken' [2014] *Nullum Crimen* 394, 396.

[585] CoC 29 November 2011 (n 550) 32. In the context of disciplinary proceedings, see CoC 25 November 2011, D.11.0016.F; B Vanlerberghe and J Verbist, 'Le droit de l'avocat de se taire en matière disciplinaire enfin reconnu par la Cour de cassation' [2012] *Revue de Jurisprudence de Liège, Mons et Bruxelles* 342, 347.

In the USA, as the text of the Fifth Amendment suggests, it only protects against self-incrimination where compulsion is present.[586] Self-incrimination is but the first of three cumulative conditions, next to a (2) compelled (3) testimonial communication.[587] The US system, like the other systems I have analysed, protects suspects and witnesses.[588] They can invoke the Fifth Amendment in any type of proceeding, be it civil, criminal, administrative, judicial, investigatory or adjudicatory.[589] Like in the other systems I have analysed and as the *Miranda* warning shows in relation to cautioned suspects, suspects can choose to stay silent as such during police interviews.

In the USA, in order to be self-incriminating,[590] the information should be of such a nature that it might subject the person providing it to the possibility of a punitive prosecution or punitive penalty, or lead to other information that could have such an effect.[591]

Therefore, understanding what amounts to a punitive case is of crucial importance. SCOTUS has addressed the distinction between what I describe in this book as punitive and non-punitive. Typically, it refers to 'civil' and 'criminal'. SCOTUS developed a test in the *Kennedy* case to distinguish the two categories.[592] The starting point is the legislator's intention.[593] Where a penalty is labelled as civil, SCOTUS can nevertheless proceed and check its true nature.[594] Several other criteria are relevant in this context.[595] SCOTUS has held that proceedings that appear to be criminal can serve a sufficient level of non-punitive interest to undo the need to apply the privilege.[596]

The privilege protects against compelled disclosure that can be directly incriminating, but also against disclosure that is a stepping stone to such information.[597] Thus, although the USA is not a party to the ECHR, its case law corresponds to the ECtHR's case law, according to which an indirect risk of self-incrimination suffices. Like in E&W, evidence which provides a link in a 'chain of evidence' needed for a conviction[598] also qualifies for protection.[599] A person needs to reasonably believe

[586] The privilege does not prevent a person from voluntarily disclosing self-incriminating evidence: *United States v Washington* 431 US 181, 186–87 (1977).

[587] *Hiibel v Sixth Judicial District Court of Nevada, Humboldt County, et al* 542 US Prelim Print 177, 189 (2004); SM Salky, *The Privilege of Silence – Fifth Amendment Protections against Self-Incrimination*, 3rd edn (ABA, 2019) 13.

[588] *McCarthy v Arndstein* 266 US 34, 40 (1924); FT Davis, *American Criminal Justice* (Cambridge University Press, 2019) 40.

[589] *Kastigar v United States* 406 US 441, 444–45 (1972); *Lefkowitz v Turley* 414 US 70 (1973); Comisky et al (n 370) 2.

[590] Although SCOTUS does often refer to incriminating, self-incrimination is what it requires: see *Washington* (n 586) 187.

[591] *Kastigar* (n 589) 445; Salky (n 587) 13.

[592] *Kennedy v Mendoza Martinez* 372 US 144 (1963).

[593] *United States v Ward* 448 US 242, 248 (1980).

[594] ibid 248–49.

[595] *Kennedy* (n 592) 168–69.

[596] *Allen v Illinois* 478 US 364, 374 (1986).

[597] *Kastigar* (n 589) 445.

[598] For example, by mentioning a potential witness's name, the prosecution may be given a lead which can help them find evidence against a suspect.

that he could (in)directly contribute to his own incrimination.[600] Also like in E&W, the risk of self-incrimination needs to be reasonable; imaginary hazards are insufficient.[601] What is required is the possibility that a punitive prosecution may follow – not a precise degree of probability, but the possibility must be realistic.[602] Generally, the threshold is considered to be met when the information that is sought would connect the person providing it to criminalised behaviour; it is uncommon for courts to preclude someone from invoking his privilege because his or her answer would not be sufficiently incriminating. The Fifth Amendment offers no protection when the possibility that a prosecution could follow is barred, either because of the statute of limitations or due to a complete defence.[603]

As I will examine in chapter six, section II, the USA has a mechanism other than the limited use provisions in use in E&W: the federal immunity statutes in the USA override the argument of a person who claims the privilege due to a risk of self-incrimination by extending immunity to that person.

The systems I have studied have all to a certain extent recognised the broad scope of 'punitive', as they have also included self-incrimination that could lead to sanctions that are not criminal *sensu stricto* within the privilege's scope. E&W adopted a wide scope as far as self-incrimination is concerned,[604] as did SCOTUS in *Boyd*. Although the focus in Belgium was on the protection against self-incrimination in relation to sanctions that are criminal *sensu stricto*, the privilege now also applies when punitive sanctions are imposed. As corporations can often face punitive sanctions, certain of which may not be criminal *sensu stricto*, it is self-evidently important that the national systems give a broad meaning to the concept of 'self-incrimination'.

All systems focus on *self*-incrimination. In order for corporations to be able to rely on a meaningful PSI, legal systems need to be willing to consider 'self' in a broad way when they deal with the corporation's privilege. By insisting that the privilege only offers 'personal' protection from compelled self-incrimination, corporations could either face a very narrow privilege, for example when a legal system only identifies a limited circle of individuals as the corporation, or be altogether excluded from it. The latter scenario arises in those legal systems that refuse to accept that a personal PSI can be exercised on behalf of a legal entity. Both in E&W and in the USA, this matter has explicitly come up in practice.

[599] *Hoffman v United States* 341 US 479, 486 (1951); *United States v Oriho* 969 F3d 917, 924 (9th Cir 2020); F Agostino and LA Sannicandro, 'Invoking the Fifth Amendment in Audits with Offshore Issues: Required Records under the Bank Secrecy Act, Greenfield and Continuation Penalties' (2016) 18 *Journal of Tax Practice & Procedure* 5, 7; Dressler and Michaels, *Criminal Procedure* (n 376) 426.

[600] SS Beale et al, *Grand Jury Law and Practice* (Clark Boardman Callaghan, 2022) §6:12, 3. In the early stages of an investigation, it is often difficult to determine who is involved in the wrongdoing, and the scope of persons who could invoke the privilege is broad, see Arlen and Buell (n 305) 717.

[601] *Marchetti v United States* 390 US 39, 53 (1968).

[602] *Hiibel* (n 587) 190.

[603] Salky (n 587) 20. It is for the party who challenges the PSI claim to show that a successful prosecution is excluded.

[604] S 14 CEA.

The issue of the geographic scope of the risk of self-incrimination is important for the prosecution of internationally active corporations or individuals. Since *Murphy*,[605] a person in the USA can rely on his privilege when he fears in a state case that the compelled evidence could lead to a federal prosecution or another state prosecution, or vice versa. This is understandable, as the court held in *Malloy* that the privilege applies also at state level through the 14th Amendment. In *Balsys*,[606] SCOTUS refused to extend the privilege so that it could be relied upon when one might only face punitive liability outside the USA. In other words, to the extent that the information could expose the person to a state or federal prosecution, the privilege can be invoked.[607] SCOTUS justified the restriction to US state or federal cases by reference to a jurisdictional argument: the protection is limited to prosecution by the country that is bound by the provision on the privilege.[608] Nevertheless, there is an exception to this rule: where the USA actively cooperates with the third state, US involvement can lead to the applicability of the PSI.[609] For example, if the USA grants immunity to a person to pass on the evidence to a third state to use it in a prosecution in that state, the Fifth Amendment can come into play. Then, the two states' cooperation leads to a situation where one state becomes the agent of the other one and the prosecution in the third state is no longer a foreign prosecution. Similarly, where evidence is gathered in a third state with the active cooperation of US officials, the later use of the evidence in the USA can lead to the Fifth Amendment's applicability to exclude the evidence obtained abroad.[610] This issue has come up in a case linked to the Libor scandal (*Allen*).[611] Ultimately, however, the district court decided the case on other grounds.

Unlike in the USA, the issue of transnational self-incrimination has received little attention in Belgium.[612] The E&W position on this issue can be found in section 14 CEA, according to which the privilege can only apply in relation to criminal offences or penalties under the law of the UK.[613] Nevertheless, in some

[605] *Murphy* (n 368).
[606] *Balsys* (n 474).
[607] ibid 672.
[608] ibid 674.
[609] ibid 698–700. Such a cooperation between the USA and the third state was not present in this case, so the Court left it open to a future case to rule clearly on this point. The existence of agreements between the USA and third states to provide mutual legal assistance in relation to war crimes does not suffice to reach the level of a cooperative prosecution.
[610] *United States v Karake* 443 FSupp2d 8 (D DC 2006).
[611] *United States of America v Anthony Allen, Anthony Conti, et al* 160 FSupp3d 684 (SD NY 2016). Although the persons concerned did not risk self-incrimination in the UK, where they made statements under compulsory questioning powers, the evidence was used indirectly in a US case. Another person had had access to the evidence during his own disciplinary proceedings in the UK. That person then entered into a plea agreement in the USA, according to which he would cooperate fully. The two employees claimed that this indirect use (as the person had had access to their statements) of their compelled testimony infringed their rights under the Fifth Amendment. That court did not address the question whether foreign compelled evidence can trigger Fifth Amendment issues as the *Kastigar* burden was in its view fulfilled.
[612] The issue was only indirectly tackled in CoC 30 April 2014, P.13.1869.F.
[613] See also *Peter John Brannigan and Others Appellants v Sir Ronald Keith Davison Respondent* [1997] AC 238; *Rottmann v Brittain* [2010] 1 WLR 67. In relation to interlocutory injunctions, see

cases, courts have accepted that a judge can use his discretionary power when deciding on disclosure orders to take into account the (foreign) self-incrimination argument.[614] In *Volaw Trust*, the Privy Council found that it is doubtful that the question (whether the PSI under Article 6 ECHR can be invoked where the pre-trial investigation takes place in another state than the trial) can be answered in categorical terms. It suggested that the answer could depend on whether the person claiming it risks suffering a flagrant denial of justice in the country seeking assistance.[615] In this case, such a denial of justice would not arise, as both Jersey and Norway adhere to the ECHR.[616] The limitation to national self-incrimination is thus common to both E&W and to the USA, subject to the aforementioned US exception regarding intense cooperation,[617] in which case the privilege can be triggered.[618] Meanwhile, a recent US CoA ruling confirmed that the Fifth Amendment applies to compelled self-incriminating evidence that is used against the person in a US case even if the compulsion was legal in the third state where the evidence was obtained.[619] Interestingly, the E&W CoA referred to the protection offered by the ECtHR through its *Saunders* ruling on the use of compelled evidence obtained in a non-punitive case in one MS, in a punitive case in another CoE MS.[620] The ECtHR itself has meanwhile shown that, where statements are obtained abroad[621] without a proper notification of the privilege to the interviewee, the state in whose courts the statements are used has a responsibility to ensure the fairness of the proceedings. In other words, evidence which was not obtained with respect for the privilege needs to be scrutinised particularly closely by the courts of the state in which it is used.[622]

The underlying reasons for the limitation to 'national' self-incrimination rely upon a variety of arguments: national judges may lack the knowledge to assess the

Arab Monetary Fund v Hashim and Others [1989] 1 WLR 565, 574. For a nuanced analysis of the issue, see Allen et al, *Practical Guide to Evidence* (n 541) 418; Glover (n 536) 530. See also Keane and McKeown (n 535) 715; J Ludlam and H Garfield, 'England and Wales' in S Spehl and T Gruetzner (eds), *Corporate Internal Investigation: A Systematic Overview of 13 Jurisdictions* (Hart Publishing, 2013) 123.

[614] *R (River East Supplies Ltd) v The Crown Court at Nottingham v Chief Constable of Nottinghamshire Police, Secretary of State for the Home Department* [2017] EWHC 1942, para 45. For example, by organising a private hearing: *Rottmann* (n 613).

[615] *Volaw Trust and Corporate Services Ltd and its Directors and others v The Office of the Comptroller of Taxes and another Volaw Trust and Corporate Services Ltd and its Directors and others (Appellants) v Her Majesty's Attorney General for Jersey* [2019] UKPC 29, para 68.

[616] Ormerod and Perry (n 540) 2799.

[617] *Balsys* (n 474) 698–700. See also *Karake* (n 610).

[618] For example, by offering immunity in the USA for a criminal offence that is also criminalised in the other state, and where that evidence is then to be used in a third state.

[619] The CoA found that the absence of protection against indirect use of compelled statements violated the Fifth Amendment: *United States v Allen* 864 F3d 63 (2nd Cir 2017). See also *In re Terrorist Bombings of US Embassies in East Africa* 552 F3d 177 (2nd Cir 2008).

[620] *Rottmann* (n 613) 74.

[621] In the context of mutual legal assistance.

[622] *Stojkovic v Belgium and France* App no 25308/08 (ECtHR, 27 October 2011) paras 49–57. In *Volaw Trust* (n 615) para 67, the Privy Council similarly found that the issue of admissibility of evidence obtained in Jersey by compulsory powers had to be handled by Norwegian courts (Norway requested assistance from Jersey).

credibility of the claim that one would incriminate oneself under foreign law.[623] The limitation has also been justified by relying on a jurisdictional argument: the protection is limited to prosecution by the state which is bound by the provision on the privilege.[624] Some have also addressed the possible detrimental effect of foreign law on domestic proceedings: should the argument of incrimination under foreign law be accepted, one may be confronted with situations whereby, for example, the banking secrecy in the third state could be used to prevent disclosure in the state where the proceedings are taking place.[625] As Stessens has pointed out, the privilege typically protects against disclosures that would connect a person to a past criminal offence, rather than in situations where the disclosure itself would amount to a new offence.[626] In any case, the limitation to national self-incrimination can put suspects in a difficult position, particularly in cases where multiple states would have an interest. This focus on national self-incrimination is not adequate. Where states provide each other with mutual legal assistance in investigations, suspects should not suffer from a restrictive approach to the privilege that would expose them to transnational incrimination. In that light, the aforementioned US *Allen* decision on appeal is to be welcomed.

My analysis shows a rather restrictive approach in multiple national systems as to the geographical scope of self-incrimination, as they restrict the privilege's protection to national self-incrimination. Cross-border cases such as *Allen* show that the limitation of the privilege to the risk of 'national' self-incrimination can be particularly prejudicial for corporations and their employees.[627] For example, a multinational corporation might be faced with the limitations of the privilege when it is required to provide information in a country if it has set up a subsidiary in a country that does not accept its refusal to provide evidence merely because it would incriminate the corporation in the state where it has its home seat. Within the countries that are to party to the ECHR, corporations face a higher level of protection, as the ECtHR requires countries to strictly ensure the fairness of the proceedings where statements have been obtained abroad through mutual legal assistance without a notification of the privilege.[628]

[623] R Pattenden, 'Self-Incrimination and the Threat of Prosecution under Foreign Law: *Brannigan v Davison*' (1998) 2 *International Journal of Evidence & Proof* 44, 46.
[624] *Balsys* (n 474) 674.
[625] On that argument, see Pattenden (n 623) 45.
[626] G Stessens, 'Buitenlandse geheimhoudingsplichten en de spreekplicht voor de Belgische onderzoeksrechter' [2003] *Tijdschrift voor Strafrecht* 193, 197.
[627] *Anthony Allen* (n 611). Rabobank employees had been interviewed under compulsory powers, pursuant to ss 174 and 177 FSMA Act 2000. S 174 largely excludes use of that evidence in criminal proceedings against them in E&W.
[628] *Stojkovic* (n 622) paras 49–57.

6

Compulsion

In the legal systems analysed, compulsion (by a public authority) plays a role in triggering the privilege.[629] The privilege does not come into play where a person makes a voluntary statement. Compulsion comes in different forms, including: the threat of a sanction, such as a fine or even imprisonment; physical or psychological compulsion exercised by police or other officers or by public officials; or the threat of loss of government employment.

I explore the requirement of compulsion in the reviewed legal systems. First, I focus on compulsion by public authorities. Then I consider whether certain types of compulsion are permitted in those systems. I also consider the issue of adverse inferences. Lastly, I tackle the issue of private compulsion, which is of particular relevance for corporations conducting internal investigations.

I. Compulsion by Public Authorities

The ECtHR requires compulsion in order for the privilege to apply.[630] Since its recognition of the privilege, the Court has considered a broad range of coercive practices to amount to forbidden compulsion.[631]

Particularly brutal is the use of evidence-gathering practices amounting to torture or inhuman and degrading treatment under Article 3 ECHR. The use of oral statements obtained in violation of Article 3 typically amounts to a violation of the PSI, regardless of the probative value and the importance of these statements in securing the person's conviction.[632] The use of real evidence discovered in light of violations of Article 3 is in principle also problematic, though the Court is less

[629] On the definition of the PSI in this book, see 5 above.

[630] *Ibrahim* (n 378) para 267; *Srsen v Croatia* App no 30305/13 (ECtHR, 22 January 2019) para 46. The ECtHR too recognises a right to silence for suspects during police and equivalent interviews, in which case a risk of self-incrimination is not required, nor a particular form of compulsion.

[631] At least three situations give rise to concerns of improper compulsion according to the Court as summarised in *Ibrahim* (n 378) para 267: threatening a suspect with sanctions in order to testify (after which testimony is given or sanctions are imposed for failure to do so); the use of physical or psychological pressure (often by means that violate Art 3 ECHR) to obtain real evidence or statements; and the use of subterfuge to obtain information they could not get during questioning. Similarly, see Lasagni, *Banking Supervision* (n 430) 253–54.

[632] *Gäfgen* (n 74) para 166; *Shlychkov v Russia* App no 40852/05 (ECtHR, 09 February 2016) para 86; *Tymchenko v Ukraine* App no 47351/06 (ECtHR, 13 October 2016) para 98; M-A Beernaert, 'La recevabilité des preuves en matière pénale dans la jurisprudence de la Cour européenne des droits de

restrictive than in the context of oral statements, at least where the violation of Article 3 is based on inhuman and degrading treatment and not on torture.[633] In a case that involved the use of inhuman and degrading treatment, the Court ruled that there was no violation of the privilege as there was a break in the causal chain.[634]

The ECtHR has also considered that other types of compulsion violate the PSI. Particularly relevant, as they are in use in numerous national systems, is the use of statutory provisions that sanction failure to provide oral statements or other evidence with fines or even imprisonment.[635] The Court has no issue with such provisions, unless they are used to compel cooperation from a person who has been charged[636] within the meaning of Article 6 ECHR or where such compelled evidence obtained prior to such a pending or anticipated charge is later used in punitive proceedings against the person.[637] Such provisions should be considered in light of the *Jalloh* test developed by the ECtHR in order to consider whether the privilege has been violated.[638] It comprises the aforementioned four criteria:

> [T]he nature and degree of compulsion used to obtain the evidence; the weight of the public interest in the investigation and punishment of the offence at issue;[639] the existence of any relevant safeguards in the procedure; and the use to which any material so obtained is put.[640]

In addition to the seriousness of the sanctions for failure to comply, the amount of information that is requested under compulsion too plays a role in the ECtHR's rulings.[641] Furthermore, such compulsion needs to occur at a moment when the compelled person can already point to a sufficiently concrete risk of self-incrimination. For example, in a case where individuals were required, while under threat of facing charges that could result in a six-month prison sentence, to account for their whereabouts during a specific time, the Court found a violation of the privilege, as its essence was extinguished.[642] The combination of the risk of a fine and up to two years' imprisonment similarly amounted to compulsion.[643]

l'homme: nouvel état de la question' in I Bouiouklíev and P Dhaeyer (eds), *La théorie des nullités en droit pénal* (Anthemis, 2014) 80.

[633] *Gäfgen* (n 74); Beernaert (n 632) 81.

[634] *Gäfgen* (n 74) para 180. On Art 3 and the PSI, see also *De Legé* (n 57) paras 67, 77 and 85.

[635] Although a corporation itself cannot face imprisonment, its officials and employees can.

[636] The Court has also considered anticipated proceedings.

[637] *Savic* (n 410) para 22. Similarly, see S De Raedt, *De draagwijdte van het recht op privéleven bij de informatie-inzameling door de fiscale administratie* (Larcier, 2017) 436.

[638] Critically on these criteria, see J Jackson, 'Re-conceptualizing the Right of Silence as an Effective Fair Trial Standard' (2009) 58 *ICLQ* 835, 840–41.

[639] This criterion has not always been referred to explicitly in the Court's later case law: eg *O'Halloran* (n 483) para 55; *Süzer v Turkey* App no 13885/05 (ECtHR, 23 April 2013); *De Legé* (n 57) para 68. It nevertheless remains relevant and seems at times to be implicitly addressed; on this issue, see Harris et al (n 35) 426. See also *Marttinen* (n 385) paras 74–75; *Ibrahim* (n 378) para 274.

[640] *Jalloh* (n 32) paras 97, 101 and 117.

[641] *O'Halloran* (n 483) para 58.

[642] *Heaney and McGuinness v Ireland* App no 34720/97 (ECtHR, 21 December 2000) paras 53 and 58.

[643] *Saunders* (n 393) 70. The Court only tackled the use of the evidence at later criminal proceedings and considered the privilege to be violated because of the use of compelled evidence. It did not rule that Mr Saunders could already have invoked the privilege when he made the statements.

In those cases where failure to provide the required evidence is only sanctioned with a fine, the Court can still conclude that such a fine, or the threat thereof, amounts to a sufficiently high level of compulsion.[644] The level of the fine is taken into account in this assessment.[645] If only limited evidence is required, the Court seems less likely to find that the necessary level of compulsion is present. In *O'Halloran*, it considered that – in the context of road traffic offences – requiring the registered car owner to inform the authorities of the identity of the driver on a specific date, with failure to do so subject to a fine, only constituted a limited inquiry.[646] In fields other than road traffic offences, the Court has not adopted a similar approach.[647] This should not come as a surprise, as the amount of evidence that is typically sought is, in most cases that come before the Court, far greater.[648] The ECtHR, in order to distinguish the scope of the required information in *O'Halloran* from its other cases,[649] referred in *Funke* to the statutory powers of 'requiring production of papers and documents of any kind relating to operations of interest to the department', as well as to the broadness of the documents at issue in *JB*.[650] Moreover, in fields other than road traffic offences, the potential sanction for non-cooperation is often higher, thus increasing the chance that the Court would find a violation of the privilege.

The CJEU's case law in relation to the privilege, in competition cases, has focused on the scope *ratione materiae* of the privilege, rather than on what level of compulsion is precluded. It has connected the privilege to coercion,[651] as voluntary self-incrimination is not covered by the privilege.[652] More recently, it has addressed the privilege as guaranteed by the CFR. The Court, with reference to case law of the ECtHR, connected the privilege to protection against improper compulsion. The CJEU considered that the prosecution should establish its case without recourse to evidence obtained by use of coercion or oppression in defiance of the will of the accused.[653] As to the types of precluded compulsion, the CJEU pointed out that obliging a suspect to testify under threat of sanctions or punishing a suspect who fails to do so amounts to an infringement of the privilege.[654] The Court extensively referred to the ECtHR's case law. The POI Directive explicitly refers to that case law in relation to compulsion.[655] Articles 6(4) and 7(4) of the Proposal which led to the adoption of that Directive stipulated that evidence obtained in breach of the Articles on the right to silence and the PSI shall be inadmissible, unless the use

[644] *Marttinen* (n 385) 73. Penalty payments too are relevant: *De Legé* (n 57) paras 79–83.
[645] *King v United Kingdom* App no 13881/02 (ECtHR, 8 April 2003) para 2; *Lückhof and Spanner v Austria* App nos 58452/00 and 61920/00 (ECtHR, 10 January 2008) para 54.
[646] *O'Halloran* (n 483) para 58.
[647] Yet, see *Savic* (n 410) para 24.
[648] In that sense, see *O'Halloran* (n 483) para 58.
[649] Andersson (n 503) 160; Veenbrink, *Criminal Law Principles* (n 386) 147–48.
[650] *Funke* (n 480); *JB* (n 491).
[651] *Fresh Del Monte* (n 382) paras 193–98; *LVM* (n 299) para 275.
[652] Andersson (n 503) 170.
[653] *DB v Consob* (n 17) paras 38–39.
[654] ibid paras 39, 45 and 57.
[655] recital 27 of the Preamble.

of that evidence does not prejudice the overall fairness of the proceedings. The adopted version does not include such an explicit approach. Article 10(2) requires the MSs to ensure in their assessment of evidence in breach of the right to silence and the PSI that the rights of defence and the fairness of proceedings are respected.

In E&W, and Belgium, the ECtHR's case law on the interpretation of the privilege has played a role in understanding how much compulsion is allowed. Yet one may wonder whether that case law has always been applied correctly.

In E&W, the applicability of the privilege also requires compulsion.[656] Statutes have on several occasions restricted the privilege, either expressly or by necessary implication.[657] Whereas the ECtHR has at times accepted restrictions of the privilege,[658] it has struck down practices leading to broad restrictions of the privilege.[659] The risk of accepting exceptions to the privilege is that the principle may be undercut as exceptions may become the norm.[660] Some statutory restrictions explicitly exclude the privilege for the purpose of that statute,[661] by strongly relying on the public interest.[662] Whereas the ECtHR in *Saunders*[663] did not accept the complexity of corporate fraud and the public interest in investigating and prosecuting it as a justification to set aside the privilege, the UKHL seemed less troubled by such considerations.[664] Other statutes are not explicit on the interaction with the privilege, so one needs to follow the guidance provided by case law.[665] It is noteworthy that the balancing exercise of the suspect's interest and the public interest has led to different conclusions being drawn by different courts.[666]

[656] *R v McGeough* [2015] UKSC 62, para 30; Keane and McKeown (n 535) 713. At the same time, a defendant has the right not to give evidence at trial and can stay silent during police questioning, without having to show any particular compulsion.

[657] *Zamira Hajiyeva v National Crime Agency* [2020] EWCA Civ 108, 2020 WL 00570014, para 51; *Beghal v DPP* (n 533); Doak et al (n 541) 179; M Lucraft (ed), *Criminal Pleading, Evidence and Practice 2021* (Sweet & Maxwell, 2020) 12-3; Veenbrink, *Criminal Law Principles* (n 386). If the privilege cannot be relied on in a particular situation by necessary implication, that implication must be established clearly and not be assumed: *R v Secretary of State for the Home Department, Ex p Simms* [2000] 2 AC 115, 131; Ormerod and Perry (n 540) 2800.

[658] Yet, national provisions that restricted the privilege and that were not accompanied by a rule that precludes the use of the compelled evidence in criminal proceedings often fail the ECtHR's scrutiny. Similarly, see Keane and McKeown (n 535) 717.

[659] Such as the broad powers to require documents in *Funke* (n 480) or the use of compelled testimony in *Saunders* (n 393).

[660] Quirk (n 25) 26.

[661] eg s 31 of the Theft Act 1968 or s 13 of the Fraud Act 2006.

[662] *R v Director of Serious Fraud Office* (n 352) 44; Dennis, *The Law of Evidence* (n 25) 159.

[663] *Saunders* (n 393) para 74. The ECtHR has ruled that fair trial rights apply irrespective of the type of offence at stake. It did not accept watering down the rights because someone is suspected of terrorism: *Butkevic v Russia* App no 5865/07 (ECtHR, 13 February 2018) para 88.

[664] *R v Director of Serious Fraud Office* (n 352) 44.

[665] In the context of insolvency law, see *Bishopgate Investment Management Ltd (In Provisional Liquidation) v Maxwell and Another* [1993] Ch 1, 20 and 39 et seq. See also *Beghal v DPP* (n 533) 344.

[666] Yet, at times, mutual influencing takes place. For example, E&W case law accepted in *Brown v Scott* 2001 2 WLR 817 that someone could be fined up to a £1000 for failing to disclose who was driving the car of which he is the registered owner. This seemingly impacts the PSI's essence, at least where the person was himself driving the car during an offence. Meanwhile, the ECtHR has itself shown more leniency towards such compulsion in relation to road traffic offences.

Unlike in E&W, compelled cooperation provisions in Belgium are in principle not equipped with a limited use rule,[667] and deciding the point at which compulsion infringes the privilege has been left to the courts.[668] Thus, where someone is required to provide testimony or hand over documents under threat of sanctions, problems can arise when this evidence is provided and admitted in a punitive case.[669] Essentially, the privilege is relevant in two ways in this context: either the person is already considered to be charged with a punitive charge, and thus the privilege applies, or he does not have this status but compelled self-incriminating evidence is subsequently used in proceedings in which he does have this status.[670]

That is clearly reflected in the CoC's ruling of 6 May 1993, which predates *Saunders*.[671] While a *sensu stricto* criminal investigation was ongoing, a parliamentary inquiry committee heard suspects under oath in a separate investigation. Later on, those statements were added to the criminal investigation and the suspects were questioned on their statements at the parliamentary hearing. Due to the mixing of the findings of the parliamentary committee with the case file, the privilege and the rights of defence were irreversibly harmed and the suspects could no longer be prosecuted.[672] The Court reasoned that as it would not be admissible to force a suspect in a *sensu stricto* criminal case to make a self-incriminating statement under oath and use it, such a statement cannot be obtained indirectly through a parliamentary committee.[673]

[667] When evidence is illegal due to violation of the privilege (eg through threats of sanctions), evidence obtained in that way can be declared null on the basis of Art 32 of the PT to the CCP. That Article provides a legal basis for the nullity of illegal evidence. The use of evidence obtained in violation of the privilege will often violate the right to a fair trial, one of the statutory nullity grounds. Similarly, compulsion can impact the evidence's reliability, another ground for exclusion. On Art 32 of the PT to the CCP, see D De Wolf, 'Recente ontwikkelingen in het bewijsrecht (2013–2019)' in F Deruyck (ed), *Strafrecht – In/uit balans* (die Keure, 2020) 50–65; J Meese, 'Onrechtmatig verkregen bewijs in strafzaken' in J Rozie, S Rutten and B Vanlerberghe (eds), *Bewijsnood na het vernieuwde bewijsrecht* (Intersentia, 2020) 63–90; Van den Wyngaert et al (n 35) 1369–84; J Van Doninck, *Het lot van onrechtmatig bewijs* (Intersentia, 2020) 20–43; Verstraeten and Verbruggen, *Strafrecht en strafprocesrecht* (n 574) 341–43. Art 13 of the Act of 9 December 2004 on the international police supply of personal data and information of a judicial nature, mutual international legal assistance in criminal matters and amending Art 90*ter* of the Code of Criminal Procedure provides the statutory framework regarding the exclusion of evidence obtained abroad.

[668] The CoC has stressed that self-incrimination as such is not forbidden, yet compelled self-incrimination is: CoC 24 May 2011, P.11.0095.N.

[669] Or when the person already has the status of suspect and is sanctioned for not providing the information. The ECtHR has often paid attention to the use in punitive proceedings of evidence that was produced under compulsion in another context: *Marttinen* (n 385) para 72; *Chambaz* (n 491) paras 54–56; *Van Weerelt v Netherlands* App no 784/14 (ECtHR, 16 June 2015) paras 60–62.

[670] A De Nauw, 'De rechten van de mens, stuwende kracht van een nieuwe golf van penalisering in het social en fiscaal strafrecht' [2001] *Tijdschrift voor Strafrecht* 216, 224–25.

[671] CoC 3 May 1993 (n 439) 465.

[672] ibid 467 and 478. Similarly, where self-incriminating statements were made pursuant to an obligation to cooperate during an administrative investigation and later used in evidence at a criminal trial: FiC Liège 5 December 2007, [2008] JLMB 197. That very strict CoC case law was criticised by Van den Wyngaert et al (n 35) 1368. The CoA of Antwerp pointed out that interrogating someone under oath in a tax case, in the absence of a pending criminal investigation, could nevertheless create risks for the viability of a later criminal procedure against the same person: CoA Antwerp 31 March 1998, [1999] TFR 163.

[673] CoC 3 May 1993 (n 439) 478. The ECtHR has held that the unavailability of the right to refuse self-incriminating questions during such a hearing is as such problematic: *Corbet* (n 430) para 33.

In a 2013 case, the CoC ruled that the 'sanction' for obtaining evidence in violation of the privilege is that it is inadmissible,[674] just like the evidence obtained as a result of that impugned evidence is inadmissible.[675] The infringement therefore does not necessarily entail the inadmissibility of the prosecution as such.[676] Liégeois and De Smet rightly point out that the use of evidence obtained by the tax authorities through compulsion by threatening with a fine can contaminate a criminal case file.[677] Similar risks exist in other fields where compelled cooperation provisions are present. In a case where the special tax inspectorate had obtained testimony thanks to compulsion, the CoC held that only where the evidence obtained in violation of the privilege is too intertwined with the other evidence is the right to a fair trial infringed.[678]

The CoC[679] also held that to assess the fairness of the procedure, the case had to be considered as a whole,[680] to check whether flaws during one stage of the procedure had been rectified later on. In this context, the possibility of challenging the authenticity of the evidence and using it during the trial and the reliability of the evidence are relevant factors, just like the public interest in the prosecution of crime can be weighed against the interest of the individual that evidence is collected in a proper way.[681] The Court further added that if the irregularity had resulted in the right of defence being deprived of its essence from the beginning or if the quality of the evidence is affected, the trial judge can reject the impugned evidence regardless of the seriousness of the facts.[682] By referring to the public interest in the prosecution of the offence, the CoC relies on one of the four *Jalloh* criteria, repeatedly used by the ECtHR to assess violations of the privilege. The

In another case, the ECtHR considered the fact that the evidence given during the parliamentary hearing could not be used in later proceedings: *Van Vondel v Netherlands* App no 38258/03 (ECtHR, 23 March 2006).

[674] See also CoC 13 February 2018, P.17.0610.N; CoC 20 November 2018 (n 1).

[675] CoC 19 June 2013 (n 1) 4. See also CoA Brussels 11 April 2014, [2015] RDPC 173, 175; Y Liégeois and B De Smet, 'Twintig jaar zuivering van nietigheden tijdens het gerechtelijk onderzoek. Tijd voor verandering of opfrissing van het systeem?' [2019–20] *Rechtskundig Weekblad* 3, 9. Similarly in the context of testimony of an accused person, provided without access to a lawyer: CoC 24 May 2016, P.15.1604.N.

[676] The criminal proceedings are only inadmissible when, regardless of the exclusion of the inadmissible evidence, it is as such impossible to continue criminal proceedings in accordance with the right to a fair trial as enshrined in Art 6 ECHR: CoC 20 November 2018 (n 1).

[677] Liégeois and De Smet (n 675) 9.

[678] CoC 2 April 2008, P.07.1744.F.

[679] CoC 30 April 2014 (n 612). A Belgian investigative judge had requested that a person be heard in France. He requested that this person was heard without taking the oath, as the person could be marked as a suspect. The Belgian police officers present during the interrogation did not intervene when French police officers interrogated the person under oath. Although the person was a suspect in a Belgian investigation, since he was not a suspect for the French authorities carrying out his interrogation, having him take the oath was not prohibited by French law.

[680] CoC 31 October 2017, P.17.0255.N.

[681] CoC 30 April 2014 (n 612).

[682] CoC 30 April 2014 (n 612) 7. B De Smet, 'De regelmatigheid van bewijs afkomstig uit het buitenland, de eed van de verdachte en te laat neergelegde conclusies' [2015–16] *Rechtskundig Weekblad* 1104, 1107. According to De Smet, this could be the case where pressure is applied before or during the interrogation, eg through violence, threats or false promises.

ECtHR has stressed in other cases that its willingness to accept the public interest argument is limited in those cases where the essence of the privilege is affected.[683]

The conclusion to be drawn from the case law is that in light of *Saunders* and later ECtHR case law, evidence obtained in a regular way in a non-punitive investigation can nevertheless result in a violation of the privilege when used in a punitive case.[684] The CoC ruled that the privilege is only violated where information obtained under compulsion in a non-punitive case is used in order to establish the offence.[685] It relied on its decision of April 2008,[686] which found that the privilege is only violated when the compelled evidence is intertwined with the other evidence. To avoid any negative consequence for the suspect, the approach taken in the CoC's ruling in *Citibank* and in certain other cases[687] is preferable: the evidence obtained in violation of the privilege should be excluded,[688] just like the evidence obtained as a result of that impugned evidence.

Even before the 2011 and 2016 Salduz legislation, the CoC had ruled, with regard to police interviews made without the assistance of a lawyer or proper information on the PSI, that a judge should decide whether a person was in a vulnerable position.[689] If that was the case, the judge should decide whether not excluding interviews conducted without the assistance of a lawyer or without proper notification of the privilege to the suspect violates the right to a fair trial.[690] It added that the right to a fair trial is not violated merely because one did not have access to a lawyer during questioning or was not properly informed of the privilege. In the end, the Court approved the ruling of the CoA and the statements were not excluded.[691] Noteworthy for corporate officials is the consideration of

[683] *Marttinen* (n 385) para 75. As I outlined before, the use of statements obtained under compulsion in a non-punitive investigation and the later use of these statements at trial did not pass the Court's scrutiny in *Saunders* (n 393).

[684] M Maus, *Handboek fiscale sanctionering* (die Keure, 2017) 177; Verstraeten, *Handboek strafvordering* (n 405) 857.

[685] And thus not where they have merely been the investigation's starting point: CoC 8 September 2010, P.08.1837.F.

[686] CoC 2 April 2008 (n 677).

[687] eg CoC 13 February 2018 (n 674) 16; CoC 19 June 2018, P.15.1275.N; CoC 20 November 2018 (n 1). In its 19 June 2018 ruling, the Court took into account that the CoA had considered that there was still sufficient evidence to assess whether the person was guilty.

[688] Similarly, see Veenbrink, *Criminal Law Principles* (n 386) 122. On this issue, see also CE Clesse, 'Aperçu de jurisprudence en droit pénal social (2013–2015)' [2016] *Droit pénal de l'entreprise* 121, 130.

[689] Currrently Art 47*bis* (6)9° CCP provides an exclusionary rule. On that issue, see C De Valkeneer, *Handboek Strafonderzoek* (Politeia, 2018) 220–21; M Giacometti and L Grisard, 'Salduz à la lumière de la jurisprudence: passé, présent et … futur ?' in V Pirson (ed), *Actualités en procédure pénale: de l'audition à l'exécution* (Anthemis, 2020) 45–48; Michiels and Falque, *Principes de procédure pénale* (n 405) 163–64; Verstraeten and Verbruggen, *Strafrecht en strafprocesrecht* (n 574) 176–78. Critically on that provision's faith in the aftermath of *Ibrahim* and *Beuze*, see Giacometti and Grisard (ibid) 54–57. Tersago rightly argues that *Beuze* should not be understood as precluding an exclusionary rule such as the one enshrined in Art 47*bis* CCP: Tersago, *Verklaringen van verdachten* (n 572) 180–81. The second *Ibrahim* criterion itself refers to the legal framework on the admissibility of evidence. Where an exclusionary rule applied, it is in the Court's view highly unlikely that the proceedings as a whole would be considered unfair.

[690] CoC 31 May 2017 (n 1); CoC 24 March 2020, P.19.0571.N.

[691] The CoA had found that there was other evidence against the person and the statements were not decisive.

the CoA of[692] the characteristics of the individual suspect in its assessment of that suspect's vulnerability. The suspect, a man of 45 years old, was the director of a company with one administrative employee, which led the CoA to decide that he had more than adequate intellectual capacities and he could be deemed to have understood the scope of his statements in the face of the facts in question.

In a recent case,[693] the CoC has meanwhile adopted a more defendant-friendly approach. It concluded that its own earlier ruling in a case[694] had not respected the right to a fair trial and the right to be assisted at all stages of criminal proceedings by an attorney.[695] In that same case, the CoC accepted that the right to a fair trial requires that a suspect who is not deprived of his liberty receives, prior to his interrogation, sufficiently explicit notice that he has the right to remain silent and that he cannot be obliged to incriminate himself. That requirement also applies in the event that such interrogation took place prior to the entry into force of Article 47*bis*(6) CCP. A conviction cannot be based wholly or partly on the defendant's statements that he has made contrary to the aforementioned requirements. The fact that the guilty verdict is not based on those statements in a decisive manner does not affect this.[696]

US case law in principle requires (public)[697] compulsion in order for the privilege to apply, although the line between public and private compulsion can be blurred.[698] In order to assess whether a person is compelled, SCOTUS requires that one verifies whether the free will of the person is overborne, either by physical force or through psychological compulsion.[699] This implies that the person is deprived of the freedom to decide whether or not to help the authorities. In order to test this, a totality of circumstances test is used, according to which everything seems relevant but nothing determinative.[700] Nevertheless, some elements have often been considered unacceptable: the use of violence,[701] or a credible threat thereof,[702] (excessive) psychological pressure.[703] Deception alone is usually not sufficient to find a violation.[704]

[692] That criterion was one of many elements the CoA took into account.

[693] The case had been handled by the ECtHR too.

[694] In its 2015 ruling, the Court had ruled that the reasons given by the CoA justified the conclusion that the absence of the assistance of a lawyer during the applicants' interrogations and without notification of the PSI did not prejudice their right to a fair trial and their right of defence in the criminal proceedings considered as a whole.

[695] The interviews took place prior to the 2011 and 2016 Acts. For a recent case in which the ECtHR concluded that Art 6 ECHR was violated due to the lack of assistance of a lawyer, see *Schurmans v Belgium* App no 33075/09 (ECtHR, 22 February 2022).

[696] CoC 1 February 2022, P.21.1286.N.

[697] Understood as opposed to compulsion by private individuals or corporations.

[698] Salky (n 587) 33.

[699] *Washington* (n 586) 188; *In re Gault* 387 US 1, 47 (1967); Salky (n 587) 23.

[700] JD Grano, '*Miranda v Arizona* and the Legal Mind: Formalism's Triumph over Substance and Reason' (1986–87) 24 *American Law Review* 243, 243.

[701] Such as slapping a suspect.

[702] Dressler and Michaels, *Criminal Procedure* (n 376) 404.

[703] Several factors need to be considered: how long the person was interrogated for; how long he was kept in custodial detention; whether the questioning took place at night; and more personal characteristics, such as the age and level of education of the person: see Dressler and Michaels, *Criminal Procedure* (n 376) 404.

SCOTUS has clearly held that not every element that tends to influence a person to make a self-incriminating statement is precluded and some level of pressure is acceptable,[705] as exercising the privilege does not need to be cost-free.[706] In that sense, the US approach corresponds to the approach taken by the ECtHR, as both courts accept some pressure. Particularly relevant for the purpose of my research are the so-called penalty cases.[707] In such cases, exercising the privilege entails a penalty that exceeds what is acceptable.[708] One specific type of penalty is the loss of (government) employment or the ability to exercise a regulated profession. A key case in this field is *Garrity v New Jersey*.[709] The appellants were police officers under investigation. Before questioning, they were told that any answer they would give could be used in *sensu stricto* criminal proceedings, that they could refuse to answer if the answer would be self-incriminating and, lastly, that refusing to answer would be a reason for dismissal. SCOTUS found that this amounted to a situation where they could not freely decide on whether to speak or not.[710] The fact that they chose to speak did not amount to a valid waiver, as choosing one of two evils does not amount to a free choice.[711] Read together with *Spevack*,[712] the conclusion of *Garrity* is that if a person is threatened with dismissal from public employment or a regulated profession for refusal to provide self-incriminating evidence, the person should benefit from use and derivative use immunity, so that the self-incriminating evidence does not contribute to their conviction.[713] If the person does not receive immunity, he cannot be fired for refusing to provide evidence.[714]

The analysis of the concept of public compulsion shows that not only compulsion, such as torture or the threat of imprisonment, can trigger the privilege's applicability: the threat of fines or other financial compulsion can do so too. Even if one would not accept that compulsion of corporate officials or employees can

[704] ibid 406. For example, SCOTUS has accepted that an anonymous police officer is placed in the same cell in order to extract information: *Illinois v Perkins* 496 US 292 (1990).

[705] SCOTUS has expressly held that the Constitution does not prohibit every element which influences a suspect to make incriminating admissions: *Washington* (n 586) 187.

[706] *McKune, Warden, et al v Lile* 536 US 24, 41 (2002). The choice between taking a blood test and having the refusal to do so used at a criminal trial is acceptable: *South Dakota v Neville* 459 US 553, 563 (1983).

[707] T Maclin, 'Long Overdue: Fifth Amendment Protection for Corporate Officers' (2021) *Boston University Law Review* 1523, 1602.

[708] Salky (n 587) 25.

[709] *Garrity v New Jersey* 385 US 493, 494–95 (1967).

[710] ibid 497; Kloeber (n 241) 652.

[711] *Garrity* (n 709) 498.

[712] *Spevack v Klein* 385 US 511 (1967). In that case, SCOTUS reversed the lower courts' judgment by holding that automatic disbarment in a disciplinary case of a lawyer who asserted his PSI was a non-criminal sanction that placed too high a burden on the person invoking the Fifth Amendment for it to be acceptable.

[713] LK Griffin, 'Compelled Cooperation and the New Corporate Criminal Procedure' (2007) 82 *New York University Law Review* 312, 354; Salky (n 587) 296.

[714] Provided that the evidence in question comes within the PSI's scope.

amount to compulsion exercised on corporations, (supra)national case law shows that financial compulsion is relevant. Corporations can be directly confronted with the threat of adverse financial consequences if they fail to cooperate, ie the aforementioned case law is relevant for them too.

II. Permitted Compulsion

Although the ECtHR has considered a broad range of practices to amount to forbidden compulsion, it allows some compulsion.[715] In *Ibrahim*, it recalled that compulsion is incompatible with the privilege if it destroys its essence and that the use to which it is put at trial is crucial.[716]

In addition to that balancing exercise, the ECtHR has also accepted that in a specific scenario the presence of compulsion does not trigger the PSI's applicability: if the evidence obtained under compulsion cannot be used in a punitive case against the person providing it.[717] Not only in *Saunders*, but also in several other cases, such a limited use rule was lacking or not yet in force.[718] In a 2015 admissibility decision,[719] the Court pointed out that where such an exclusionary provision applies,[720] a person can be required through summary proceedings to provide the tax administration with information in order to assess its tax situation. The advantage of such a rule is that interested parties, including a creditor in bankruptcy proceedings or the tax authorities, can have access to relevant evidence, while the compelled person gets a guarantee that the evidence is not used against him in a punitive case.

The aforementioned case law of the ECtHR, particularly in light of the CJEU's limited case law, is relevant for the interpretation of the privilege implicitly included in the CFR and explicitly included in the POI Directive. In *DB v Consob*, the CJEU was mindful of the use of compelled evidence to establish liability in a subsequent punitive case. The Court found that even if penalties imposed by a supervisory authority would not qualify as punitive,[721] the need to respect the privilege during

[715] *Van Vondel* (n 673) para 1; *O'Halloran* (n 483) para 53; *Van Weerelt* (n 669) para 56; *Ibrahim* (n 378) para 269; *Jurgelaitis v Lithuania* App no 9464/14 (ECtHR, 10 October 2017) para 35. On *O'Halloran*, see JR Spencer, 'Curbing Speed and Limiting the Privilege' (2007) 66 *CLJ* 531. More generally, see Harris et al (n 35) 422 et seq.

[716] *Ibrahim* (n 378) para 269.

[717] *Heaney and McGuinness* (n 642) paras 53 and 58; *Van Vondel* (n 673) para 1; *Marttinen* (n 385) para 75.

[718] eg *Marttinen* (n 385) para 75 or *Chambaz* (n 491) para 56.

[719] *Van Weerelt* (n 669) para 60.

[720] The Dutch Supreme Court limited the use of the information to the 'levying of taxes' and excluded its use for imposing tax fines or bringing a criminal prosecution. In *Wanner* (n 378), the Court found that a person whose conviction was final and who was interviewed as a witness in relation to those facts could not rely on the PSI as he could not face criminal liability in light of the *ne bis in idem* principle.

[721] The Court referred to criminal in nature. The preceding paragraphs indicate that the *Engel* criteria determine whether the penalties are criminal in nature.

the investigation could stem from the possibility[722] that evidence could later be used in punitive proceedings to establish that a criminal offence was committed.[723]

The three national systems at times permit compulsion. I focus here on the issue of compelled cooperation provisions.

These provisions typically amount to compulsion. As far as Belgium and E&W are concerned, one can hardly deny the impact of the ECtHR's case law. In light of cases such as *Funke*, *Saunders*, *Marttinen* and *Chambaz*, compelled disclosure provisions can be problematic once the person is charged in a punitive case. Just as the concept of a 'punitive' case is particularly broad, the notion of being 'charged' is similarly broad. Moreover, cases such as *Saunders* have highlighted that the use in a punitive case of evidence obtained pursuant to such compelled cooperation provisions in a non-punitive context is hard to reconcile with Article 6 ECHR.

In order to settle the different interests involved, E&W extensively equipped compelled cooperation provisions with 'limited use' rules.[724] The latter largely[725] exclude the use of compelled statements against the same person in *sensu stricto* criminal cases.[726] The reference in these exclusionary rules to statements or admissions suggests that the exclusion does not cover documentary evidence.[727] Whereas several statutes, such as section 31 of the Theft Act 1968, traditionally contained limited use provisions, after *Saunders* their number has greatly increased. The Youth Justice and Criminal Evidence Act 1999 amended a significant number of statutes that had restricted the privilege.[728] Prior to *Saunders*, the approach in several statutes was that compelled evidence gathered in a non-punitive context could be transmitted to the prosecuting authorities.[729] Thus, immunity was often lacking.[730] Even nowadays not all compelled disclosure provisions include such a rule.[731] Furthermore, they typically do not exclude indirect use of the

[722] The Court deduced from the preliminary reference that no limited use rule precluded the use of information provided to Consob in the course of criminal proceedings.

[723] *DB v Consob* (n 17) para 44.

[724] With some exceptions, such as s 2 CJA and s 62 SOCPA, these statutes regulate non-criminal investigations.

[725] In principle, its use is restricted to false statement charges and cases where the defence brings it up.

[726] eg s 31(1) Theft Act 1968; s 72(3) Senior Courts Act; s 434(5A) Companies Act 1985; s 2(8) CJA; s 362F Proceeds of Crime Act 2002; s 13(2) Fraud Act 2006. On that matter, see Keane and McKeown (n 535) 721–24; Ormerod and Perry (n 540) 2801–04.

[727] *R (River East Supplies Ltd)* (n 614) para 59; Dennis, *The Law of Evidence* (n 25) 160.

[728] B Emmerson et al, *Human Rights and Criminal Justice* (Sweet & Maxwell, 2012) 623. Roles considers that legislative changes have put undue hindrance on the ability to investigate and prosecute corporate fraudsters: Roles (n 82) 174.

[729] Dennis, *The Law of Evidence* (n 25) 159.

[730] ibid 159.

[731] eg s 71(2) EPA 1990; s 172(2) Road Traffic Act 1998; s 2(1) Schedule 7 Terrorism Act 2000; *Beghal v DPP* (n 533) para 63. A second mechanism to resolve improper compulsion is the use by the trial judge of s 78 PACE and thus the exclusion of evidence. In *Beghal*, the UKSC referred (para 65) to the latter provision in concluding that there is no real risk of prosecution on the basis of statements given pursuant to s 2(1). Lord Kerr (paras 117–18) was not convinced by the argument, and in his Dissenting Opinion he found that using s 78 PACE to exclude compelled statements does not afford the same protection as allowing one to invoke the PSI. Similarly, see Lucraft (n 657) 12-2c. The absence of a limited use provision and the subsequent use of compelled evidence does not in all cases result in an Art 6 ECHR violation: Keane and McKeown (n 535) 717–19; Ormerod and Perry (n 540) 2803.

compelled evidence,[732] and in this sense it does not provide an equivalent protection to the privilege.[733]

Unlike E&W, Belgian provisions on compelled disclosure usually do not include a limited use provision and the matter is mainly addressed through case law. The result is a complex body of jurisprudence, which requires persons to make difficult choices.[734] What seems clear in Belgium is that compelled disclosure provisions cannot in general[735] force someone to make a statement that is self-incriminatory;[736] yet the CoC has in some cases been more lenient towards the use of compelled cooperation provisions in relation to documents that are to be kept pursuant to a statutory obligation.[737] At the same time, it has excluded the use of documents for which there was no statutory retention obligation but that were obtained through a compelled cooperation provision.[738] In another case, the court held that it needs to be checked whether the case as a whole was fair.[739] This case law highlights the uncertainties that persons face in the absence of statutes that grant immunity or include limited use provisions.

Practice in Belgium stands in stark contrast with the US system, where compelled disclosure is typically accompanied by grants of immunity to overcome the Fifth Amendment claim. By granting immunity, a person receives assurances that such evidence will not be used against him,[740] and in this sense immunity is a substitute for the privilege.[741] In E&W,[742] too, a person can be provided with

[732] That issue came up in the aforementioned *Allen* and *Conti* cases.

[733] Roles (n 82) 156–57.

[734] For example, when he has to decide whether or not to provide his smartphone password.

[735] Both the CoC and the ConsC accept that even a suspect can be required to provide his password to access for instance a smartphone: CoC 4 February 2020 (n 428); ConsC 20 February 2020 (n 396).

[736] CoC 29 November 2011 (n 550).

[737] CoC 21 April 2015, P.13.1258.N. The Court found that the deliberate non-delivery of data carriers containing social data or data to be created, maintained or stored in accordance with the law to a social inspector who has requested them may constitute the offence of obstruction of supervision. The Court found it irrelevant whether the inspectors had used their investigative powers to obtain these documents. Similarly, see CoC 7 March 2018, P.17.0558.F. In another ruling, it found that Art 209 CCVSL did not criminalise the mere refusal to provide social documents to social inspectors without resisting the search for these documents by the inspectors: CoC 6 November 2018, P.18.0339.N.

[738] CoC 19 June 2013 (n 1).

[739] CoC 30 April 2014 (n 612).

[740] Except for a prosecution for perjury, giving a false statement or otherwise failing to comply with the order.

[741] *United States v Mandujano* 425 US 564, 576 (1976).

[742] Admittedly E&W courts can substitute the PSI with a different protection if it can be considered adequate; see *AT & T* (n 413) 63–64. In civil proceedings, a court had ordered disclosure, but equipped it with protection against compelled self-incrimination, by including the following sentence: 'No disclosure made in compliance with paragraphs 18 to 32 inclusive of this order shall be used as evidence in the prosecution of an offence alleged to have been committed by the person required to make that disclosure or by any spouse of that person.' The UKHL took into consideration a letter from the prosecution service that they understood as an acceptance by that service that they could only use material which they had already gathered before the disclosure order was made and material obtained independently from the material disclosed under the disclosure order. The underlying reasoning is that if such adequate protection is put in place, a person cannot rely on the PSI due to the lack of a real and appreciable risk of self-incrimination. On this issue, see also Ormerod and Perry (n 540) 2798; Keane

immunity, although the use of immunity notices is somewhat limited.[743] Under section 71 SOCPA, a specified prosecutor can[744] give a written immunity notice to a person when he thinks that it is appropriate to do so for the purpose of the investigation or prosecution of an offence.[745] Once such a notice is given, the receiver of the immunity notice cannot be prosecuted for an offence of a description specified in the notice.[746]

In the USA, the type of immunity that the person can require to set aside his Fifth Amendment claim has varied over time. The three main types of immunity are:[747] transactional immunity; use immunity; and use and derivative use immunity. Transactional immunity essentially guarantees that the person will not face prosecution for any crime to which his testimony is connected. Use immunity only protects against the use of the compelled evidence as such and not against prosecution. Nor does it protect against the use of the compelled evidence to find other evidence. Use and derivative use immunity guarantees the person that neither his immunised evidence nor any evidence to which it may lead can lead to a prosecution against him. Unlike transactional immunity, use and derivative use immunity still allows for the prosecution of the person providing the immunised evidence.

Until 1970, transactional immunity was the required standard of immunity.[748] Since 1970, the relevant applicable federal statute,[749] limits the immunity's scope to a use and derivative use immunity.[750] Unlike in its older case law,[751] SCOTUS found in *Kastigar* that such use and derivative use immunity suffices to require a person to testify.[752] The Court essentially ruled that transactional immunity offers

and McKeown (n 535) 713 and 724. On assurances given by the CPS, see *R (DPP) v Leicester Magistrates' Court* [2015] EWHC 1295, paras 11–16.

[743] T Stocker et al, 'United Kingdom' in J Seddon et al, *The Practitioner's Guide to Global Investigations – Volume II: Global Investigations around the World*, 4th edn (Law Business Research, 2019) 532.

[744] According to the CPS, immunity is only warranted in the most exceptional cases. The criteria are available at www.cps.gov.uk/legal-guidance/queens-evidence-immunities-undertakings-and-agreements-under-serious-organised-crime.

[745] Under s 72 a prosecutor can grant a conditional undertaking that information provided by an individual will not be used against him in criminal proceedings. S 73 provides the possibility of offering a sentence reduction in order to secure an offender's cooperation.

[746] With the exception of circumstances laid down in the notice. The notice's protection is lost if the person fails to comply with the notice's conditions.

[747] TR Tarvin, 'The Privilege against Self-Incrimination in Bankruptcy and the Plight of the Debtor' (2014) 44 *Seton Hall Law Review* 47, 60–62.

[748] *Counselman v Hitchcock* 142 US 547, 584–86 (1892); J Dressler and AC Michaels, *Understanding Criminal Procedure – Volume 2: Adjudication* (Lexis Nexis, 2006) 275.

[749] 18 USC §6002.

[750] Immunity can also be offered informally by any attorney for the USA, instead of following the statutory track. Informal immunity only binds the authority that offers it, whereas court ordered immunity binds all prosecutors. Not all courts have applied the *Kastigar* burden with the same stringency to informal immunity: Salky (n 587) 302 et seq.

[751] *Counselman* (n 748) 586.

[752] *Kastigar* (n 589).

more protection than the privilege itself. The privilege ensures that a person is not personally compelled to provide self-incriminating evidence. It does not prevent the prosecution from proving his guilt with the help of other evidence. By being offered transactional immunity, the person thus received more than what the privilege itself accorded him: he obtained a guarantee that he will not face prosecution as such. In *Kastigar*, SCOTUS put the burden of showing that, where the prosecution brings a case against a person who benefited from an immunity order, 'the evidence it proposes to use is derived from a legitimate source wholly independent of the compelled evidence'.[753] This so-called *Kastigar* burden can make it particularly difficult,[754] though not impossible,[755] in practice for the prosecution to bring a case against an immunised person.

The wording of 18 USC §6002[756] clarifies that the protection offered only applies in a *sensu stricto* criminal case. Therefore, immunity does not protect against other negative effects, such as use of the evidence in a civil case,[757] the imposition of additional punishment for a past conviction[758] or discharge from employment.[759] Particularly in the context of economic crime, where both civil and *sensu stricto* criminal enforcement are often available, immunity can put a person in an uneasy position: under the granted immunity, he is required to provide evidence that cannot be used against him in a *sensu stricto* criminal case, yet at the same time he may be contributing to civil enforcement against himself. Moreover, if the immunised person commits perjury in the testimony that he gives pursuant to the immunity order,[760] the grant of immunity does not protect him against perjury charges.[761] This resembles the approach taken in E&W, where the limited use provisions do not preclude prosecution due to false statements. Where the person refuses to provide evidence, although he has received immunity, he can face contempt charges.[762]

[753] ibid 460.

[754] *United States v North* 910 F2d 843 (DC Cir 1990); Arlen and Buell (n 305) 718. The prosecution's case failed, even though it had taken great care of showing that its evidence had been obtained before the immunised testimony was given, as one of the witnesses who was called had heard the defendant's immunised testimony.

[755] Sometimes this can be due to the fact that courts may find that violations of the immunity order constitute harmless error if the *Chapman* burden is met. See H Goldstein and SM Witzel, *Grand Jury Practice* (Law Journal Press, 2015) 10–55.

[756] The immunity foreseen by 18 USC is formally requested by the prosecutor and granted by a court, most commonly during a grand jury proceeding: Dressler and Michaels, *Understanding Criminal Procedure* (n 748) 274.

[757] *United States v Cappetto, et al* 502 F3d 1351, 1359 (7th Cir 1974); Goldstein and Witzel (n 755) 10–44.

[758] *Reina v United States* 364 US 507, 513 (1960).

[759] *Ullmann v United States* 350 US 422, 430–31 (1956).

[760] Prosecutions for false statements made before the immunity order, cannot be based on the immunised testimony: *United States v DeSalvo* 26 F3d 1216, 1222 (2nd Cir 1994).

[761] *United States v Apfelbaum* 445 US 115, 130–31 (1950).

[762] 18 USC §6002 *in fine*.

The inherent compulsion of the US RRD is not restricted by a limited use provision. That doctrine is considered in chapter seven.

The overview of the different approaches to immunity and limited use provisions is highly relevant for my research for two reasons. First, immunity is an important tool in the hands of law enforcement: it can use it to obtain evidence that persons would often otherwise not provide. Selective use of immunity or of compelled cooperation provisions equipped with a limited use provision allows authorities to gather evidence against persons other than the one providing it. With the exception of E&W, where a number of statutes declare that the limited use provision also benefits the spouse or civil partner, the other national systems limit the protection to the person providing the evidence.[763] In a corporate setting, the selective use of immunity poses a risk for the corporation, as well as for its employees: by offering immunity to key individuals, the authorities can gather information that is admissible in evidence against the corporation. At the same time, the authorities could immunise the corporation,[764] and use the evidence against the corporate employees or officials. In this way, immunity can help overcome difficulties in the evidence-gathering process. In this sense, one can counter arguments[765] against a corporate PSI by reference to immunity statutes and limited use provisions. Moreover, the evolution in the USA from transactional immunity to use and derivative use immunity indicates that the price for overcoming the PSI has decreased: whereas previously immunity ended the possibility of prosecuting the immunised natural or legal person, this is no longer the case, provided that the *Kastigar* burden is met.

III. Adverse Inferences

Adverse inferences constitute a particular type of compulsion. Under certain conditions, a number of legal systems accept them. My definition of the privilege also comprises the right not to have negative inferences drawn from the choice to remain silent. A person can indeed feel compelled to speak if he knows that staying silent can be interpreted as an indication of his guilt. Negative inferences imply that the choice not to answer questions or not to make statements at trial are used as evidence of a person's guilt.

The question whether exercising the privilege can give rise to negative consequences at a punitive trial was repeatedly addressed by the ECtHR.[766] *John Murray v United Kingdom*[767] has, unsurprisingly,[768] demonstrated that under certain conditions

[763] Admittedly, more general provisions such as Art 156 CCP or the spousal privilege in the USA may provide protection to certain family members.

[764] Or use other incentives.

[765] Such as the argument that a corporate PSI would make it impossible to prosecute a corporation.

[766] On this issue, see Jackson and Summers (n 273) 544 et seq.

[767] *Murray* (n 380).

[768] Unsurprisingly, as the privilege is not absolute in the ECtHR's view: *Ibrahim* (n 378) para 269.

adverse inferences can indeed be drawn.[769] In cases clearly calling for an explanation by the accused, this silence can be taken into account when considering the evidence against him.[770] The Court recently considered this matter with regard to a corporation.[771] It found that extensive evidence had been put forward by the competition authority and that the corporation had failed to refute the credibility or reliability of that evidence, as well as of the conclusions drawn by that authority from it.

In order to determine whether such an inference is acceptable, several factors are relevant, including the weight attached to the inferences in the assessment of the evidence and the situations where they may be drawn, as well as the degree of compulsion inherent in the situation.[772] In *Murray*,[773] the ECtHR held that the level of compulsion was not as high as in, for example, *Funke*, where a penalty was indeed attached to remaining silent. It considered that there was some indirect compulsion connected to a warning to a suspect that adverse inferences could be drawn from his refusal to provide testimony, in light of the weight of the case against him. Furthermore, it has highlighted that adverse inferences can only be accepted where there is a sufficiently strong prima facie case,[774] so that one can consider that the situation calls for the suspect's explanation,[775] and that his silence means that he has no good explanation to counter the case against him.[776] In other words, a conviction cannot exclusively or mainly be based on the suspect's choice to remain silent.[777] Relevant in this context is also whether safeguards were in place and whether the suspect had access to counsel from the early stages of the case and especially at the interrogation.[778] As far as the privilege guaranteed by the CFR is concerned, reference can be made here to the ECtHR's case law on the topic.

There is limited CJEU case law on the topic of adverse inferences in the context of the PSI as a general principle of EU law. The most relevant case law in this context relates to the potential impact on the fine of a refusal to answer questions. The Court has accepted that, where an undertaking refuses to answer a question in a context where its privilege is applicable, it may not be compelled to do so by the EC. Yet, the EC may, for the purpose of setting the amount of the fine, consider

[769] The Court found that adverse inferences from an accused person's failure to give evidence, at the investigative stage or at trial, are not as such incompatible with fair trial requirements: *Tabbakh v United Kingdom* App no 40945/09 (ECtHR, 21 February 2012) para 24; *O'Donnell v UK* App no 16667/10 (ECtHR, 7 April 2015) para 48.

[770] *Murray* (n 380) para 47; *SA-Capital Oy* (n 9) paras 108–10; Gray (n 480) 547.

[771] *SA-Capital Oy* (n 9) paras 108–10.

[772] *Murray* (n 380) para 47; *O'Donnell* (n 769) para 51; Ormerod and Perry (n 540) 3053.

[773] On this issue, see Ashworth (n 395) 754 et seq.

[774] *O'Donnell* (n 769) para 49.

[775] *Murray* (n 380) para 51, *Averill* (n 392) para 51. This condition is not always fulfilled: *Krumpholz* (n 430) para 40.

[776] *Telfner v Austria* App no 33501/96 (ECtHR, 20 March 2001) para 17.

[777] *Condron v United Kingdom* App no 35718/97 (ECtHR, 2 May 2000) para 56; *Tabbakh* (n 769) para 25.

[778] ibid.

the assistance given by the undertaking in establishing the existence of a competition law violation.[779] In other words, just as the use of leniency provisions can help incentivise alleged wrongdoers to come clean and facilitate the EC's task of enforcing EU competition law,[780] rewarding a cooperative attitude through a lower fine can be a helpful tool.

Articles 7(1)–(2) and particularly Article 7(5) POI Directive suggest that the privilege as incorporated in that Directive is strong, since exercising it cannot lead to negative inferences. Article 7(5) explicitly spells out the fact that a suspected or accused person exercising his privilege cannot have this choice used against him and it is not to be considered as evidence.[781] At the same time, Article 7(4) consolidates the practice of taking the defendant's (un)cooperative attitude into account for the purpose of sentencing. Nevertheless, it seems that by including 'in itself' in recital 28, adverse inferences are not completely excluded. That recital suggests that where other evidence is present, the defendant's silence could again be relevant. Yet, it should be stressed that recital 28 does not have the same normative value as Article 7(5) and thus should not be used to reduce the value of the prohibition enshrined in that provision. At the same time, the absence of a strong exclusionary rule in the Directive does not strengthen Article 7(5)'s position.[782]

In E&W, adverse inferences were mainly treated by case law until the 1990s.[783] They were not generally allowed at common law.[784] Since the criticised reform by the CJPOA, the issue of adverse inferences is largely regulated by statute.[785] The introduction of statutory provisions should be seen in the light of the ebb and flow of support for defence rights,[786] as well in the context of attempts to tackle rising crime rates around the time of its introduction.[787] Section 34 et seq CJPOA have been criticised for the lack of persuasive evidence that warranted these restrictions of the privilege.[788] The regime put in place by the CJPOA was supported by

[779] Joined Cases C-65/02 P and C-73/02 P *ThyssenKrupp v Commission* ECLI:EU:C:2005:454, paras 50–51; *Timab* (n 440) para 84.

[780] The EC's leniency notice requires an extensive disclosure of relevant information: EC Notice on Immunity from fines and reduction of fines in cartel cases [2006] OJ C298/17. On the conditions for immunity, see C Hödlmayr and L Ortiz Blanco, 'Investigation of Cases (I)' in Ortiz Blanco (n 16) 343 et seq.

[781] Indeed, this seems to go beyond the criticised *Murray* (n 380) case law, which accepts, under certain conditions, negative effects of the choice to stay silent.

[782] Cras and Erbežnik argue that the *Murray* ruling of the ECtHR is 'still hanging (a bit) around': Cras and Erbežnik (n 523) 32.

[783] Dennis, *The Law of Evidence* (n 25) 169–74.

[784] Ormerod and Perry (n 540) 3051. Under certain conditions, adverse inference could nevertheless be drawn: Ormerod and Perry (n 540) 3064–65 and 3075–76.

[785] S 34(5)(b) nevertheless does not preclude 'the drawing of any inference from any such silence or other reaction of the accused which could properly be drawn apart from this section'.

[786] Quirk (n 25) 2. Quirk is sceptical about there being a flow for the privilege any time soon: ibid 175 et seq.

[787] ibid 25.

[788] ibid 41 and 73.

a strong police campaign,[789] and it can be understood as a reaction to the defence safeguards that were strengthened by PACE, including access to a lawyer.[790]

Section 34(1) and (2) CJPOA allows for the drawing of inferences that appear proper,[791] under three specific scenarios: where the accused, (i) after being cautioned[792] but before being charged, was questioned and failed to mention a fact that he later relied on in his defence;[793] (ii) or once charged or informed that he might be prosecuted, failed to mention a fact that he relied on in his defence;[794] or (iii) in the context of post-charge questioning in relation to terrorism offences, failed to mention a fact that he relied on in his defence.[795] Adverse inferences can also be drawn where a defendant relies on a fact which he did not state himself at the trial stage but where, for instance, that fact has been established by a witness for the defence or by a prosecution witness.[796] The aim of the section is the deterrence of late fabrication, as well as encouraging early disclosure of genuine defences.[797] Section 34 aims to tackle those situations where an accused person presents a defence after having remained silent or comes with a new, ambush defence not disclosed during interviews.[798] The section essentially comes into play where a fact is relied upon that was not mentioned before.[799] The provision does not allow for adverse inferences purely because one remained silent.[800]

[789] Munday additionally refers to political anxiousness to appear tough on law and order: R Munday, *Evidence*, 10th edn (Oxford University Press, 2019) 458. On the background to the CJPOA: Keane and McKeown (n 535) 506–07.

[790] S 58 PACE. The idea that the CJPOA needed to restore the balance in favour of law enforcement, seems flawed: Quirk (n 25) 51 and 87.

[791] Not only in relation to someone's guilt, but also for other purposes, such as the purpose of deciding whether there is a case to answer: s 34(2)c CJPOA.

[792] PACE, Code C, para 10.5: 'You do not have to say anything. But it may harm your defence if you do not mention when questioned something which you later rely on in court. Anything you do say may be given in evidence.'

[793] On the condition that the fact was a fact which the accused under the circumstances that existed at the time of questioning could have been reasonably expected to mention. Circumstances should be understood broadly in this context as including circumstances related both to the interviewee and to the interview: *Argent* [1997] 2 CrAppR 27; Dennis, *The Law of Evidence* (n 25) 181.

[794] And which he, similarly to scenario (i), could have reasonably been expected to mention.

[795] And which he could have reasonably been expected to mention.

[796] Ormerod and Perry (n 540) 3055. On this topic, see Munday (n 789) 472.

[797] *R v Smith* [2011] EWCA Crim 1098, para 17; Crown Court Compendium – Part I (August 2022), 17-1, www.judiciary.uk/wp-content/uploads/2020/12/Crown-Court-Compendium-Part-I-August-2021.pdf; Munday (n 789) 461.

[798] *Smith* (n 797). Further statutory changes have meanwhile been made to that effect: s 5(5) of the Criminal Procedure and Investigations Act 1996 requires the defence to make a defence statement prior to the trial, after previously undisclosed material was disclosed by the prosecution. On this matter, see Keane and McKeown (n 535) 526–31. This statement has not been considered to violate the privilege as it does not require self-incrimination, but merely disclosure of what will be said at trial: *R v Rochford* [2011] 1 WLR 534, 540. On the defence statement's adequacy, see *Ludovic Black v R* [2020] EWCA Crim 915.

[799] Ormerod and Perry (n 540) 3051. The CoA has suggested that it is wiser to avoid a s 34 direction when a defendant has set up a line of reasoning in interview and then introduces additional details later connected to that line of reasoning: *Adam Johnsen v R* [2017] EWCA Crim 191, para 28.

[800] *T v DPP* [2007] EWHC 1793, para 20; Billing (n 356) 172; Ormerod and Perry (n 540) 3052.

Similarly, in order for an adverse inference to be drawn, the specific fact which was not mentioned and which is relied upon at trial needs to be identified.[801] The requirement that the person could have been reasonably expected to mention the fact(s) at issue has raised several questions.[802] It presupposes that one checks whether an ordinary person with the same characteristics as the accused would have disclosed the fact or not.[803] Moreover, can a person reasonably be expected to disclose a fact where his lawyer advised him not to do so? If legal advice would suffice to exclude section 34 CJPOA's applicability, the section's impact could easily be restricted.[804] Legal advice is still a relevant factor for juries to consider, but it does not immunise a defendant from adverse inferences.[805] Another tool that offers some protection against adverse inferences is the use of a pre-prepared statement.[806]

Section 35 CJPOA deals with inferences from silence at trial. Where the defendant stays silent, or refuses without good reason to answer questions after having been sworn, the trial court can draw inferences that appear proper. For the provision to apply, it should have been made clear to the defendant that he can give evidence.[807] Such inferences cannot be made unless the defendant has had the chance to give evidence.[808] The prosecution bears the burden of establishing a prima facie case before the issue of inferences can come into play.[809] The strength of the case against the defendant is paralleled by the incentive to provide answers.[810] The reference to inferences as 'appear proper' gives a broad power of discretion to the trial judge.[811] Sections 36 and 37 address inferences in cases where the suspect does not have an explanation for items and marks, as well as with regard to his presence at a certain place.[812]

Although inferences can be allowed, the CJPOA precludes convictions based solely on them.[813] The effect of these provisions is that suspects are pushed into cooperating,[814] both at the investigation stage and at trial. Although a conviction

[801] *R v Aftab Ulhaq Khan* [2020] EWCA Crim 163, paras 26–27; Ormerod and Perry (n 540) 3055.

[802] Dennis, *The Law of Evidence* (n 25) 183. This matter was recently considered by the CoA: *Ludovic Black* (n 798).

[803] Dennis, *The Law of Evidence* (n 25) 183–84.

[804] *Condron and Condron* [1997] 1 CrApp R 185, 191; Munday (n 789) 465; on the two-stage test that is to be applied, see Dennis, *The Law of Evidence* (n 25) 190. Critically, see Quirk (n 25) 129.

[805] Munday (n 789) 465.

[806] A suspect can decide to stay silent during interview but hand in a pre-prepared statement to the interviewing officers. On this issue, see Munday (n 789) 468–70.

[807] Munday (n 789) 482.

[808] Moreover, inferences under s 35 CJPOA cannot be drawn in certain cases, eg where the accused's physical or mental condition would make it undesirable for the person to testify: s 35(1) CJPOA.

[809] Ormerod and Perry (n 540) 3073.

[810] Crown Court Compendium (n 797) 17–24, para 16: 'The nature of the inference available will depend on the way in which the evidence has developed and the strength of the prosecution case. The stronger the case, the more powerful the incentive to provide an answer, if there is one.'

[811] Keane and McKeown (n 535) 521.

[812] On that matter, see Ormerod and Perry (n 540) 3066–68.

[813] S 38(3) CJPOA. Nor can the suspect be held in contempt if he decides not to testify at trial: s 35(4) CJPOA.

[814] Billing (n 356) 171.

may not be solely based on adverse inferences, the potential impact of the adverse inference provisions does increase the pressure on suspects and its adoption was highly controversial.[815] In the meantime, the ECtHR has had the opportunity to address the adverse inference regime both under the CJPOA and the Criminal Evidence (Northern Ireland) Order 1988.[816] The Court has at times been lenient towards the idea, provided that the inferences are drawn in situations where the case clearly calls for an explanation of the suspect[817] and the necessary safeguards are put in place,[818] with a particular emphasis on access to a lawyer[819] and proper jury directions.[820] The current situation, particularly in relation to section 34, has strongly weakened the privilege and the suspect is put in a difficult spot, as deciding whether to rely on the privilege has become a difficult choice, for example, due to the complicated caution.[821] Put differently: exercising the privilege now comes, in certain cases, at a price. This has also impacted on the relation between lawyers and their clients, as lawyers may have to take the stand to justify why they advised to rely on the privilege.[822] In light of the lack of substantially increased charge, plea and conviction rates, one may seriously wonder whether the restrictions imposed on suspects' privilege are justified.[823] Moreover, more widespread availability of video surveillance, communication interception and other techniques may reduce the importance of the compulsion that is exercised by adverse inferences.[824]

Unlike E&W, the issue of adverse inference in Belgium is principally tackled through case law.[825] Similarly to the ECtHR, Belgian case law has at times accepted adverse inferences from the person's silence, but only where there are sufficiently strong indications against the suspect that call for an explanation.[826] The defendant's silence can then be taken into account by the court, together with other leads, in the court's assessment of the available evidence.[827] The CoC has ruled that the right of defence and the POI are not violated when the objections against the defendant are overwhelming and the judge draws unfavourable conclusions from

[815] Dennis, *The Law of Evidence* (n 25) 176.

[816] Billing (n 356) 170.

[817] *Adetoro v United Kingdom* App no 46834/06 (ECtHR, 20 April 2010) para 49.

[818] *Murray* (n 380) and *Condron v United Kingdom* (n 777). The Art 6 violation in *Condron v United Kingdom* seemed to be based on the faulty direction, and not on the CJPOA regime as such: Dennis, *The Law of Evidence* (n 25) 177. The ECtHR's case law nevertheless impacted the CJPOA regime, eg in relation to access to a lawyer.

[819] Billing (n 356) 173.

[820] Emmerson et al (n 728) 630 and 631.

[821] Quirk (n 25) 4.

[822] ibid 5 and 115–16.

[823] ibid 5 and 155. On this issue also, see Munday (n 789) 487–88.

[824] Quirk (n 25) 27 and 161.

[825] Rozie et al, 'Het zwijgrecht als tweesnijdend zwaard' (n 431) 479.

[826] CoC 5 April 2000, P.00.0250.F, 2000/1 Pas 708; CoC 2 September 2008, P.08.0393.N, 4; CoC 5 October 2010, P.10.0703.N, 7; de la Serna (n 25) 13–14; Rozie et al, 'Het zwijgrecht als tweesnijdend zwaard' (n 431) 479; Verstraeten, *Handboek strafvordering* (n 405) 859.

[827] Tersago, *Verklaringen van verdachten* (n 572) 102.

his silence or unsatisfactory statements by way of factual presumptions.[828] Lastly, the suspect should not be punished for his choice of defence strategy.[829]

A US defendant can decide to rely on his PSI and choose not to testify at trial.[830] The PSI offers protection against adverse comments by a trial judge, prosecutors[831] or counsel for other defendants.[832] In *Griffin*,[833] SCOTUS prohibited inferences of guilt based on the defendant's choice to invoke his privilege. This would constitute improper compulsion, since it would amount to a court-imposed penalty for relying on a constitutional privilege and this would cut down on the privilege as it makes its assertion costly.[834] The US system considers adverse inferences at trial in principle incompatible with the privilege. The *Griffin* rule also applies at sentencing.[835] Yet, it is not an unqualified rule.[836] Adverse comments by a prosecutor can be accepted if they constitute harmless errors.[837] SCOTUS has established a fair response exception to the rule.[838] The *Griffin* rule only covers silence at trial and not silence in the context of police questioning. What happens if a suspect does not speak until trial, where he is suddenly willing to testify? Can reference be made to his silence? If the suspect has stayed silent after he has been arrested and given the *Miranda* warnings, such a reference is not allowed.[839] This makes sense since the person has (implicitly) been given reasons to believe in light of those warnings that he will not be 'punished' for staying silent in this scenario.[840] Given the difference in wording of the US caution as compared to the one in use in E&W, that is unsurprising. References to pre-arrest silence for impeachment purposes[841] or to silence in the absence of the *Miranda* warnings are allowed.[842]

[828] CoC 5 May 2020, P.20.0036.N.

[829] CoC 24 May 2011 (n 668) 18; CoC 7 February 2012, P.11.1732.N; Beernaert et al (n 405) 37; Van den Wyngaert et al (n 35) 761; Verstraeten and Verbruggen, *Strafrecht en strafprocesrecht* (n 574) 293. In the former case, it held that judges are only bound by the right to silence insofar as they are deciding on guilt. Once a person has been found guilty, his silence can be taken into account, as long as he is not punished for his defence strategy. In a later ruling, it quashed a ruling of the CoA that had taken into account the defendant's lack of remorse or insight: CoC 7 January 2014, P.12.1653.N.

[830] Salky (n 587) 108.

[831] *United States v Hills, Tyleman and Winters* 618 F3d 619 (7th Cir 2010).

[832] L Barker et al, *Civil Liberties and the Constitution – Cases and Commentaries*, 9th edn (Routledge, 2011) 424; Salky (n 587) 108.

[833] *Griffin v California* 380 US 609, 613–14 (1965).

[834] ibid 614; WP Signorelli, *Criminal Law, Procedure and Evidence* (CRC Press, 2011) 61.

[835] *Mitchell v United States* 526 US 314 (1999).

[836] *Chapman v California* 386 US 18 (1967).

[837] In order for such comments to be accepted, the prosecutor must show, beyond reasonable doubt, that the defendant would have been found guilty in any event. Comments by another defendant's counsel are more likely to amount to a harmless error: Salky (n 587) 113.

[838] *United States v Robinson* 485 US 25 (1988); Salky (n 587) 110. That fair response exception has widely been accepted, see Salky (n 587) 110–11.

[839] *Doyle v Ohio* 426 US 610 (1976); JJ Duane, 'The Extraordinary Trajectory of *Griffin v California*: The Aftermath of Playing Fifty Years of Scrabble with the Fifth Amendment' (2015) 3 *Stanford Journal of Criminal Law and Policy* 1, 4.

[840] *Doyle* (n 839) 618.

[841] *Jenkins v Anderson* 447 US 231 (1980).

[842] *Fletcher v Weir* 455 US 63 (1982); *Salinas v Texas* 570 US 178 (2013).

In relation to adverse inferences, a particular challenge comes up in relation to corporations. From whose silence can one draw adverse inferences against the corporation? That specific question has not been clearly answered in the examined legal systems.

IV. Private Compulsion

In all studied systems, case law mainly focuses on public compulsion, rather than on compulsion by private parties, such as a private employer. This aspect is increasingly relevant in the context of internal investigations, where individuals often face pressure to cooperate. During such investigations, corporate officials and employees are regularly interviewed by private individuals, often lawyers from the law firm in charge of the corporation's internal investigation. If an individual makes a self-incriminating statement, that statement could later turn up in a punitive case against him, provided the authorities gain access to the findings of the internal investigation. Corporations may decide to share these findings to obtain cooperation credit. The analysis made here is an example of the conflicts of interest between the corporation and the individuals on which it relies[843] and the connected issue of the use of economic power by the corporation.

Prior to conducting interviews with corporate officers or employees in the course of an internal investigation, corporate counsel should ascertain that such interviews are allowed and whether they are subject to specific conditions.[844] In cases that cover multiple legal systems, that exercise is all the more important, in order to avoid, for instance, that evidence would turn out to be inadmissible.

Neither the ECtHR nor the CJEU has properly addressed whether compulsion by a private party suffices to trigger the PSI's applicability.[845] This question is relevant for my research. One may argue that an individual cannot invoke his privilege in an internal investigation as Article 6 ECHR does not apply to statements made to a private party,[846] provided that the private party is not acting under the authority of the authorities. For example, in *Allan*,[847] the ECtHR found a violation of the privilege where the police had put an informant whom they had closely coached in

[843] Griffin (n 713) 337.

[844] C Day and L Hodges, 'Witness Interviews in Internal Investigations: The UK Perspective' in J Seddon et al, *The Practitioner's Guide to Global Investigations – Volume I: Global Investigations in the United Kingdom and the United States*, 4th edn (Law Business Research, 2019) 148; JT Wells, *International Fraud Handbook* (Wiley, 2018) 182.

[845] The ECtHR has ruled on other aspects of internal investigations, such as the use of camera surveillance in case of employee theft allegations: *López Ribalda and Others v Spain* App nos 1874/13 and 8567/13 (ECtHR, 17 October 2019). Similarly relevant for the purpose of internal investigations is the Court's ruling on electronic surveillance by an employer of messages exchanged by an employee: *Bărbulescu v Romania* App no 61496/08 (ECtHR, 5 September 2017).

[846] This is the position adopted by the CoC: CoC 20 April 2015 (n 331).

[847] *Allan* (n 395). On this case, see Zeeman (n 80) 324–26. See also the Opinion of the AG Timperman in the Belgian case that resulted in the aforementioned 2015 CoC ruling.

a suspect's cell to elicit evidence. In *Bykov*, where an individual was equipped with a wire and coached to talk to another individual, the ECtHR found that coercion or oppression was lacking. It took several factors into account, including the fact that the person wearing the wire was a subordinate of the person who was being recorded.[848]

Establishing a similar link between the corporate internal investigation and the authorities will not always be easy, unless, for example, the cooperation between the authorities and the corporations is so close that the authorities give instructions as to how to conduct the internal investigation. Where the employee's interview has already been conducted prior to consultation between the corporation and the authorities, it is difficult to attribute the compulsion to the government. Secondly, one may wonder whether an individual can claim at his trial that his privilege is violated by the use of evidence given during the internal investigation. As the pressure in such investigations is of a private nature, I am not certain such a claim will be successful at the CJEU and the ECtHR. Yet, a close nexus between the corporation's internal investigation and the authorities may nevertheless play a role.

At the same time, an employee could also challenge the voluntariness of his statement. Several mechanisms can help preserve the statement's voluntariness, such as providing a notification of the interviewee's rights and the facts on which he will be interviewed, allowing the interviewee to be assisted during the interview, for example, by an attorney or by a trade union representative.[849] It should at all times be clear that, if the interviews are conducted by an attorney, he acts for the corporation and not as counsel to the interviewee. The interviewee should understand that the corporation may decide to share the information obtained during the interview with the authorities.[850] Furthermore, in order to make sure that the individual feels at ease, the interview should be set up in a place where the interviewee feels comfortable and safe, though the interviewer should be in control of the environment.[851] The interviewee should not feel restricted by any

[848] *Bykov* (n 395) para 102.

[849] T Bauwens et al, 'Belgium' in S Lach et al, *European Investigations Guide 2018* (Hogan Lovells International LLP, 2018) 41–42; J Hofkens and Y Lenders, 'Belgium' in D Kelly and C Black, *Corporate Investigations 2021* (ICLG, 2021) 41. On the right of US private employees who are members of a union and at risk of disciplinary action to be assisted by a union representative, see Arlen and Buell (n 305) 719.

[850] In the USA, such a notification is referred to as an *Upjohn* warning in light of the SCOTUS decision in *Upjohn Co v United States* 449 US 383 (1981). On that matter, see Griffin (n 713) 337–38; AM Tompkins et al, 'Witness Interviews in Internal Investigations: The US Perspective' in Seddon et al, *The Practitioner's Guide to Global Investigations – Volume II* (n 743) 153; TP Tran et al, 'Managing Cross Border Internal Investigations' (2020) 24 *Currents: Journal of International Economic Law* 52, 57. *Upjohn* warnings help ensure that employees do not mistakenly believe that the interviewing attorney acts on their personal behalf. Sometimes an employee can rely on the attorney-client privilege if he can show that the corporation's attorney acted as his individual counsel; admittedly, he faces a high evidentiary burden: Kloeber (n 241) 649–51. Green and Podgor advocate that courts should go beyond the mere application of that test and they propose a 'fair dealing' approach: BA Green and ES Podgor, 'Unregulated Internal Investigations: Achieving Fairness for Corporate Constituents' (2013) 54 *Boston College Law Review* 73.

[851] Wells, *International Fraud Handbook* (n 844) 183.

physical barrier, also to prevent the interviewer and the corporation from incurring liability, for instance, for false imprisonment.[852]

US courts have repeatedly assessed whether a person was facing unacceptable private compulsion. As the Fifth Amendment focuses on public compulsion,[853] the privilege provides little protection in a private employment context:[854] if an employer threatens employees with dismissal for failure to cooperate, eg during an internal investigation, this does not, in principle, amount to public compulsion.[855] US employees are very often employed through an at-will mechanism,[856] which makes termination easy, except where specific protection applies.[857] The corporation usually conducts internal investigations with the help of outside help, typically including a law firm.[858]

Being threatened with dismissal for not cooperating is compelling, yet it does not amount to government compulsion, even when the compelled evidence is later shared with the government by the corporation in order to prevent the corporation from being convicted. Thus, employees can[859] face a trilemma during an internal investigation:[860] refusing to answer questions might make them look guilty and could result in termination of their employment[861] or disciplinary measures;[862] answering questions could have an adverse impact on their defence if that information is subsequently disclosed to the prosecuting authorities;[863] and false denial could amount to a criminal offence.[864] Moreover, depending on the nature of the evidence and the employee's involvement in the wrongdoing, the corporation could still dismiss them. As I will analyse later in chapter 10, several legal systems have put mechanisms in place that encourage corporate cooperation.

[852] ibid 183; T Harvey, 'United Kingdom' in Wells, *International Fraud Handbook* (n 844) 370; MJ Kranacher and R Riley, *Forensic Accounting and Fraud Examination*, 2nd edn (Wiley, 2019) 76.

[853] Arlen and Buell (n 305) 719. MH Baer, 'Law Enforcement's Lochner' (2021) 105 *Minnesota Law Review* 1667, 1690–98.

[854] Several authors consider that the Sixth Amendment right to counsel does not apply to interviews by private entities: see Kloeber (n 241) 645 and 652; Kranacher and Riley (n 852) 76. Yet, the interviewee remains free to consult a lawyer.

[855] Kranacher and Riley (n 852) 76.

[856] Arlen and Buell (n 305) 719.

[857] JL Achilles et al, 'United States' in Seddon et al, *The Practitioner's Guide to Global Investigations – Volume II* (n 743) 574.

[858] As this too can entail the attorney–client privilege's protection.

[859] Where an employee is likely to be fired anyway for his involvement in the offences under investigation, he could decide not to provide detailed answers during the internal investigation.

[860] Interviewees can be assisted by their personal attorney at such interviews: Achilles et al (n 857) 578; JA Brown and RA Burlingame, 'USA' in Kelly and Black (n 849); ML Williams et al, 'Employee Rights: The US Perspective' in Seddon et al, *The Practitioner's Guide to Global Investigations – Volume I* (n 844) 259. High-level employees or corporate officials may be able to rely on indemnification of legal fees provided by the corporation.

[861] Arlen and Buell (n 305) 719; Achilles et al (n 857) 574; Brown and Burlingame (n 860) 144; Kloeber (n 241) 645.

[862] Garrett, 'Corporate Confessions' (n 303) 918; Williams et al (n 860) 256. Corporations may have policies on cooperation with internal investigations: Tompkins et al (n 850) 156.

[863] Carpenter (n 331) 221–22.

[864] Griffin (n 713) 355.

Some individuals have challenged this particularly precarious situation by invoking a violation of their PSI. Such claims rarely succeed, and only where the cooperation between the corporation and the authorities is very close does the chance of success increase. Case law of SCOTUS on other Constitutional Amendments[865] highlights that in order for the actions of a private party to amount to state action there needs to be[866] 'such a close nexus between the state and the challenged action that seemingly private behaviour may be fairly treated as that of the state itself'.[867] Determining whether this is the case can be difficult, and there seems to be no fixed set of circumstances that suffices, since there can be counter-indications against concluding that the action involved can be attributed to the state.[868] Relevant questions in this context are: is the action of the private party caused by the use by the state of its coercive power? Are there important, open or covert incentives given by the state? Does the private actor assume the role of a wilful participant in a joint activity with the state? Has a public function been delegated by the state?[869]

Currently, there is very little case law that has accepted such a close nexus in relation to the PSI.[870] The privilege only comes into play to the extent that there is sufficient government involvement in order for the private compulsion to be attributable to the authorities.[871] Arlen and Buell consider that as long as the corporation leads the investigation, without direction from the prosecuting authorities, a claim of state action will not succeed.[872] *United States v Stein* is one of the key cases on this matter.[873] KPMG and several of its employees were under investigation in the USA for their involvement in alleged abusive tax shelters. KPMG feared suffering the same fate as Arthur Andersen, which had collapsed after a conviction. Therefore, it attempted to avoid being indicted and the prosecution relied on that fear.[874] KPMG's policy included paying the legal fees of its employees for civil suits or *sensu stricto* criminal charges related to their employment for KPMG. The corporation had to ensure that its employees cooperated with the prosecution to avoid an indictment.[875] KPMG then threatened the employees concerned

[865] eg the 14th Amendment.
[866] On this topic, see Griffin (n 713) 365–71.
[867] *Brentwood Academy v Tennessee Secondary School Athletic Association* et al 531 US 288, 295 (2001).
[868] ibid 295–96 and 303.
[869] ibid 296.
[870] Calls have been made to broaden employee protection in the course of internal investigations: Griffin (n 713) 357; Kloeber (n 241) 657. Critically on providing private employees with *Garrity* immunity: Buell, 'Criminal Procedure Within the Firm' (n 371) 1642–46. Lowell and Man (n 240) at v suggest that instead of considering the level of government involvement that amounts to state action, the authorities should point out that corporations are expected to respect employees' constitutional rights. Compliance with that requirement should in their view be achieved by refusing any credit to corporations who do not abide by that demand.
[871] R Kent and J Thomas, 'United States of America' in Spehl and Gruetzner (n 613) 426.
[872] Arlen and Buell (n 305) 720.
[873] *United States v Stein* 440 FSupp2d 315 (SD NY 2006).
[874] On that case, see Griffin (n 713) 338–39, 358–59 and 365; Lowell and Man (n 240) ix–xi and xx.
[875] KPMG entered into a DPA in August 2005.

with refusal to pay their legal fees – or even dismissal – if they were uncooperative. During this time, there was extensive contact between the company and the authorities. The district court found a sufficiently close nexus and some compelled evidence provided by the individuals was excluded. On appeal, the exclusion of evidence was not confirmed as the appellate court ruled that the indictment against all 13 defendants had to be dismissed.[876] The court found that KPMG's actions were a direct consequence of the influence of the government and that KPMG's action amounted to state action,[877] and it found a violation of the Sixth Amendment.

More recently,[878] the 2nd Circuit CoA rejected allegations by two dismissed employees that their employer's request to attend interviews directed by external counsel[879] and answer potentially incriminating questions in the framework of an internal investigation amounted to state action.[880] This claim was made in light of cooperation between their employer and the authorities.[881] The court found that the request to attend the interview was reasonable as the employees had been implicated in a conspiracy related to acts within their scope of employment which put the corporation at risk and it accepted that they were fired for cause.[882] In its reasoning, the court referred to the corporation's duty towards the shareholders to investigate potentially criminal employee conduct. It also considered the fact that the requests for interviews predated a meeting of the authorities with the corporation's representative. The court refused to adopt a rule according to which 'acts that are taken by a private company in response to government action, and that have as one goal obtaining better treatment from the government, amount to state action'.[883] It found that corporations can cooperate and anyway have independent interests in setting up internal investigations and cooperating with the authorities.[884]

In *United States v Connolly and Black*, a US district court took a strong stance on involvement of the authorities in an 'internal' investigation.[885] DB had received a demand by the CFTC in the context of possible LIBOR manipulation to conduct

[876] *United States v J Stein and others* 541 F3d 130 (2nd Cir 2008).

[877] ibid 147–51.

[878] See also *United States v J Vorley and C Chanu* 2020 WL 1166185 (ND Ill 2020).

[879] One of the plaintiffs claimed he was asked to attend an interview (without counsel) with a lawyer of the Attorney General, yet his employer denied this.

[880] *WW Gilman and EJ McNenney v Marsh & Mclennan Companies, Inc, Marsh Inc, Marsh USA Inc, Marsh Global Broking Inc and Michael Cherkasky* 826 F3d 69 (2nd Cir 2016).

[881] No criminal prosecution of the corporation would occur in exchange for its cooperation in the ongoing investigation, including waiver of attorney-client privilege and work-product immunity.

[882] The employees did not attend the interviews into criminal bid-rigging, though they had attended an earlier interview when a civil case was ongoing. Both employees were fired the day after they refused an interview. On for cause dismissal in case of failure to cooperate with an internal investigation, see Arlen and Buell (n 305) 719.

[883] It distinguished this case from *Stein* by arguing that KPMG was forced by the authorities to abandon its policy of paying attorney fees for its employees, while it was not planning to do so if it had not been put under pressure.

[884] On this issue, see Kloeber (n 241) 655.

[885] *United States v M Connolly and GC Black* 2019 WL 2120523 (SD NY 2019).

an internal investigation by outside counsel and it had been instructed as to the matter that was to be investigated. At the same time, DB had been informed of the conditions under which cooperation credit could be obtained. The bank coordinated extensively with the CFTC, the DOJ and the SEC during the internal investigation, which took about five years, and in addition to regular updates to the authorities, the bank received directions in terms of what and how it should look into the matter.[886] It was clear to the employees that failure to attend interviews would have resulted in termination. The court took issue with the fact that the authorities heavily relied on the bank and did not undertake a proper investigation of their own. It considered that:

> In short, while the record before the Court is incomplete (at the Government's choice), everything I have read suggests that the United States outsourced its investigation to Deutsche Bank and its lawyers. The inference one draws from a lack of evidence from the Government is not an inference that is favorable to the Government.

The court accepted that the *Garrity* doctrine applies to a private employer's conduct if it is fairly attributable to the government, which was the case here as there was a sufficiently close nexus between the state and the challenged action,[887] adding that 'the "controlling factor" is not whether the state directed the constitutionally prohibited conduct, but whether the state "involved itself in the use of a substantial economic threat to coerce a person into furnishing an incriminating statement"'. The court highlighted the fact that DB faced significant pressure, as an indictment would have ruined it. Although the court accepted that a *Garrity* violation had occurred, Black did not obtain relief as his compelled statements had not been directly or indirectly used against him. The case is a warning for authorities who fail to conduct a proper independent investigation and demand an internal investigation, paid for by the corporation whose future can be ruined by a criminal indictment,[888] but (co-)directed by the authorities.

In E&W, employees or corporate officers do not typically have to be informed of the PSI prior to an interview in an internal investigation, yet interviewers may decide to inform them.[889]

Individuals who, in the course of an internal investigation, carry out an interview of a person who might become a suspect would most likely not be under a duty to comply with section 67(9) PACE.[890] In order for that section to apply to

[886] Lowell and Man would undoubtedly argue with regard to such case that 'in a literal sense and at least in spirit, the corporations are acting as agents of the government': Lowell and Man (n 240) iv. DB obtained a DPA in 2015. A subsidiary agreed to plead guilty on one count of wire fraud. Connolly and Black's convictions were overturned on appeal.

[887] Reference was made to the *Stein* criteria: 'i) exercises coercive power; (ii) is entwined in the management or control of the private actor; (iii) provides the private action with significant encouragement, either over or covert; (iv) engages in a joint activity in which the private actor is a wilful participant; (v) delegates a public function to the private actor; or (vi) entwines the private actor in governmental policies.'

[888] Kloeber (n 241) 638.

[889] L Naidoo and R Vandercruyssen, 'United Kingdom' in Lach et al (n 849) 266.

[890] See Day and Hodges (n 844) 138.

internal investigators, interviews of suspects regarding criminal offences should have been delegated to them, and even then only to the extent that they can be considered to act on behalf of the authorities.[891] That is unlikely to occur since authorities in E&W are reluctant to delegate interviews of suspects to the corporation, particularly when seeking first accounts.[892]

In the absence of formal requirements for interviews in the course of internal investigations, practitioners in E&W consider it advisable to provide information to the interviewee, including: the context of the investigation; the fact that it may be used in litigation; whether the interviewer considers that the interviewee is implicated in wrongdoing; where the interview is carried out by an attorney, the interviewee should be notified that he acts on behalf of the corporation; and it should be clear that the corporation may choose to share its findings with the authorities.[893] Putting pressure on employees to admit guilt is to be avoided.[894] It is recommended that interviewees are permitted to be assisted by their personal counsel if they choose to retain one.[895] In principle, requests to assist an internal investigation will amount to reasonable management instructions, and a refusal to comply with such a request can qualify as employee misconduct.[896] Employees can be required to attend interviews and cooperate with the persons conducting the internal investigation and they can face disciplinary action if they fail to do so.[897]

In Belgium, in one case, the CoC refused to apply Article 6 ECHR to an internal investigation, as that article does not apply to statements made to a private party at a time when no criminal charge is pending.[898] In my view, an exception must be made where the private party is cooperating so closely with the authorities that the internal investigation can no longer be considered as mere private compulsion.[899] The Court further checked whether any undue pressure was exerted on the individual and ruled that this was not the case and that the testimony obtained in the internal investigation could be used at trial.[900] The case thus suggests that even where there is no sufficiently close connection between the authorities and the internal investigation, declarations should still be excluded if they are involuntary.

[891] ibid 138.

[892] ibid 138.

[893] Stocker et al (n 743) 553–54.

[894] ibid 546.

[895] ibid 554. According to these authors, ethical reasons can make it preferable, where a risk of self-incrimination exists, that employees are advised to consult a lawyer.

[896] ibid 546.

[897] Day and Hodges (n 844) 130; Ludlam and Garfield (n 614) 124. Naidoo and Vandercruyssen (n 889) 265. Whether dismissal is acceptable depends on the overall context, including the employee's seniority: Stocker et al (n 743) 546.

[898] CoC 20 April 2015 (n 331). Recently the CoC also found that the PSI did not apply in relation to a civil servant who supervised a convict as that person was neither a prosecuting or judicial authority: CoC 1 September 2021, P.21.1078.F.

[899] In his 2015 Opinion, AG Timperman accepted that if the corporation had acted as a state agent when it obtained the statement, that could result in the evidence's inadmissibility or exclusion.

[900] An employee had signed a written declaration in the CEO's office, in the presence of a manager and the attorney assisting the corporation.

It should be emphasised that if the CoC would have found that the statement had to be excluded, the impact on the *sensu stricto* criminal proceedings in this specific case would have been detrimental: the internal investigation resulted in the filing of a complaint by the corporation, which was the victim of an offence by the employee. The application of the 'fruit of the poisonous tree' doctrine could have resulted in the exclusion of all or at least most of the evidence as it likely built upon the statement given during the internal investigation.

It has been argued that employees owe a duty of loyalty to their employer under Article 17(2) of the Act of 3 July 1978 on labour contracts and thus must abide by all legitimate orders of the employer. Staying silent during interviewing can be punished by a disciplinary sanction or give rise to termination.[901]

The Belgian Minister of the Interior has announced that the Private Detective Act of 1991 will face reform and modernisation. If the reform is adopted, interviewing a person in such a private investigation will only be possible where the person consents to be interviewed.[902] The legislator might seize this opportunity to explicitly allow interviewees to be accompanied by a person of their choice and to require that they are provided with information on, for instance, the purpose of the interview and their rights during the interview.

With the exception of a few US cases, the case law has proven to be rather lenient towards the use of internal investigations in relation to the PSI of corporate officers and employees. In the absence of very close cooperation between the corporation and the authorities, the privilege would not tend to offer much protection to individuals. Even though internal investigations can be an effective tool for corporations to gather information, which they may consider providing to the authorities in order to obtain cooperation credit, they should not pressure the individual too much as this could endanger the voluntary nature of his statement.

[901] E Soetens and S De Cock, 'Verslagen studienamiddag van 23 november 2017 – Vereniging voor de Studie van het Mededingingsrecht – Mededingingsrecht met een arbeidsrechtelijk staartje' [2018] *Competitio* 219, 223. Hofkens and Lenders (n 849) 41 consider that employees cannot be compelled to cooperate, yet not doing so can be considered as disloyal behaviour, which might qualify as cause for dismissal.

[902] L Bové, 'Privédetectives krijgen niet langer vrij spel' *De Tijd* (14 January 2021) www.tijd.be/politiek-economie/belgie/algemeen/privedetectives-krijgen-niet-langer-vrij-spel/10277150.html.

7

The Privilege against Self-Incrimination and Different Types of Evidence

In this chapter, I examine which types of evidence are covered by the PSI. Assessing whether the privilege protects only oral statements or also other types of evidence is of particular relevance for corporations. Admittedly, they are not so concerned by questions such as whether the privilege protects urine samples or DNA, or whether a person can invoke the privilege to refuse to submit to a breathalyser test, yet other types of evidence are highly relevant to them: can a corporation refuse to submit documents by claiming that this would tend to incriminate it? Can a CEO refuse to unlock his smartphone as doing so would give the authorities access to evidence of the corrupt practices of the corporation?

I. Oral Statements

As far as oral statements are concerned, the ECtHR's case law is clear: such statements are covered by the privilege.[903] As I outlined in the introduction, my working definition of the PSI includes a right to silence. The ECtHR often treats the right to silence and the PSI together.

By comparison to the ECtHR's approach, the protection offered by the CJEU in terms of material scope of the privilege in competition cases is very narrow. That case law precludes compelling undertakings to provide information through decisions calling for information[904] to an extent that would undermine their rights of defence.[905] Compelling an undertaking to provide answers that might involve an admission of the existence of a competition law infringement is a red line that should not be crossed according to the CJEU.[906] Requiring answers to factual questions is permitted according to the CJEU. Yet, certain factual questions can be prohibited if they would in fact lead to an admission of guilt. This could be the case

[903] *Ibrahim* (n 378) 266–68; *De Legé* (n 57) para 75.

[904] Also during inspections carried out under Art 20(4) of Regulation 1/2003 undertakings cannot be required to admit competition law infringements: *Deutsche Bahn and others* (n 504) para 82; A Lamadrid de Pablo and M Kellerbauer, 'Investigation of cases (II)' in Ortiz Blanco (n 16) 461; Veenbrink, *Criminal Law Principles* (n 386) 149.

[905] *Orkem* (n 439) para 34.

[906] ibid para 35; Ortiz Blanco and Jörgens (n 16) 37.

where a company is required to disclose the names of undertakings it has warned about a possible investigation by the competition authorities.[907]

In *DB v Consob*, the CJEU confirmed that the privilege implicitly enshrined in the second paragraph of Article 47 and Article 48 CFR is not limited to admissions of wrongdoing or directly incriminating remarks, but also covers information on factual questions which can later be used to support the prosecution and which are thus relevant towards a conviction or a penalty.[908] The Court, like AG Pikamäe,[909] expressly distinguished the setting in *DB v Consob* from EU competition proceedings. It reaffirmed that in competition proceedings undertakings cannot be compelled to give answers which might involve an admission of the existence of an infringement, by the undertaking, of competition law. According to the Court, its case law in competition cases[910] cannot be applied by analogy to the privilege of individuals in proceedings for an offence of insider dealing.[911]

Article 7(1)–(2) POI Directive is relevant in relation to the material scope of the privilege. As far as oral evidence is concerned, there is little doubt that it is covered by the Directive, most likely with the exception of routine questions.[912]

In E&W, too, oral statements come within the PSI's scope.[913] As I have outlined, several statutes in E&W restrict the privilege as they require (compelled) cooperation. Often, but not always, these provisions are equipped with a limited use rule according to which statements obtained in that way are not to be used against the person providing that information.

Like in E&W, in Belgium the privilege covers oral statements. Yet, as I have highlighted, several statutory provisions include a compelled cooperation duty. Unlike in E&W, these provisions are typically not equipped with a limited use clause. In a case concerning such a provision, the CoC has ruled that the offence of obstruction of supervision does not preclude a person from refusing to make a self-incriminating statement.[914]

In the USA, testimonial communications come within the material scope of the privilege. There is no definition of that concept, but it is broader than just

[907] *SGL Carbon* (n 15) paras 66–69. For examples of further forbidden questions: Lamadrid de Pablo and Kellerbauer (n 904) 395.

[908] *DB v Consob* (n 17) para 40.

[909] AG Pikamäe (n 59). He pointed out that when a charge is punitive, as defined in ch 1, the full range of guarantees under the criminal head of Art 6 ECHR, including the PSI, applies. He referred to ECtHR case law. He convincingly argued that it is not at all certain that the ECtHR would accept adopting its *Jussila* approach in relation to the PSI, given its place at the heart of the concept of a fair trial. In *De Legé* (n 57) the ECtHR did not use the *Jussila* approach in order not to find a violation of the PSI.

[910] The Court found that the case law concerns procedures that can result in penalties for undertakings and associations of undertakings.

[911] *DB v Consob* (n 17) para 48.

[912] Recital 26 suggests that the reference to the criminal offence of which the person is suspected or accused of having committed is used to make sure that the person can still be required to answer certain questions, eg to identify himself.

[913] *R v Director of Serious Fraud Office* (n 352) 30–31; Billing (n 356) 159 et seq; Roberts and Zuckerman (n 273) 539–40.

[914] CoC 29 November 2011 (n 550) 31–32. This case dealt with another act, yet the offence description corresponds to the one of the 1985 Act.

oral evidence.[915] Case law seems to indicate that 'expression of the contents of one's mind is testimonial communication'.[916] The communication needs 'to explicitly or implicitly relate a factual assertion or disclose information'.[917] Oral evidence typically falls within the scope of this definition.

II. Documentary Evidence

In relation to real evidence, the ECtHR's position is not crystal clear, yet the Court's Fourth Section has tried to clarify that position. Such evidence exists, unlike oral statements, independently of the suspect's will. It includes, for example, blood, urine or DNA samples, as well as, and more importantly for the purpose of this book, pre-existing documentary evidence. I will focus mainly on documentary evidence here.

It is important to distinguish pre-existing documents, which already existed before a person is required to hand them over, and documents that are created after a person is compelled to produce them.[918] Pre-existing documents exist independently of the will of the person who is required to hand them over. When the handing over of such documents is required, that person is not required to incriminate himself by creating documents that did not exist before. The same argument cannot hold true with regard to documents that are created in response to compulsion. There the person is required to create evidence.

Most of the ECtHR's case law in relation to the privilege and documents has addressed the issue of compelled production of pre-existing documents. Nevertheless, one may wonder what its position is on statutory obligations to, for example, keep accounting documents or file a tax declaration. Failing to create and file such documents can typically lead to a punitive charge. Such documents should be distinguished from documents that a person is required to create once he is under concrete suspicion, such as a questionnaire on one's price-fixing agreements with competitors. Documents such as tax declaration typically need to be created before any suspicion is present and at a time when no punitive charge is pending or anticipated.[919] The Court has held that the ECHR does not preclude obligations to inform the authorities as such, as it recognises that they play a role in several fields, such as tax law,[920] and that in the absence of such obligations

[915] Requiring an individual to sign a consent form to authorise his bank to provide information on his bank account does not meet that criterion in the Court's view, as it did not force him to express the contents of his mind: *Doe v United States* 487 US 201 (1988).

[916] ibid 210, fn 9.

[917] ibid 210.

[918] Pre-existing in this context means already in existence at the time the compulsion is used. Where a person is required to hand over his email exchange of the last two months, one can say that these documents are pre-existing documents. In case he is required to provide written answers to a questionnaire, the filled-out questionnaire would not constitute a pre-existing document as it is created in response to the compulsion. See *De Legé* (n 57) para 75.

[919] De Raedt (n 637) 432.

[920] *King* (n 645) para 2.

difficulties could arise in practice as to the effective functioning of these fields.[921] The privilege thus does not preclude regulatory reporting requirements as such.[922] The case law on such statutory documents typically tackles cases where someone has provided such a document, but has included false information in it.[923] The ECtHR has thus accepted that where someone lies in such a document, the privilege does not protect him if he is later punished. It has concluded that such a case cannot be equated to cases where someone is punished for not providing self-incriminating pre-existing documents that could be used against him in criminal proceedings.[924]

Before I tackle the Court's first landmark ruling on the matter, *Funke*, I briefly consider whether the compelled handing over of pre-existing documents can really amount to self-incrimination. If one merely focuses on the result that handing over such documents has, one can argue that there is no difference between forcing someone to hand over self-incriminating documents and compelling someone to provide self-incriminating testimony, in terms of result: they both lead to self-incrimination. From this point of view, the applicability of the privilege is defendable. At the same time, one could also take a different approach and focus on the fact that pre-existing documents exist independently of the will of the person who is required to hand them over. Then, one can argue that as long as they are not created under compulsion, the privilege should not apply. The former approach focuses on the element of compulsion linked to the handing over of the documents, and it is suspect- and defendant-friendly: it allows them to be free from compelled oral self-incrimination and it also protects them from self-incrimination by handing over documents. In that sense, that approach ensures that a person can freely set up his defence strategy.[925]

In *Funke*,[926] the ECtHR provided protection against the compelled production of pre-existing documents. During a house search, customs officers found documents linked to foreign banks, and Mr Funke had admitted having had several bank accounts abroad, for personal and professional reasons. He was asked to hand over documents[927] related to his accounts and share portfolio at these banks. His refusal to do so led to punitive proceedings against him in order to secure his conviction and a fine, and further penalties until he produced the documents.[928]

[921] *Weh* (n 484) para 45; *Marttinen* (n 385) para 68; *Van Weerelt* (n 669) para 56.

[922] *Allen v UK* App no 76574/01 (ECtHR, 10 September 2002) para 1; Berger, 'Self-Incrimination' (n 386) 518.

[923] Berger, 'Self-Incrimination' (n 386) 518.

[924] *Eklund v Finland* App no 56936/13 (ECtHR, 8 December 2015) para 50. In such cases, the person is not required to hand over evidence that would show that he committed, for example, tax evasion in the past. Whereas in *JB* the focus is on protection against self-incrimination for past criminal offences, in *Allen* and *Eklund*, the issue was that false information was provided, which in itself constitutes the offence. Similarly, see De Raedt (n 637) 443.

[925] Zeeman (n 80) 723.

[926] *Funke* (n 480) para 44. On the issues left open by *Funke*, see Emmerson et al (n 728) 615.

[927] Statements and chequebooks from foreign banks.

[928] The applicable cooperation duty, incorporated in Art 65 of the French Customs Code, was very broad: 'Customs officers with the rank of at least inspector (*inspecteur* or *officier*) and those performing

The ECtHR found that securing this conviction was aimed at getting the documents that the authorities believed to exist but they could not or did not want to get by other means.[929] They thus attempted to compel him, through the use of a production order, to provide evidence of alleged offences. According to the ECtHR, this amounted to an unjustifiable breach of the privilege. At the time the compulsion was applied, Mr Funke had not been formally charged in a punitive case, and the only pending proceedings were those that were brought to compel him to hand over the documents sought by the authorities.[930] Nevertheless, the Court handed down its ruling based on the assumption that he was charged with a punitive offence, within the sense of Article 6 ECHR.[931]

The *Funke* approach was quickly called into question[932] when the Court decided *Saunders*. That case is particularly relevant in relation to two issues: the privilege's role in the interaction between non-punitive and punitive proceedings, and the types of evidence covered by it. The ECtHR held that the privilege is primarily concerned with respecting the accused person's will to remain silent, thereby finding that the privilege does not cover the use in punitive proceedings of material gathered from him by using compulsory powers but which exists independently of his will.[933] Among other types of real evidence,[934] such as blood samples or tissue for DNA testing, the Court referred to 'documents acquired pursuant to a warrant'.[935] The lack of clarity on concepts such as the 'will of the person' and 'material with an independent existence' is not helpful.[936]

According to some, this ruling allows practices that require suspects to hand over pre-existing documents,[937] even if they are self-incriminating and are used in punitive proceedings. To reach that conclusion, it is helpful to bear in mind the two aforementioned approaches to self-incrimination and incriminating documents. According to the one, requiring someone to hand over self-incriminating documents is no different from requiring that person to make self-incriminating statements, since they both imply a risk of self-incrimination. According to the other, documents exist independently of the person's will, and as long as they do not come into existence due to compulsion, the person is not required to create

the duties of collector may require production of papers and documents of any kind relating to operations of interest to their department …' Failure to comply could lead to imprisonment of 10 days to one month and a fine of 600–3000 French francs. Moreover a 10 franc/day penalty could be imposed.

[929] Funke himself suggested that the authorities could have relied on international cooperation to have access to the documents.

[930] Yet his house had been searched and he was told that the authorities considered that he had unlawfully transferred money to another country: Treschel (n 27) 343.

[931] *Funke* (n 480) para 44.

[932] Berger, 'Self-Incrimination' (n 386) 514; Treschel (n 27) 353–54.

[933] *Saunders* (n 393) paras 68 and 69. In *Jalloh* (n 32) para 113, the Court accepted that real evidence such as drugs hidden inside the suspect's body can be covered by the privilege where it is recovered in defiance of the suspect's will.

[934] Such as voice samples: *PG and JH v United Kingdom* App no 44787/98 (ECtHR, 25 September 2001) para 80.

[935] *Saunders* (n 393) para 69; *De Legé* (n 57) para 67.

[936] Choo (n 30) 44.

[937] Dissenting Opinion of Martens in *Saunders* (n 393) para 12.

self-incriminating evidence. Martens's reading of *Saunders* fits into the second category, which focuses on the voluntary creation of the documents to argue that no compelled self-incrimination takes place when the documents are produced.

How should one reconcile *Saunders* and *Funke*? Were the French authorities mounting a fishing expedition in *Funke*,[938] as the authorities were not entirely certain of the documents' existence?[939] Or was the ECtHR simply trying to prevent the privilege from becoming a burdensome obstacle to prosecuting crime? Alternatively, one could argue that 'warrant' in *Saunders* refers to search warrants.[940] Since search warrants, as opposed to production orders,[941] do not compel a person to actively hand over documents, they are not directly problematic in light of the privilege.[942] At the same time, the use of search warrants may increase if the privilege is understood as covering self-incriminating documents.[943] Nevertheless, focusing on the reference to search warrants does not fully address the ECtHR's reference in *Saunders* to 'evidence which has an existence independent of the will of the accused'. Documents, once created, exist independently of the accused's will.

In *JB*, tax authorities imposed fines in the course of tax-evasion proceedings for failure to hand over documents they sought. The ECtHR reconfirmed its protective approach to self-incriminating documents. It stressed that the privilege presupposes that authorities make their case without using evidence obtained through coercion or oppression in defiance of the charged person's will.[944] The privilege thus helps to ensure that one can freely decide on one's defence strategy.[945] It added that *JB* 'did not involve material of this nature, which like that considered in *Saunders*, has an existence independent of the person concerned and is not, therefore, obtained by means of coercion and in defiance of the will of that person'.[946] In this sense, *JB* seems to confirm that *Saunders* only refers to documents obtained pursuant to a search warrant.

In *Jalloh*, where intrusive chemicals were used to force a suspect to regurgitate drugs, the ECtHR referred to *Funke* and *JB*, and added that in those cases, like in *Jalloh*, real evidence was retrieved in disregard of the applicant's will,[947] thereby again suggesting that the privilege would protect against the compelled production

[938] According to De Raedt, the privilege protects against fishing expeditions, but not against the production of documents whose existence is known to the authorities: De Raedt (n 637) 443.

[939] *JB* (n 491) para 69. According to Treschel, allowing production orders where the authorities are certain of the documents' existence should not be accepted: Treschel (n 27) 354.

[940] Choo (n 30) 44; Zeeman (n 80) 305–06 and 724. On the distinction between documents sought with and without warrants, see Berger, 'Self-Incrimination' (n 386) 526.

[941] Critically, see Treschel (n 27) 354.

[942] Redmayne (n 351) 214 and 215.

[943] See AG Darmon's analysis in *Orkem*: Case 374/87 *Orkem v Commission* ECLI:EU:C:1989:207, para 155. On that topic, see also G Stessens, 'The Obligation to Produce Documents versus the Privilege Against Self-Incrimination: Human Rights Protection Extended Too Far?' [1997] *EL Rev* 22 Supp, 45–62.

[944] *JB* (n 491) para 64.

[945] Zeeman (n 80) 347.

[946] *JB* (n 491) particularly paras 66 and 68.

[947] *Jalloh* (n 32) para 113.

of self-incriminating documents. Interestingly, the Court distinguished different types of real evidence on the basis of the different levels of compulsion on the person involved.[948]

In *Chambaz*, the ECtHR repeated that the PSI was violated after the applicant had been fined,[949] as these fines amounted to pressure on him to submit documents and that he could not rule out that these documents might harm his position in a tax evasion case.[950] The Swiss authorities were well aware of Mr Chambaz's assets, held in a number of bank accounts and managed by a third party, as well as of the operations carried out with those assets.[951]

In *Van Weerelt*, the Court approved the Dutch Supreme Court's approach. The latter had endorsed an order in summary injunction proceedings. The tax and customs administration had sought an order, while administrative tax proceedings were pending with regard to a tax adjustment, to obtain accurate information from a taxpayer on which the tax adjustment was to be based. The order was granted and penalties were provided in case of failure to disclose the information.[952] The ECtHR particularly took into account that the Supreme Court had restricted the use of the information that the taxpayer had to provide to the levying of taxes, thereby excluding its use for punitive purposes. That restriction applied 'in so far as the information to be provided by the applicant concerned material the existence of which was dependent on his will'.[953]

It thus seems that the ECtHR is willing to offer protection where the compelled handing over of self-incriminating documents is ordered. Nevertheless, its reference in *Saunders* to evidence independent of the will has cast some doubts. Arguments have been made to suggest that cases such as *Funke* and *JB* should not be interpreted so broadly that one can rely on them to refuse to hand over any potentially self-incriminating document.[954] Some argue that these cases show that the ECtHR merely wants to protect suspects from fishing expeditions.[955] According to this argument, the national authorities in *Funke* and *JB* did not have sufficiently precise information on the documents' existence and they were trying

[948] ibid para 114. Taking hair samples does not require the same level of compulsion as the use of tubes and chemicals as was the case in *Jalloh* to obtain drugs swallowed by the suspect.

[949] The fines were imposed in the course of an administrative objection by Mr Chambaz to imposed taxes. The tax administration considered that he had not declared all of his income. The tax evasion proceedings were only initiated several years later.

[950] *Chambaz* (n 491) paras 53–58.

[951] ibid paras 31 and 53.

[952] The penalties could amount to €500,000.

[953] *Van Weerelt* (n 669) paras 60, 62 and 63.

[954] De Raedt (n 637) 443–45; Stessens, 'The Obligation to Produce Documents' (n 943) 55. Contra, see F Koning, 'Cour. Eur. D.H., Chambaz contre Suisse, 5 avril 2012 Prohibition de l'auto-incrimination' [2012] *Revue générale du contentieux fiscal* 403, 414. According to Huysmans, the individual documents obtained by a judicial order are not covered unless the authorities are not certain of its existence or are unable to gain access to it themself: Huysmans, *Legitieme verdediging* (n 405) 805.

[955] De Raedt (n 637) 443; Stessens, 'The Obligation to Produce Documents' (n 943) 56; Wissink (n 501) 92. Zeeman strongly disagrees with such an analysis. He points to the absence of a fishing expedition in *Chambaz* (n 491) to argue that the ECHR's protection is not limited to protection against fishing expeditions: Zeeman (n 80) 371–73 and 725.

to compel them from the suspects.[956] Then, the privilege would only provide protection against the compelled handing over of self-incriminatory pre-existing documents if the authorities would otherwise not have access to them.[957] Thus, where the authorities could, for example, gain access to those documents by means of a search warrant, the privilege would not provide for protection. This approach would imply that the production of documents cannot be required when the authorities are not sure of their existence.[958] In order to check whether the authorities are not setting up a fishing expedition, the authorities' request should be sufficiently specific.[959]

In *De Legé* the ECtHR's Fourth Section took the view that pre-existing documents are only protected against fishing expeditions.[960] Admittedly, it also found that the PSI is engaged when, regardless of whether or not the authorities are aware of the existence of documents or other material evidence, this has been obtained by methods that violate Article 3 ECHR.[961] In my view it is not evident that a taxpayer who fails to declare foreign assets, would retain those documents more than five or ten years later.[962] Nevertheless, The Fourth Section considered that this was not a fishing expedition. It strongly relied on the fact that the Dutch authorities were aware of the fact that the individual had held a bank account in Luxembourg. Yet, there are reasons to remain cautious with regard to such an interpretation of the Court's case law. The Court has, in its case law, repeatedly stressed the importance of respecting the will of the person concerned.[963] This suggests that the Court defends a broad privilege,[964] and one may wonder whether its case law can thus be understood as being restricted to protection against fishing expeditions. It should be recalled that in *Funke*, the compelled person had admitted to having bank accounts abroad, and at that time chequebooks and paper statements were common documents for bank account holders. The accused's will is defied when documents that the authorities cannot sufficiently show they are aware of are required, but also when documents which the authorities can clearly show they know the existence of are sought. The suspect's autonomy to define his defence strategy is affected in both cases.[965] In *Chambaz*, the Swiss authorities were well aware of the specific financial dealings of Mr Chambaz with regard to the bank accounts. If the ECtHR's case law on orders to produce documents only offered protection against fishing expeditions, it is unlikely that it would

[956] In support of that argument, see *Funke* (n 480) para 44; *JB* (n 491) para 69.
[957] Macculloch (n 398) 231; Stessens, 'The Obligation to Produce Documents' (n 943) 54.
[958] *De Legé* (n 57) para 76; Stessens, 'The Obligation to Produce Documents' (n 943) 56.
[959] ibid; Veenbrink, *Criminal Law Principles* (n 386) 26–27.
[960] *De Legé* (n 57) para 76.
[961] *De Legé* (n 57) para 77.
[962] In 2007 the Dutch tax authorities required a taxpayer to produce documents, including bank statements from Luxembourg covering the period between 1 January 1996 and 31 December 2000.
[963] *Jalloh* (n 32) para 113; *Chambaz* (n 491) para 52.
[964] A De Nauw, 'Het zwijgrecht in het strafrecht van het bedrijfsleven' in F Moeykens et al, *De Praktijkjurist XVI* (Story Publishers, 2010) 265.
[965] De Nauw, 'Het zwijgrecht in het strafrecht' (n 964) 267; Zeeman (n 80) 725.

have found a violation of Chambaz's privilege.[966] Its finding that the privilege was violated suggests that the PSI protection, for other sections than the ECtHR's Fourth Section, goes further than protection against fishing expeditions. One may also wonder what is implied by an 'existence independent of the will of a suspect' and whether this concept warrants a differentiation between the handing over of documents subject to a legal retention obligation and the handing over of other documents.[967] Essentially, one may argue that 'existence independent of the will of the suspect' applies to both types of documents, once they have been created, and that the only difference between them is the motive that led to their creation.[968] The confusing double use of the concept of 'will' is not helpful in understanding the privilege's limits,[969] as *Van Weerelt* demonstrates.[970] The Court ruled that the privilege presupposes that the case is built against a person without using evidence obtained through methods that defy the accused's will,[971] while, on the other hand, it has held that the privilege does not extend to the use in criminal proceedings of material which may be obtained through the use of compulsory powers, but which exists independently of the will of the suspect, such as, inter alia, documents acquired pursuant to a warrant.[972] The Court then jumps to the conclusion: 'Thus it was that the Court found Article 6 §1 to have been violated by the bringing of a prosecution with a view to obtaining incriminating documents from the accused himself.'[973]

Regardless of some of its suspect-friendly case law in relation to documentary evidence and the privilege, the ECtHR has developed a test, the *Jalloh* test,[974] to verify whether the privilege has been violated.[975] In *Chambaz*, a post-*Jalloh* case, the Court did not explicitly refer to that test, whereas it did in *De Legé*.[976] If one applies that test to documentary evidence and provided those criteria are met, then the suspect will not be protected against compelled self-incrimination. Nevertheless,

[966] Zeeman (n 80) 371–73 and 436.

[967] De Raedt argues that the privilege is not relevant for documents that need to be kept pursuant to a statutory duty, as the authorities know that they must exist: De Raedt (n 637) 444–45. Koning strongly opposes this view: Koning, 'Cour. Eur. D.H., Chambaz' (n 954) 414.

[968] On this point, see De Nauw, 'Het zwijgrecht in het strafrecht' (n 964) 267.

[969] EJ Koops and L Stevens, 'JB versus Saunders. De groeiende duisternis rond nemo tenetur' [2003] *Delikt en Delinkwent* 281, 293. See also D Dewandeleer, 'Misdrijven en strafonderzoek in de IT-context' in R Verstraeten and F Verbruggen (eds), *Themis Straf- en strafprocesrecht* (die Keure, 2010) 158–59.

[970] Vanderkerken summarises the ECtHR's position on pre-existing documents after that decision as follows: documents, including bank statements, seem to exist independently of one's will, but they cannot be used against a person for punitive aims if he handed them over under compulsion: C Vanderkerken, 'Dwangmaatregelen in het fiscaal onderzoeksrecht: de zaak VW en het actueel belang ervan' [2020] *Tijdschrift voor Fiscaal Recht* 35, 41.

[971] *Van Weerelt* (n 669) para 54.

[972] ibid para 55.

[973] ibid para 55.

[974] These criteria are also listed in the more extensive, albeit still non-exhaustive, list of criteria that should be considered when assessing the criminal proceedings' overall fairness, summarised in *Ibrahim* (n 378) para 274.

[975] Critically on these criteria, see Jackson (n 638) 840–41.

[976] *De Legé* (n 57) para 78. Succinctly on this point, see S Lamberigts, 'The Privilege against Self-Incrimination: A Chameleon of Criminal Procedure' (2016) 7 *New Journal of European Criminal Law* 418, 431–32.

the ECtHR has not accepted that the public interest, the complexity of certain types of crime[977] or the specific characteristics of some fields of law[978] justify provisions that extinguish the privilege's essence.[979] Moreover, the Court has at times been more likely to conclude that the privilege is violated where the contested evidence has played a decisive role in the person's conviction.[980] Moreover, where compulsion to provide the documents is high in terms of possible fines, penalty payments or imprisonment, the chance that the privilege's essence is infringed increases.

In sum, the ECtHR's case law on documentary evidence and the privilege is ambiguous, and one needs to be cautious when drawing conclusions from it. It is clear that *Saunders* did not result in a complete overturning of *Funke*. Post-*Saunders*, pre-existing documents can still benefit from protection under the PSI. What is less clear is how broad that protection is. Some argue that the privilege only applies where the authorities are mounting a fishing expedition and thus lack sufficiently concrete information on the documents. In my view, that reading is too narrow even though the ECtHR's Fourth Section adopted that view in *De Legé*. In light of *Jalloh*, the focus seems to be more on the element of compulsion to defy the person's will than on the type of evidence.[981] The Court has also repeatedly paid attention to the (un)availability of limited use rules. The *Jalloh* test, moreover, does not exclude that the privilege can cover documentary evidence. In *De Legé* the ECtHR confirmed that compelling one to create new documents does not respect the person's will to remain silent.

As a general principle of EU law, as applied in EU competition cases by the CJEU, the privilege does not in principle offer protection to pre-existing documents. The Court has held that it does not allow a person to refuse to hand over real evidence, such as pre-existing documents.[982]

As for the protection offered to documentary evidence by the privilege, implicitly enshrined in the CFR, reference can be made to the case law of the ECtHR analysed above.

Article 7(3) and recital 29 of the POI Directive show that the Directive adopts a similar approach to the ECtHR's ruling in *Saunders*.[983] In that case, the ECtHR adopted a restrictive view with regard to evidence existing independently of the accused's will, thereby enabling limitations of the protection provided by the privilege. According to *Saunders*, evidence that has an existence independent of the will of the accused covers documents acquired pursuant to a warrant. Recital 29 of

[977] eg corporate crime.

[978] eg the special features of customs law.

[979] See *Jalloh* (n 32) para 97; *Marttinen* (n 385) para 75; Treschel (n 27) 345.

[980] *Jalloh* (n 32) para 121; *Bykov* (n 395) para 103; *Zaichenko* (n 478) para 59; *Yaremenko v Ukraine (no 2)* App no 66338/09 (ECtHR, 30 April 2015) para 67. See also *Gäfgen* (n 74) para 186.

[981] *Jalloh* (n 32) para 113. Van Toor considers the use of improper compulsion as the determining criterion to establish whether a PSI violation has taken place. The type of evidence (material existing independent of the will of the person versus will dependent evidence) is not decisive in his view: DAG van Toor, *Het schuldige geheugen? Een onderzoek naar het gebruik van hersenonderzoek als opsporingsmethode in het licht van eisen van instrumentaliteit en rechtsbescherming* (Kluwer, 2017) 395.

[982] *Qualcomm* (2021) (n 15) para 143.

[983] *Saunders* (n 393) para 69.

the Preamble to the Directive refers to material acquired pursuant to a warrant, as well as to material in respect of which there is a legal obligation of retention and production upon request. The scope of the term 'legal powers of compulsion' in Article 7(3) can be understood in different ways. An MS may interpret it as allowing blood tests, yet nothing precludes an MS from understanding it as allowing the use of production orders to obtain documents from a suspect under threat of a sanction for failure to comply with the order. As a result, the POI Directive does not seem to preclude MSs from keeping provisions in place under which suspects can be required to hand over self-incriminating documents, which can then be used against them. Self-evidently, such practices can be strongly questioned in light of the ECtHR's case law because the ECtHR has repeatedly extended protection to documentary evidence. That case law is reflected in recital 25, according to which suspects or accused persons should not be forced to produce documents that could lead to self-incrimination. Therefore, in order to stay within the limits set out by the less than crystal clear ECtHR case law, MSs should be careful when implementing this provision, as the Directive can in no way be used to adopt a standard of protection lower than that offered by the ECHR.[984] Article 10(2) of the Directive requires that the fairness of the proceedings and the rights of the defence be respected where statements obtained in violation of the privilege are used, which is a less strong wording than an absolute exclusionary rule.

Provided the other conditions to invoke the PSI are met, compelling someone to create new self-incriminating documents would amount to compelled self-incrimination in the three national systems, as it presupposes the use of one's mind. For example, requiring someone to fill out a questionnaire during a punitive investigation detailing one's involvement in a corrupt practice scheme would typically come within the privilege's scope. At the same time, the national systems are all familiar with reporting duties which, in case of failure to comply, can result in sanctions, eg the filing of a tax declaration or documents related to the operation of a factory. Refusing to comply with such reporting duties by relying on the privilege is unlikely to be successful in the three national systems (E&W, Belgium and the USA). Purposely filling out wrongful information to hide the truth is similarly not protected by the privilege. Nevertheless, refusing to fill out specific parts of a document where the person can convincingly argue that this specific point would incriminate him can come within the scope of the privilege, or it might need to be excluded as evidence in a punitive case.

In relation to pre-existing documents, the three national systems' approaches have varied over time.

In E&W, the privilege's applicability to pre-existing documentary evidence has given rise to significant debate, which has been strongly influenced by the reference in *Saunders* to material which has an existence independent of the will of the suspect.[985] It has been argued that applying the privilege to such evidence is

[984] Art 13.

[985] *R v Kearns* [2002] 1 WLR 2815, 2823; *C plc and another v P (Attorney General intervening)* [2008] Ch 1, 14–15.

not warranted by the underlying rationales[986] of protecting against ill-treatment and the production of dubious confessions.[987] Moreover, it has been argued that it would not make much sense in practice as police would be able to acquire the documents through searches and seizures.[988] That argument is unconvincing as it underlines that the privilege does not necessarily render evidence gathering impossible.[989] The fact that authorities can gather documents through a search is an element that any person who thinks about invoking his privilege needs to consider.[990] It may be pragmatic to cooperate with the authorities for different reasons. Prior to *Saunders*, the privilege was repeatedly applied to pre-existing documentary evidence in E&W.[991] In some cases, the courts accepted that the privilege covers documents, but did not apply it because equivalent protection had been available. This was the case where the order of a judge ordering the disclosure of evidence in a non-punitive case provided that the evidence would not be admissible in a punitive case against the person disclosing it.[992]

The issue was considered post-*Saunders* in a *sensu stricto* criminal case involving production orders under section 9 PACE. Although one judge dissented,[993] the others agreed that that provision by necessary implication allowed production orders that could infringe a person's privilege.[994] In that case no guarantees were offered to the person concerned that he would not be prosecuted. The trial judge nevertheless retained the possibility of excluding the compelled material under section 78 PACE.[995] In other words, in the absence of a statutory provision excluding the compelled evidence from use in a punitive case against the person providing it, the person concerned had to hope for ex post protection by the trial judge. In *R (Malik) v Manchester Crown Court*,[996] the divisional court confirmed that a trial judge has the power to exclude evidence under section 78 PACE.[997] In that case, a list of non-exhaustive criteria were put forward to determine whether one should be required to disclose material: (i) assessment of the true benefit of the

[986] On these rationales, see *C plc* (n 985) 13; *AT & T* (n 413) 53.
[987] *AT & T* (n 413) 52 and 57; Zuckerman (n 353) 397.
[988] Zuckerman (n 353) 397.
[989] Admittedly that depends on the specifics of the case: where the documents could be found at a person's house through a search, that holds true. Where the documents are stored in another country with a low tendency to help foreign law enforcement agencies, a search cannot so easily be carried out.
[990] Claes and Horseele (n 555) 395.
[991] *AT & T* (n 413) 49; *Rio Tinto Zinc Corporation and Other Appellants v Westinghouse Electric Corporation Respondents v et a contra* [1978] AC 547.
[992] *AT & T* (n 413) 55 and 57. On this case, see Keane and McKeown (n 535) 724.
[993] Judge LJ in *R (Bright) v Central Criminal Court* [2001] 1 WLR 662, 683–84.
[994] ibid 697.
[995] ibid 694.
[996] The Court seemed to accept that the ECtHR's case law offers some protection to documentary evidence: 'They are somewhat problematic and we find it difficult to extract from them a clear statement of principle as to whether the privilege against self-incrimination applies to pre-existing documents. We are inclined to accept the submissions of Mr Eadie that they seem to indicate that the privilege against self-incrimination protected by Art 6 is in play even where the potential for self-incrimination derives from pre-existing documents.'
[997] *R (Malik) v Manchester Crown Court* [2008] EWHC 1362, para 83.

material which is sought;[998] (ii) the importance of the privilege should be borne in mind as forgoing the protection of the privilege requires a convincing justification; (iii) the gravity of the offence;[999] (iv) the risk of prosecution;[1000] and (v) the possibility for the trial judge to use section 78 PACE.

The compatibility with Article 6 ECHR of the use in a punitive case of documents produced under compulsion in a non-punitive procedure was considered in *Attorney-General's Reference (No 7 of 2000)*.[1001] The CoA found that this practice did not infringe Article 6 ECHR. Its conclusion relied strongly on *Saunders*, and particularly on the reference to 'material which may be obtained from the accused through the use of compulsory powers but which has an existence independent of the will of the suspect'.[1002] According to the CoA, pre-existing documents fall in that category of evidence and the privilege thus does not apply to it.[1003] This reasoning is questionable. Suffice it to say that whereas at the time of the CoA's case there was limited ECtHR case law on the issue of documentary evidence,[1004] more recent cases demonstrate that documents do benefit from a certain level of protection under the ECHR.[1005] The lack of clearness in the ECtHR's reasoning seems to have inclined E&W courts towards the adoption of a position which may not be consistent with the ECtHR's case law.[1006]

Later case law similarly relies on the argument that pre-existing documents are already in existence, unlike statements.[1007] The compulsory powers only allow for the evidence to come to the court's attention; their existence and quality are independent of a production order.[1008] This case law suggests that pre-existing documents would no longer benefit from the privilege's protection. This is also the case, for example, in the context of IP rights.[1009] In such cases, the protection offered to documentary evidence has strongly been reduced.[1010]

[998] When considering this first criterion, one should take into account whether the evidence could be obtained through other means, a disclosure in stages should be considered, as well as redaction to exclude the parts which create the risk of self-incrimination.

[999] More serious offences require more serious justification.

[1000] The Court considered that the prosecution may offer immunity.

[1001] [2001] EWCA Crim 888. Documents had been handed over in the context of a bankruptcy. Some of these documents referred to the person's gambling. Failure to deliver them was a punishable offence. He was later prosecuted for having contributed to his insolvency through gambling. On this case, see Emmerson et al (n 728) 624.

[1002] *Saunders* (n 393) para 69.

[1003] Restrictively on the privilege and documents, see Keane and McKeown (n 535) 719–20.

[1004] The CoA essentially found that to the extent that *Saunders* and *Funke* were at odds with each other, it rather relied on *Saunders*.

[1005] Similarly, see Emmerson et al (n 728) 625.

[1006] ibid 626.

[1007] *R v Hundal and Dhaliwal* [2004] EWCA Crim 389.

[1008] ibid. The CoA considered that the statutory provision (in the context of terrorism) was a proportionate measure, justified by security and safety interests.

[1009] S 72(1) Senior Courts Act 1981. S 72(3) counters the risk of self- or spouse incrimination by excluding statements or admissions from being used in the prosecution of offences or recovery of penalties. Nevertheless, this protection seems inapplicable to documentary evidence. Similarly, see Zuckerman (n 353) 399. In *C plc* (n 985), the CoA took a restrictive position in relation to protection of 'real evidence' by the privilege.

[1010] *C plc* (n 985).

Yet, even though the CoA has interpreted the protection offered to documents restrictively,[1011] it accepted that a trial judge can use his exclusionary powers under section 78 PACE to exclude documents where the fairness of the proceedings would be affected. In *Kearns*,[1012] emphasis was put on the proportionality of the use in a punitive case of evidence obtained in a non-punitive one in light of the social or economic problem that the statute is trying to tackle. The courts have at times been willing to use that provision to exclude evidence in a punitive tax evasion case where it had been obtained under threat of contempt charges, holding that imprisonment would not be proportionate to fight tax evasion.[1013]

At the same time, UKSC case law still accepts that the privilege provides protection to self-incriminating documents.[1014] It thus seems that although the privilege at common law would still provide protection against the compelled handing over of documents,[1015] a statutory provision may exclude the privilege in a specific context. Such a restriction of the privilege can be done expressly or by necessary implication (provided the implication is clear and it is not to be assumed).[1016] Admittedly, in *R (River East Supplies Ltd)* the divisional court concluded that the common law PSI does not apply to 'independent' documents.[1017] In its view, the ECtHR's case law clearly distinguishes between material that is 'independent' and material that is not. It interpreted the *C plc* case[1018] as a confirmation that the privilege does not apply to will-independent material.

Evidence of knowledge of documents can, even if one were to consider that pre-existing documents benefit from little protection, as such still be covered by the privilege.[1019]

Meanwhile, the Privy Council addressed the issue of pre-existing documents and the PSI in *Volaw Trust*.[1020] It considered that, notwithstanding *Saunders*, the privilege can in principle apply to real evidence too. It found that it is too categorical to state that Article 6 ECHR is not engaged by compulsion to produce pre-existing

[1011] According to Veenbrink, pre-existing documents are not protected by the PSI in E&W: Veenbrink, *Criminal Law Principles* (n 386) 120.

[1012] *Kearns* (n 985).

[1013] *R v K* [2009] EWCA Crim 1640.

[1014] Unless the privilege has been restricted by statute in relation to those documents: *Beghal v DPP* (n 533) para 60. The ECtHR found in *Beghal* that the person had not faced a criminal charge. At the same time, it held that it would not exclude the possibility that Art 6 ECHR would be engaged if statements made under the compelled cooperation provision at issue would have been used in a criminal proceedings: *Beghal v United Kingdom* (n 484) para 122.

[1015] M Hannibal and L Mountford, *Criminal Litigation 2020–2021* (Oxford University Press, 2020) 390; Sime (n 541) 347.

[1016] *Beghal v DPP* (n 533) para 61.

[1017] *R (River East Supplies Ltd)* (n 614) para 102.

[1018] *C plc* (n 985).

[1019] *R v S* [2009] 1 WLR 1489; Lucraft (n 657) 12-2a.

[1020] *Volaw Trust* (n 615). The challenges against the production of documents were brought at the investigatory stage. On that case, see K Laird, 'Fair Trial: Volaw Trust and Corporate Services Ltd v Office of the Controller of Taxes; Volaw Trust and Corporate Services Ltd v HM Attorney General for Jersey Privy Council: Lords Reed, Kerr, Sumption, Carnwath, Hodge, Kitching and Lady Arden: 17 June 2019; [2019] UKPC 29' [2020] *Crim LR* 75; Lucraft (n 657) 12-2a; Ormerod and Perry (n 540) 2805.

documents.[1021] It considered that the four *Jalloh* criteria had to be applied. It distinguished *Volaw Trust* from *Funke* by holding that no prosecution was brought for failure to produce documents, though a fine could be imposed in case of non-compliance. It considered that the corporation could challenge the compelled evidence's admissibility at trial. Having applied the *Jalloh* criteria, it rejected the complaint based on Article 6 ECHR. The approach taken by the Privy Council more correctly takes into account the ECtHR's case law.

Belgian courts, similarly to their E&W counterparts, have been strongly influenced by the unclear ECtHR case law.[1022] Belgian courts, including the CoC, have in principle accepted that the privilege covers pre-existing documents.[1023]

At the same time, part of the case law suggests distinguishing between different categories of documents.[1024] If the authorities have sufficient knowledge of the existence of certain documents, due to the legal obligation to create and keep them,[1025] such as accounting documents,[1026] they are not covered by the PSI

[1021] *Volaw Trust* (n 615) para 44. The Council took into account more recent ECtHR case law: 'The respondents' submission that the privilege protected by article 6 is not engaged by compulsion to produce pre-existing documents is therefore too categorically stated. In so far as the CoA favoured a similar view of the scope of the privilege in Attorney General's Reference (No 7 of 2000), *R v Kearns* and *C plc v P*, the more recent case law of the European court indicates that a more nuanced approach should be adopted.'

[1022] See also C Conings, 'Statusupdate: Belgische opsporing- voelt zich #verward bij het speuren in sociale media' in E Lievens et al (eds), *Sociale media anno 2015: Actuele juridische aspecten* (Intersentia, 2015) 293–94.

[1023] CoA Brussels 21 May 2012 (n 1); CoC 19 June 2013 (n 1); CoC 20 November 2018 (n 1); HD Bosly, 'Le droit au silence pendant la phase administrative de la surveillance du respect des lois sociales' in CE Clesse (ed), *L'auditorat du travail: compétences civiles et pénales (Liber amicorum Robert Blondiaux)* (Larcier, 2012) 435; Beernaert et al (n 405) 31 and 34; I de la Serna, 'Le droit au silence' [2015] *Le Pli juridique* 3, 6 and 8; Huybrechts (n 584) 396 and 397; F Kéfer, 'L'employeur est-il tenu d'être présent et actif lors d'un contrôle social?' [2013] *Revue de Jurisprudence de Liège, Mons et Bruxelles* 1861, 1862. In that 2018 case, the CoC accepted that the person had to provide access to his books as he was not facing a criminal charge at the time access was sought. The CoC referred to the CoA's consideration that at the stage of the check of the bookkeeping, no concrete threat was made in terms of fines for refusal of production of documents, as included in Art 329 GCEA.

[1024] CoA Antwerp 13 February 2002, [2002–03] RW 1062, 1065 and 1066; CoA Antwerp 24 February 2009, FJF 2010 276, www.monkey.be, 8/14; CoA Ghent 15 June 2010, [2012] TGR-TWVR 65. According to the Court in the 2002 case, the privilege could only come into play when the person, by handing over documents, would be giving evidence to the authorities it would otherwise not have access to (through a search). Along the same lines, see Van den Wyngaert et al (n 35) 755. These authors admit that *Chambaz* is to be understood as implying that incriminating documents should be obtained through measures that do not require any active cooperation, such as searches, seizures and/or by requesting them from third parties, such as banks. Verstraeten suggests that orders to hand over specific documents would fall outside the scope of the privilege, whereas requests for documents that are not properly specified would come within the scope of the privilege: Verstraeten, *Handboek strafvordering* (n 405) 857. Some even suggest that the privilege does not cover documents at all: P Bekaert, 'De rechten van verdediging in strafzaken' in X, *De Praktijkjurist XX* (Story, 2013) 226.

[1025] CoA Antwerp 24 February 2009 (n 1024) 8/14; CE Clesse and JC Heirman, *Procédure pénale sociale* (Larcier, 2020) 132–33; J Speecke, *Fiscaal strafrecht en strafprocesrecht* (Kluwer, 2021) 98; C Van de Heyning and J Coppens, 'Het bevel tot medewerking van artikel 88quater Sv, het zwijgrecht en het verbod op zelfincriminatie' [2016] *Tijdschrift voor Strafrecht* 260, 264. Nevertheless, a legal obligation does, as such, not guarantee that documents will be created.

[1026] CoA Ghent 15 June 2010 (n 1024).

according to that line of case law,[1027] whereas other documents would be covered. The CoC has considered that the privilege does not apply to information that can be obtained from the accused by the use of coercive powers but which exist independently of the will of the suspect,[1028] specifically in a case where documents were sought in relation to which a statutory record-keeping requirement applied.[1029] This approach reflects a vision, too restrictive in my opinion, that cases such as *Funke* imply that documents are only covered by the privilege when the authorities are carrying out a fishing expedition for documents of whose existence they are not certain or which they do not know how to get access to.[1030] The legal obligation to create documents is not perfect as a distinguishing criterion: broad record-keeping obligations may tend to strongly limit the privilege's scope.

Several authors have pointed out that broad cooperation duties are also risky for another reason: persons would risk sanctions for being unwilling to cooperate where, in reality, they cannot cooperate.[1031]

From a technical point of view, this distinction raises questions: once documents exist, they exist independently of the person's will,[1032] but in order for them to exist, the person's will to create them is needed.[1033] This reasoning applies to documents for which there is a legal obligation to keep them and for other documents alike. Thus, from this point of view, the distinction is odd. Moreover, one may also imagine cases where the authorities are aware of the existence of documents for which there is no legal duty to create and keep. At the same time, it holds true for both types of documents that the will of a suspect can be defied if he is forced to hand them over,[1034] and thus one could argue that the privilege could cover both categories.

Other authors and case law do not seem to make a distinction based on the knowledge of the authorities of the existence of documents and accept a broad privilege in relation to documents.[1035] This finding is at times based on the argument

[1027] De Nauw has argued by reference to *Saunders* that documents in relation to which a legal retention obligation exists, have an existence independent of the accused person's will: De Nauw, 'De rechten van de mens' (n 670) 225. More nuanced: De Nauw, 'Het zwijgrecht in het strafrecht' (n 964) 267 and 268.

[1028] The ConsC came to a similar conclusion in a case involving on-site visits by civil servants of the tax administration: ConsC 12 October 2017 (n 405) B.14.4.

[1029] CoC 7 March 2018 (n 735). The Court also came to this conclusion in a case where a suspect pointed out the location of weapons. The Court found that these weapons could in any case be found since search warrants were being executed: CoC 14 March 2017 (n 462).

[1030] CoA Antwerp 13 February 2002 (n 1024) 1065–66; CoA Liège 16 May 2013, [2013] JLMB 1858, 1860; M Delanote, 'Het zwijgrecht van een tot medewerking gehouden belastingplichtige' in B Peeters et al, *Liber Amicorum Stefaan van Crombrugge* (RMG, 2020) 271; M Delanote, 'Hof van Justitie erkent ruime draagwijdte van het zwijgrecht' [2021] No 7 *Fiscale Actualiteit* 5; De Nauw, 'De rechten van de mens' (n 670) 225. Delanote refers to foreign accounts' bank statements as an example of documents that could qualify as documents which are protected (if their discovery is will-dependent).

[1031] For example, because the person does not have the documents that are being required, or at least no longer has them. On this issue, see Conings, 'Statusupdate' (n 1022) 294.

[1032] Koops and Stevens (n 969) 293.

[1033] Kéfer (n 1023) 1867.

[1034] T Byl et al, *Financieel rechercheren* (Politeia, 2020) 100.

[1035] CoA Brussels 21 May 2012 (n 1); CoC 19 June 2013 (n 1); Beernaert et al (n 405) 34; de la Serna, 'Le droit au silence' (n 1023) 3, 6 and 8; Huybrechts (n 584) 396 and 397; Kéfer (n 1023) 1862.

that the privilege not only includes the right not to testify against oneself, but also the right not to cooperate to one's own incrimination.[1036] Moreover, it has been argued that the case law of the ECtHR, and in particular *Chambaz*, does not seem to make a distinction between the two types of documents.[1037] *Van Weerelt* also seems to stress the need to respect the will of the person, and the Court outlined that it was the fact that a prosecution was brought against a person to obtain incriminating documents from the accused person himself that led to its conclusion that the PSI was violated in *Funke*.[1038]

The distinction between documents created and kept pursuant to a legal obligation and other documents has also been included in certain legislative acts. Article 209 CCVSL distinguishes between these two categories of documents for the purpose of the offence of obstruction of supervision: it is only a *sensu stricto* criminal offence when one impedes supervision with regard to the first type of documents.[1039] The distinction between the two categories was inspired by the ECtHR's case law in *Funke*.[1040] That offence description is particularly broad: those who (with the required *mens rea*)[1041] obstruct the supervision established on the basis of the CCVSL or any of its executive orders come within the scope of the offence. The word 'obstruct' in particular is rather vague, and it includes both acts and omissions.[1042] In any case, it cannot be interpreted so broadly that it would preclude the privilege from being invoked.[1043] In an earlier ruling, the CoC ruled that the cooperation duty does not infringe the POI; however, the Court gave little reasoning for this finding.[1044] This judgment seemingly takes a more restrictive approach than the CoC's *Citibank* ruling of 2013, where the Court recognised a broad privilege.[1045] More recently, the CoC has found that simply refusing to hand

[1036] CoC 19 June 2013 (n 1); CoC 27 September 2018, D.17.0015.F; CoC 20 November 2018 (n 1).

[1037] Maus (n 684) 178; LCA Wijsman and M Delanote, 'Het zwijgrecht en niet-meewerkrecht in de rechtspraak van het EHRM met enkele reflecties vanuit het Belgisch fiscaal (sanctie)recht' in M Delanote et al, *Fiscaal en sociaal strafrecht – wegwijzer doorheen het labyrint* (Story Publishers, 2021) 410.

[1038] *Van Weerelt* (n 669) para 55. Therefore, it is not surprising that where evidence, including documents, is found during a search, the Court does not find the privilege to be violated. *Kalneniene* (n 387) para 52.

[1039] Art 209, combined with Arts 28 and 29 CCVSL.

[1040] MvT *ParlSt* Kamer 2005–06, 51-2518/001, 159.

[1041] Knowingly and voluntarily. On this point, see B Elias and S Van de Perre, *Sociale inspectie* (Intersentia, 2021) 170; O Michiels and G Falque, 'L'infraction d'obstacle à la surveillance sous le spectre du droit au silence et du droit de ne pas s'auto-incriminer' [2016] *Orientations* 2, 4.

[1042] Elias and Van de Perre (n 1041) 169; Michiels and Falque, 'L'infraction d'obstacle' (n 1041) 3.

[1043] At the same time, the privilege in this context does not go so far that it allows one to be absent at the business premises after repeatedly announced visits of the inspectors, nor to refuse them access to the premises. See CoA Antwerp 11 October 2001, [2003] TStrafr 297; CoA Mons 9 September 2015, [2016] Dr pén entr 227; CoA Liège 14 April 2016, [2016] Dr pén entr 341, 342. Similarly, see Clesse (n 688) 129. In contrast, see FiC Brussels 19 April 2010, [2011] RDPC 209; Kéfer (n 1023) 1865.

[1044] The applicant did not explicitly claim that this offence violated his privilege, yet he relied on the POI: CoC 21 April 2015 (n 737) (2015). The employer was repeatedly absent when the competent inspectors showed up or he failed to provide the documents when he was present. On this case, see also Clesse and Heirman (n 1025) 130.

[1045] CoC 19 June 2013 (n 1).

over documents to labour inspectors, without resisting when they search for the documents themselves, does not qualify as an obstruction of supervision.[1046]

Other legislative acts that contain cooperation duties or penalise the obstruction of supervision do not distinguish, for the purpose of cooperation duties, between documents for which there is a legal obligation to create and retain them and other documents.[1047] This practice is risky in light of the case law of the ECtHR.[1048] The CoC's ruling in *Citibank* and its ruling of 6 November 2018 support the view that, provided that the conditions to invoke the privilege are met,[1049] simply refusing to hand over requested documents does not constitute the offence of obstruction or hindrance of supervision.[1050] At the same time, other provisions not only penalise the obstruction or hindrance of supervision, but penalise failure to provide documents as such.[1051]

For a long time, US case law focused on the compulsion linked to the handing over of the documents and not on the manner in which these documents were

[1046] CoC 6 November 2018 (n 737). In another 2018 case, the Court did not quash a CoA ruling finding a person guilty of the obstruction of supervision offence. The person had not delivered the promised documents to the labour inspectors and he had missed appointments with those inspectors: CoC 7 March 2018 (n 737). The CJEU has also ruled that the PSI does not justify every failure to cooperate, such as a refusal to appear at a hearing or delaying tactics designed to postpone it: *DB v Consob* (n 17) para 41.

[1047] eg Arts 6 *in fine* and 10(1), 1° of the Act of 15 July 1985 on the use of materials containing hormonal, anti-hormonal, beta-adrenergic or production-stimulating effects; Art XV.3(1)5° CEL. Art XV.126 CEL criminalises the voluntary obstruction or hindrance of the exercise of civil servants or police officials; Art 203 GCEA. On this matter, see also A Baert, *Douane en accijnzen* (Wolters Kluwer, 2021) 270–71; Art 188/2 CCVSL; Arts 315 and 316 ITC provide extensive cooperation duties, including the production of documents and replying to requests for information: I De Troyer and L Vandenberghe, *Fiscale procedure inkomstenbelasting* (Intersentia, 2020) 39–46. Discussions can arise as to the extent of the documents that need to be kept and produced, eg with regard to letters or emails related to one's professional activity: F Vanbiervliet and A Visschers, *Taxatie- en geschillenprocedure* (Gompel & Svacina, 2020) 43. Art 445 ITC allows the administration to impose an administrative fine in case of infringements of that code, and where one refuses to provide on-site access to documents with the required intent, one can face prosecution on the basis of the general offence description of Art 449 ITC: Delanote, 'Het zwijgrecht van een tot medewerking gehouden belastingplichtige' (n 1030) 273; Art 36/19 of the Act of 22 February 1998 establishing the organic statute of the National Bank of Belgium grants the bank far-reaching powers. It can impose daily penalty payments of €250–50,000 in case one fails to provide the information (capped at €2,500,000). Obstructing the National Bank's investigations is a punishable offence under Art 36/20 of the Act. See O Voordeckers and S Lamberigts, 'Belgium' in S Allegrezza (ed), *The Enforcement Dimension of the Single Supervisory Mechanism* (Wolters Kluwer, 2020) 214–16. With regard to obstruction of investigations by the FSMA, see Arts 41(1) 3° and 87 of the Act of 2 August 2002 on the Supervision of the Financial Sector and Financial Services. The FSMA has accepted that persons can exercise the PSI during questioning: Sanctions Committee 28 April 2010, 8, www.fsma.be/sites/default/files/legacy/sitecore/media%20library/Files/sanc/fr/2010-04-28_abusdemarche.pdf; CoA Brussels 13 December 2011, [2012] Bank Fin R 212, 215.

[1048] De Nauw, 'Het zwijgrecht in het strafrecht' (n 964) 269.

[1049] In its ruling of 20 November 2018, the CoC considered the PSI not to be applicable to purely administrative enquiries whose sole purpose is to make material findings with a view to ensuring compliance with the applicable regulations, without the person who is the subject of the enquiry being accused of an offence or facing the threat of criminal prosecution.

[1050] A Bloch, 'Ook de eenhoorn bestaat en hij kan spreken' [2019] No 382 *Juristenkrant* 13. In *Citibank*, even the Prosecutor's Office had considered that failure to produce documents amounted to the offence of obstruction of supervision. Clesse and Heirman consider that failure to produce social documents can amount to the offence of obstruction of supervision: Clesse and Heirman (n 1025) 132–33.

[1051] Art 203 GCEA.

created,[1052] finding that the privilege offers protection to the compelled handing over of documents. In *Boyd*,[1053] SCOTUS considered that there is no difference between compelling a person to incriminate himself through oral testimony and compelling him to hand over self-incriminating private documents.[1054] This suspect- and defendant-friendly approach allows them to be exempt from both oral and documentary self-incrimination. The ruling seemed to pay particular attention to the privacy argument in order to offer protection to voluntarily created documents.[1055] What made *Boyd* even more interesting is that the document at issue was not a very personal document, such as a diary. Instead, the document sought was an invoice for crates of plated glass, as the relevant import duties were supposedly not paid. In other words, the notion 'private papers' had a very broad meaning in this case and if an invoice, established by another party, can fall under it, a great number of business documents could too. By adopting this broad approach to the PSI and documentary evidence, SCOTUS adopted a similar position as the early E&W cases mentioned in chapter two.

By interpreting private papers very broadly in *Boyd* and by accepting that documentary evidence falls within the PSI's scope, SCOTUS initially adopted a protective approach.[1056] In the following decades, case law turned on the question whether a document was private or public, as only the former were protected by the Fifth Amendment.[1057] That protection was quickly reduced by the Court's rulings in *Hale* and *Wilson*.[1058] The RRD[1059] further reduced *Boyd*'s impact as it excludes a significant number of documents from the privilege's scope altogether:[1060] a person cannot invoke the privilege in relation to records that he is required to keep as a condition of voluntarily engaging in a highly regulated activity,[1061] even where this would expose a link in a chain of evidence.[1062] This rule traditionally played a role in regulated business fields,[1063] but later case law has extended its application to other fields.[1064] A parallel can be drawn between Belgian case law,

[1052] Thus, the fact that the documents are created voluntarily was not essential. It is the compulsion to hand them over that is key.

[1053] *Boyd v United States* 116 US 616 (1886).

[1054] ibid 633–35; Salky (n 587) 260.

[1055] Salky (n 587) 134. See also its later cases that shortly predate *Fischer* (n 472), eg *Bellis v United States* 417 US 85, 91 (1974).

[1056] On this topic, see L Sacharoff, 'Unlocking the Fifth Amendment: Passwords and Encrypted Devices' (2018) 87 *Fordham Law Review* 203, 211–20.

[1057] Horowitz and Wirth (n 233) 514.

[1058] Hale (n 247); *Wilson* (n 247).

[1059] *Shapiro v United States* 335 US 1, 4 (1948).

[1060] On its restrictive effect, see PS Diamond, *Federal Grand Jury Practice and Procedure* (Juris Publishing, 2014) 6–22.

[1061] Dressler and Michaels, *Understanding Criminal Procedure* (n 748) 277; SA Saltzburg, 'The Required Records Doctrine: Its Lessons for the Privilege Against Self-Incrimination', (1986) 53 *University of Chicago Law Review* 6, 31.

[1062] *United States v Chen* 815 F3d 72, 78 (1st Cir 2016); Dressler and Michaels, *Understanding Criminal Procedure* (n 748) 278.

[1063] J Israel and W LaFave, *Criminal Procedure, Constitutional Limitations in a Nutshell* (West Academic, 2014) 462. In *Shapiro* (n 1059), the person needed a licence.

which excludes documents created pursuant to a statutory duty from the privilege's scope, and the American RRD. The result of the RRD and the Belgian case law that distinguishes between documents for which there is a legal retention duty and other documents is the same, as they restrict the privilege's scope. Admittedly, US case law is more detailed in defining when the RRD applies. That doctrine is a classification tool to label certain documents as public and thus not protected by the Fifth Amendment.[1065]

As such, requiring record-keeping is an understandable and justifiable practice.[1066] Yet, one can easily imagine that a broad record-keeping obligation, coupled with the obligation to present these records upon request, could also be a useful tool for punitive law enforcement,[1067] and the question thus is what limitations apply to the RRD.[1068] This doctrine developed through case law and, considering the Fifth Amendment's wording, it seems that the only way to make it constitutionally sound[1069] is by excluding required records from the privilege's scope as statutory restrictions to the privilege are difficult in light of the particularly broad wording of the privilege.

To prevent the records from resulting in self-incrimination, one could imagine that a person who is required to keep the records and produce them upon request can benefit from use and derivative use immunity. This way, the records could still be relevant for the purpose of civil liability or for revoking the licence of an airline company that does not take safety regulations seriously, but not for prosecution of a punitive case.[1070] Under such a model, a statutory provision could require a person who has a foreign bank account to keep records on this account and failure to keep these records could constitute an offence,[1071] whereas a punitive prosecution for tax evasion could not rely on these records produced

[1064] *Baltimore Department of Social Services v Bouknight* 493 US 549, 555–56 (1990) extended the scope to a conflict between the social services and a mother, as the mother's custodial duties related to production and the production of the child were required as part of a non-criminal regulatory scheme.

[1065] Horowitz and Wirth (n 233) 524 and 529; C Rule, 'United States v Greenfield: A Triumph of the Fifth Amendment's Act of Production Privilege; or Confirmation that the Privilege Can be entirely Abrogated by Any Act of Congress, or Even by a Treasury Regulation' (2018) 71 *Tax Law* 335, 356. At that time, *Boyd* (n 1053) extended the PSI's protection to private papers.

[1066] For example, checking whether an airline company complies with safety regulations would become significantly more difficult were the company not required to keep records on the maintenance of its planes.

[1067] In his dissent in *Shapiro*, Justice Jackson pointed out that if every citizen was required to keep a diary of his whereabouts and activities, this would facilitate criminal enforcement (provided that it is combined with an obligation to produce it upon request).

[1068] *Chen* (n 1062) 79. The risks of an overly broad RRD were already clear to Justice Jackson, who dissented in *Shapiro* and pointed out the risks posed by the RRD's expansion.

[1069] Provided that one accepts that documents as such fall within the scope of the wording of the Fifth Amendment.

[1070] One could foresee an exception so that failure to keep and produce the records is still a punishable offence, in order to ensure that they are indeed kept.

[1071] In a case where a person is merely prosecuted for failure to keep the records, the privilege is not necessarily infringed, provided that the records could not have been admissible in evidence for a criminal conviction. When a person does not keep records and is convicted for not keeping them, he cannot claim that by keeping and producing them he would have been forced to contribute to his own incrimination.

by the person himself. Admittedly, such immunity would confront the government with a situation where it has incriminating information, which it cannot use, and therefore the required records would lose a significant part of their usefulness for punitive enforcement.[1072] Yet this is not a novelty: in cases where a person is granted immunity, this is similarly the case under US federal law. It is nevertheless true that these two types of immunity are not entirely comparable: whereas a court order granting immunity is granted only upon request,[1073] the immunity for record-keepers would be automatic.[1074] The immunity for required record-keepers would not entirely exclude prosecutions, but it would make them more difficult, as the prosecution would need to show, eg in a punitive tax evasion case, that it has not relied on the information provided by the suspect and it would need an independent source for its evidence.[1075]

SCOTUS did not grant immunity to required record-keepers in *Shapiro*.[1076] It held that federal legislation obliging certain licensed businesses to keep records of their business,[1077] as well as produce them for inspection when asked to do so, was constitutional.[1078] It also held that the privilege does not apply to documents that are required to be kept for the benefit of the public and for public inspection.[1079] The petitioner in *Shapiro*,[1080] confronted with a prosecution for tie-in sales,[1081] had claimed immunity. SCOTUS held that the Emergency Price Control Act did not merely impose the keeping of required records in order to obtain information, but that they were imposed to allow enforcement of the statute and that the legislator had not intended to limit the use of these records for enforcement purposes by granting immunity to the record-keeper.[1082] The aforementioned Belgian case law resembles the US approach as it does not provide for immunity either.

Depending on how broadly one defines required records, it is quite clear that many documents that would qualify as 'private documents' under *Boyd* would be

[1072] It could nevertheless still be relevant for general information-gathering purposes, civil liability, revoking of licences and non-criminal enforcement mechanisms.

[1073] Thus, the prosecution can deliberately choose to request immunity for a person in whose prosecution it is less interested, in order to secure evidence against persons whose prosecution it accords higher importance.

[1074] A further difference is that immunity orders are granted in cases where the Fifth Amendment is available, whereas required records fall outside that Amendment's scope.

[1075] Saltzburg (n 1061) 27.

[1076] Several judges dissented and blamed the majority for 'deleting and reshaping' the relevant statutory provision. See Justice Frankfurter's dissenting opinion in *Shapiro* (n 1059) 43. He points out that the immunity provision in the statute in question essentially had as its purpose ensuring that the government could gather the necessary information for price regulation while not being hindered by Fifth Amendment claims. In other words, by offering immunity to those who provided the required records, there would be no Fifth Amendment claims that obstructed the information gathering process: Frankfurter in *Shapiro* (n 1059) 49.

[1077] The documents sought in this case were vast: 'all duplicate sales invoices, sales books, ledgers, inventory records, contracts and records relating to the sale of all commodities from September 1st, 1944, to September 28, 1944': *Shapiro* (n 1059) 4.

[1078] ibid.

[1079] ibid 17–19.

[1080] A fruit and produce wholesaler.

[1081] A violation of the Emergency Price Control Act.

[1082] *Shapiro* (n 1059) 15.

required records, and would thus fall outside the privilege's scope. *Shapiro* did not set out these limits, but SCOTUS later developed a three-prong test to check the RRD's applicability.[1083]

First, the interest of the government should derive from a regulatory scheme rather than from a *sensu stricto* criminal law enforcement purpose;[1084] the inquiry must essentially be regulatory.[1085] This first criterion has the potential to restrict the RRD's impact. By requiring the inquiry to be essentially regulatory instead of *sensu stricto* criminal,[1086] the doctrine seemingly precludes the disguising of a *sensu stricto* criminal inquiry beneath the cloak of administrative regulation.[1087] In principle,[1088] it does not suffice that there is some (accessorial) regulatory purpose in order to satisfy this condition.[1089] Yet, this does not answer the question of just how much of an element of *sensu stricto* criminal law enforcement may cause the inquiry to lose its essentially regulatory nature.[1090]

This issue came up in cases[1091] where an individual was ordered to produce required records on his foreign financial accounts.[1092] By producing these records, he would expose his failure to report the existence of such an account and thus admit a *sensu stricto* criminal offence. Interestingly, the sections requiring the records to be kept derive their authority from the Bank Secrecy Act.[1093] That act specifically states that the purpose of the relevant sub-chapter is to 'require certain reports or records that are highly useful in criminal, tax, or regulatory investigations, risk assessments or proceedings'.[1094] The express reference to usefulness in criminal investigations or proceedings raises the question whether this exceeds the RRD's limits.[1095] Nevertheless, the 9th Circuit CoA, as well as other appellate courts,[1096] considered that the records fitted within an essentially regulatory

[1083] *Grosso v United States* 390 US 62 (1968); *Marchetti* (n 601); Beale et al (n 600) §6:15, 2–3. According to Rule, SCOTUS did not intend to set three factors that always had to rigidly be analysed by courts to assess the RRD's applicability: Rule (n 1065) 360.

[1084] Israel and LaFave (n 1063) 463; Salky (n 587) 272.

[1085] *Grosso* (n 1083) 67–68; Agostino and Sannicandro (n 599) 7.

[1086] *In re Grand Jury Subpoena Duces Tecum (Underhill)* 781 F2d 64, 67 (6th Cir 1986).

[1087] For example, in *California v Byers* 402 US 424, 427–28 (1971), SCOTUS found that the requirement for drivers, involved in an accident, to stop and provide their name and address was not aimed at facilitating criminal convictions, but at promoting the settling of civil liabilities.

[1088] The strictness of this condition can be questioned in light of the case law on the required record-keeping of foreign bank accounts.

[1089] CM Ferguson, 'The Required Records Doctrine, the Fifth Amendment Privilege under Attack' (2011) 115 *Journal of Taxation* 218, 224.

[1090] The fact that the record-keeping requirement has criminal implications is not sufficient to exclude the RRD's applicability: *Byers* (n 1087) 428; *Chen* (n 1062) 80. In the context of SEC regulations, the mere possibility of incrimination has similarly been held to be insufficient: *SEC v Fehn* 97 F3d 1276, 1291 (9th Cir 1996).

[1091] eg *In re Grand Jury Investigation MH* F3d 1067 (9th Cir 2011).

[1092] Those records need to be kept under 31 CFR 1010.420.

[1093] Ferguson (n 1089) 220.

[1094] 31 USC 5311.

[1095] There are further indications that the criminal enforcement aspect plays an important role, eg the required retention period corresponds with the statute of limitations for the prosecution for the criminal offence of wilfully not reporting a foreign account: Ferguson (n 1089) 224.

[1096] Since the 9th Circuit's 2011 ruling, the majority of the federal CoAs have similarly held that the RRD is applicable and attempts to obtain a SCOTUS ruling have so far been denied: *United States v Chabot* 793 F3d 339, 341 and 345 (3rd Cir 2015); *Chen* (n 1062) 76; Rule (n 1065) 339.

regime because the area concerned was not permeated with *sensu stricto* criminal statutes, nor was it aimed at a highly selective group of people.[1097] This finding can be criticised particularly in light of the history of the Bank Secrecy Act, which shows that attention was paid to white-collar crime, terrorism and the role of foreign bank accounts.[1098] It gives a very wide latitude to the RRD's first prong. The 3rd Circuit CoA, in another case on required records of a foreign account, dismissed criticism that the RRD would allow for a more general abrogation of the PSI by creating a host of record-keeping or reporting obligations. It emphasised the legitimate non-criminal purposes of the records.[1099]

According to the second requirement, 'information is to be obtained by requiring the preservation of records of a kind which the regulated party customarily kept'.[1100] In the aforementioned 9th Circuit case, it was suggested that this requirement can be based in part on the requirement to report the account as such and in part on the need to have this information to access the account.[1101] Because one is required to keep them according to law, they become records that the regulated party customarily keeps. This reasoning seems to be at odds with *Grosso* and *Marchetti*, as these cases suggest that the records at issue would have been kept anyway, and thus not because there is an obligation to keep them.[1102] Moreover, one may wonder what exactly is implied by the reference to records 'of a kind which the regulated party customarily kept'.[1103] If, for example, a person keeps information on his accounts and he is then required to keep additional details that he would not keep if he were not obliged to, one may wonder whether the second prong is fulfilled.[1104] Moreover, 31 CFR 1010.420 may actually require the creation of new records, as foreign bank statements may not even include all the information that needs to be kept.[1105]

Thirdly, the records should have acquired some 'public aspects' which render them at least analogous to public documents.[1106] A statutory requirement to keep certain records does not give them the requisite 'public aspects'.[1107]

[1097] The Court considered that having such an account was not unlawful nor that there was an inherently criminal element in the elements required to be recorded: *In re Grand Jury Investigation MH* (n 1091) 1074; *Chen* (n 1062) 79.

[1098] Ferguson (n 1089) 225. This was explicitly acknowledged by the 1st Circuit in *Chen* (n 1062) 76. It nevertheless concluded that the first prong of the test was fulfilled. It indicated that the justifications for the required record-keeping went far beyond the criminal sphere and that purposes were diverse.

[1099] *Chabot* (n 1096) 344.

[1100] *Grosso* (n 1083) 68.

[1101] *In re Grand Jury Investigation MH* (n 1091) 1076. The latter part is incorrect, as intermediaries such as attorneys or advisors are often relied upon to access the accounts.

[1102] Ferguson (n 1089) 229.

[1103] Critically, see Saltzburg (n 1061) 22–23.

[1104] Similarly, see Ferguson (n 1089) 229.

[1105] Rule (n 1065) 361. It is unlikely that individuals who were not declaring foreign accounts would create additional records of their own free will. Banks in secrecy jurisdictions often did not even send bank statements to US account holders. Rule refers to the fact that foreign bank statements might not even refer to the account holder's name but merely to a number.

[1106] *Grosso* (n 1083) 68.

[1107] *Marchetti* (n 601) 57; Ferguson (n 1089) 230. Against, see *In re Grand Jury Investigation MH* (n 1091) 1077. The 3rd Circuit CoA considers that several other CoAs have accepted public aspects to be present once the test's first prong is met: *Chabot* (n 1096) 348.

Where the documents sought were linked to licensing, their public aspects have been accepted.[1108] One can hardly imagine that foreign bank account records are comparable to the records of a produce-seller such as Shapiro, who was openly selling goods.[1109] Yet public aspects have even been accepted with regard to such records, and it has surprisingly been held that voluntarily engaging in foreign banking constitutes a waiver of the PSI with regard to bank records.[1110] Arguing that documents have public aspects since they are required to be kept to support the enforcement of a valid regulatory scheme seems to turn things around. If merely requiring the records to be kept is sufficient to make them public, then the legislator could give a very wide circle of documents public aspects, just by imposing a legal duty to keep them. In other words, if this were to be the case, I would be living in a glasshouse.[1111]

The initial generous approach towards documentary evidence received a further blow by the so-called *Fischer* doctrine. Even though the RRD and the CED severely restricted the protection offered by the privilege to documentary evidence, other documents were still protected.[1112] This changed when SCOTUS took a different approach in *Fischer*,[1113] as it largely abandoned the privilege's privacy justification in relation to documents. According to this new approach, the focus is no longer on the compulsion involved in the production of the documents. Instead, the question is whether the documents were voluntarily created.[1114] That reasoning corresponds to what certain authors and national courts have argued in the aftermath of *Saunders*. It greatly restricted the finding in *Boyd* by limiting the protection offered by the privilege to the compelled creation of documents[1115] or the act of affirming the truth of the incriminating content of documents. The documents' content does not benefit from protection under the privilege.[1116] The Court's new approach thus does not focus on the distinction between private and public documents introduced by *Boyd*. The new approach only offers protection if the act of producing the documents itself amounts to a testimonial communication.[1117] The reasoning behind this protection is that by handing over

[1108] Ferguson (n 1089) 230.
[1109] Rule (n 1065) 378.
[1110] *Chabot* (n 1096) 348–49. Critically, see Rule (n 1065) 383–89.
[1111] Dissenting Opinion of Justice Frankfurter in *Shapiro* (n 1059) 51.
[1112] For confirmation that documents still benefited from the PSI's protection in the 1960s, see *Schmerber v California* 384 US 757, 763–64 (1966).
[1113] *Fischer* (n 472); Dressler and Michaels, *Understanding Criminal Procedure* (n 748) 276–77. The documents sought were papers used in the preparation of a taxpayer's tax return and these tax returns were supposedly fraudulent.
[1114] This reasoning played a role in SCOTUS's new approach: *Fischer* (n 472) 409–10; *United States v Doe* 465 US 605, 611–12 (1984); Horowitz and Wirth (n 233) 532.
[1115] Compelling a person to create documents as opposed to producing pre-existing documents would still be protected post-*Fischer*, except where the RRD applies.
[1116] RJ Allen et al, *Criminal Procedure: Adjudication and the Right to Counsel* (Wolters Kluwer, 2020) 1130; Salky (n 587) 260; Horowitz and Wirth (n 233) 534; Rule (n 1065) 339. On the discussion of whether purely private papers such as diaries would benefit from more protection, see Dressler and Michaels, *Understanding Criminal Procedure* (n 748) 277.
[1117] Rule (n 1065) 345; Salky (n 587) 259.

the documents the person who produces them tacitly concedes the existence of the sought documents, their possession or control, as well as the belief that the documents produced are those requested by the subpoena.[1118]

In a post-*Fischer* case, *Doe*,[1119] SCOTUS refused to grant protection on the ground that the content of the documents requested under a subpoena were potentially self-incriminating. SCOTUS did accept that, given the case's specifics, the act of production of the documents would involve testimonial self-incrimination because it would involve admitting the existence and possession, as well as the authentication, of the documents.[1120]

The key question is whether the existence of the documents and the possession of the documents are a foregone conclusion or not,[1121] as an affirmative answer to this question would likely lead to the conclusion that the documents' production is not testimonial.[1122] In *Fischer*, SCOTUS found that the documents' existence and location amounted to a foregone conclusion, while adding that the individual added little or nothing to the sum total of the government's information by admitting possession of the documents.[1123] Under a reasonable particularity standard, the government must, in order for the foregone conclusion to be accepted, show its knowledge[1124] as to (i) the existence of the documents, (ii) the possession or control of the documents[1125] and (iii) the authenticity of the documents.[1126] In that sense, the *Fischer* doctrine resembles what some European authors and the ECtHR's Fourth Section have argued post-*Funke*: they read it as precluding the compelled handing over of documents only in those cases where the authorities mount a fishing expedition. Where the act of production itself would amount to a

[1118] *Fischer* (n 472) 410; Horowitz and Wirth (n 233) 515; JG Palmer, 'The Fifth Amendment Act of Production Doctrine and the Collective Entity Rule: A Primer' (2018–19) 33 *Criminal Justice* 22, 22–23.

[1119] *United States v Doe* (n 1114) 611–12.

[1120] ibid 613–14; *Chabot* (n 1096) 342.

[1121] *Fischer* (n 472) 411; Allen et al, *Criminal Procedure* (n 1116). It is in the government's interest to provide concrete elements to support a foregone conclusion argument: *Oriho* (n 599) 927–28. In *United States v Hubbell* 540 US 27, 45 (2000), SCOTUS refused to accept the argument that a businessman such as the respondent always possesses general business and tax records included in the broadly worded categories listed in the subpoena.

[1122] *Fischer* (n 472) 411.

[1123] ibid.

[1124] At the time the summons was issued: *United States v Fridman* 974 F3d 163, 175 (2nd Cir 2020); Rule (n 1065).

[1125] *United States v Greenfield* 831 F3d 106 (2nd Cir 2016) demonstrates that even if the authorities can show existence, control and authenticity at one point in time, a foregone conclusion can only be drawn if control and existence can be shown at the time the summons was issued.

[1126] In ibid 118 the 2nd Circuit CoA held, with regard to authenticity, that: (i) authentication can be done implicitly when a person produces the requested documents and in doing so implicitly testifies that he owns or at least possesses the documents. The authorities need to establish that the documents 'are in fact what they purport to be' and that the person will not be compelled to 'use his discretion in selecting the responsive documents, thereby tacitly providing identifying information'; and (ii) authentication can be demonstrated independently, for instance by third parties familiar with the type of documents. See also *United States v Ponds* 454 F3d 313, 324 (DC Cir 2006); *Fridman* (n 1124) 174.

testimonial communication, the authorities can still under US federal law compel the documents' production by providing immunity for the act of production.[1127]

Hubbell[1128] has helped clarify the *Fischer* doctrine's impact. In that case, a person had received a subpoena to hand over a wide range of documents.[1129] At the same time, he received immunity in relation to the act of production of these documents. The person produced the documents and was later indicted. SCOTUS found that the testimonial element of the act of production was the first step in a chain of evidence needed for his prosecution.[1130] The Court refused to accept that the production of the documents was only a physical act. It stressed the need for Hubbell to make extensive use of the contents of his mind in the identification of the relevant documents.[1131] Interestingly, it compared putting together all these documents to giving the combination of a safe, rather than to giving the key to access a vault. In other words, the use and derivative use immunity does in the end offer some protection to the content of the documents. According to the *Kastigar* burden,[1132] the prosecution can only rely on the documents' content produced through an immunised act of production, when it can show that it had an independent source to show existence and possession of the documents.

A further question is whether a person who has created the documents can claim protection in cases where the existence and possession are a foregone conclusion, merely because by producing the documents he would implicitly authenticate them. The answers by the lower courts are divided on this issue, and while some accept it,[1133] other courts refuse to do so.[1134]

Taking stock of the RRD and the CED, both developed before *Fischer*, as well as the rulings that built upon *Fischer*, one may wonder whether the RRD is still relevant. Somehow, the answer seems to be affirmative, since SCOTUS applied the doctrine in *Bouknight*,[1135] and more recent rulings by lower courts have taken a similar approach.[1136] The willingness of numerous federal appellate courts to

[1127] Dressler and Michaels, *Understanding Criminal Procedure* (n 748) 279.
[1128] *Hubbell* (n 1121).
[1129] 13,120 pages, divided into 11 categories.
[1130] *Hubbell* (n 1121) 42.
[1131] ibid 43. See also *United States v Sideman & Bancroft*, LLP 704 F3d 1197, 1203 (9th Cir 2013). Courts need to distinguish subpoenas or demands for documents that merely seek the production of documents whose existence and possession qualify as a foregone conclusion from those that require the use of the content of one's mind in the identification and production process of the documents: Rule (n 1065) 347; Salky (n 587) 263. The question is whether a case is more like *Fischer* or *Hubbell*: *Greenfield* (n 1125) 116. A repatriation order (of funds) can trigger the PSI as it can force a person to show to which bank accounts (and allegedly illicit assets) he has access and control: *Oriho* (n 599) 925–26.
[1132] *Kastigar* (n 589).
[1133] *Greenfield* (n 1125) 120.
[1134] For the former approach, see *In re Grand Jury Subpoena Dated April 18, 2003* 383 F3d 905, 912–13 (9th Cir 2004). See also Salky (n 587) 265–67.
[1135] *Bouknight* (n 1064) 555. Horowitz and Wirth (n 233) 543 consider that this ruling cannot be accepted as 'authority for the revitalization of the required-records-doctrine'.
[1136] *In re Grand Jury Investigation MH* (n 1091); *In re Grand Jury Subpoena* 21 F3d 226, 229 (8th Cir 1994); *Chabot* (n 1096) 343. Critically, see Rule (n 1065) 357.

apply the required records exception in relation to foreign bank accounts suggests that the protection offered by the *Fischer* doctrine, also known as the act of production privilege, only applies where the legislator or a federal agency has not overridden the Fifth Amendment by imposing record-keeping requirements.[1137] Applying a doctrine developed at a time when the relevant criterion of distinction for the purpose of protection was the private/public nature of documents, after *Fischer* limited protection to an act of production privilege, is not convincing.[1138] Nevertheless, several justifications have been put forward in order to justify the continued application of the RRD: engaging in an activity that is subject to a record-keeping requirement is considered as a waiver of the PSI; since a record-keeping duty is in place, one concedes little in terms of control or authentication by handing over the documents; or the doctrine is vital to protect the government's interest in using the required records.[1139] The argument that since the act of production case law, the focus no longer is on the regulatory scheme but on the testimonial aspects of producing the documents[1140] has failed to gain acceptance.

In the USA, the PSI's material scope has gradually become more limited. The CED and the RRD reduced protection by the PSI of documentary evidence, and the act of production case law has largely ended protection of the content of documentary evidence. Under this case law, compelling someone to create new incriminating documents would still lead to the applicability of the privilege, at least to the extent that the documents are not required records. *Hubbell* has nevertheless indirectly increased the protection offered to the content of documents through a backdoor: where a person has received act of production immunity, the use of the content of the documents to build a case against him is only possible where the prosecution can meet its *Kastigar* burden to show that it had an independent source to show the existence and possession of the documents. Failure to do so would amount to a violation of the derivative use immunity.

In sum, the ECtHR and national courts have struggled with answering the question whether the PSI provides protection against the compelled handing over of documents. Whereas several ECtHR rulings confirm that the privilege offers protection to documents, that case law is not crystal clear, and the reference in *Saunders* to material which has an existence independent of the will of the suspect has also in national case law resulted in a restriction of the protection offered by the PSI. E&W courts have repeatedly accepted that statutes can restrict the privilege and thus require the compelled production of documents or oral statements.

[1137] Rule (n 1065) 337 and 342. In *Greenfield* (n 1125), the requirement of 31 CFR 1010.420 did not prevent the act of production privilege from applying. The aforementioned regulation provides a five-year retention period and many of the documents went beyond the requirements of that regulation. The CoA indicated at fn 6 that 'The documents sought in the instant case do not fall under the so-called "required records exception" to the act-of-production doctrine'. See also Agostino and Sannicandro (n 599) 8.

[1138] Horowitz and Wirth (n 233) 516.

[1139] *Chabot* (n 1096) 343.

[1140] Salky (n 587) 273.

As the economic activities of corporations are often regulated by statutory provisions, such provisions have a direct impact on the PSI's scope also with regard to corporations. In Belgium, too, numerous provisions provide for compelled cooperation, regularly in fields relevant to corporations. In addition to these provisions, several courts have often found that where there is a statutory duty to keep records, the PSI does not protect against their compelled production. A similar doctrine, the RRD, applies in the USA. There, the level of protection offered to documents has significantly decreased since *Boyd*, through the RRD, the CED and the *Fischer* doctrine. Whereas the focus was on the element of compulsion linked to the handing over of the documents, the lack of compulsion in the documents' creation has played a role in the shift towards less protection.

III. Encrypted Evidence

A topical issue connected to the PSI is the use of passwords or encryption to prevent access to smartphones, other electronic devices, applications and data.[1141] For instance, an individual might have secured the data carrier containing documents connecting him to money laundering or other offences with multiple passwords.[1142] Access to such protected[1143] data is considered to be an important challenge for law enforcement.[1144] For example, Apple made headlines as allegations were made that it had dropped end-to-end encryption of iCloud back-ups due to pressure by the FBI.[1145] Encryption evidently has legitimate purposes.[1146] In light of revelations by Edward Snowden and others, it comes as no surprise that increased recourse is taken to the protection of information.[1147] Indeed, several legitimate reasons justify the use of encryption. It is, for example, crucial for safe e-commerce,[1148] or for protection against repression by a dictator.[1149]

[1141] 94% of Americans aged 18–29 carry smartphones, often with encryption enabled: OS Kerr, 'Compelled Decryption and the Privilege against Self-Incrimination' (2019) 97 *Texas Law Review* 767, 768.

[1142] R De Keersmaecker and G Verbeke, '"Obstruction of Justice": een eerste stap(je) op Belgische bodem?' [2020] *Politie & Recht* 202.

[1143] Different mechanisms of protection are used: in addition to protecting access to eg a USB key by adding a password, one can go further by encrypting data so that it cannot be ordinarily understood: I Walden, *Computer Crimes and Digital Investigations*, 2nd edn (Oxford University Press, 2016) 291.

[1144] Walden (n 1143) 290.

[1145] Alternative explanations for the halting of such encryption have appeared: www.bbc.com/news/technology-51207744.

[1146] Commission to the European Parliament, the Council, the European Economic and Social Committee and the Committee of the Regions, 'Protecting Fundamental Rights in the Digital Age – 2021 Annual Report on the Application of the EU Charter of Fundamental Rights' COM(2021) 819 final, 30.

[1147] See also Walden (n 1143) 292.

[1148] BB Chatterjee, 'New but Not Improved: A Critical Examination of Revisions to the Regulation of Investigatory Powers Act 2000 Encryption Provisions' (2011) 19 *International Journal of Law and Information Technology* 264, 265.

[1149] Van de Heyning, 'Het zwijgrecht in digitale tijden' (n 435) 308.

Requiring someone to decrypt evidence or to provide the password to do so can facilitate the evidence-gathering process to mount a punitive case against that person. Therefore, one may wonder whether an individual or a corporation can invoke the PSI when asked to decrypt information. Case law of the three selected countries has been struggling with this issue, and specific case law of the ECtHR and the CJEU is currently lacking.[1150]

In E&W, the contested[1151] sections 49–56 RIPA regulate this matter.[1152] According to section 49, a person who has received permission from a competent judge[1153] can order disclosure of the protected information in an intelligible form.[1154] Thus, this order is in principle not limited to giving the key to the protected information,[1155] though in some cases the only way to comply is by giving the key.[1156] The requirement to disclose protected information can be imposed on the person believed to have possession of the key to access the protected information. Several conditions need to be met before such an order can be imposed.[1157] First, there have to be reasonable grounds to believe that a specific person has the key to the protected information.[1158] Secondly, the order should be necessary in the interests of national security, for the purpose of preventing or detecting crime; in the interests of the UK's economic well-being; or for the purpose of securing effective exercise or proper performance of a statutory power or duty by a public authority.[1159] Furthermore, imposing disclosure should also be proportionate to what it aims to achieve. Lastly, there should be no reasonable alternative to gaining access to the information, other than giving the order.[1160] Where multiple persons are in possession of the key or the protected information and where one of them has possession of it as an officer or employee to the corporation or firm and another of those persons is the corporation or firm itself or another officer, employee or partner of the corporation or firm, the order should be given to a senior officer, a partner or the most senior employee.[1161] Where it is not reasonably practicable to give the order to do so, the order can be given to the officer or employee.

[1150] These courts will most likely address that issue in the near future. A case has already been communicated to the ECtHR: *Minteh v France* App no 23624/20 (ECtHR, pending).
[1151] Chatterjee (n 1148) 266 et seq.
[1152] These rules should not be circumvented by relying on other provisions: *Love v National Crime Agency* [2016] 5 WLUK 173.
[1153] Sch 2, para 1 RIPA. Written approval is also needed from the National Technical Assistance Centre. On this issue, see Walden (n 1143) 303.
[1154] S 49(2) RIPA.
[1155] Yet the order's target can choose to give the key instead: s 50(2) RIPA.
[1156] S 51(4)–(5) RIPA; Walden (n 1143) 296.
[1157] Walden (n 1143) 294 et seq. In addition to the mandatory information that should be given to the subject of the order: see s 49(4) RIPA.
[1158] S 49(2)a RIPA.
[1159] S 49(2)b and s 49(3) RIPA.
[1160] S 49(2)d RIPA. In practice, it seems that often convictions for the underlying offences can be secured in other ways: Chatterjee (n 1148) 273.
[1161] S 49(5)–(7) RIPA.

In order to ensure compliance with the order to disclose protected information, it is a punishable offence to knowingly fail to comply with such an order,[1162] punishable by a fine and/or imprisonment of up to two years, or even five years in a national security or child indecency case. One may wonder how effective these sanctions are in practice:[1163] if someone is facing a higher penalty for the underlying offence, he may prefer the penalty for failure to disclose the encrypted information.[1164]

In the absence of explicit ECtHR case law on the issue, assessing whether sections 49–56 RIPA comply with the ECHR is challenging. The sanctions for failure to comply are sufficiently high to qualify as compulsion. One may argue that these sections can lead to the disclosure of (in)directly incriminating real evidence or testimony. The evidence of which disclosure is required is real evidence, and it can include images, sounds, documents and other data. In those cases where one is only required to disclose protected information and not the key that protects it, the privilege still seems to apply: this disclosure shows that the person had access to the information, and in this sense it can be self-incriminating. In those cases where disclosure of a key or keys is required, I believe that the key(s) should not be considered independently of the underlying information. Yet, the applicability of the privilege does not necessarily imply that every restriction is forbidden. Both common law and the ECtHR have accepted statutory limitations of the privilege. The *Jalloh* criteria provide guidance in this context. As a prison sentence of up to two (or five) years can be imposed, the nature and degree of compulsion is high. At the same time, RIPA does provide a number of applicable safeguards. First of all, the disclosure order can only be given by a person who has received a judge's permission. Thus, some judicial control is available to avoid excessive use of the measure. Moreover, the order can only be given where it is necessary in light of one of the listed grounds, such as the prevention or detection of crime. Yet some of these grounds are worded particularly broadly and thus offer little protection. For example, 'preventing or detecting crime' is not restricted to very serious offences, nor can it be said that 'the interests of the economic well-being of the United Kingdom' is a narrow ground. Therefore, there is a risk that the disclosure orders are used for less serious offences.[1165] More protection is offered by the required proportionality between the issuing of the order and its aims, and by the requirement that it may not reasonably be practicable to access the information in another way.[1166] Some important safeguards are nevertheless missing: there is no specific protection for suspects in order not to receive a disclosure order as it is

[1162] S 53 RIPA.
[1163] Chatterjee (n 1148) 271.
[1164] For example, a terrorism suspect may not be willing to hand over the encrypted information or the key if this may be used against him for terrorism charges. See Chatterjee (n 1148) 282.
[1165] Chatterjee (n 1148) 277.
[1166] The meaning of reasonable is particularly relevant: in certain cases, encryption can indeed be cracked, but this may be costly. Yet, one may wonder whether the fact that such 'cracking' is costly suffices to say that it is not reasonably practicable to otherwise get the information.

not limited to witnesses or third parties, and there is no exclusion of the disclosed evidence from punitive proceedings against the person making the disclosure. The availability of that second safeguard has influenced the ECtHR's finding that the privilege was not violated. Moreover, the disclosure order is not limited to the password, but also covers the encrypted information. In this sense, the order has a broad scope, regardless of the requirement of section 49(4)b RIPA to describe the information to which the notice relates. As the ECtHR has stressed several times, the seriousness of a certain type of crime cannot justify restrictions that affect the privilege's essence. Thus, arguing that the person to whom a disclosure order has been given is involved with serious offences does not as such justify a possibly broad disclosure order. The consideration of the final *Jalloh* criterion, the use to which the compelled evidence is put, will depend on the importance of the protected information to the prosecution's case, and is thus case specific; it will also depend on the extent to which one does or does not connect the data to the password. The weight of this criterion depends on the other evidence available: if there is a compelling set of evidence that supports the guilt of the person that is required to hand over the password, the chance that the PSI is violated is reduced.[1167]

Sections 49–56 RIPA have passed judicial scrutiny. *R v S*[1168] addressed these provisions in light of the PSI.[1169] Charges had already been brought under the Terrorism Act 2000 when the disclosure orders were given.[1170] The CoA strongly emphasised the available safeguards, and the fact that the authorities already need to have possession of the protected electronic data was considered important.[1171] It then recalled the non-absolute character of the privilege and the numerous statutory restrictions. The CoA rightly pointed out that before considering restrictions, one should first examine whether the privilege applies as such. It once more relied on the reference in *Saunders* to 'material … which has an existence independent of the will of the suspect' to hold that the protected data, as well as the key that protected it, exist independently of the suspect's will.[1172] Whereas this is not surprising in relation to the protected information, it raises challenges in relation to the key itself. If the key has not been put on paper or on any other medium, and thus can only be found in the suspect's mind, the notion of 'existence independent of the will' is tested. The CoA equated the key to a classic key to a drawer.[1173] This analogy is flawed:[1174] whereas a physical key to a drawer really does exist independently of the suspect's will, a password that has not been put on paper or on another medium is indistinguishable from the suspect's mind.[1175] The fact that a

[1167] *Jalloh* (n 32) para 121; *Bykov* (n 395) para 103; *Zaichenko* (n 478) para 59.
[1168] n 1015.
[1169] On the case, see S Mason, 'Electronic Evidence: Dealing with Encrypted Data and Understanding Software, Logic and Proof' [2014] *ERA Forum* 25, 28–30.
[1170] *R v S* (n 1019) 1492.
[1171] ibid 1493–94.
[1172] Similarly, see *Greater Manchester Police v Andrews* [2011] EWHC 1966 (Admin).
[1173] *R v S* (n 1019) 1496.
[1174] Chatterjee (n 1148) 281.
[1175] ibid 281.

key exists in the sense that it has been created[1176] does not, in my view, alter this finding. The use of one's mind is still required in the production process. Regardless of the key's status (dependent or independent of the will), the ECtHR's case law has shown that real evidence, such as documents, too can be protected. In *Jalloh*, the Court accepted that swallowed drugs can also be covered. The CoA did accept that the mere knowledge of the key as such can be incriminating,[1177] eg where child sexual abuse material is found on a protected hard disk.[1178] Relying strongly on the safeguards put in place by RIPA and the judge's power to exclude evidence on the basis of section 78 PACE, the CoA concluded that there was sufficient protection against improper compulsion. The powers under that section, the statutory safeguards under RIPA and the proportionality requirement satisfied the Court.

Like E&W, the Belgian legislator and courts have struggled with the interrelation between the PSI and the compelled providing of a key or access to protected electronic evidence.[1179] The ConsC and the CoC both handed down rulings on the issue in 2020.[1180] The legislator has attempted to anticipate the risk of compelled self-incrimination: Article 88*quater* CCP[1181] distinguishes two types of obligations: an investigative judge can order anyone[1182] whom he presumes to have specific knowledge of the IT system which is the object of a search, its extension or the services used to secure or encrypt the data stored on it to provide information on the functioning of the system, as well as on the way to access it and to gain access in an understandable way to the data (Article 88*quater*(1) CCP). This includes the disclosure of the password to the IT system.[1183] Secondly, the investigative judge or a delegated individual can order any suitable person to operate the IT system, to search for relevant data, to render them (in)accessible, to copy them or to remove them. This second, broader obligation cannot be imposed on the suspect or on most of his family members. The preparatory works justify this distinction by arguing that the second obligation would not be compatible with the privilege, whereas the first one is ECHR compatible.[1184] Similarly to E&W, the competence

[1176] For example, when one sets up a smartphone, one typically needs to create a password (or use fingerprints or facial recognition to unlock the smartphone). Once set, it does as such exist, even if it is not written down.

[1177] *R v S* (n 1019) 1497 and 1498.

[1178] The Court found that if the data was neutral or innocent, knowledge of the key to access it would also be neutral or innocent.

[1179] On this issue, see C Conings, 'De medewerkingsplicht van houders van kennis (Art 88quater en 90quater, §4 Sv)' in J Kerkhofs and P Van Linthout, *Cybercrime 3.0* (Politeia, 2019) 542–43, 561–66.

[1180] On these rulings, see F Koning, 'Droit au silence et à ne pas s'incriminer: quo vadis?' [2020] *Journal des Tribunaux* 204; Meese, 'Recht om te zwijgen' (n 437); Royer and Yperman (n 436); De Keersmaecker and Verbeke (n 1142).

[1181] The preparatory works show concerns about the fast-developing technologies, the lack of expertise within government services and the lack of experts. Therefore, it was considered crucial to be able to force people with a specific expertise to help the authorities.

[1182] This includes corporations: De Keersmaecker and Verbeke (n 1142) 204.

[1183] See the preparatory works to the Act that introduced Art 88*quater* CCP: MvT *ParlSt* Kamer 1999–2000, 500213/001, 27; Van de Heyning and Coppens (n 1025) 261. On Art 88*quater* CCP, see Conings, 'Statusupdate' (n 1022) 288–304.

[1184] MvT *ParlSt* Kamer 1999–2000 (n 1183) 27–28. The preparatory works refer to *Saunders* (n 393) on this point. The ConsC has meanwhile annulled another provision of the CCP (Art 464/24, paras 2 and 3)

to compel one to provide access to a protected system has been reserved to a judge. This constitutes a relevant safeguard. Similarly, it should be shown that the person to whom one wants to give an order to cooperate has specific knowledge of the IT system or the encryption software. Discharging that burden of proof raises interesting questions in a corporate setting: a computer whose locked screen refers to the name of its primary user suggests that that individual will know the password to access the computer. Identifying possible other individuals who know how to gain access may be less simple: law enforcement will not necessarily know in advance which individuals within the IT service have access to tools to, for instance, reset the password on that computer, which creates the risk that the order would have to be addressed to the corporation as such. Even more challenges arise when law enforcement seeks access to data stored on the corporation's network. Not all employees or officers will necessarily have access to the whole network.

Whether the distinction made between different categories of persons in Article 88*quater* CCP ensures an ECtHR[1185] and CJEU proof solution is uncertain. The CJEU can indeed be called upon to provide its view as, for instance, the POI Directive is of direct relevance for the compelled providing of an electronic key. Non-compliance with an order pursuant to Article 88*quater*(1) CCP can be sanctioned by a prison sentence of up to three or even five years, and/or a fine of up to €20,000 or even €50,000.[1186] Like the applicable sanction in E&W, this amounts to a sufficiently heavy sanction to qualify as compulsion.[1187] Secondly, for the privilege to apply, the compulsion should be aimed at obtaining evidence directly or indirectly[1188] incriminating to the compelled person.[1189] One can wonder in this context whether the obligation to provide the password should be addressed in light of the case law on real evidence, the case law on testimony or both.[1190] That discussion has also arisen in E&W. Conings rightly analysed this issue from the perspective of both categories:[1191] the evidence that can potentially be found on the IT system is real evidence, whereas telling the authorities the key to access the system falls into the second category, regardless of the status of the key (real evidence or not). One can argue that by handing over the password, one gives away not merely the password, but also the evidence it protects.[1192] If one

that imposed a duty to operate the IT system under threat of penalty, insofar as it compelled persons whom can be considered to be suspected of an offence other than the one they have already been convinced of: ConsC 17 December 2015, 178/2015, B.53.

1185 Also on this issue, see Dewandeleer (n 969) 368–69.

1186 The fine is to be multiplied by eight (fines in Belgium are multiplied to protect them against inflation).

1187 Conings, 'Statusupdate' (n 1022) 299.

1188 *Saunders* shows that evidence that can be used to discredit the suspect's credibility can also be relevant for the privilege and thus not only directly incriminating evidence.

1189 Conings, 'Statusupdate' (n 1022) 292.

1190 According to De Keersmaecker and Verbeke (n 1142) 204, the password does not amount to evidence and should therefore be compellable.

1191 Conings, 'Statusupdate' (n 1022) 299–300.

1192 On this issue also, see BJ Koops et al, *Zoeken in computers naar Nederlands en Belgisch recht* (Wolf Legal Publishers, 2016) 91.

accepts this close nexus between the password and the protected data, one can argue that the cooperation duty seeks to compel the production of evidence.[1193] Other authors have challenged this view by arguing that the authorities have to find the IT system themselves and, even when the password has been handed over, are required to search the data themselves.[1194] The CoC meanwhile accepted that a judge can issue an order to provide passwords to a suspect.[1195] The Court considered the fact that the IT system has to be located by the authorities without compulsion in its ruling, as well as the fact that the prosecuting authority had to show that there was no reasonable doubt as to the person's knowledge of the password and that the requested information was proportionate in light of the investigation into the facts. It considered that the PSI in the first place serves to safeguard the right to a fair trial by excluding incorrect statements obtained under compulsion. In fact, the justifications of the PSI go far beyond protection against unreliable compelled evidence.[1196] It even referred, unconvincingly,[1197] to the anti-abuse clause of the ECHR, enshrined in Article 17 ECHR.[1198] It considered, like the ConsC, that the password existed independently of the person's will,[1199] and also that there was no risk of unreliable evidence.[1200] In light of the existence of kill codes and technical possibilities to display different information depending on which code is entered, a real risk of unreliable evidence does, in my view, exist.[1201] I also think that cutting the nexus between the password and the data it protects is somewhat artificial.[1202] What the authorities are looking for is the data on the IT system, rather than the password.[1203] Admittedly, as the E&W CoA has held, knowledge of the password itself too can have an incriminating value. If one analyses the cooperation duty as an obligation to provide oral testimony, I believe that

[1193] Van de Heyning, 'Het zwijgrecht in digitale tijden' (n 435) 314.

[1194] Conings, 'Statusupdate' (n 1022) 299 points out that the data can be well hidden on the IT system, eg through the use of hidden maps or misleading files names.

[1195] CoC 10 July 1916 (n 427).

[1196] See ch 4; Meese, 'Recht om te zwijgen' (n 437) 1322; Van de Heyning, 'Het zwijgrecht in digitale tijden' (n 435) 317.

[1197] *Lawless v Ireland* App no 332/57 (ECtHR, 1 July 1961) para 75.

[1198] Koning, 'Droit au silence' (n 1180) 205; Meese, 'Recht om te zwijgen' (n 437) 1322.

[1199] ConsC 20 February 2020 (n 396) B.3.1 and B.6.2; Conings, 'De medewerkingsplicht (n 1179) 547.

[1200] Similarly, see CoA Ghent 7 June 2019, C/621/2019, not published, 14; Conings, 'De medewerkingsplicht (n 1179) 551.

[1201] De Keersmaecker and Verbeke (n 1142) 207; Royer and Yperman (n 436) 444. The former authors suggest that a person who provides the kill code would have complied with the judicial order. In contrast, see Conings, 'De medewerkingsplicht (n 1179) 567; Conings and De Keersmaecker (n 430) 173.

[1202] Similarly, see Royer and Yperman (n 436) 444. In contrast, see Conings and De Keersmaecker (n 430) 173.

[1203] How should *Funke* be applied to this type of case? Some authors have read *Funke* as precluding fishing expeditions in the context of documentary evidence. Considering that the authorities often do not know what data is stored on the IT system, one may wonder whether compelled cooperation does not amount to helping the authorities with a fishing expedition. Does it suffice for the authorities to have located the IT system to refute this criticism? Finding an encrypted IT system does not necessarily show that there will be incriminating data on the system. Similarly, see FiC Dendermonde (n 549) 258; Van de Heyning, 'Het zwijgrecht in digitale tijden' (n 435) 316.

it can qualify as an incriminating statement: even if the key to the IT system is itself not incriminating (it is merely a list of numbers, signs or letters),[1204] it has the potential to be indirectly incriminating: it shows that the person who provided the key has been able to access the incriminating data that can be found on the IT system.[1205] Thus, drawing a parallel with cases such as *O'Halloran*, where the ECtHR found no violation, in light of the limited nature of the disclosure and the fact that the person was required to state a simple fact, cannot be accepted: stating the key to an IT system needs to be considered together with the data to which it gives access.[1206] The CoC did not draw links between the 'neutral' password and the incriminating data. Equating the password, which is in most cases only known to the person who set it,[1207] to DNA samples[1208] or documents obtained pursuant to a (search) warrant is not convincing.[1209] An individual is actively required to use the contents of his mind to provide the password.[1210] One author considers that one can invoke his statutory entitlement to stay silent during interviews, enshrined in Article 47*bis* CCP, when he is prosecuted for failure to provide his password.[1211] He considers that the aforementioned article can be qualified as a cause of justification, enshrined in Article 70 CC.[1212]

Yet, (public) compulsion and self-incriminating evidence can merely give an indication that the obligation stipulated by Article 88*quater* CCP can be at odds with the privilege. As the ECtHR has shown, where the essence of the privilege is not infringed,[1213] such a compulsory practice may pass its *Jalloh* test.[1214] In light of the heavy sanction one faces,[1215] it is clear that the nature and degree of

[1204] Conings, 'Statusupdate' (n 1022) 300.

[1205] eg stolen information on bank accounts. In the same sense, see Conings, 'Statusupdate' (n 1022) 300; Van de Heyning, 'Het zwijgrecht in digitale tijden' (n 435) 314.

[1206] See *O'Halloran* (n 483). More restrictively, see Conings, 'Statusupdate' (n 1022) 301.

[1207] Conings, 'De medewerkingsplicht (n 1179) 542. ISPs are typically not aware of the encryption used in case of end-to-end encryption: Conings and De Keersmaecker (n 430) 164. On encryption as a best practice, see Van de Heyning, 'Het zwijgrecht in digitale tijden' (n 435) 307. On encryption workarounds, see OS Kerr and B Schneider, 'Encryption Workarounds' (2018) 106 *Georgetown Law Journal* 989.

[1208] CoA Ghent 7 June 2019 (n 1200) 15.

[1209] Koning, 'Droit au silence' (n 1180) 205; Meese, 'Recht om te zwijgen' (n 437) 1322.

[1210] CoA Ghent 14 May 2019, C/520/2019, not published, 14; Royer and Yperman (n 436) 444; Van de Heyning, 'Het zwijgrecht in digitale tijden' (n 435) 315. Very few elements would amount to will-dependent elements if one accepts the CoC's and the ConsC's reasoning. Similarly, see Royer and Yperman (n 436) 443. In contrast, see Conings and De Keersmaecker (n 430) 172.

[1211] Conings considers that requiring cooperation under Art 88*quater* CCP does not qualify as an interview and therefore considers Art 47*bis* CCP not to be applicable: Conings, 'De medewerkingsplicht (n 1179) 537.

[1212] Except for offences provided for in Book II, Title I*bis*, there is no crime when the act is prescribed by law and ordered by the government. 'And' should be read as 'or': Koning, 'Droit au silence' (n 1180) 204.

[1213] Van de Heyning, 'Het zwijgrecht in digitale tijden' (n 435) 310.

[1214] Both the CoC and the ConsC explicitly referred to these criteria.

[1215] De Keersmaecker and Verbeke (n 1142) 209 refer to unpublished case law in which courts applied Art 65 CC, which, inter alia, provides that if several offences that are the successive and continuous execution of the same criminal intent are submitted simultaneously to the same court, only the most severe penalty is pronounced. Even where some offences are submitted to the court at a later time,

compulsion are serious. As to the applicable safeguards, it is relevant that the cooperation order is given by the investigative judge or people mandated by him and the requirement of proof of a specific knowledge of the IT system or the services to secure or encrypt the data provides some protection.[1216] As to the use to which the compelled evidence is put, reference can be made to the analysis in relation to RIPA. Lastly, as for the weight of the public interest in the investigation and punishment of the offence at issue, the ECtHR has ruled that neither the public interest, nor the complexity of certain types of crime, eg corporate crime or the specific characteristics of some fields of law, can be accepted as justification for provisions that extinguish the PSI's essence.[1217] The CoC considered the wide availability of encryption applications as an (almost) insurmountable obstacle, which renders the communication of the password essential.[1218] It remains to be seen whether the ECtHR and the CJEU will be willing to accept that in light of the rapid development of encryption software and its use by criminals of all sorts, including terrorists, people can be compelled to hand over their password under threat of penalties. Conings rightly stresses that if an obligation to hand over the password would be incompatible with the privilege, recourse will probably be taken to more far-reaching measures to get access to the data.[1219] One could consider the use of (limited) adverse inferences as an alternative to the hefty penalties that currently apply.[1220]

US courts have repeatedly applied the aforementioned act of production doctrine in cases involving the compelled production of an electronic key. Such compelled cooperation is usually sought through the use of more general subpoena powers,[1221] rather than through specific legal provisions, such as the ones in use in E&W and Belgium. The Third Circuit CoA found that the Fifth Amendment was not violated.[1222] It accepted the reasoning of the lower court that had ruled that any testimonial element of the production of decrypted devices amounted to a foregone conclusion.[1223] The 11th Circuit CoA, similarly to the CoA in E&W, accepted that

the court should take the previously imposed sentence into account at sentencing. CoA Ghent has also applied Art 65 CC in such a case: CoA Ghent 7 June 2019 (n 1200). See also Royer and Yperman (n 436) 445.

[1216] The authorities should credibly show the person's knowledge of the password before ordering him to give the password: Conings, 'Statusupdate' (n 1022) 301; Koops et al (n 1192) 94.

[1217] In this context, see *Jalloh* (n 32) para 97; *Marttinen* (n 385) para 75.

[1218] Similarly, see De Keersmaecker and Verbeke (n 1142) 203. The ConsC too paid attention to technological developments: ConsC 20 February 2020 (n 396) B.4.

[1219] More restrictively, see Conings, 'Statusupdate' (n 1022) 302. One could imagine, for example, the use of immunity for another person who provides access: Koops et al (n 1192) 96. Brutal forcing is not considered as a viable option by a number of authors, eg De Keersmaecker and Verbeke (n 1142) 202.

[1220] On that issue, see Van de Heyning, 'Het zwijgrecht in digitale tijden' (n 435) 310.

[1221] 28 USCA §1651.

[1222] On the interpretation by state courts and the role of state constitutions, see DR Rangaviz, 'Compelled Decryption & State Constitutional Protection' (2020) 57 *American Criminal Law Review* 157.

[1223] *United States v Apple MacPro Computer* 851 F3d 238, 248 (3rd Cir 2017). The authorities found evidence related to child pornography on some of the suspect's devices and had a witness confirm that she had seen child pornography on one of the devices. See also *United States v Gavegnano* 305 FedAppx 954 (4th Cir 2009); *United States v Spencer* 2018 WL 1964588 (ND Cal, 2018). Sacharoff suggests that courts should only order decryption of files whose possession is already known by the

the files on an encrypted device as such are not testimonial.[1224] It also confirmed that the physical key to a lock does not amount to a testimonial communication, as it does not compel a person to make use of the contents of his mind.[1225] Unlike the use of a physical key, decrypting and handing over a drive would be testimonial in the Court's view.[1226] Moreover, the lack of sufficient knowledge on the side of the authorities of the existence of any file on the protected drive and of the suspect's ability to access the encrypted part of the drive led to the conclusion that this was not a foregone conclusion case.[1227] Thus, whereas the E&W system focuses, like its US counterparts, on the fact the protected data exists independently of the will of the person, it too provides some limited protection as it accepts that knowledge of the key can have some incriminating value.

When a corporation is faced with an order to provide access to its IT systems, the tension between the PSI and compelled production of electronic keys is similarly crucial. Amongst the three national systems, only that of E&W has foreseen a specific set of rules as to whom should provide the electronic key.

authorities, provided that they can be described with reasonable particularity: Sacharoff (n 1056) 208. Kerr argues that the PSI does not preclude compelled decryption, provided the authorities have independent evidence that the suspect knows the password: Kerr (n 1141) 769–70. Kerr rightly points out that the issue becomes even more complex when hidden volumes are used: ibid 784.

[1224] *In Re Grand Jury Subpoena Duces Tecum* 670 F3d 1335, 1342 (11th Cir 2012).

[1225] ibid 1345.

[1226] It would not merely be a physical act, but instead would require the use of one's mind. Kerr accepts that entering one's password to unlock a device amounts to testimony: Kerr (n 1141) 779. In *In Matter of Search of a Residence in Aptos, California* 2018 WL 1400401 (ND Cal 2018), the district court concluded that the individual's knowledge of the encryption passwords amounted to a foregone conclusion in this specific case and it compelled him to decrypt. In other cases, district courts (*In the matter of the Search of (redacted) Washington District of Columbia* 317 FSupp3d 523 (D DC 2018) and *In Re Search Warrant No 5165* 470 FSupp3d 715 (ED Ky 2020)) decided that providing biometric features to access devices was not testimonial and distinguished them from providing a password. Other district courts (*US v Wright* 431 FSupp3d 1175 (D Nev 2020) concluded that unlocking a smartphone with one's face was testimonial. See also *In the matter of the Search of a residence in Oakland California* 354 FSupp3d 1010 (ND Cal 2019). That court, moreover, concluded that the foregone conclusion was not applicable as the government inherently lacked the requisite prior knowledge of the information available on the device.

[1227] *In Re Grand Jury Subpoena Duces Tecum* (n 1224) 1346, 1348 and 1351. This case is relevant as the court made it clear that use and derivative use immunity needs to be provided to overcome the Fifth Amendment claim.

8

The Applicability of the Privilege against Self-Incrimination *Ratione Temporis*

This book focuses on the privilege in punitive cases, as defined by the *Engel* criteria. Its scope is not limited to *sensu stricto* criminal cases. In order to understand the effectiveness of the PSI's protection, it is essential to determine as of what stage of (non)-punitive proceedings a person can invoke it. The very early availability of the privilege, which is before one even faces a punitive case, can impact on other public and private interests. If the privilege is available in such cases, other parties may face restrictions in terms of accessing evidence, eg where they allege IP infringements or bring a civil case for damages in relation to fraud. At the same time, if in non-punitive cases evidence can be gathered under compulsion, this can harm one's ability to set up an effective defence in a punitive case if that evidence is admissible in a punitive case.

The ECtHR has labelled a broad range of cases as punitive, and as it easily considers someone to be charged in such a case, the PSI can at times be applicable at a very early stage of an investigation.[1228] In relation to non-punitive cases, two scenarios often come up: information obtained in non-punitive cases, under threat of sanctions, is later admitted in a punitive case;[1229] or a person is already implicated in a punitive case, or such a case is anticipated, while a non-punitive case is similarly pending.[1230]

As to the first scenario, the ECtHR has confirmed that the privilege does not as such preclude the use of compulsory powers to obtain information outside punitive proceedings.[1231] The landmark case on this issue is *Saunders*.[1232] The Court found that the privilege was infringed by the use at the *sensu stricto* criminal trial stage of statements previously obtained by DTI inspectors in a non-punitive investigation.[1233]

[1228] The ECtHR stresses the importance of rights that are practical and effective: *Chambaz* (n 491) para 41; Zeeman (n 80) 424–25. See also ch 5 on this topic.

[1229] eg *Saunders* (n 393).

[1230] eg *JB* (n 491); *Marttinen* (n 385). The Court has accepted an early applicability of the PSI in cases where documents were sought: *JB* (n 491) para 66 and *Chambaz* (n 491) para 54.

[1231] *Savic* (n 410) para 22; *Weh* (n 484) para 45.

[1232] *Saunders* (n 393).

[1233] ibid paras 67–76; Wissink (n 501) 93.

The statements had been given under compulsion as Mr Saunders faced up to two years' imprisonment should he have failed to cooperate.[1234] *Saunders* provides a good example of the modern equivalent of the historical threat to self-preservation encountered in chapter two: failure to give evidence to the inspectors could result in a punitive charge, whilst providing the evidence could lead to self-incrimination and providing false information would also be punishable. The Court stressed that the purpose of the investigation by those inspectors, an investigation which did not come within the scope of Article 6(1) ECHR,[1235] was to check facts which could later pave the way for action by regulatory, disciplinary or legislative authorities, or by the prosecution service.[1236] The Court confined its analysis to the use of the statements in the *sensu stricto* criminal case.[1237] Part of the interviews' transcripts were read out at trial and they played a significant role in the case against Saunders. This infringed the PSI. Therefore, where someone cannot claim the privilege's protection because he cannot yet indicate a sufficiently concrete risk of self-incrimination, *Saunders* can still be helpful in having evidence excluded at a later stage.[1238] Some years after *Saunders*, the Court reconfirmed its ruling in *Kansal*, a case involving the official receiver.[1239]

That case law found support in the CJEU's case law on inapplicability of the privilege in purely civil proceedings between two companies.[1240] The Court has confirmed that national courts are not required to apply the general principle of EU law established in *Orkem*,[1241] as these civil proceedings could not (in)directly lead to a penalty handed down by a public authority. It ruled that where such information would be passed on, for example, to the EC or to a national authority to take action, it would be inadmissible[1242] and could not form the basis for opening an investigation.[1243] In relation to investigations by EU competition authorities, the CJEU has recognised that the privilege can be invoked at the investigation stage.[1244]

[1234] *Saunders* (n 393) para 70. Such compulsion is not present where someone, in the course of the assessment of his status as a refugee, admits a criminal offence while he is supposed to substantiate his claim of needing refugee status: *H and J v The Netherlands* App nos 978/09 and 992/09 (ECtHR, 13 November 2014) para 75.

[1235] *Saunders* (n 393) para 67.

[1236] At the same time the Court recognised that an administrative investigation can involve the determining of a 'criminal charge'.

[1237] *Saunders* (n 393); Ashworth (n 395) 756.

[1238] Stessens, 'The Obligation to Produce Documents' (n 943) 58–59.

[1239] *Kansal v United Kingdom* App no 21413/02 (ECtHR, 27 April 2004). With respect to DTI inspectors, it had already done so: *IJL, GMR and AKP v United Kingdom* App nos 29522/95, 30056/96 and 30574/96 (ECtHR, 9 September 2000).

[1240] K Jörgens and L Ortiz Blanco, 'Opening of the File' in Ortiz Blanco (n 16) 315. One company was a customer of the other company.

[1241] Case C-60/92 *Otto BV v Postbank NV* ECLI:EU:C:1993:876, para 16.

[1242] ibid para 20. The Court refers to *Orkem* to come to this conclusion.

[1243] CA Jones, 'Into the Parallel Universe: Procedural Fairness in Private Litigation after the Damages Directive' in P Nihoul and T Skoczny (eds), *Procedural Fairness in Competition Proceedings* (Edward Elgar, 2015) 225.

[1244] *Orkem* (n 439) para 34.

In *DB v Consob*, the CJEU accepted that an individual can invoke the privilege in an investigation[1245] into insider dealing that can lead to penalties of a punitive nature. It added that the need to respect the privilege in an investigation by a supervisory authority which cannot lead to a penalty that is punitive in nature could also stem from the possibility that evidence is later used in punitive[1246] proceedings against that person.

The ECtHR has repeatedly addressed the second scenario, parallel proceedings.[1247] In *Marttinen*, it held that the privilege in such a setting can also be invoked in the non-punitive case. The issue is that the suspect fears that by providing the required information in the non-punitive case, he will harm his defence in the punitive one. This risk can be resolved by providing a limited use rule so that information provided under compulsion in a non-punitive investigation cannot be used in the punitive case itself.[1248] Such a rule is criticised as it leads to the worst outcome: one has evidence but cannot use it for the purpose of the punitive case.[1249]

In punitive cases[1250] where someone is 'charged' as interpreted by the ECtHR, he can rely on the privilege.[1251] This is also the case where a person who is in reality a suspect is interrogated as a witness, regardless of his status under national law.[1252] There is no need to be in the formal setting of a police station in order for it to be applicable.[1253] It is, however, of critical importance[1254] that the police or other interviewers inform the suspect of his privilege[1255] as soon as he can be considered to be 'charged'. Failure to do so may result in an untimely notification of the privilege – which can be problematic.[1256] Similarly, the Court has often stressed the importance of early access to a lawyer in order to ensure an effective privilege, as well as to protect the suspect from ill-treatment.[1257] The Court has paid considerable attention to the particular vulnerability of a suspect at the early stages of a case.[1258] Not only is he exposed to a stressful situation, he is

[1245] The investigation was carried out by a supervisory authority and not by a prosecutor or judge.
[1246] The Court referred to criminal proceedings.
[1247] eg *JB* (n 491); *Marttinen* (n 385).
[1248] *Van Weerelt* (n 669) paras 60–62.
[1249] Sedley (n 362) 120.
[1250] Only to the extent that these punitive proceedings are labelled as criminal in the sense of the POI Directive can one rely on the Directive too.
[1251] On the privilege and the early stages of a case, see Roberts and Zuckerman (n 273) 542–43.
[1252] *Brusco* (n 486) para 50.
[1253] eg *Zaichenko* (n 478).
[1254] Arts 3 and 4 of Directive 2012/13/EU on the right to information in criminal proceedings, as well as recitals 31–32 of the POI Directive.
[1255] *Navone and others v Monaco* App nos 62880/11, 62892/11 and 62899/11 (ECtHR, 24 October 2013) para 74. This notification should be done clearly to avoid confusion: *Grinenko v Ukraine* App no 33627/06 (ECtHR, 15 November 2012) para 96.
[1256] *Zaichenko* (n 478) paras 53 and 59; *Kaçiu and Kotorri v Albania* App nos 33192/07 and 33194/07 (ECtHR, 25 June 2013) para 119; *Schmid-Laffer* (n 479) para 31.
[1257] *Leonid Lazarenko v Ukraine* App no 22313/04 (ECtHR, 28 October 2010) para 50. Regardless of their complementarity, the Court has stressed that these are two separate rights: *Navone* (n 1255) para 74.
[1258] *Stojkovic* (n 622) para 53.

moreover confronted with ever more complex legislation.[1259] Therefore, the Court has ruled that, in principle, a suspect should have access to a lawyer[1260] as of the first interrogation,[1261] except where the specific circumstances of a case give rise to a compelling reason to restrict access. Where the right to access to a lawyer is structurally precluded,[1262] Article 6 ECHR can at times even be violated where the suspect remained silent.[1263] The Court has stressed the importance of initial confessions for the further development of a case, regardless of the availability of other evidence.[1264]

The privilege is, unsurprisingly, also applicable at the trial stage of a punitive case.[1265] Nevertheless, a question that often arises in this case is whether exercising the privilege at this stage should be free of 'costs': can the choice to remain silent result in adverse inferences?[1266]

In E&W, the privilege is applicable at both the pre-trial and trial stages,[1267] and also in non-punitive proceedings.[1268] Should the defendant decide to testify at his *sensu stricto* criminal trial, he is precluded from hiding behind his privilege in relation to questions that would incriminate him as to offences with which he is charged in the proceedings,[1269] as his decision to testify exposes him to cross-examination.[1270] Section 14(1) CEA provides that a person can, in any legal proceedings other than criminal proceedings,[1271] refuse to answer questions or provide documents or things if this would expose him to proceedings for an offence or the recovery of a penalty.[1272] This privilege is confined to offences and penalties under E&W law,[1273] but in legal proceedings other than

[1259] *AT v Luxembourg* App no 30460/13 (ECtHR, 9 April 2015) para 64. In order to assist the suspect with the issue of adverse inferences from silence, a lawyer can be helpful: *Murray* (n 380) para 66.

[1260] In principle, a lawyer of his choice: *Pavlenko* (n 387). Where the police prevent the lawyer of choice from having access to his client and where a confession is made in the presence of another lawyer, Art 6 can be violated: *Dvorski v Croatia* App no 25703/11 (ECtHR, 20 December 2015) para 111.

[1261] *AT* (n 1259) para 63; *Simeonovi* (n 388) para 109.

[1262] eg *Borg v Malta* App no 37537/13 (ECtHR, 12 January 2016) paras 59–63.

[1263] *Dayanan v Turkey* App no 7377/03 (ECtHR, 13 October 2009) para 33; *Simeonovi* (n 388) para 110. Yet see ibid paras 114–16.

[1264] *Chopenko v Ukraine* App no 17735/06 (ECtHR, 15 January 2015) para 52.

[1265] *Murray* (n 380) paras 47–51.

[1266] See ch 6, s III.

[1267] Dennis, *The Law of Evidence* (n 25) 155; Keane and McKeown (n 535) 714; Matthews and Malek (n 535) 396. See also s 7(7) of the Civil Procedure Act 1997.

[1268] Macgregor et al (n 535) 325. Yet, on extrajudicial proceedings, see 150–152 below; Keane and McKeown (n 535) 720–21.

[1269] Keane and McKeown (n 535) 714. Witnesses, including the defendant, cannot be required to answer questions that would expose them to the possibility of a future prosecution: Hannibal and Mountford (n 1015) 390.

[1270] S 1(2) Criminal Evidence Act 1898 and s 72 Criminal Justice Act 1982; Allen et al, *Practical Guide to Evidence* (n 541) 84.

[1271] The privilege in criminal proceedings was originally mainly regulated by common law and has been influenced by statutes.

[1272] Which codifies common law: *Rio Tinto* (n 991) 636 and 637.

[1273] Zuckerman (n 353) 395.

sensu stricto criminal ones[1274] it is not limited to self-incrimination as it equally covers situations where one would incriminate one's spouse or civil partner.[1275] Several statutory restrictions have, however, been introduced. Many of these should be considered in light of the argument that limited use provisions can be used, on the one hand, to protect the interests of the person who would be required to self-incriminate, while at the same time, other parties would still have access to evidence.[1276] Such an approach does indeed remedy the ECtHR's criticism in *Saunders*.

The CoA's ruling in *R v Kearns* reflects the relevance of such a limited use provision in non-punitive bankruptcy proceedings. The Court held that Article 6 ECHR is concerned with the fairness of a trial where an adjudication takes place, and thus not with extrajudicial investigations as such.[1277] It stressed the possibility of restricting the privilege where there is an identifiable social or economic problem that can be addressed by the restriction, to the extent that the measure is proportionate to that problem.[1278] The Court reaffirmed that the privilege does not protect against the compelled production of pre-existing documents. It then stressed that where information is sought for an extrajudicial inquiry or for an administrative purpose, the chance that the privilege will be infringed is small. Yet, the privilege could in its view be infringed where such information is later used at trial.[1279] Criteria to be used in that context are, according to the CoA, whether it is an admission of guilt that is sought or only factual information, and whether the request for information and its use at trial are proportionate to the particular social or economic problem.[1280] It concluded, having taken into account the fact that no punitive charge was pending when the information was requested and that the information could not be used in a punitive case, that the privilege had not been infringed.

Compulsory questioning powers that criminalise failure to comply have also been introduced in relation to certain investigations in which the prosecution of crime and thus a punitive aim are at stake. The prime example of this approach is section 2 CJA. It authorises the SFO's Director to require a person to provide oral

[1274] Yet, see Glover (n 536) 531.

[1275] Keane and McKeown (n 535) 717. This is broader than the common law privilege: *Rio Tinto* (n 991) 637–38.

[1276] Dennis, *The Law of Evidence* (n 25) 157. See, eg s 31 of the Theft Act 1968 or s 13 of the Fraud Act 2006.

[1277] *Kearns* (n 985) 2829. This reasoning does find some support in *Saunders* (n 393) para 67. At the same time, the Court has found violations of the privilege where no judicial proceedings were brought, eg in *Funke*. The ECtHR is also attentive to the early stages of a case, as is demonstrated by *Ibrahim* (n 378) para 253.

[1278] *Kearns* (n 985) 2830.

[1279] ibid 2830.

[1280] In the CoA's view, bankruptcy can be considered as such as problem: ibid 2830. The ECtHR has, eg in *Jalloh*, listed the public interest as a criterion to be taken into account when considering restrictions of the privilege. It has repeatedly refused to accept restrictions of the privilege by accepting such a societal problem as a justification: *Marttinen* (n 385).

answers, as well as documentary evidence, when dealing with serious or complex fraud.[1281] A notice pursuant to section 2(3) cannot be issued against a foreign company without a UK presence[1282] to produce documents held in the USA.[1283] Failure to comply with such an order constitutes an offence under section 2(13) CJA.[1284] In order to balance the different interests, section 2(8) CJA limits[1285] the use of such compelled evidence to cases where it turns out to be untrue and one is charged in accordance with section 2(14) CJA and is an inconsistent statement in the prosecution for other offences if contradictory evidence is supplied by the defendant.[1286] Yet, this limited use rule only applies to oral statements and not to self-incriminating documents handed over pursuant to such an order.[1287] The CJA does not expressly provide what is to happen to evidence derived from the compelled statements.[1288] The main protection that seems available in relation to such derived evidence is the possibility of excluding it under section 78 PACE.[1289]

In relation to investigations by authorities other than classic law enforcement, a limited use rule is lacking at times, as *R v Herts CC Ex p Green Environmental Industries* demonstrates.[1290] A company and its director had been asked to provide factual information on waste that had been found, without providing them with assurances that such information would not be used in punitive proceedings for infringement of the EPA. Failure to respond to this request from the local authorities was criminalised.[1291] The privilege was not held to be applicable as the investigation was considered to be extrajudicial[1292] and the *Saunders* case law did not apply

[1281] S 2(2)–(3) CJA 1987.
[1282] The US company had no registered office or fixed place of business there, nor had it carried out business there.
[1283] *R (KBR Inc) v Director of the SFO* [2021] UKSC 2.
[1284] An individual who was not a suspect was recently convicted for failing to provide all the requested documents: www.sfo.gov.uk/2020/01/30/anna-machkevitch-found-guilty-of-failing-to-comply with-a-section-2-notice/.
[1285] Furthermore, a trial judge could also rely on s 78 PACE: Billing (n 356) 182.
[1286] Billing (n 356) 181. Similarly, see s 65 SOCPA.
[1287] ibid 183.
[1288] For example, a person's statements can lead the authorities to incriminating documents.
[1289] On s 78 PACE, see Billing (n 356) 186–94.
[1290] [2000] 1 All ER 773 HL.
[1291] S 71(3) EPA.
[1292] Pinto and Evans (n 4) 216. The Privy Council has taken a more nuanced stance in *Volaw Trust* (n 615) para 72: 'That is true as a generalisation, but as the Board has explained, a breach of article 6 can also arise in consequence of the punishment of a person for refusing to incriminate himself in the course of extrajudicial inquiries (as in *Funke v France, Heaney and McGuinness v Ireland, JB v Switzerland, Shannon v United Kingdom* and *Chambaz v Switzerland*). It is also necessary to bear in mind that the nature of extrajudicial inquiries can itself prejudice the fairness of trial proceedings for the purposes of article 6. An example given in Ibrahim, at para 253, was where "national laws may attach consequences to the attitude of an accused at the initial stages of police interrogation which are decisive for the prospects of the defence in any subsequent criminal proceedings". The case of *Ex p Green Environmental Industries Ltd* was not, however, concerned with a situation of that kind, or with the situation considered in the *Funke* or *Heaney and McGuinness* line of authorities.' See also Laird (n 1020) 78; Ormerod and Perry (n 540) 2801.

as there was no adjudication.[1293] The UKHL furthermore paid attention to the fact that the local authorities' request was aimed at getting only factual information, rather than an admission of wrongdoing. This decision underlines the difficult distinction between cases where the privilege is applicable and cases where one is not charged (yet) and is under a duty to cooperate. Where the authority involved is merely looking into facts, without having the power to launch a punitive case, the E&W courts seem less willing to hold that the privilege applies.[1294] This ruling was far-reaching, as no provision prohibited the use of that compelled evidence in a future punitive case.[1295] The same approach was taken in the aforementioned *Attorney-General's Reference (No 7 of 2000)* case in relation to documents.[1296] A person had been required to hand over documents in the context of bankruptcy proceedings, which later laid the foundations for his prosecution. The CoA distinguished pre-existing documents and statements made under compulsion, arguing that in the former case no compulsion is used to create self-incriminating evidence, as the documents already exist. Whereas, in relation to the statute at issue in *Attorney-General's Reference*, a limited use provision applied to statements, there was no equivalent protection to documents handed over under compulsion in a non-punitive set of proceedings.

Determining the applicability of the privilege *ratione temporis* is not self-evident in Belgium, particularly where the aim of the proceedings, whether punitive or not, is not clear from the outset.[1297] Furthermore, whereas the CCP does not in general provide for a sanction where a suspect refuses to testify or to hand over self-incriminating documents,[1298] specific legislation often imposes a cooperation duty,[1299] typically not equipped with a statutory limited use rule such as the one I have encountered in my analysis of a number of ECtHR cases and the E&W approach.[1300]

[1293] The CoA also relied on the case in *Kearns* (n 985) 2828.

[1294] Dennis, *The Law of Evidence* (n 25) 164. See also *Kearns* (n 985).

[1295] P Bogan, 'Self-Incrimination, the Privilege, and the Reverse Burden of Proof' in M Colvin and J Cooper (eds), *Human Rights in the Investigation and Prosecution of Crime* (Oxford University Press, 2009) 347, 357.

[1296] Above n 1001.

[1297] On this topic, see Y Liégeois and M Bockstaele, 'Over "toezicht" en "opsporing" door bijzondere inspectiediensten' [2016] *Nullum Crimen* 406, 406–07 and 413. Often civil servants of inspection services can check whether the specific legislation for which they are competent (eg social or environmental law) has been respected, while they can also detect and analyse offences that they have noticed and it may thus be difficult to decide in which capacity they are acting. Once there is a reasonable suspicion of an offence, there is a punitive investigation: ConsC 1 October 2015, 134/2015, B.11.1.

[1298] Michiels and Falque, 'L'infraction d'obstacle' (n 1041) 2.

[1299] The CCP itself includes cooperation duties, which are often relevant for third parties such as financial institutions or (tele)communication operators. Art 88*quater*(1) CCP is considered to apply to suspects.

[1300] C Franssen and T Litannie, *Manuel de procédure fiscale* (Anthemis, 2019) 796; J Spreutels et al, *Droit pénal des affaires*, 2nd edn (Larcier, 2021) 1157–58. Franssen and Litannie, moreover, refer to the obligation of tax officials to report offences to the prosecutor's service. Vanbiervliet and Visschers (n 1047) 51 conclude that due to the absence of such a limited use rule, taxpayers should be able to rely on the PSI.

The CoC considers the privilege to be available once a criminal investigation is pending or anticipated. It considers the PSI to be inapplicable in purely administrative investigations aimed at making material findings to ensure compliance with applicable regulations, while the person who faces such investigation is not accused of an infringement or faces the threat of prosecution.[1301]

These issues have often arisen in the context of income tax, as well as in other fields of Belgian tax law,[1302] where tax payers are often obliged to cooperate.[1303] Striking a balance between the authorities' rights and those of the taxpayers is complex.[1304] Failure to reply to the requests from the tax authorities for information can be sanctioned in different ways, including an administrative fine of €50–1250 for violations of the ITC,[1305] tax increases or, where fraudulent intent or the intent to harm can be shown, *sensu stricto* criminal penalties can be imposed.[1306] At times, the tax authorities have tried to compel persons to provide information by obtaining an order to pay penalty payments.[1307] The starting point of the primary privilege[1308] in the context of Belgian tax cases has been interpreted differently by different authors and by the courts. The starting point depends on when one has the status of a 'charged' person.[1309] One can acquire this status while the case is still under examination by the tax authorities,

[1301] CoC 20 November 2018 (n 1); Byl et al (n 1034) 100 consider this approach to be stricter than the ECtHR's approach in *Chambaz* (n 491).

[1302] Artis 315–17 of the ITC contain broad obligations to produce existing documents (Art 315 ITC) or provide written or oral explanations (Arts 316–17 ITC). The obligation to provide existing documents includes all books and other documents needed for the determination of the taxable income. As for the explanations that can be required, all information can be sought, provided they are being asked to determine the person's tax situation. The information sought under Arts 315 and 316 needs to be linked to the transactions in which the person has participated (Art 317 ITC). On requests for information, see F Eerens, 'De vraag om inlichtingen: vraag maar raak?' [2015] *Tijdschrift voor Fiscaal Recht* 386; C Franssen and E Traversa, 'La demande de renseignements adressée au contribuable à l'impôt sur les revenus et le droit de se taire' [2012] *Revue générale du contentieux fiscal* 3, 3–46. Moreover, as far as belated or incomplete tax declarations or failure to declare tax as such are concerned, the administration can impose tax increases of 10–200% (Art 444 ITC).

[1303] CoA Antwerp 16 June 2015, 2014/AR/312, www.monkey.be, 6/12; M Daube, 'Nouvelles obligations de déclaration fiscale: exigence légitime ou auto-incrimination prohibée?' [2013] *Revue générale du contentieux fiscal* 249, 267; Franssen and Traversa (n 1302) 3–4; S Gnedasj, 'Wat zijn de gevolgen op fiscaal vlak als speurders het zwijgrecht miskennen?' [2014] No 18 *Fiscale Actualiteit*; Spreutels et al (n 1300) 1155; V Vercauteren et al, 'De controle' in A Tiberghien, *Tiberghien. Handboek voor Fiscaal Recht*, 40th edn (Kluwer, 2021) 1082.

[1304] Spreutels et al (n 1300) 1149.

[1305] Art 445 ITC; De Troyer and Vandenberghe (n 1047) 79. The ConsC has confirmed that such fines are punitive within the meaning of Art 6 ECHR: ConsC 14 October 2021, 143/2021, B.3.1.

[1306] Art 449 ITC. Although the case law of the ECtHR is case specific, the potential sanctions seem to be sufficiently high to amount to compulsion.

[1307] De Troyer and Vandenberghe (n 1047) 81; Eerens (n 1302) 402. The Brussels CoA has refused to do so as it questioned its competence to intervene at the administrative phase of the case before taxes had been imposed: CoA Brussels 5 January 2011, [2015] JLMB 1872, 1878–79. Some lower courts have accepted the use of penalty payments, eg, FiC Liège 9 October 2002, [2003] TFR 277. A legislative reform in 2022 has provided for an explicit legal basis, including Art 381 ITC.

[1308] In the sense of being entitled to refuse to reply or to provide documents.

[1309] Maus (n 684) 175–76.

before a *sensu stricto* criminal case is pending.[1310] In light of *Chambaz*,[1311] some authors have argued that the privilege can be invoked once the person who faces an investigation by the tax authorities receives a request for information. Given the broad availability of sanctions under Belgian tax law, the person under investigation could not exclude that he would expose himself to a punitive charge.[1312] Applying the privilege as early as at the start of a tax investigation can make assessing the tax situation more difficult.[1313] Regardless, the very early applicability of the PSI in tax cases has received some support in case law.[1314] Several authors accept that, once a notification is given, the applicable time limits are extended due to indications of tax evasion;[1315] or once a notification of a tax increase of 50 per cent is announced, the privilege becomes applicable; or it becomes applicable once a *sensu stricto* criminal case is pending.[1316] Some lower courts have found the privilege to apply only to tax cases, once the information sought is intended to be used to support a complaint before a *sensu stricto* criminal court.[1317] The Antwerp CoA was similarly restrictive and did not consider that a pending investigation of an investigative judge discharged the person from cooperating with the tax authorities. It held that the obligation to answer questions that merely relate to his tax assessment remains applicable, even if

[1310] T Afschrift, 'Le rôle du fisc dans la procédure pénale' [2006] *Revue générale du contentieux fiscal* 283, 300; Byl et al (n 1034) 97; Delanote, 'Hof van Justitie erkent ruime draagwijdte van het zwijgrecht' (n 1030) 4/5; Franssen and Traversa (n 1302) 34–36. Provided that one is 'charged' within the autonomous ECHR meaning of that term.

[1311] *Chambaz* (n 491) does not imply that the tax authorities can no longer request information, provided that they make no references to sanctions for failure to do so and that no so such sanctions are imposed after a refusal to hand over the evidence: Huybrechts (n 584) 396.

[1312] Daube (n 1303) 269–70; N Muyshondt, 'Zwijgrecht in fiscale zaken: wat zijn wilsafhankelijke gegevens?' [2012] No 1302 *Fiscoloog* 7. Also on this issue, see Maus (n 684) 171. Maus supports the PSI's early applicability, but is more nuanced as to the PSI's extent in this context.

[1313] Some authors consider that when the PSI is applicable, the taxpayer can refuse to produce documents, including documents whose creation and retention is provided by statute: Franssen and Litannie (n 1300) 797; Koning, 'Cour. Eur. D.H., Chambaz' (n 954) 414. In contrast, see De Raedt (n 637) 444–45; De Troyer and Vandenberghe (n 1047) 80; Speecke (n 1025) 98.

[1314] Support for this approach can mainly be found in some case law of the FiC and CoA of Liège: CoA Liège 31 March 2010, [2012] JLMB 1679, 1680 (the same day as the request for information was received, a notification was given that the tax authorities had indications of fraud, and that tax increases were planned); FiC Liège 9 February 2012, [2012] RGCF 465, 466. More recently, the CoA did not accept that the privilege was applicable: CoA Liège 25 March 2016, [2016] RGCF 477. It found that the tax authorities did not clearly have the intention to gather evidence for a criminal complaint, or that it was going to impose a sanction itself, nor did the tax authorities refer to the use of false documents.

[1315] CoA Mons 12 December 2017, 2016/RG/664, www.taxwin.be. Franssen and Litannie (n 1300) 797; Maus (n 684) 177; Spreutels et al (n 1300) 1158. In contrast, see FiC Brussels 29 January 2015, FiscKoer 2015/16, 797–800. The person had been notified of indications of tax evasion, yet the tax authorities had informed him that they did not have any intention to have a criminal investigation opened against him.

[1316] Eerens (n 1302) 404; Franssen and Traversa (n 1302) 43; Spreutels et al (n 1300) 1161.

[1317] FiC Mons 15 January 2008, 04/2989/A, www.monkey.be, 5; FiC Hasselt 1 April 2010, [2010] TFR 704, 706.

this would lead to the disclosure of an offence.[1318] More recently, the same CoA has accepted that the PSI can be applicable where a tax increase of 50 per cent is imposed, in relation to testimony that had been provided under compulsion during the administrative investigation.[1319] Other lower case law seems to limit the privilege to its secondary role of justifying the exclusion of evidence in *sensu stricto* criminal cases, where it had been obtained under compulsion.[1320] Noteworthy in this context is a case of the CoA of Brussels that accepted the applicability of the privilege to administrative VAT fines.[1321]

Another question that has come up is whether the privilege applies to questions in the tax declaration as such, for example when one is asked whether he or she has foreign bank accounts or specific financial instruments.[1322] Daube has defended the applicability of the privilege in such cases, as not respecting the obligation can lead to administrative fines, tax increases and/or *sensu stricto* criminal penalties (provided the right *mens rea* can be shown).[1323] How this should be done in practice is less clear: if one falsely answers that one has no foreign bank accounts, whereas one does in fact have such a bank account, one would, in light of the ECtHR's case law in *King* and *Allen*, not be protected. The privilege does not provide one with the right to create false documents. Therefore, one would have to leave this point in the tax declaration empty, which will in practice draw the authorities' attention to this point of the declaration. One may equally wonder whether the privilege applies this early on, as one can in principle not claim to be (already) charged with a criminal offence at the time of filing the tax declaration.[1324]

The aforementioned questions have come up not only in the context of tax law; other fields of Belgian law too have struggled to find a balance between cooperation duties and the privilege. Unsurprisingly, the issues have arisen in the context of labour law, where several sanctioned obligations to create, retain and produce records[1325] to the competent authorities are in place. Case law on

[1318] CoA Antwerp 20 March 2012, [2013] FJF; CoA Antwerp 10 December 2013, www.monkey.be, 8/12; Maus (n 684) 178. The Court, in its 2012 judgment, reiterated the position discussed before: documents (invoices) that one is legally required to keep exist independently of the will and their production cannot be refused. Similarly, see Maus (n 684) 173. Only where the information that is being required would only be relevant for the purpose of punishing the person concerned would the privilege apply. At the same time, Maus admits that compelled evidence cannot be used for imposing penalties.

[1319] CoA Antwerp 16 June 2015 (n 1303) 10/12.

[1320] FiC Brussels 15 October 2008, [2010] RGCF 54, 56.

[1321] CoA Brussels 2 October 2013, [2014] FJF 333.

[1322] eg Art 307 ITC.

[1323] Daube (n 1303) 272. According to her, the fact that no civil servant threatens the person with any sanction is not an issue. The mere presence in the code of these sanctions suffices.

[1324] On this matter, see *Rodriguez-Porto Perez v Spain* App no 25069/03 (ECtHR, 22 March 2005) para 1. The privilege may be relevant if the references made in the declaration are later used in a criminal case, provided the references were truthful. Similarly, see F Kuty, 'Le droit au silence, les investigations de l'administration fiscale et l'enquête pénale' [2008] *Journal des Tribunaux* 386, 387.

[1325] On this topic, see Royal Decree no 5 of 23 October 1978 on the retention of social documents; W Van Eeckhoutte, *Sociaal Compendium 2016–2017* (Kluwer, 2016) 2815–25.

this topic often deals with interviews by civil servants of the social inspection service and in the context of requests to produce documents. As to interviews by those inspectors, the CoA in labour matters of Antwerp ruled, in a discussion on the payment of social contributions on the salary, that the privilege is not applicable when no punitive charge is pending.[1326] It is also noteworthy that, unlike the CCP, the provisions in the CCVSL do not list the privilege as a right that one has to be informed of.[1327] In labour matters, one of the tricky challenges is to determine whether deciding to invoke the PSI exposes one to prosecution for obstruction of supervision.[1328]

The tension between the PSI and cooperation duties similarly came up in the context of health safety investigations. Article 6 *in fine* and Article 10(1), 1° of the Act of 15 July 1985 on the use of materials containing hormonal, anti-hormonal, beta-adrenergic or production-stimulating effects grant civil servants the competence to require any information or document they need for carrying out checks. The Act includes sanctions[1329] for anyone who opposes requests for information or documents, or who provides incorrect information or documents. Nevertheless, case law of the CoC has interpreted this offence of obstruction of supervision as not precluding someone from refusing to make a self-incriminating statement.[1330] Not handing over requested documents or providing false testimony or documents does fall within the scope of the offence.[1331] It should be recalled that interpreting the privilege so narrowly that it would not provide protection to documentary evidence at all is likely at odds with the ECtHR's case law.[1332]

Another field where a broad offence of obstruction of supervision is applicable is in the context of the CEL. Interestingly, Articles XV.3, XV.126 and XV.126/1 CEL do not make a distinction between documents for which there is a legal obligation

[1326] CoA Antwerp (labour) 27 January 2012, [2012] RABG 973. The court found that they only acted within their capacity to check whether the legislation in question had been respected, not whether an offence had been committed. See CoC 20 March 2000, [2000–01] RW 623. According to the CoC, such reports are merely aimed at establishing that a criminal offence took place in view of punishment and it does not amount to a punitive charge as it does not charge the person, nor require him to take measures to defend himself. See the critical case note of De Smet, who rightly points out that this strict approach of the Court may not be compliant with ECtHR case law. See B De Smet, 'Het beginpunt van de redelijke termijn in zaken van sociaal strafrecht' [2000–01] *RW* 623.

[1327] Art 62. Yet, see Guideline 15/2014 of the College of Prosecutors general at the Courts of Appeal (2 June 2016). On this point, see also Elias and Van de Perre (n 1041) 111–15; Liégeois and Bockstaele (n 1297) 415–16.

[1328] Elias and Van de Perre (n 1041) 174.

[1329] On this offence, see also M Sterkens, 'Hormonen: de misdrijven' in Postal (n 554) H122/11–H122/12.

[1330] CoC 29 November 2011 (n 550) 31–32.

[1331] CoA Ghent 26 November 2008 (n 554). It considered that at the time of the administrative investigation, no charge was pending against the person concerned. It thus focused on the PSI's applicability *ratione temporis*. Yet, it reasoned more broadly, and it seems to exclude documentary evidence as such from its scope. The judgment suggests the Court would not accept the privilege's applicability to situations where someone hands over documents under compulsion before having been labelled as a suspect, and where this evidence is used in a punitive case. This is not a correct interpretation of the, admittedly at times unclear, case law of the ECtHR. Similarly to the CoA, see FiC Dendermonde 9 May 2008, [2008] TStrafr 476, 478.

[1332] *Funke* (n 480) addressed a situation where the authority had broad powers to demand documents.

to keep, even though the Code and the 2010 predecessor of these articles have been adopted well after the ECtHR handed down the *Funke* and *JB* rulings.[1333] In *Citibank*,[1334] the CoC addressed the tension between the privilege and the obstruction of supervision offence, which can now be found in Articles XV.126 and XV.126/1 CEL, and concluded that the privilege includes the right not to cooperate in one's own incrimination. It found that the evidence which had been produced after repeated warnings from special inspectors and the prosecutor that a sanction would be imposed for failure to do so had to be excluded from the case.

Legislative changes, as well as guidelines by the College of Prosecutors General,[1335] that followed the developments in the ECtHR's case law as well as in EU law strengthened the privilege during police, judicial or equivalent interviews: the right to have access to a lawyer during questioning has been significantly extended, first in 2011 and more importantly in 2016. Guidelines from the College of Prosecutors General now cautiously recommend applying these safeguards from an early stage, also where the choice is made for administrative enforcement rather than *sensu stricto* criminal enforcement in order to avoid evidence later being deemed inadmissible due to a violation of a safeguard such as the PSI. The College correctly understood that the former type of enforcement would often be punitive in light of the *Engel* criteria.[1336]

Within the context of *sensu stricto* criminal investigations, several provisions of the CCP impose duties upon service providers to provide different types of information to the prosecutor and/or the investigative judge under threat of imprisonment or fines in case of non-compliance.[1337] To the extent that they are not charged themselves, their PSI is not engaged. To the extent that such obligations are imposed on persons that can provide this information without incriminating themselves[1338] or the corporation that employs them,[1339] such obligations raise no particular issues for the privilege.[1340] Thus, if a bank or a telecom operator has customers that are suspected of criminal wrongdoing, providing the requested information will in principle not lead to the self-incrimination of those institutions. Yet, one may imagine that there can be cases where complying with such

[1333] ibid; *JB* (n 491).
[1334] CoC 19 June 2013 (n 1).
[1335] Guideline 15/2014 of the College of Prosecutors general at the Courts of Appeal (2 June 2016).
[1336] ibid 21–22.
[1337] For example, in relation to bank accounts (Art 46*quater* CCP *in fine*) and to telecommunication (Art 46*bis* CCP *in fine*).
[1338] ConsC 14 February 2013, 6/2013, B.17.
[1339] To the extent that these persons come within the scope of persons that can exercise the corporation's PSI. On this issue, see Dewandeleer (n 969) 160.
[1340] Yet other practical concerns can arise: service providers will not necessarily be enthusiastic to cooperate with law enforcement. See, eg the *Yahoo* case: CoC 1 December 2015, P.13.2082.N, [2016] RABG 485. Extensively, K De Schepper and F Verbruggen, 'Ontsnappen space invaders aan onze pacmannen? De materiële en formele strafrechtsmacht van België bij strafbare weigering van medewerking door elektronische dienstverleners' [2013] *Tijdschrift voor Strafrecht* 143.

obligations to provide information could lead to self-incrimination on the side of the institution concerned, provided that it is involved in its customers' wrongdoing,[1341] or where providing the requested information would otherwise incriminate them. In those cases, the privilege of these institutions can come into play.

Unsurprisingly, the privilege not only applies during the criminal investigation *sensu stricto*, but also at the trial stage of the case.[1342] Belgian law allows accused persons to choose to answer certain questions at their trial and invoke the privilege in relation to other questions.[1343] Thus, they are not obliged to face cross-examination during which they are required to tell the truth,[1344] unlike in E&W and in the USA.[1345] At the same time, in Belgium, choosing to answer only some questions and refusing to answer others can reflect badly on the defendant where evidence is available against him.

In the USA, a person can invoke the privilege in any type of case, provided that the evidence sought is within the scope of the privilege, is self-incriminating and compulsion is present. SCOTUS has adopted this broad position essentially to avoid a person being compelled in a non-punitive case to provide self-incriminating evidence that can be used in a punitive case. In other words, when a person cannot face such a punitive case, the PSI does not apply.

In practice, persons are often required to distinguish between statements that would expose them to self-incrimination and those that would not, as they can only rely on the privilege with regard to the former.[1346] Particularly in non-punitive cases, the privilege does not apply to the same extent as during questioning by the police or at a *sensu stricto* criminal trial. In the context of regulatory demands in a non-punitive case, it cannot be used as a general way of preventing the government from gaining access to information in a blanket fashion.[1347] For example, in a tax context, that implies that a person cannot refuse to submit a tax return as such, though he can refuse to fill out specific points in the tax return where those would tend to incriminate him.[1348] In order to correctly do so, the person should claim the privilege in his tax return.[1349] As I pointed out in relation to Belgium,

[1341] Which is not to be excluded, eg in money laundering or tax fraud cases.

[1342] L Huybrechts and M Rozie, 'De rechten van de verdediging bij de behandeling ten gronde' [2008] *Nullum Crimen* 106, 120. As far as the trial stage is concerned, the CoC has ruled that where an accused person is assisted by a lawyer during the trial phase, the lawyer can inform his client of his privilege. The judge is thus not required to inform the accused person of his privilege: CoC 17 November 2015, P.14.1274.N, 3.

[1343] Tersago, *Verklaringen van verdachten* (n 572) 95.

[1344] Beernaert et al (n 405) 33.

[1345] S 1(2) Criminal Evidence Act 1898; *Brown v United States* 356 US 148 (1958), 154–55.

[1346] JL Kestler, *Questioning Techniques and Tactics*, 3rd edn (Clark Boardman Callaghan, 2022) §6:2.50, 1. In the context of tax cases, see Comisky et al (n 370) 38; NC Skarlatos, 'The Fifth Amendment Privilege Against Self-Incrimination and Tax Returns: Oil and Water or Peanut Butter and Jelly?' (2016) 18 *Journal of Tax Practice & Procedure* 15, 15–16 and 53.

[1347] Tarvin (n 747) 71–72.

[1348] *United States v Sullivan* 274 US 259, 263 (1927).

[1349] *Garner v United States* 424 US 648, 651 (1976).

one risks attracting the authorities' attention by making such a claim. An attempt to claim later on that filling out the tax return amounted to compulsion in order to exclude the tax return from a punitive case is not advisable.[1350] As I have highlighted previously, in the USA, the RRD has led to the exclusion of several types of documents from the privilege's scope. Thus, even where the person may have a valid Fifth Amendment claim, the RRD can still lead to a compelled production of the underlying documents.[1351]

In the context of police questioning, SCOTUS has distinguished custodial[1352] and non-custodial interviews.[1353] The former are governed by *Miranda v Arizona*.[1354] SCOTUS established a set of warnings that should precede such interrogations to protect the privilege, including the availability of the PSI as such.[1355] Unless it is shown that the person was given these warnings and voluntarily, knowingly and intelligently waived these rights, no evidence given during such a custodial questioning can be admitted at trial.[1356] This enhanced protection of persons during custodial interviews is, in the Court's view, needed to protect the person against the inherently compelling pressures of such interviews.[1357] Suffice it to say at this point that *Miranda* has led to many questions, such as: what happens if the warnings are not given in a correct way?[1358] Are there exceptions to the *Miranda* rule? Non-custodial police interrogations are not subject to the *Miranda* rule, as there is no similar presumption that the individual is under the same level of pressure that would prevent him from choosing freely between talking or staying silent.[1359] Thus, in such interviews, the person will not necessarily be informed of his privilege, yet he can exercise it, provided he is aware of it. In that sense, the current US approach, like the E&W one,[1360] offers less protection than the

[1350] On this matter, see Comisky et al (n 370) 6–7 and 39–42. Although SCOTUS accepted that a person is generally compelled to make a tax declaration, it stressed that this did not prevent him from claiming the privilege in relation to specific self-incriminating points on the declaration.

[1351] In other words, even if the person can refuse to fill out a certain point of his tax return, he may still have to provide the documents, such as foreign bank account records, linked to the income. See *In re Grand Jury Proceedings, No 4-10* 707 F3d 1262 (11th Cir 2013); *In re Grand Jury Subpoena Dated February 2 2012* 741 F3d 339 (2nd Cir 2013).

[1352] Defined in *Miranda* (n 446) 444 as: 'Questioning initiated by law enforcement officers after a person has been taken into custody or otherwise deprived of his freedom of action in any significant way'.

[1353] Comisky et al (n 370) 11.

[1354] *Miranda* (n 446). The case's merits should be considered in its historical context: at that time, defence attorneys in the interrogation room were absent and, due to an outcry over the use of violent tactics, a shift had been made to psychological tricks to get suspects to cooperate. Thus, adding a lawyer to the equation, and a strict set of warnings coupled with an exclusionary rule, had the potential to shift the balance in favour of the suspect's position.

[1355] *Miranda* (n 446) 478–79.

[1356] ibid 444 and 479.

[1357] ibid 467. See also *New York v Quarles* 467 US 649, 654 (1984); Dressler and Michaels, *Criminal Procedure* (n 376) 443–44.

[1358] *Michigan v Tucker* 417 US 433, 452 (1974).

[1359] Salky (n 587) 91.

[1360] PACE, Code C, note 10A: 'There must be some reasonable, objective grounds for the suspicion, based on known facts or information which are relevant to the likelihood the offence has been committed and the person to be questioned committed it.'

current provisions in place in Belgium. Belgian witnesses and suspects are both informed that they cannot be required to incriminate themselves. Only suspects are informed of their broader right to stay silent as such and thus not only when they would incriminate themselves during questioning.

The privilege is available in grand jury proceedings too,[1361] yet there is no decision similar to *Miranda* that requires that the person be informed about it.[1362] SCOTUS admitted that a grand jury witness is under oath to tell the truth and the context of a grand jury hearing encourages them to tell the truth, but SCOTUS nevertheless did not find it necessary that they be reminded of the privilege.[1363] In order to invoke his PSI, the individual has to appear before the grand jury and invoke it after each question that would tend to incriminate him, or he should try to get the subpoena annulled as answers would be protected under the Fifth Amendment.[1364] Meanwhile, the JM authorises prosecutors to abstain from insisting on the hearing of a person to whom the subpoena was addressed.[1365] If he does not appear, he risks exposing himself to contempt of court charges.[1366]

At a *sensu stricto* trial, the privilege is strong: the defendant enjoys an unqualified right (not) to testify.[1367] If he chooses not to provide testimony, no adverse comments can be made on this choice by the judge, the prosecutor or the lawyer of a co-defendant.[1368] Yet, one should pay particular attention when deciding whether to make statements or whether to rely on the privilege: once a defendant decides to make statements on the merits, like in E&W, he faces cross-examination in relation to questions properly within the, generally broad,[1369] scope of cross-examination. Once a court has found the defendant guilty, this does not necessarily mean that his Fifth Amendment privilege ceases to apply: he retains his privilege during the sentencing hearing, and this is particularly so where he can still appeal the judgment.[1370]

[1361] The grand jury checks whether there are sufficient grounds to indict a person for a crime. To do so, it has the power to require witnesses to testify or to produce items, such as documents, through the use of subpoenas: *United States v Calandra*, 414 US 338, 346 (1974); Salky (n 587) 93.

[1362] Internal guidelines require federal prosecutors to notify subpoenaed persons of it: JM 9-11.151.

[1363] *Minnesota v Murphy* 465 US 420, 431 (1984).

[1364] Salky (n 587) 94.

[1365] JM 9-11.154.

[1366] In practice, in federal grand jury cases, witnesses who make it clear that they will invoke the privilege in response to every question that would tend to incriminate them can often be excused from having to appear.

[1367] Salky (n 587) 108.

[1368] ibid.

[1369] *Brown v United States* (n 1345) 155–56.

[1370] Salky (n 587) 120.

9

Waiver of the Privilege against Self-Incrimination

The privilege protects a person against compulsion, and in certain cases allows him to stay silent altogether. A person protected by the privilege can and often does decide to cooperate and to provide evidence by waiving the privilege. This chapter considers the (supra)national approaches to waiver.

The ECtHR has accepted that one can validly waive the PSI, while stressing the importance of the voluntary character of the waiver. In order to be valid, it must be unequivocal and surrounded by minimum safeguards, and the waiver must not run counter to an important public interest.[1371] The Court has pointed out that the person making the waiver should have been in a position where he could have reasonably foreseen the consequences of the waiver.[1372] This is not the case where the person did not have a translator to have questions translated and where the charges were not made as clear and as precise as possible.[1373] For example, the Court has taken into account the fact that a suspect was himself a lawyer, as well as the fact that the statement given after the waiver was reconfirmed at a later time, in determining the validity of the waiver.[1374] The Court rightly confirmed that there cannot be a valid waiver if the suspect has been subject to ill-treatment.[1375] Another element that is relevant in the assessment of the validity of the waiver is whether the person has been informed of his privilege.[1376] The fact that the person has signed a document that confirms that he has been reminded of his privilege is as such not sufficient to establish a valid waiver.[1377]

[1371] *Shlychkov* (n 632) para 85.
[1372] *Hakan Duman v Turkey* App no 28439/03 (ECtHR, 23 March 2010) para 48; B Rainey, P McCormick and C Ovey, *The European Convention on Human Rights*, 8th edn (Oxford University Press, 2021) 308–09.
[1373] *Baytar v Turkey* App no 45440/04 (ECtHR, 14 October 2014) para 54.
[1374] *Paskal v Ukraine* App no 24652/04 (ECtHR, 15 September 2001) para 78.
[1375] *Turbylev v Russia* App no 4722/09 (ECtHR, 6 October 2015) para 96.
[1376] ibid. On the importance of the notification of the privilege, see *Ibrahim* (n 378) paras 270–73.
[1377] *Plonka v Poland* App no 20310/02 (ECtHR, 31 March 2009) para 37.

CJEU case law on waiver of the privilege is scarce. Implicitly,[1378] by stating that the privilege in competition law protects against compulsion,[1379] the Court has confirmed that voluntary self-incriminating statements are not precluded and that a suspect can thus waive his privilege, eg in order to cooperate and attempt to obtain a lenient treatment.

As for the POI Directive, there is, unlike the Access to a Lawyer Directive,[1380] no article that deals expressly with the issue of waiver. In order to be ECHR-compliant, such a waiver should fulfil the criteria set out above.

In E&W, the privilege can be waived, both pre-trial and at trial.[1381] An issue that remains unanswered is whether a person can contractually waive his privilege in connection to that contract.[1382] If such clauses would be accepted, one may imagine that they would be included in employment contracts. Case law in relation to persons acting as a fiduciary has rejected the suggestion that one implicitly agrees not to rely on the privilege, just like it has been rejected that an agent cannot rely on the privilege.[1383] On the other hand, provisions on the membership of the Institute of Chartered Accountants that preclude relying on the privilege have passed judicial scrutiny.[1384] As I have outlined before, testifying at trial as a defendant amounts to waiver of the privilege as one exposes oneself to cross-examination.

Belgian case law and doctrine accept, similarly to the ECtHR, that the privilege can be waived.[1385] At least one Belgian court has applied the idea of voluntary waiver in a particularly broad way: by engaging in a regulated activity, one waives one's privilege.[1386] That approach seems to be at odds with the ECtHR's approach in *Saunders*.[1387] This Belgian approach disregards that a situation may change over time and it would thus be particularly stringent to force someone to waive his privilege before he has any concrete information on a potential charge. For the same reason, waiving the privilege at the time of signing the employment contract or at the time of accepting a position as a corporate official seems difficult to reconcile

[1378] The issue is briefly addressed in AG Szpunar's Opinion in Case C-162/15 P *Evonik Degussa GmbH v Commission* ECLI:EU:C:2017:205, para 122. He confirms that the privilege can be waived.

[1379] *LVM* (n 299) para 288.

[1380] Art 9 of Directive 2013/48/EU of the European Parliament and of the Council of 22 October 2013 on the right of access to a lawyer in criminal proceedings and in European arrest warrant proceedings and on the right to have a third party informed upon deprivation of liberty and to communicate with third persons and with consular authorities while deprived of liberty.

[1381] Matthews and Malek (n 535) 408.

[1382] *Bishopgate* (n 665).

[1383] ibid; *Tate Access Floors Inc v Boswell* [1991] Ch 512, 518.

[1384] *R v Institute of Chartered Accountants of England and Wales, Ex p Taher Nawaz* [1997] PNLR 433, confirmed on appeal: [1997] CLY 1.

[1385] CoC 29 November 2011 (n 550) 32; Michiels and Falque, 'L'infraction d'obstacle' (n 1041) 5.

[1386] FiC Liège 12 February 2015, [2015] JLMB 1855, 1859.

[1387] The reference in *O'Halloran* (n 483) to a regulatory regime has been mostly limited to traffic cases, though a reference was made in a case involving a cooperation duty linked to gambling legislation: *Savic* (n 410) para 24.

with the requirement that the person makes a voluntary waiver, as he lacks the necessary information on the impact of his waiver and on the possible charges he faces.

Under US federal law, too, one can waive the privilege, yet any waiver is proceedings-specific, which means that the waiver is limited to the proceedings in which the person appears.[1388] The notion 'proceedings' often has a narrow meaning. For example, two appearances at different points in time before the same grand jury have been considered as separate proceedings,[1389] just like an appearance before a grand jury and at the *sensu stricto* criminal trial,[1390] and the rule of the proceedings-specific waiver also applies to statements made in an informal setting.[1391] The underlying rationale is that the situation may change due to the passage of time or the occurrence of events, which can lead the person to understand that compelled disclosure could expose him to self-incrimination.[1392] That understanding seems to be missing in the aforementioned Belgian first instance case.

Like with the ECtHR, waiver should be the result of a free choice also in the USA.[1393] Situations where a person under compulsion needs to choose between his privilege or an important benefit are likely to be considered as an involuntary waiver. Somewhat surprisingly, SCOTUS has held that in situations not covered by the *Miranda* rule, a person may forego his privilege without knowingly making a waiver, including in grand jury proceedings.[1394] Due to rules on cross-examination, at the trial stage one should, like in E&W, pay particular attention when deciding whether to make statements or whether to rely on the privilege. US case law is tolerant towards poor Fifth Amendment protection of employees, at least in cases where an internal investigation is ongoing. Only in rare cases are US courts willing to strike down practices where a private sector employee risks losing his employment for failure to waive the privilege.

Where the privilege of an individual is concerned, it is self-evident that the individual decides whether to waive his privilege. Admittedly, in some of the national orders he is precluded from invoking it because the privilege does not apply, for example because he has been granted immunity. The issue of waiver raises a particular challenge in the context of corporations. Some legal systems accept that a corporation can invoke the PSI. First, one needs to establish which individuals can

[1388] *United States v Cain* 544 F2d 1113, 1117 (1st Cir 1976); *In re Vitamins Antitrust Litig* 120 FSupp2d 58, 66 (D DC 2000).

[1389] *United States v Miranti* 253 F2d 135, 140–41 (2nd Cir 1958).

[1390] *United States v Licavoli* 604 F2d 613, 623 (9th Cir 1979). The opposite rule applies in the DC Circuit: *Ellis v United States* 416 F2d 791, 800 (DC Cir 1969).

[1391] For example, statements made to an officer investigating a case do not imply a waiver of the PSI at later criminal proceedings: *Nationwide Life Ins Co v Richards*, 541 F3d 903, 911 (9th Cir 2008).

[1392] Salky (n 587) 221.

[1393] ibid 227.

[1394] *Rogers v United States* 340 US 367 (1951).

invoke the corporation's privilege. Only then can someone consider the implications of a waiver of the privilege. To the extent that only one person can exercise the privilege, that seems rather straightforward. If the corporate privilege can be exercised by multiple individuals and one of them decides to waive the corporation's privilege, one may wonder whether that deprives the other individuals of the chance to invoke it. In any case, if one individual has waived the corporation's privilege and subsequently submits documents that incriminate the corporation, the effectiveness of the corporation's privilege is harmed. Considering the importance attached by the different legal systems to the waiver's voluntary character, one may wonder whether one can challenge the waiver's voluntariness if one individual has waived the privilege against the will of the other individuals who can invoke the corporation's privilege.

10

Corporations and the Privilege against Self-Incrimination

In this chapter, I consider the different approaches at the (supra)national level regarding the corporate PSI.

First, I briefly consider the models of CCL in use or promoted by the different legal systems considered in my book. I then test my hypothesis.[1395] At the end of the chapter, I consider a number of tools used in the different legal systems to incentivise corporate cooperation.

I. (Supra)national Models of Corporate Criminal Liability

The question whether corporations can be held liable, criminally or by other means, has been on the agenda of the CoE for decades, as first reflected in soft law instruments and later in conventions.[1396] As long ago as 1988, the Committee of Ministers adopted a Recommendation on the topic.[1397] It was particularly concerned by the rise of corporate misconduct, the difficulty of identifying the individual responsible and the difficulty for several European countries of holding corporations criminally liable. It recommended that responsibility be put where the benefit from the offence is.[1398] In order to do so, it recommended the adoption of CCL or other liability mechanisms, such as administrative liability.[1399] It proposed liability for offences committed in the exercise of a corporate activity, even where the offence was outside the undertaking's purpose, regardless of the

[1395] See 10.
[1396] G De Vel, 'La responsabilité pénale des personnes morales dans les instruments juridiques du Conseil de l'Europe' in S Adam et al (eds), *Corporate Criminal Liability in Europe* (La Charte, 2008) 343.
[1397] Recommendation R (88) 18, available along with the explanatory memorandum: https://rm.coe.int/CoERMPublicCommonSearchServices/DisplayDCTMContent?documentId=09000016804c5d71. Some of the Recommendations adopted before had briefly referred to the mechanism of CCL or equivalent mechanisms. eg point 6 of Recommendation R (82) 15.
[1398] Recommendation R (88) 18, pp 5 and 6.
[1399] I.3, a and b, as well as I.3.20 of the Memorandum.

possibility of identifying an individual.[1400] Yet, the Committee recommended that no corporate liability be imposed where the management[1401] was not implicated in the crime[1402] and where it took the necessary measures to prevent it.[1403]

Interestingly, as it predates the ECtHR's case law on the PSI, the Recommendation provided that legal persons should enjoy rights and guarantees equivalent to those enjoyed by natural persons suspected of crime. Nevertheless, this should not be an issue, as the privilege was known in the MSs of the CoE before those cases were handed down, admittedly to different degrees in the different states. Similarly, in a Recommendation of 2 March 2016,[1404] the Committee stressed that investigations into human rights abuses should comply with the ECHR's effectiveness criteria and, where necessary, give rise to prosecution. This requirement of effective investigations and, if necessary, prosecutions applies irrespective of whether the alleged perpetrator is a natural person or a legal person. No reference was made to a reduced level of procedural protection where the alleged culprit of human rights abuses is a corporation.

From the 1990s onwards, the CoE adopted several conventions that explicitly provide for corporate liability mechanisms and thus consolidate the Recommendation.[1405] The Convention on the Protection of the Environment through Criminal Law started this trend.[1406] It requires states to adopt either CCL or other mechanisms for offences covered by the Convention.[1407] According to Article 9, such liability should be available where a member of a corporate organ or another representative commits an offence covered by the Convention.[1408] The explanatory report confirms that a breach of supervisory duty can trigger corporate liability.[1409]

The CoE's Criminal Law Convention on Corruption[1410] requires (criminal or non-criminal) effective, proportionate and dissuasive sanctions for corporate wrongdoing and reconfirms that broad approach.[1411] In order to trigger the corporation's liability, an offence covered by the Convention needs to have

[1400] I.1 and 2.
[1401] On the liability of managers: I.5.
[1402] Implicated includes situations where the management itself is not directly involved in the offence, yet is aware of it and accepts the profits that are derived from it.
[1403] I.4.
[1404] Para 46 of Recommendation CM/Rec(2016)3, https://wcd.coe.int/ViewDoc.jsp?p=&Ref=CM/Rec(2016)3&Language=lanEnglish&Ver=original&BackColorInternet=DBDCF2&BackColorIntranet=FDC864&BackColorLogged=FDC864&direct=true.
[1405] V Mitsilegas, *Money-Laundering Counter-Measures in the European Union* (Kluwer, 2003) 123.
[1406] 4 November 1998.
[1407] In a 2016 Recommendation, the Committee of Ministers recommended criminal liability or equivalent liability for business-related human rights abuses: para 44 of Recommendation CM/Rec(2016)3.
[1408] According to the explanatory report, the relevant question is whether these persons are legally or factually in such a position that can trigger the liability of the legal person. See https://rm.coe.int/CoERMPublicCommonSearchServices/DisplayDCTMContent?documentId=09000016800cce43.
[1409] Page 15 of the report.
[1410] 27 January 1999.
[1411] Art 19.

been committed for the corporation's benefit or on its behalf.[1412] The corporation's liability can be triggered either by the commission of a covered offence by a person who has a leading position or where that person's lack of supervision or control has allowed a natural person under its authority to commit such an offence.[1413] Subsequent CoE conventions include the same technique of establishing liability.[1414]

The corporate liability model that has been widely used in EU legislative acts corresponds to that of the CoE's Corruption Convention.[1415] It first appeared in detail in the Second Protocol to the Convention on the protection of the European Communities' financial interests (the PIF Convention). Article 3(1) of that Protocol introduced corporate liability for the covered offences[1416] where the offence is committed for the corporation's benefit[1417] by an individual who acts individually, or as part of an organ of the legal person, provided that the individual has a leading position within the legal person due to its power of representation, its authority to take decisions on the legal person's behalf or its authority to exercise control within the legal person. Moreover, like the aforementioned CoE Convention, Article 3(2) of the Second Protocol adds corporate liability for those cases where a lack of supervision or control of one of the aforementioned individuals has made it possible for a natural person under the legal person's authority to commit one of the covered offences for that legal person's benefit.

The Second PIF Protocol and the later instruments that copied its approach require MSs to ensure that legal persons can be punished by effective, proportionate and dissuasive sanctions, while leaving the MSs free to determine whether to impose criminal liability or other liability mechanisms.[1418]

1412 Art 18 and p 18 of the explanatory report, https://rm.coe.int/CoERMPublicCommonSearchServices/DisplayDCTMContent?documentId=09000016800cce44.

1413 Art 18(2) of the Convention.

1414 Art 12 of the Convention on Cybercrime, 23 November 2001; Art 10 of the CoE Convention on Laundering, Search, Seizure and Confiscation of the Proceeds from Crime and on the Financing of Terrorism, 16 May 2005; Art 18 of the CoE Convention on the Manipulation of Sports Competitions, 18 September 2014; Art 13 of the CoE Convention on Offences relating to Cultural Property, 19 May 2017.

1415 Art 8 of Directive 2014/57/EU of the European Parliament and of the Council of 16 April 2014 on criminal sanctions for market abuse (Market Abuse Directive); Art 6 of Directive (EU) 2017/1371 of the European Parliament and of the Council of 5 July 2017 on the fight against fraud to the Union's financial interests by means of criminal law; Art 7 of Directive (EU) 2018/1673 of the European Parliament and of the Council of 23 October 2018 on combating money laundering by criminal law; M Engelhart, 'Corporate Criminal Liability from a Comparative Perspective' in Brodowski et al (n 5) 54–55; A Klip, *European Criminal Law*, 4th edn (Intersentia, 2021) 278–80; S Peers, *EU Justice and Home Affairs Law – Volume II: EU Criminal Law, Policing and Civil Law*, 4th edn (Oxford University Press, 2016) 199–200.

1416 Fraud, active corruption and money laundering.

1417 Flore has pointed out that the French version of the Second Protocol uses 'pour leur compte', like other instruments such as the Market Abuse Directive, while other instruments refer to 'au bénifice de': D Flore, *Droit pénal européen*, 2nd edn (Larcier, 2014) 255. See, eg Art 5(1) of Council Framework Decision 2003/568/JHA of 22 July 2003 on combating corruption in the private sector.

1418 Klip (n 1415) 278–79; Roef (n 7) 370.

The traditional English model of CCL,[1419] at least for offences requiring a blameworthy mental state such as knowledge,[1420] developed in the middle of the twentieth century.[1421] It limits the circle of individuals whose behaviour may trigger CCL. According to the controlling mind model, also known as the identification doctrine,[1422] only the acts and *mens rea* of senior officers can be taken into account for the purpose of CCL, as these acts and *mens rea* are considered to be the corporation's.[1423] Such an individual needs to be in control of (part) of the corporation's activities and should be independent in the sense that he should not have to justify his way of discharging his obligations to another person within the corporation.[1424]

[1419] *R v St Regis Paper Co Ltd* [2011] EWCA Crim 2527; *R v A Ltd* [2016] EWCA Crim 1469; *SFO v Barclays Plc* [2018] EWHC 3055 (QB); Pinto and Evans (n 4) 49 and 65.

[1420] Vicarious liability is typically applied in E&W to regulatory offences, often strict liability offences. Vicarious liability has been used since the end of the 19th century. See Roef (n 7) 342; C Wells, 'Economic Crime in the UK' in Ligeti and Tosza (eds), *White Collar Crime* (n 298) 257. Regulatory schemes apply to 'sellers' or 'persons', which include natural and legal persons: sch 1 of the Interpretation Act 1978. That rule was enshrined in an 1827 statute, but it was a settled rule since much longer: Pinto and Evans (n 4) 3. A legal person can thus commit statutory offences that refer to a person unless 'contrary intention' appears. Contrary intention can be deduced from the corporation's inability to commit the *actus reus*: D Ormerod and K Laird, *Smith, Hogan, and Ormerod's Criminal Law*, 13th edn (Oxford University Press, 2020) 274. As Pinto and Evans indicate, vicarious liability had by that time also applied to offences that required some mental element: Pinto and Evans (n 4) 33.

[1421] ibid 29–45.

[1422] Directors and senior officers, the minds of the corporation, are identified with it: Wells, 'Economic Crime in the UK' (n 1420) 258. On the model's shortcomings, see Ormerod and Laird (n 1420) 776–77; Pinto and Evans (n 4) 45–47; Roef (n 7) 349–52. A narrow definition of that circle makes it easy for larger corporations to escape liability: if the board of directors is not directly involved in the day-to-day operations, they typically lack criminal conduct which qualifies as the corporation's. The Law Commission was asked in November 2020 to consider the matter and provide different options for reform: www.lawcom.gov.uk/project/corporate-criminal-liability/. An option paper was published on 10 June 2022.

[1423] *R v ICR Haulage Ltd and others* [1944] KB 551, 559; Ormerod and Laird (n 1420) 774; Ormerod and Perry (n 540) 124; Pinto and Evans (n 4) 33; Roef (n 7) 346; C Wells, 'Corporate Criminal Liability in England and Wales: Past, Present and Future' in Pieth and Ivory, *Corporate Criminal Liability* (n 3) 98.

[1424] *Tesco Supermarkets Ltd v Nattrass* [1972] AC 153; Pinto and Evans (n 4) 43; Wells, 'Corporate Criminal Liability (n 1423) 287. In *Tesco*, a branch manager of a supermarket did not qualify as part of the circle of individuals qualifying as the controlling mind. The memorandum and articles of association were considered as essential sources to identify the individuals who are to be treated as the company. Action taken by the directors or the general meeting should not be overlooked when conducting that exercise: Pinto and Evans (n 4) 44–45. A more pragmatic approach was adopted by the Privy Council in *Meridian Global Funds Management Asia Ltd Appellant v Securities Commission Respondent* [1995] AC 500, 508. In *Re Supply of Ready Mixed Concrete (No 2)* [1995] 1 AC 456, the UKHL held the corporation liable for a restrictive practice after local managers had acted in violation of orders of the board of directors. In *Attorney General's Reference (No 2 of 1999)* [2000] 3 All ER 182, the CoA ruled that evidence establishing the guilt of an identified individual for the offence was required to convict the corporation. In *SFO v Barclays* (n 1419), individuals, including directors, did not qualify as the directing mind and will of the corporation: 'On that basis, derived from the prosecution's own case, those individuals did not with regard to these transactions have "full discretion" to act independently and they were "responsible to another person [viz the BFC] for the manner in which they discharged their duties …"' Knowledge and approval of one director does not necessarily equate to knowledge and approval of the board: Ormerod and Perry (n 540) 125.

In addition to the identification doctrine and 'simple' vicarious liability, qualified vicarious liability has been introduced more recently, through failure to prevent offences.[1425] Section 7 of the Bribery Act 2010 introduced such qualified vicarious liability by providing a defence of adequate procedures.[1426] Sections 45 and 46 of the Criminal Finances Act 2017 similarly include a failure to prevent offence, while providing a defence where reasonable prevention procedures are in place.[1427]

Moreover, the CMCHA has introduced, by considering management failure, a more 'realistic' approach to CCL than the traditional identification doctrine.[1428]

Compared to the other two national systems, CCL has only been introduced in Belgium recently.[1429] It was introduced by the Act of 4 May 1999 in Article 5 CC. The approach taken by the legislator in terms of offences that can be committed by corporations is particularly broad: provided that the *mens rea* and *actus reus* required for the offence are present, they can be held liable for all offences.[1430]

[1425] Ormerod and Laird (n 1420) 778–80; Roef (n 7) 344; Wells, 'Economic Crime in the UK' (n 1420) 260.

[1426] Wells, 'Economic Crime in the UK' (n 1420) 260–61. The organisation carries the reverse burden of proof as it needs to establish on the balance of probabilities that it had such procedures in place. At the same time, that statute also includes other offences in ss 1, 2 and 6 which apply to corporations through the identification doctrine. A guidance document has been made available by the Ministry of Justice: www.justice.gov.uk/downloads/legislation/bribery-act-2010-guidance.pdf.

[1427] Or where it would not be reasonable in all the circumstances to expect the entity to have preventive procedures in place. Roef (n 7) 345–46; Wells, 'Economic Crime in the UK' (n 1420) 273–74. Generally, see J Fischer and A Clifford, *The Criminal Finances Act 2017* (Informa Law from Routledge, 2019) 73–95.

[1428] Roef (n 7) 352–53. Instead of focusing on finding a senior officer who can be identified as the corporation, a qualified attribution principle is applied. In s 1(3), the CMCHA says: 'An organisation is guilty of an offence under this section only if the way in which its activities are managed or organised by its senior management is a substantial element in the breach referred to in subsection 1.' On this topic, see J Herring, *Criminal Law* (9th edn, Oxford University Press, 2020) 767–68; Ormerod and Laird (n 1420) 780–93; C Wells, 'Corporate Manslaughter: Why Does Reform Matter?' (2006) 123 *African Law Journal* 648.

[1429] Prior to the 1999 Act, the CoC had accepted that legal persons could commit offences, yet only natural persons could be punished: CoC 8 April 1946, [1946] ArrCass 137, 138. Unsurprisingly, one of the elements that played a role in the debate on the introduction of CCL was the issue of *mens rea* in the context of a corporation: Van den Wyngaert et al (n 35) 131. On the pre-1999 era, see N Colette-Basecqz and N Blaise, *Manuel de droit pénal général*, 4th edn (Anthemis, 2019) 327–28; F Kuty, *Principes généraux du droit pénal belge. Tome III: l'auteur de l'infraction pénale*, 2nd edn (Larcier, 2020) 75–81; F Roggen, 'La responsabilité pénale des personnes morales' in X, *Droit pénal et procédure pénale* (Kluwer, 2015) 99–103.

[1430] CoC 20 December 2005, P.05.1220.N; Van den Wyngaert et al (n 35) 139; P Waeterinckx, 'Strafrechtelijke verantwoordelijkheid van en binnen de onderneming (bestuurders, bedrijfsleiders en rechtspersonen)' in P Waeterinckx et al (eds), *Strafrecht in de onderneming*, 3rd edn (Intersentia, 2016) 187. On the legal persons that were excluded from the scope of Art 5 CC prior to the 2018 modification, see A Masset, 'La responsabilité pénale des personnes morales' [2011] *Droit pénal de l'entreprise* 3, 4; Roggen (n 1429) 105–08. On the personal scope after the Act of 11 July 2018, see Colette-Basecqz and Blaise (n 1429) 330–31; Kuty, *Principes généraux* (n 1429) 89–116. On that Act more generally, see P Waeterinckx and R Van Herpe, 'De wettelijke regeling i.v.m. de strafrechtelijke verantwoordelijkheid van de rechtspersoon ontdoet zich na 19 jaar van twee groeipijnen' [2018] *Nullum Crimen* 541.

Belgium opted for an anthropomorphic CCL concept, assimilating legal persons with natural persons.[1431] The corporation[1432] is considered to be a real actor, who can commit offences, and the corporation's liability can be triggered even in the absence of the identification of a specific individual.[1433] The model introduced in Article 5 CC was envisaged as an autonomous criminal liability by the legislator.[1434] In principle, the Belgian model should thus be a more 'independent' liability model than the main models employed in the two other national systems.

To attribute the offence to the corporation, judges will typically[1435] have to rely on the three criteria included in Article 5(1) CC: whether there is an intrinsic link between the offence and the objective of the legal person; whether there is an intrinsic link between the offence and the interests of the legal person; and whether there are concrete circumstances that show the offence has been committed on the corporation's account.[1436] These criteria are not cumulative; it suffices for just one of them to be fulfilled.[1437] If the legislator had only referred to the first one, it would be too easy for the corporation to escape liability: a narrowly defined aim would suffice to do so.[1438] The second criterion covers a broad range of interests and goes beyond mere economic interests.[1439] The third criterion is broad, but nevertheless has some limits: where the offence is committed by an individual who, for example, abuses his employer's tools for purely personal reasons that in no way have the potential to benefit the corporation, this criterion should not result in corporate liability. In other words, the corporation should not be punished when offences are merely committed through it.[1440]

[1431] CoC 28 April 2015, P.14.1655.N; ConsC 18 January 2018 (n 66) (2018) B.1.2; CoC 30 January 2018, P.17.0102.N; Colette-Basecqz and Blaise (n 1429) 329; Kuty, *Principes généraux* (n 1429) 85; Van den Wyngaert et al (n 35) 134.

[1432] Art 5 CC refers to legal persons and a number of entities are equated to legal persons by Art 5(2) CC.

[1433] C Bulteel et al, 'Arbeidsveiligheid en aansprakelijkheid' in X, *Aanwerven. Tewerkstellen. Ontslaan* (Kluwer, 2019) 79; Kuty, *Principes généraux* (n 1429) 86; Verstraeten and Verbruggen, *Strafrecht en strafprocesrecht* (n 574) 55.

[1434] CoC 20 December 2005 (n 1430) 3; F Deruyck, *Overzicht van het Belgisch algemeen strafrecht* (die Keure, 2021) 83; Kuty, *Principes généraux* (n 1429) 84; Spreutels et al (n 1300) 120; D Van Gerven, *Handboek vennootschappen – Algemeen deel* (Larcier, 2020) 958; Waeterinckx, 'Strafrechtelijke verantwoordelijkheid' (n 1430) 192.

[1435] Yet, there can be cases where a statute defines the persons that can be liable for the offence, such as the employer or the director.

[1436] According to the CoC, it is not required that the offences committed by the natural person acting on behalf of the legal person are intended only to benefit or at least not harm the legal person, or actually only benefit or at least not harm the legal person: CoC 17 December 2019, P.19.0845.N.

[1437] Kuty, *Principes généraux* (n 1429) 121; Verstraeten and Verbruggen, *Strafrecht en strafprocesrecht* (n 574) 56; Waeterinckx, 'Strafrechtelijke verantwoordelijkheid' (n 1430) 193.

[1438] Verstraeten and Verbruggen, *Strafrecht en strafprocesrecht* (n 574) 56.

[1439] ibid 56.

[1440] Masset (n 1430) 7; P Waeterinckx, 'De eenpersoonsvennootschap en de grenzen van het antropomorfisme. Botst de autonome strafrechtelijke verantwoordelijkheid van de rechtspersoon werkelijk op haar grenzen bij de eenpersoonsvennootschap, of is dit het gevolg van rechtspraak die het antropomorfisme niet volledig doortrekt?' [2016] *Nullum Crimen* 58, 60–61; Waeterinckx, 'Strafrechtelijke verantwoordelijkheid' (n 1430) 195.

In order for the corporation to be liable, not only should the *actus reus* be present, but so should the right *mens rea*,[1441] in light of the *nullum crimen sine culpa* principle.[1442] From the outset, it was clear that the aim was not to introduce a strict liability regime.[1443] In order for the company to have the required moral element, it should be shown that an intentional decision was taken within the corporation[1444] or that a corporate negligence[1445] has a causal link with the offence.[1446] Thus, even where the offence is imputed to a leading individual within the corporation, this does not by itself suffice to find the corporation guilty,[1447] as an own fault of the corporation remains necessary.[1448] As this is a factual question,[1449] the legislator has left it to the courts,[1450] who in practice have at times struggled in applying the autonomous CCL as corporations always act through individuals.[1451] Therefore, it is essential that sufficient attention is paid during the investigation to the search for a fault of the

[1441] Bulteel et al (n 1433) 80 and 86–87; Declercq, *Beginselen van strafrechtspleging* (n 549) 13; S Van Dyck and V Franssen, 'De strafrechtelijke verantwoordelijkheid van vennootschappen: wie, wanneer en hoe?' in Departement Permanente Vorming van de Orde van Advocaten van de Balie van Kortrijk, *De vennootschap in de verschillende takken van het recht* (Larcier, 2013) 20; Waeterinckx, 'Strafrechtelijke verantwoordelijkheid' (n 1430) 193.

[1442] Masset (n 1430) 8; Van Dyck and Franssen (n 1441) 25; Waeterinckx, 'De eenpersoonsvennootschap' (n 1440) 59.

[1443] Toelichting bij het Wetsvoorstel tot invoering van de strafrechtelijke verantwoordelijkheid van rechtspersonen, *ParlSt* Senaat 1998–99, 1-1217/1, 5; Bulteel et al (n 1433) 80; Colette-Basecqz and Blaise (n 1429) 339; Kuty, *Principes généraux* (n 1429) 87; Masset (n 1430) 7; Van Gerven (n 1434) 958; Waeterinckx, 'Strafrechtelijke verantwoordelijkheid' (n 1430) 193.

[1444] On this matter, see Van Dyck and Franssen (n 1441) 26–28. The corporation's special intent is established when it is shown that the management bodies were aware of the intent to carry out the offence and consented to it: CoC 20 April 2011, P.10.2026.F; CoA Antwerp 6 November 2019, 2018/CO/614, not published, 12. The Court considered that a court can, without giving further reasons, where no briefs were filed on behalf of the defendant, infer intent from the fact that a legal person does not pay attention to compliance with the regulations when operating: CoC 15 October 2019, P.19.0329.N.

[1445] A solid internal organisation, employing the right person for the right task and exercising supervision and control, is key: Waeterinckx, 'Strafrechtelijke verantwoordelijkheid' (n 1430) 196–97. A lack of attention to workplace safety, lack of training and the use of unfit tools are key elements taken into account in finding a corporation guilty: CoC 29 October 2019, P.19.0409.N.

[1446] Toelichting bij het Wetsvoorstel tot invoering van de strafrechtelijke verantwoordelijkheid van rechtspersonen (n 1443) 5; CoC 30 April 2013, P.12.1290.N, 13; V Franssen and R Verstraeten, 'La volonté et la faute de la personne morale' [2010] *Journal des Tribunaux* 65, 70–73; Van Dyck and Franssen (n 1441) 25; Waeterinckx, 'Strafrechtelijke verantwoordelijkheid' (n 1430) 194. This includes, for example, a faulty internal organisation, a lack of safety measures or an unreasonable restriction of the relevant budgets. If a technician of a corporation is under such time pressure that he only has a couple of minutes to check a customer's system, thereby missing a critical issue, this shows that the company's organisation is poor and that it commits the most serious fault: CoC 4 September 2013, P.13.0368.F, [2014] JDSC 282, 283.

[1447] CoC 9 February 2013, P.12.1072.N; V Franssen, 'Daderschap en toerekening bij de rechtspersoon' [2009] *Nullum Crimen* 227, 241.

[1448] CoC 23 September 2008, P.08.0587.N, 3; CoC 15 September 2020, P.20.0150.N; Van Dyck and Franssen (n 1441) 21; Waeterinckx, 'Strafrechtelijke verantwoordelijkheid' (n 1430) 194–95.

[1449] B Meganck, 'Strafrechtelijke verantwoordelijkheid eenmansvennootschap: het eigen schuldpatroon van de rechtspersoon' [2015] *Tijdschrift voor Strafrecht* 81, 82.

[1450] Toelichting bij het Wetsvoorstel tot invoering van de strafrechtelijke verantwoordelijkheid van rechtspersonen (n 1443) 5.

[1451] Meganck (n 1449) 81.

corporation,[1452] as failure to do so can result in an acquittal of the corporation.[1453] Admittedly, the CoC's case law suggests that the fault of the individual and the corporation can at times be closely connected.[1454] The issue of the corporation's own guilt is particularly challenging in single person corporations. In such cases, it will be difficult to determine a corporate moral element,[1455] different from the one of the individuals behind the corporation.[1456] The CoC has nevertheless held that even in the case of single person corporations a proper corporate guilt can be determined.[1457] The fact that the acts or omissions of its only shareholder or director are taken into account in that context does not prevent that conclusion. It thus seems that the Court's case law accepts the use of elements considered for the determination of the individual's guilt in the determination of the corporation's guilt, as an own fault of the corporation can be established.[1458]

The legislator was aware of the risk of conflicts of interests between the corporation and the individuals that embody it. Yet, originally, a particular mechanism was put in place that risked reinforcing such conflicts: the so-called *decumul* rule.[1459] The aim of this special rule was to avoid automatic double convictions of the individual and the legal person, and to avoid a strict liability system,[1460] as well as to protect the employee.[1461] The rule was abolished by an Act of 11 July 2018, which entered into force on 30 July 2018.[1462] The *decumul* issue could in

[1452] H Van Bavel, 'De strafrechtelijke aansprakelijkheid van vennootschappen en leidinggevenden – De lege lata, de lege ferenda' [2017] *Tijdschrift voor Strafrecht* 3, 18; Van den Wyngaert et al (n 35) 141; Waeterinckx, 'Strafrechtelijke verantwoordelijkheid' (n 1430) 195.

[1453] CoA Brussels 21 May 2012 (n 1) 163; CoA Antwerp 21 November 2012, C/1821/2012, not published. The CoA of Liège has, along with other elements, considered the lack of proper attention by the investigators of measures taken by the corporation in a recent acquittal: CoA Liège 10 November 2021, 2018/AG/34, not published, 13. The CoC has ruled that the (trial) court shall determine whether the information submitted suffices to enable it to make an informed judgement on the attribution of *mens rea* to the corporation. The attribution of *mens rea* to the corporation does not always require a specific investigation: CoC 8 February 2022, P.21.1278.N. That case seems mostly relevant for smaller corporations.

[1454] CoC (n 1439) 3; CoC 25 May 2016, P.16.0486.F; CoC 8 February 2022 (n 1453). On this point, see Franssen, 'Daderschap en toerekening' (n 1447) 241; Kuty, *Principes généraux* (n 1429) 142; Meganck (n 1449) 81.

[1455] Franssen, 'Daderschap en toerekening' (n 1447) 241.

[1456] See CoC 3 March 2015, P.13.1261.N, [2016] NC 57 and [2015] TStrafr 80.

[1457] ibid.

[1458] Meganck (n 1449) 83.

[1459] Former Art 5(2) CC. On the decumul rule, see A Jacobs and J-F Dister, 'Responsabilité pénale des personnes morales' in X, *Postal Mémorialis. Lexique du droit pénal et des lois spéciales* (Kluwer, 2019) R 130/9–11; Roggen (n 1429) 117–28; G Van De Mosselaer, 'Sociaal strafrecht- aansprakelijkheid van de rechtspersoon' [2014] *Oriëntatie* 58, 61–63.

[1460] Toelichting bij het Wetsvoorstel tot invoering van de strafrechtelijke verantwoordelijkheid van rechtspersonen (n 1443) 6; Verstraeten and Verbruggen, *Strafrecht en strafprocesrecht* (n 574) 57.

[1461] Verslag namens de commissie voor de justitie, *ParlSt* 1998–99, 2093/5, 25.

[1462] Art 2 of the Act of 11 July 2018 Act amending the Criminal Code and the preliminary title of the Code of Criminal Procedure as regards the criminal liability of legal persons. See MJ Horseele, S Van Dyck and V Franssen, 'Requiem voor de decumulregel (oud artikel 5, lid 2 Strafwetboek)' [2020] *Tijdschrift voor Strafrecht* 3. The decumul rule remains relevant for offences committed prior to 30 July 2018. Art 19 of the Bill establishing a new Penal Code is in that sense a copy & paste of the current version of Art 5 CC: Wetsvoorstel tot instelling van een nieuw Strafwetboek (boek 1 en 2), *ParlSt* Kamer 2019–20, 55 1011/001, 8.

practice only come up if a strict set of conditions were fulfilled. Moreover, it could not come into play if the identified natural person committed the offence knowingly and willingly.[1463] Where the *decumul* rule applied, only the corporation or the individual could be convicted. This could generate a conflict of interest, as both the corporation and the individual involved would have an interest in minimising their own fault. Yet, this was not always the case: one could imagine that both of them were convinced that neither of them was to blame, or that the corporation may have been willing to protect its employees. The determination of the most serious fault was left to the courts. In light of the difficulties to which the *decumul* rule gave rise, its abolition is unsurprising.[1464]

SCOTUS developed the federal standard of CCL in the early 1900s, long before CCL was introduced in Belgium and several other European states. The model has faced extensive criticism,[1465] yet has remained largely unchanged. Although it is easy to trigger, in practice, the number of corporate convictions is low.[1466] The US model, vicarious in nature, in principle greatly differs from the Belgian model. It also differs from the E&W identification doctrine, as it does not focus on the leading individuals within the corporation.

Its development has strong ties with the growth of corporations in a rapidly industrialising world[1467] at the end of the nineteenth and the beginning of the twentieth century, with rising interstate commerce. At the same time, federal criminal law was rising too,[1468] often in order to tackle problems linked to, for example, interstate commerce. In this context, there was a strong call for CCL, also because jurors were not likely to impose heavy sentences on employees when the crime essentially benefited only the company.[1469] The landmark case is *New York Central R Co v United States*.[1470] It dealt with illegal price reduction connected to the transport of goods in light of the Elkins Act. SCOTUS refused to accept that the provisions of the Elkins Act were unconstitutional because the corporation faced punishment for its employees' acts but not for those of the corporation, and

1463 CoC 4 March 2003, P.02.1249.N, 3; CoC (n 1448) 3; CoC 26 September 2017, P.16.1232.N; Meganck (n 1449) 82.

1464 The abolition was also proposed in Art 17 of The Draft Bill of book 1 of the Criminal Code: J Rozie and D Vandermeersch, *Commissie voor de hervorming van het strafrecht. Voorstel van voorontwerp van boek 1 van het strafwetboek* (die Keure, 2017) 4 and 73–78.

1465 Alschuler (n 288). Critically on this criticism, see Beale, 'A Response to the Critics' (n 269).

1466 M Baer, 'Three Conceptions of Corporate Crime (and One Avenue for Reform)' (2020) 83 *Law and Contemporary Problems* 1, 10; SS Beale, 'The Development and Evolution of the US Law of Corporate Criminal Liability', 1, http://scholarship.law.duke.edu/cgi/viewcontent.cgi?article=5910&context=faculty_scholarship. In German: SS Beale, 'Die Entwicklung des US-amerikanischen Recht der strafrechtlichen Verantwortlichkeit von Unternehmen' (2014) 126 *Zeitschrift für die Gesamte Strafrechtswissenschaft* 27.

1467 In which railroads played a key role by connecting different states.

1468 Beale, 'The Development and Evolution of the US Law' (n 1466) 2–3.

1469 ibid 3.

1470 *New York Central R Co v United States* 212 US 481 (1909). CCL for strict liability offences had been accepted earlier on, similarly to E&W: A Babin, 'Corporate Criminal Liability' (2021) 58 *American Criminal Law Review* 671, 679; M Diamantis, 'The Body Corporate' (2020) 83 *Law and Contemporary Problems* 133, 140.

because the corporation's punishment would deprive shareholders of their belongings without due process; nor did it accept that this would violate the corporation's due process.[1471] SCOTUS relied strongly on an author of those days, who considered that:

> Since a corporation acts by its officers and agents, their purposes, motives, and intent are just as much those of the corporation as are the things done. If, for example, the invisible, intangible essence or air which we term a corporation can level mountains, fill up valleys, lay down iron tracks, and run railroad cars on them, it can intend to do it, and can act therein as well viciously as virtuously.[1472]

Accepting the argument that corporations cannot commit crime would, according to SCOTUS, imply a strong limitation on the enforcement of abuses.[1473] In light of corporations' growing power, SCOTUS adopted a pragmatic approach by accepting CCL on public policy grounds.[1474] Although it hinted that corporations cannot commit some offences, without specifying which ones, CCL can be applied to a broad range of offences and, in principle, there is no explicit need for a criminal statute to refer to CCL for it to be available.[1475]

Tort law strongly inspired the federal CCL standard, which comes down to a *respondeat superior* model. The underlying idea is that the corporation is in the best position to supervise employees and prevent them from breaking the law.[1476] A private policing role is imposed on the corporation.[1477] It faces vicarious liability for the acts and omissions of its officers, agents and employees[1478] in the course of their employment. These acts and omissions need to be within the scope and nature of the person's employment,[1479] provided that the act partly or wholly benefits the

[1471] *New York Central* (n 1470) 492.

[1472] ibid 492–93.

[1473] ibid 496. Back then, civil enforcement by public bodies was much more limited than it currently is. This also explains the focus on the importance of CCL. See Beale, 'The Development and Evolution of the US Law' (n 1466) 6 and 11 for certain authors' criticism of SCOTUS's focus on criminal liability. Gobert and Punch argue that the possibility of imposing criminal liability on corporations, combined with awarding damages under civil liability law, has the potential to push corporations to properly control their employees: Gobert and Punch (n 248) 56.

[1474] Diamantis (n 1470) 141.

[1475] 1 USC §1 confirms CCL's broad applicability. On the broad application by lower courts in the aftermath of *New York Central*, see W Thomas, 'Corporate Criminal Law Is Too Broad – Worse, It's Too Narrow' (2021) 53 *Arizona State Law Journal* 199, 210.

[1476] BL Garrett, *Too Big to Jail* (Harvard University Press, 2014) 4.

[1477] Gobert and Punch (n 248) 56.

[1478] Babin (n 1470) 674; Baer, 'Three Conceptions of Corporate Crime' (n 1466) 9. There is no principled limitation to high-ranking employees, so any employee can trigger CCL: Gobert and Punch (n 248) 57; VP Nanda, 'Corporate Criminal Liability in the United States: Is a New Approach Warranted?' (2010) 58 *American Journal of Comparative Law* 605, 612; Thomas (n 1475) 202.

[1479] Babin (n 1470) 675; M Baer, 'Corporate Criminal Law Unbounded' in RF Wright et al (eds), *The Oxford Handbook of Prosecutors and Prosecution* (Oxford University Press, 2021) 478. This criterion is often applied broadly: IK Bleustein et al, 'Corporate Criminal Liability' (2015) 52 *American Criminal Law Review* 851, 854.

corporation.[1480] The condition that the employee needs to act within the scope of his employment implies that he had actual or apparent authority to take a certain action.[1481] The corporation can even face liability when the individual violated corporate policy.[1482] No actual benefit is needed in order to fulfil the second criterion; the individual's intent to in part benefit the corporation suffices.[1483]

In principle, this broad model should make it rather easy to prove an offence against the corporation. A single employee can trigger the corporation's criminal liability.[1484] No proof of *mens rea* at the level of corporate management is required.[1485] The idea that a single rogue employee could nevertheless lead to CCL has often been invoked in order to attack the current CCL model.[1486]

Federal courts have at times[1487] made it even easier to prove an offence against corporations by applying the collective knowledge doctrine where no employee fulfilled all the offence requirements. This doctrine combines the knowledge and acts of multiple employees in order to find the corporation guilty.[1488] For example, if one employee knows that certain transactions should be notified to a competent authority but is unaware that those transactions are happening, while another employee is executing the transactions without being aware of the notification duty, these two elements can be put together to conclude that the corporation had the required knowledge of what was going on.[1489]

This model reflects SCOTUS's view that CCL is an essential enforcement tool. As I stressed before, the US model does not use an anthropomorphic approach like Belgium. Instead, it focuses on effective enforcement and essentially derives the corporation's liability from that of the individual. Unlike the E&W identification

[1480] JM 9-28.210; AM Rose, 'Public Enforcement: Criminal versus Civil' in J Gordon and W-G Ringe (eds), *The Oxford Handbook of Corporate Law and Governance* (Oxford University Press, 2015) 9; Garrett, *Too Big to Jail* (n 1476) 4.

[1481] Bleustein et al (n 1479) 855.

[1482] J Albano and A Sanyshyn, 'Corporate Criminal Liability' (2016) 53 *American Criminal Law Review* 1027, 1034; Babin (n 1470) 676; Baer, 'Three Conceptions of Corporate Crime' (n 1466) 9.

[1483] JM 9-28.210; Arlen and Buell (n 305) 700; Babin (n 1470) 678; Baer, 'Three Conceptions of Corporate Crime' (n 1466) 9; Baer, 'Corporate Criminal Law Unbounded' (n 1479) 479; Thomas (n 1475) 210. The individual may even have acted primarily for personal benefit: Albano and Sanyshyn (n 1482) 1034; L Cole, 'Reexamining the Collective Entity Doctrine in the New Era of Limited Liability Entities – Should Business Entities Have a Fifth Amendment Privilege?' [2005] *Columbia Business Law Review* 1, 64.

[1484] Garrett, *Too Big to Jail* (n 1476) 4; Kloeber (n 241) 639.

[1485] Babin (n 1470) 680.

[1486] Guidelines for prosecutors point out that such a corporate prosecution may not be suitable: JM 9-28.500.

[1487] This doctrine has not been generally shared and several circuits approach it critically: *United States v Science Applications International Corp* 626 F3d 1257, 1274 (DC Cir 2010); Baer, 'Corporate Criminal Law Unbounded' (n 1479) 479; Thomas (n 1475) 213.

[1488] Babin (n 1470) 680; Beale, 'The Development and Evolution of the US Law' (n 1466) 9. Where specific intent is needed, additional evidence is needed, or an individual agent needs to possess such intent: Babin (n 1470) 681.

[1489] eg *United States v Bank of New England* 821 F2d 844 (1st Cir 1987).

doctrine, the US model does not examine whether the person that triggered the corporation's liability embodies its will and it is not restricted to high-ranking officials or employees.

II. Corporations and the Privilege against Self-Incrimination

Some of the analysed legal systems have made clear and explicit choices as to the PSI's (in)applicability to corporations. Others, such as the ECtHR's case law, are less explicit on the matter. The ECtHR situates the privilege at the heart of a fair procedure, without, however, elevating it to an absolute right. It has not handed down rulings that explicitly confirm that the privilege applies or does not apply to corporations.[1490] In the absence of such case law, the rationales of the privilege identified by the Court offer guidance.

As I previously examined, it considers the privilege as an important safeguard against different types of improper compulsion.[1491] Such compulsion comes in various forms.[1492] Very relevant for corporations are the cases where a suspect is required to provide oral statements or other evidence, or face sanctions for refusing to do so. The ECtHR has addressed cases where a suspect was punished for failure to do so, as well as cases where the person did provide the required evidence. The sanctions that could be imposed vary and include imprisonment and, more relevantly for corporations, since they cannot be imprisoned, fines. In a number of the cases where the Court has concluded that the privilege was violated, such compulsion was at play.[1493] If one were to apply these cases *mutatis mutandis* to corporations, it is likely that the ECtHR would accept that corporations could be subject to such compulsion and thus be worthy of the PSI's protection. The level of fines will be a relevant factor. The second type of compulsion, where psychological or physical pressure is involved, at times amounting to a violation of Article 3 ECHR, at first sight seems less relevant to corporations. As pointed out in chapter three, in the strictest sense, corporations cannot have their arm twisted. To the extent that the privilege protects against such compulsion, one may think that this provides an argument against applying it to corporations. Nevertheless, such types

[1490] Andersson (n 503) 162; Lasagni, *Banking Supervision* (n 430) 247; Ortiz Blanco (n 16) 36; AG Pikamäe (n 59) para 97. In a 2013 case on Art 8 ECHR and corporations, the applicant referred to the PSI in the context of forced 'consent' to the handing over of a backup tape, yet the ECtHR did not address this argument in depth: *Bernh* (n 254) para 138. In 2014, a company explicitly relied on the privilege in the context of its forced cooperation with a competition authority during a search, but the Court did not decide on this claim as it was inadmissible due to the lack of exhaustion of domestic remedies: *Delta Pekarny AS v Czech Republic* App no 97/11 (ECtHR, 2 October 2014) paras 104–14.

[1491] *Ibrahim* (n 378) para 267.

[1492] ibid.

[1493] eg *Saunders* (n 393); *JB* (n 491); *Marttinen* (n 385); *Chambaz* (n 491).

of compulsion may indirectly remain relevant in cases where it is exercised on individuals in their capacity of corporate officer or employee.[1494] The case law on damages, cited below, shows that the ECtHR is willing to look beyond the paper entity. What is nevertheless unclear is how the Court will rule on the concept of 'defying the will of the accused' in relation to corporations. It remains to be seen whether the Court would be willing to accept my argument that the use of indirect compulsion can defy the corporation's choice not to cooperate. At least in situations where corporations would be threatened with sufficiently high fines or other sanctions in order to give up self-incriminating evidence,[1495] the ECtHR's rationale of protecting persons against improper compulsion advocates in favour of applying the privilege.

The second rationale, which focuses on the connection between the PSI and the POI, is relevant for corporations. The underlying idea of the ECtHR's reasoning is that the government should itself do the work of providing the evidence against the person;[1496] it also applies in the context of corporations. If the privilege is an essential feature that allows a party to freely set up its defence strategy, corporations could similarly benefit from it. Nevertheless, as I have pointed out, this rationale at times considers the privilege as a protection of the balance between the state and private parties. The state has significant power when it builds a case against someone, including the use of searches and seizures, electronic surveillance and the power to arrest individuals. Critics may argue that the issue of finding a fair balance between the state and private parties does not apply to the same extent where the state confronts a corporation, as corporations can have great economic power and vast resources to fight a case. In my view, that argument is not so clear-cut: first of all, not all corporations are multinationals with a well-filled war chest to hire a large defence team. Many corporations are much smaller and do not have unlimited resources to mount a defence. Moreover, even with regard to bigger corporations, one may critically remark that the use of compulsion by the authorities also impacts them: searches at the corporate premises, arrests of key officials, an official decision to charge the corporation, combined with media coverage, can quickly have a big impact. Arguing that the POI does not apply to corporations because of their economic power is a slippery slope: one could then similarly argue that the POI would not need to be applied as stringently in connection to a very wealthy individual, as in the case of a poor one.[1497] Lastly, focusing

[1494] The Court concluded that Art 6 ECHR was violated where individuals testified due to serious coercion and where this evidence was used against another person. Where, for example, an employee would face grave coercion, the use of evidence obtained as a result of it against a corporation could impact the fairness of the corporation's trial. Case law addresses this point in relation to individuals: *Harutyunyan v Armenia* App no 36549/03 (ECtHR, 28 June 2007) paras 58–66; *Kaçiu and Kotorri* (n 1256) paras 126–28.

[1495] Similarly to the situation of individuals, the level of compulsion should be assessed not only in light of the level of the fines, but also in light of the extent of the evidence sought.

[1496] Harris et al (n 35) 422.

[1497] Critically, see O'Neill (n 464) 135.

on corporations' wealth in order to set them apart of individuals is also misguided as it fails to acknowledge that as long as they can both face punitive liability, they face a similar risk. The POI and the privilege are thus relevant for both categories. In sum, attacking the applicability of the privilege to corporations by referring to arguments that suggest that one of the justifications for the privilege, the POI, is not fully applicable to corporations is, in my view, erroneous.

Although the ECtHR did not have to address the privilege's applicability to corporations in *Saunders*, the case is still relevant. Mr Saunders was chief executive of a corporation that attempted to take over another corporation. In its struggle to do so, unlawful methods were used, such as a covert share support operation. Saunders clearly acted in his capacity of corporate official. Nevertheless, the ECtHR did not restrict his privilege, and added that the complexity of corporate fraud did not suffice to allow a practice under which compelled evidence, obtained in a non-punitive setting, could be used at Saunders's *sensu stricto* criminal trial. This suggests that the Court does not find that by accepting a position of corporate official one waives one's personal PSI in relation to those corporate activities.[1498] Moreover, the refusal to accept the complexity of corporate fraud as an overriding reason to restrict the privilege may suggest that the Court would accept the inclusion of corporations within its scope. Similarly, the Court has accepted that the privilege can be invoked in relation to all types of criminal offences.[1499] It would be a long leap to conclude that this implies that all types of persons, including corporations, can invoke the privilege in relation to all offences. Nevertheless, it is indicative of the Court's willingness to find the privilege applicable in a broad range of cases.

At the same time, one may wonder whether *O'Halloran*[1500] will impact on the ECtHR's reasoning as to the privilege's applicability to corporations. In that case, which was on the disclosure of a driver's identity, the Court found that those who own and use cars accept certain responsibilities and obligations as part of the regulatory regime linked to motor vehicles. Could one say that by choosing to operate one's business through a corporate form, which entails advantages such as limited liability, one subjects oneself to a regulatory regime? If the answer is affirmative, one of the obligations this could entail is that one has to comply when potentially incriminating evidence is sought against the corporation and the individuals behind it. In my view, such an approach would be too far-reaching, as it entails that one waives one's privilege by taking up the corporate form. The ECtHR replied negatively to that question in *Saunders*.[1501] In fact, the regulatory regime argument to restrict the PSI is, at the time of writing, only firmly established in relation to road traffic offences.[1502]

[1498] Implementing such an approach in practice would be difficult. See Dine (n 234) 282–86.
[1499] *Zaichenko* (n 478) para 39; Jackson and Summers (n 273) 257.
[1500] *O'Halloran* (n 483).
[1501] *Saunders* (n 393) para 64 and 74.
[1502] *Krumpholz* (n 430) para 36; *Lückhof and Spanner* (n 645) para 53. Reference was made to it in *Savic* (n 410) para 24.

Certain elements in the ECtHR's case law may cast doubt on its willingness to apply the privilege to corporations. First, it cannot be excluded that some of the *Jalloh* criteria, such as the nature and degree of compulsion, are applied more leniently when the applicant is a corporation. This could result in a very restrictive approach to the privilege of corporations, or possibly even a refusal to apply it to them. For example, the fact that corporations cannot face imprisonment could be considered when assessing the nature and degree of compulsion.[1503] Nevertheless, depending on the level of the fines, or the availability of other sanctions that could have a 'life'-threatening impact on a corporation, one can argue that the level of compulsion is also high with regard to corporations.

In addition to the application of the *Jalloh* criteria to corporate suspects, a second threat lurks around the corner for corporations wishing to rely on the PSI, at least in the context of 'punitive charges' that are not part of the hard core of criminal law. The ECtHR has recognised that its interpretation of what constitutes a punitive case has resulted in a broad list of cases being labelled as criminal.[1504] Similarly, it has recognised that not all criminal cases amount to the hard core of criminal law.[1505] *Menarini*, a case introduced by a corporate applicant, is one of those cases.[1506] Taking this into account, one may wonder what the impact is on corporate claims to the PSI. Where corporations face a hard-core criminal case, this case law does not pose a threat to their PSI. In non-hard-core cases, the reasoning in *Menarini* could theoretically result in a restrictive approach to the corporation's privilege. Nevertheless, this will not necessarily be the case: the Court has stressed the privilege's importance.[1507] Also with regard to other Article 6 rights, the Court has not systematically lowered its protection because the applicant was a corporation.[1508] Overall, the ECtHR has been critical of restrictions on the PSI, particularly where they harm the essence of the privilege.

Outside the context of the PSI, the ECtHR has held several Article 6 ECHR procedural safeguards to be applicable to corporations and has accepted corporations' entitlement to a fair trial.[1509] The Court's conclusion that the POI

[1503] In this context, see *King* (n 645) para 2. The Court pointed out that the applicant at most faced a financial penalty. Nevertheless, it has repeatedly found a violation where, in practice, only a fine was imposed. See, eg *JB* (n 491); *Marttinen* (n 385).

[1504] *Jussila* (n 54) para 43.

[1505] ibid para 43; *Grande Stevens* (n 41) para 120; *A and B* (n 38) para 133; *Nodet v France* App no 47342/14 (ECtHR, 6 June 2019) para 42.

[1506] *Menarini* (n 49).

[1507] On this matter, see Ligeti and Tosza, 'Challenges and Trends' (n 298) 29. AG Pikamäe (n 59) paras 107–17 makes a strong case against blindly applying the *Jussila* approach to the PSI, admittedly of natural persons. In *De Legé* (n 57) the ECtHR did not use the *Jussila* approach in order not to find a violation of the PSI.

[1508] eg *Özmurat* (n 57); *Produkcija Plus* (n 9); *Vegotex* (n 47) para 157–158.

[1509] *Paykar* (n 10); *Menarini* (n 49); *Al-Dulimi and Montana Management Inc v Switzerland* App no 5809/08 (ECtHR, 21 June 2016); *Özmurat* (n 57) para 37; *Xero Flor w Polsce sp zoo v Poland* App no 4907/18 (ECtHR, 7 May 2021) paras 173 and 291; *Bio Farmland Betriebs SRL v Romania* App no 43639/17 (ECtHR, 13 July 2021) para 57. See also Gilliaux (n 10) 73; van Kempen (n 10) 373; Tilleman and Van Damme (n 9) 351.

applies to legal persons is of particular relevance.[1510] Since the Court has on several occasions connected the privilege to the POI, the applicability of the POI to corporations provides some indication as to whether the Court considers the privilege applicable to corporations. Moreover, the Court has repeatedly confirmed the importance of rights that are effective.[1511] Thus, given the central importance accorded to the privilege by the Court, one can argue that a corporation's entitlement to the POI would not be effective if it is unable to rely on the PSI.

In other cases dealing with legal aid and taxes that have impacted on a corporation's access to a court, the ECtHR has at times referred to the lack of consensus in the CoE's MSs on the topic of legal aid for corporations, without, however, attaching decisive value to this argument.[1512] Some of the Court's case law suggests that it would accept more restrictions in relation to corporations than in relation to individuals. In a case where a company complained about the excessiveness of court fees, the Court found that the diligence that can be required of an entity may be greater than that demanded of a natural person.[1513]

At the same time, the ECtHR has at times applied Article 6(1) ECHR broadly. In a case on the excessive delay of a court to decide a case, the Court accepted that a corporation can be the victim of an Article 6 ECHR violation where such a delay occurs.[1514] It accepted that it cannot be excluded that commercial companies receive compensation for non-pecuniary damage.[1515] The Court highlighted the need to interpret the Convention in such a way that it ensures practical and effective rights. Such non-pecuniary damage can be based on the company's reputation, uncertainty in decision-planning or disruption in the company's management.[1516] Moreover, the anxiety and inconvenience caused by the delay to the members of the management team and to the shareholders[1517] are also factors to be considered, albeit, in the Court's view, not at the same level as the previous factors. The factors to which the Court has pointed are particularly relevant as they tend to overlap with some of the elements that come up in the context of the prosecution of corporations. The Court's willingness to consider these elements in relation to the issue of excessive delay may indicate that it would be willing to do so too in cases where corporations claim the PSI.

[1510] *Aannemersbedrijf* (n 11) para 1; *Vastberga* (n 11) para 122; *SA-Capital Oy* (n 9) para 107.

[1511] *Ibrahim* (n 378) para 270.

[1512] *Granos Organicos Nacionales SA v Germany* App no 19508/07 (ECtHR, 22 March 2012) para 47. For a case where a violation of Art 6 was found due to the restriction imposed on corporations to have access to a court due to a court access tax, see *Agromodel OOD and Mironov v Bulgaria* App no 68334/01 (ECtHR, 24 September 2009) para 48.

[1513] *Elcomp sp zoo v Poland* App no 37492/05 (ECtHR, 19 April 2011) para 41. The company had not been particularly diligent when presenting its financial situation to the national court.

[1514] *Comingersoll SA v Portugal* App no 35382/97 (ECtHR, 6 April 2000) para 25; *Vegotex* (n 47) paras 100–06.

[1515] *Comingersoll* (n 1514) para 35.

[1516] ibid; *Lupeni Greek Catholic Parish and Others v Romania* App no 76943/11 (ECtHR, 29 November 2016) para 182.

[1517] *Comingersoll* (n 1514) para 36.

The ECtHR's case law on Article 8 ECHR, which is particularly relevant in the context of evidence gathering through, for example, searches of corporate premises, or seizure of documents or electronic files, provides some interesting insights. In *Société Colas*, the Court accepted to extend the right to respect for the home to corporations, acknowledging that the applicants were legal persons.[1518] The Court recalled that it had already found that the French version of the Convention allowed for a broader understanding of 'domicile' that could cover the office of someone.[1519] Its willingness to accept that corporations could claim a violation was based on the aforementioned argument that the Convention is a living instrument, which needs to be interpreted according to current conditions.[1520] At the same time, the Court, picking up on some of the French government's reasoning, accepted that more far-reaching interferences may be accepted with regard to legal persons than to natural persons.[1521] Nevertheless, the absence of relevant safeguards still led the Court to conclude that Article 8 ECHR was violated due to a lack of proportionality.[1522]

Colas is not only relevant for its ruling on the applicability of Article 8 ECHR to corporations. It also provides some insights that may be helpful in understanding the ECtHR's reasoning in relation to the applicability of ECHR safeguards to corporations and the possible differences in reasoning between the ECtHR and the CJEU. The CJEU adopted, in the context of competition cases, a restrictive approach in relation to the applicability of the PSI of corporations. Similarly, in relation to the right to the inviolability of the home, the CJEU strongly relied on the 'not inconsiderable divergences' between the approaches of the MSs to the nature and degree of protection given to business premises against the state.[1523] Instead of following the CJEU's restrictive example, the ECtHR stressed the Convention's status as a living instrument and accepted that corporations can be protected by Article 8 ECHR. In any case, the Court's approach to Article 8 ECHR does not imply that corporations will always enjoy more limited rights.[1524] After a change to its national procedural framework, the Court again found a violation of Article 8 ECHR in a case against France.[1525] The Court attached particular importance to the absence of sufficiently strong judicial control where the corporations

[1518] *Société Colas Est and others v France* App no 37971/97 (ECtHR, 16 April 2002) para 40 et seq.
[1519] ibid para 40.
[1520] ibid para 41.
[1521] ibid para 49. See also *Bernh* (n 254) para 159; ConsC 12 October 2017 (n 405) B.5.1.
[1522] The Court concluded that Art 8 was violated in a case where a search warrant had been executed at the premises of a publishing company, due to the warrant's over-broadness: *Saint-Paul Luxembourg SA v Luxembourg* App no 26419/10 (ECtHR, 18 April 2013) para 61.
[1523] Nevertheless, the CJEU accepted that it was a principle of Community law at that time that protection must be foreseen against arbitrary or disproportionate intervention in the private activities of natural or legal persons: Joined Cases 46/87 and 227/88 *Hoechst AG v Commission* ECLI:EU:C:1989:337, paras 17–19.
[1524] Oliver, 'Companies and their Fundamental Rights' (n 235) 678.
[1525] *Vinci Construction and GTM Génie Civil and Services v France* App nos 63629/10 and 60567/10 (ECtHR, 2 April 2015).

contested the seizure of specific pieces of evidence during a search.[1526] Meanwhile, it seems to be accepted that corporations can indeed claim the protection of Article 8 ECHR in relation to the right to respect for home and correspondence[1527] where they are subjected to a search of business premises and the search and seizure of electronic data.[1528]

Unlike the ECtHR, the CJEU has handed down rulings in which it has expressed its view on the PSI in relation to undertakings. This line of competition law cases[1529] started off with *Orkem*.[1530] A limited liability company had challenged an EC decision calling for information on several grounds, including a breach of the rights of defence.[1531] According to the company, the decision compelled it to incriminate itself by admitting an infringement of competition law.[1532] Since the applicable Regulation at the time[1533] did not explicitly provide for a PSI, the CJEU turned to Community law's general principles. It considered the fact that there was neither a judgment of the ECtHR recognising a privilege nor an express provision in the ECHR on it.[1534] Moreover, its analysis of the MS's law on the issue showed that the privilege was primarily reserved to natural persons in *sensu stricto* criminal proceedings and not for legal persons committing infringements in the economic sphere.[1535] When *Orkem* was decided, numerous EU countries had not yet introduced CCL, so that finding should be considered in that context. The Court nevertheless found that the power of the EC to compel undertakings to provide it with information and documents may not go so far that it would, by means of a decision calling for information, undermine the undertaking's rights of defence.[1536] It then held that compelling

[1526] ibid para 79.

[1527] *Wieser and Bicos Beteiligungen GmbH v Austria* App no 74336/01 (ECtHR, 16 October 2007) para 45. In *Vinci*, the Court even referred to private life in the context of a corporate case: *Vinci* (n 1525) para 63.

[1528] However, not every claim will necessarily be successful: *Bernh* (n 254).

[1529] *Orkem* (n 439). For the reconfirmation of the privilege as a general principle, see *LVM* (n 299) para 273.

[1530] *Orkem* (n 439). On this judgment, see K Lenaerts, 'Procedural Rights of Private Parties in the Community Administrative Process' (1997) 34 *CML Rev* 531, 549–51.

[1531] The EC can ask undertakings for information either through a request for information or through a decision. Where a simple request is issued, no penalties will be imposed for failure to reply, only for incorrect or misleading information (Arts 18(2) and 23 of Regulation 1/2003). Failure to provide information after a decision calling for this information has been adopted can result in a fine (Art 23(1)b), as well as periodic penalty payments (Art 24(1)d). See 8-11/15 of the Commission's Antitrust Manual of Procedures section on requests for information (n 383).

[1532] ibid para 18.

[1533] Implementing Arts 85 and 86 of the Treaty. These matters are governed by Regulation 1/2003.

[1534] *Orkem* (n 439) para 30.

[1535] See the extensive analysis of AG Darmon in *Orkem*, starting at para 97, as well as para 29 of the judgment.

[1536] *Orkem* (n 439) para 34; Lamadrid de Pablo and Kellerbauer (n 904) 406. The rights of the defence have been recognised as a general principle of EU law, eg *Erste* (n 499) para 270.

an undertaking to provide answers that might involve an admission of the existence of a competition law infringement on its part could not be accepted.[1537]

Nowadays, the position in the CJEU's case law on competition cases is, as outlined above (109–110 and 118), that requiring answers to (some) factual questions and the handing over of pre-existing documents is acceptable,[1538] whereas requiring an oral or written[1539] admission of a violation of EU competition law is not. This approach is in general more restrictive than the ECtHR's case law, which also applies to statements which are in themselves not directly incriminating. The exception made to that position in *O'Halloran*,[1540] in relation to road traffic offences, has not been firmly extended beyond that field and thus does not suggest that the two courts have a similar approach to factual questions. Similarly, it is more restrictive than the ruling in *DB v Consob*, in which the CJEU addressed a natural person's PSI.[1541] The obligation to hand over pre-existing documents is interpreted broadly by the EC. Its 2019 Manual of Procedures refers to minutes of cartel meetings as an example of the type of documents that can be required pursuant to an Article 18(3) Decision.[1542] With regard to documents, the CJEU, while acknowledging the importance of the rights of the defence, seems to be satisfied that the undertaking can argue that the documents have a different meaning to that claimed by the EC.[1543] In other words, as long as it can challenge the EC's interpretation of these documents, the Court does not consider such compelled production as problematic.

This privilege is limited in terms of the evidence that falls within its scope. The privilege recognised by the CJEU leads to difficult distinctions in practice between admissible questions and forbidden questions[1544] which might involve an admission on the part of the undertaking of the existence of an infringement.[1545] In order to safeguard the PSI's effectiveness, it is imperative to critically assess

[1537] ibid para 35. Andersson (n 503) 167 argues that *Orkem* implies that leading questions or requiring the compilation of information that establishes an undertaking's guilt are precluded. On the relevance of this case law for OLAF investigations, see J Inghelram, *Legal and Institutional Aspects of the European Anti-Fraud Office (OLAF)* (Europa Law Publishing, 2011) 159–60.

[1538] *SGL Carbon* (n 15) para 48; *Qualcomm* (2021) (n 15) para 143; Lamadrid de Pablo and Kellerbauer (n 904) 380. See also 12/15 of the Manual. 'Document' is understood broadly by the EC, so that it includes not only written notes, but also electronically stored documents. A proper document retention policy is relevant with regard to possibly exculpating evidence. On an undertaking's 'duty of care' in competition cases, see Case C-611/16 P *Xellia Pharmaceuticals Aps and Alpharma v Commission* ECLI:EU:C:2021:245, paras 151–57.

[1539] Written in the sense that the EC would require the creation of a new document that contains such an admission: Jones and Sufrin (n 21) 223. In *Qualcomm* (2019) (n 500), the GC stated at para 192 that an undertaking cannot claim a violation of its privilege in case it has to compile information into a document in response to questions considered as factual by the GC. The CJ concluded that the undertakings did not have to admit that they committed an infringement of competition law: ibid para 147.

[1540] *O'Halloran* (n 483) para 194.

[1541] *DB v Consob* (n 17) para 40.

[1542] 7/15 of the section requests for information in the Antitrust Manual of Procedures (n 383).

[1543] *SGL Carbon* (n 15) para 49; Lamadrid de Pablo and Kellerbauer (n 904) 410.

[1544] 12/15 of that section.

[1545] eg Opinion of AG Wahl in Case C-267/14 P *Buzzi Unicem SpA* ECLI:EU:C:2015:696, paras 73–91.

whether a question does in fact, rather than in form, require an admission of a competition law breach.[1546] This could be the case where a company is required to disclose[1547] the names of undertakings it has warned about a possible investigation by the competition authorities. *Orkem* was later incorporated into recital 23 of Regulation 1/2003.[1548] The CJEU has not fundamentally altered its case law in light of the case law of the ECtHR, although it acknowledged the developments in the ECtHR's case law in *LVM*.[1549] One may wonder whether the CJEU's position is in line with the ECtHR's: not only has the ECtHR ruled repeatedly that the privilege can protect documentary evidence, it has also rejected the view that only directly incriminating evidence comes within the PSI's scope. Yet, in the absence of an explicit ECtHR case confirming the entitlement of corporations to the privilege, one can try to explain the difference between *Orkem* and the ECtHR case law simply by referring to the fact that *Orkem* dealt with legal persons, whereas the ECtHR's cases deal with natural persons,[1550] and that *Orkem* did not deal with a criminal case in the Court's view. In *LVM*, it specified that the privilege can only come into play where coercion is involved.[1551]

Since *Orkem*, the CJEU has been concerned that accepting a broad PSI could be an obstacle for the effective enforcement of competition law.[1552] The focus on the effectiveness of enforcement has thus resulted in a narrow privilege, which does not include self-incriminating documents in the possession of the undertakings under investigation,[1553] and is limited as far as testimony goes to admissions of guilt.[1554] The persons who can invoke the privilege on the corporation's behalf have not been fully identified in the case law. According to the aforementioned Manual, the information that is being required from the undertaking should be supplied by its owners, and in the case of legal persons or associations (without legal personality), this duty is to be executed by the person who can represent the legal person or the association.[1555] It makes sense that those individuals should

[1546] *LVM* (n 299) para 273 *in fine*.
[1547] *SGL Carbon* (n 15) paras 66–69.
[1548] The Antitrust Manual of Procedures provides that addressees of an Art 18(3) Decision are to be reminded of their privilege as defined by the CJEU: see 7/15 of the request for information section; Lamadrid de Pablo and Kellerbauer (n 904) 401. In the context of a voluntary interview, on the basis of Art 19 of Regulation 1/2003, the Manual recommends drawing the attention of the interviewee to the self-incriminating nature of a question, as well as the implications of answering it: 4/6 of the section on the power to take statements.
[1549] *LVM* (n 299) para 274. At the time this ruling was handed down, the ECtHR had already decided *Funke* (n 480); *Saunders* (n 393); *JB* (n 491).
[1550] P Whelan, *The Criminalization of European Cartel Enforcement – Theoretical, Legal and Practical Challenges* (Oxford University Press, 2014) 125–26.
[1551] *LVM* (n 299) para 275; Case C-407/04 P *Dalmine v Commission* ECLI:EU:C:2007:53, paras 31–35; Lamadrid de Pablo and Kellerbauer (n 904) 408; Wissink (n 501) 93.
[1552] *Orkem* (n 439) para 34; Veenbrink, *Criminal Law Principles* (n 386) 146.
[1553] Recital 23 of Regulation 1/2003; *SGL Carbon* (n 15) para 48.
[1554] Ward et al (n 502) 1148–1149.
[1555] Antitrust Manual of Procedures, 8/15 of the requests for information section; M Veenbrink, 'The Privilege against Self-Incrimination in EU Competition Law: A Deafening Silence?' (2015) 42 *Legal Issues of Economic Integration* 119, 134 et seq.

be able to invoke the corporation's privilege. Where associations of undertakings are involved, members of the association cannot claim that their privilege is infringed when the association gives evidence against them, as this would, in the Court's view, prejudice the effectiveness of competition enforcement.[1556] The privilege's perceived impact on the effectiveness of enforcement is a recurring argument that is also present in certain national case law. Similar questions as those that have been raised in the field of competition cases could come up in other fields of EU law, such as banking supervision.[1557]

The privilege is also tackled through the second paragraph of Articles 47 and 48 CFR. The provisions, at the very least, mirror Article 6 ECHR. One may wonder whether, within the scope of cases to which those articles apply, they also guarantee a PSI to corporations and, if so, what extent. A first question that needs to be briefly answered is whether corporations can invoke Charter provisions as such.[1558] It does not contain an explicit rule as to which CFR provisions apply to legal persons – perhaps surprisingly, as it was adopted decades after the first fundamental rights treaties' adoption[1559] and in light of the high number of cases tackled by the CJEU involving legal persons claiming freedoms and rights. Although some provisions focus on individuals rather than legal persons,[1560] it has meanwhile become clear that several provisions are applicable to legal persons, including the freedom to conduct a business[1561] and the right to property covered by Article 17 CFR.[1562] In light of the ECtHR's case law on Article 8 ECHR on the right to respect for the home, the CJEU has accepted Article 7 CFR's applicability to legal persons in cases addressing the right to home.[1563] Nevertheless, the CJEU has also picked up on the ECtHR's more permissive attitude in relation to intrusion when a legal person's right to respect for the home is at stake rather than an individual's.[1564] Moreover, the CJEU has not excluded that a legal person can rely

[1556] Joined Cases C-204/00 P, C-205/00 P, C-211/00 P, C-213/00 P, C-217/00 P and C-219/00 P *Aalborg Portland A/S and Others v Commission* ECLI:EU:C:2004:6, paras 206–09.

[1557] Arts 9–11 of Council Regulation (EU) of 15 October 2013 conferring specific tasks on the European Central Bank concerning policies relating to the prudential supervision of credit institutions. See S Allegrezza and I Rodopoulos, 'Enforcing Prudential Banking Regulations in the Eurozone: A Reading from the Viewpoint of Criminal Law' in K Ligeti and V Franssen (eds), *Challenges in the Field of Economic and Financial Crime in Europe and the US* (Hart Publishing, 2017) 238; Lasagni, *Banking Supervision* (n 430) 257–65; G Lasagni, 'Investigatory, Supervisory and Sanctioning Powers within the SSM' in Allegrezza (n 1047) 86–89.

[1558] See 3 above.

[1559] Oliver, 'Companies and their Fundamental Rights' (n 235) 680. Nevertheless, some specific articles do indicate that they also apply to legal persons: see Arts 42–44.

[1560] Such as Art 1.

[1561] Case C-70/10 *Scarlet Extended SA v Sabam* ECLI:EU:C:2011:771, para 46.

[1562] ibid.

[1563] Case C-583/13 P *Deutsche Bahn AG and Others v Commission* ECLI:EU:C:2015:404, paras 19–20; J Vested-Hansen, 'Respect for Private and Family Life (Private Life, Home and Communications)' in Peers et al (n 509) 158–59.

[1564] Case C-94/00 *Roquette Frères SA* ECLI:EU:C:2002:603, para 29.

on Articles 47 and 48 CFR, for example, to support their claim for legal aid.[1565] The Court has relied strongly on the principle of effective judicial protection and the rights of the defence,[1566] nowadays enshrined in the Charter, in this context.[1567] The Court's case law shows that the POI enshrined in Article 48(1) CFR is applicable to corporations, also in competition cases.[1568]

In addition to examining the ECtHR's case law and national approaches when considering the applicability of Charter provisions to legal persons, the CJEU has also accepted with regard to Article 47 CFR that the use in multiple language versions of the word 'person(s)'[1569] can be an indication that they cover legal persons.[1570] Furthermore, the Court pays attention to the title of the Charter in which a provision can be found; for example, it paid attention to the fact that Article 47 is part of Title VI of the Charter, which deals with justice, and to the fact that other principles of that title apply to natural as well as legal persons.[1571]

The CJEU may offer wider protection to legal persons than the ECtHR. At the same time, Article 52(3) CFR precludes the CJEU from applying a more restricted approach to legal persons where the CJEU applies fundamental rights covered by both the ECHR and the CFR. Admittedly, there is no explicit ECtHR case law that has accepted the privilege's applicability to corporations. At the same time, even if the ECtHR were to decide that Article 6 ECHR does not grant corporations a PSI, this would not necessarily imply that corporations cannot benefit from such a privilege on the basis of Articles 47 and 48 CFR. Nor would a ruling of the ECtHR granting corporations a more restricted privilege than that guaranteed to individuals on the basis of Article 6 ECHR[1572] imply that the CJEU would necessarily have to come to the same conclusion as the ECtHR.

The implications of *DB v Consob* for corporations are not entirely clear.[1573] AG Pikamäe emphasised that the PSI's rationales, as recognised by the ECtHR, are strongly connected to human dignity. Therefore, he considers that the ECtHR's case law, as it stands, cannot be transposed to legal persons.[1574] The

[1565] *DEB* (n 14) para 59. The Court left it to the national court to check whether the national conditions for the obtention of legal aid constituted a restriction on the right to access to a court which undermined that right's core.

[1566] The latter are part of the principle of effective judicial protection: Case C-199/11 *Europese Gemeenschap v Otis NV and others* ECLI:EU:C:2012:684, para 48.

[1567] *Texdata* (n 14) paras 70 and 76; Case C-203/21 *Delta Stroy* 2003 ECLI:EU:C:865.

[1568] Case C-243/12 P *FLS Plast A/S v Commission* ECLI:EU:C:2014:2006, paras 23–27; *'Eturas'* (n 14) para 38.

[1569] This is the case, for example, for the German and French versions of Arts 47(1) and 47(2). The English version refers to 'everyone' in Arts 47(1) and 47(2) and to 'those' in Art 47(3). Similarly, the Dutch version refers to 'everyone' and to 'those'.

[1570] *DEB* (n 14) paras 38–39.

[1571] ibid para 40.

[1572] Delanote, 'Hof van Justitie erkent ruime draagwijdte van het zwijgrecht' (n 1030) 5/5 considers chances of such a decision as slim.

[1573] ibid 5/5.

[1574] AG Pikamäe (n 59) paras 97–99.

CJEU has, unsurprisingly, extensively referred to natural persons in its ruling. Do those references imply that corporations can, in the CJEU's view, never, even in *sensu stricto* criminal cases, claim a more extensive PSI than the one recognised in *Orkem*? Considering that the preliminary reference was made in a case involving a *natural* person,[1575] the Court did not have to answer that thorny[1576] question.[1577] The Court therefore seemingly limited its reasoning by focusing on natural persons. At the same time, the Court made reference to its *Orkem* case law in paragraphs 46–48. The Court concluded that that case law cannot be applied 'by analogy when determining the scope of the right to silence of natural persons who, like DB, are the subject of proceedings for an offence of insider dealing'. Those parts of the judgment show that the CJEU does not want to strip the EC of effective investigative tools in competition cases.[1578] In my view, the quoted section does not necessarily imply that corporations can only benefit from a 'light version' of the PSI in punitive cases, other than competition ones, particularly where those cases are *sensu stricto* criminal cases. The Court specifically referred to natural persons who 'are the subject of proceedings for an offence of insider dealing'. The specificities of the field of competition law versus other fields seems of great relevance. In any case, the CJEU has accepted that a limited privilege is guaranteed on the basis of a general principle of EU law in the field of competition law,[1579] a field traditionally not considered to be criminal in nature by that Court,[1580] and it has accepted that legal persons can rely on the rights of defence and to effective judicial protection.[1581]

The POI Directive explicitly excludes corporations from its scope.[1582] This contrasts with the Directives previously adopted in the framework of the roadmap for strengthening procedural rights in criminal proceedings,[1583] which are

[1575] The Italian Constitutional Court referred to individuals, not to legal persons.

[1576] Given the diverging views, at the national level but also between different EU institutions, on that matter.

[1577] Para 34 of the ruling shows the Court understood it was only asked to clarify the situation of natural persons. The same holds true for *FN* (n 17). In that case, the administrative sanction procedure was launched against three natural persons.

[1578] The concepts 'undertakings' and 'associations of undertakings', used in para 48 of the judgment are typical concepts of (EU) competition law.

[1579] *DB v Consob* (n 17) para 47.

[1580] Lasagni, *Banking Supervision* (n 430) 237.

[1581] eg Case C-176/13 P *Council v Bank Mellat* ECLI:EU:C:2016:96, para 49. The Court has affirmed that 'In all proceedings in which sanctions, especially fines or penalty payments, may be imposed, observance of the rights of the defence is a fundamental principle of Community law which must be complied with even if the proceedings in question are administrative proceedings': Case C-194/99 P *Thyssen Stahl AG v Commission* ECLI:EU:C:2003:527, para 30; *Texdata* (n 14) para 79.

[1582] Art 2 POI Directive and recitals 13–15. See also S Lamberigts, 'The Directive on the Presumption of Innocence. A Missed Opportunity for Legal Persons?' [2016] No 1 *Eucrim* 36; Lasagni, *Banking Supervision* (n 430) 65; A Pivaty et al, 'Opening Pandora's Box: The Right to Silence in Police Interrogations and the Directive 2016/343/EU' (2021) 12 *New Journal of European Criminal Law* 328, 333.

[1583] Resolution of the Council of 30 November 2009 on a Roadmap for strengthening procedural rights of suspected or accused persons in criminal proceedings.

applicable to suspects or accused persons and do not explicitly exclude legal persons.[1584] Legal persons were not excluded from the POI Directive's scope by accident. Instead, it was an explicit choice of the EU legislator.[1585] The legislative history of the Directive shows that the EP tried to include legal persons withing its scope.[1586] However, the Council, supported by the EC, rejected this approach.[1587] In support of its arguments, the Council and the EC referred to several considerations that have now been incorporated into the Directive's recitals.[1588] The EU legislator considered that the needs and levels of protection for individuals and legal persons with regard to certain aspects of the POI are different. The EU legislator relies on the CJEU case law in competition cases. Ultimately, the recitals indicate that, in light of national law, as well as Union law and national case law, legislative action with regard to legal persons is considered premature, as there is a lack of consensus. These arguments raise several interesting issues. First, referring to case law handed down in a punitive administrative context to exclude legal persons from a Directive that seems to be focused on *sensu stricto* criminal cases is questionable. Unlike classic criminal cases, punitive administrative cases do not always give rise to the most stringent application of safeguards developed with classic criminal cases in mind. The EU legislator does not seem to give a clear justification for this differentiated treatment of legal persons; why should legal persons facing a classic criminal case not benefit from a higher level of procedural safeguards than when they face punitive administrative proceedings?

Secondly, the EU legislator seems to overlook the increasing importance of CCL. Since AG Darmon referred to the situation in the EU MSs on the applicability of the privilege to legal persons in the 1980s, a lot has changed: several MSs have since introduced CCL.[1589] Investigations involving the financial interests of the EU can focus on 'economic operators',[1590] making legal persons the object of investigations and prosecution. Therefore, including legal persons in the POI Directive's scope would have reflected this new reality and led to an increased level of legal certainty, in light of the diverging national approaches.[1591]

[1584] eg Art 1 of Directive 2010/64/EU on the right to interpretation and translation in criminal proceedings and Arts 1 and 2 of Directive 2012/13/EU on the right to information in criminal proceedings.

[1585] The legal basis used for the POI Directive, Art 82(2)(b) TFEU, refers to 'the rights of individuals in criminal procedure'. Should this be understood as limiting the EU legislator's competence to procedural safeguards that apply only to natural persons and thus not to legal persons? Other language versions of the TFEU, such as the Dutch and French versions, refer to 'persons' and seem less restrictive in their wording. Moreover, the use of the term 'individuals' in Art 82(2)(b) TFEU does not seem to have been an issue during the negotiations on the POI Directive.

[1586] EP Document of 20 August 2015, A8-0133/2015, amendments 9 and 39, www.europarl.europa.eu/sides/getDoc.do?pubRef=-//EP//NONSGML+REPORT+A8-2015-0133+0+DOC+PDF+V0//EN.

[1587] See Council doc of 29 July 2015, 11112/15, p 4, n 1, http://data.consilium.europa.eu/doc/document/ST-11112-2015-INIT/en/pdf.

[1588] Recitals 13–15 POI Directive.

[1589] Vermeulen et al (n 2) 34–35.

[1590] Art 2(6) of Regulation (EU, Euratom) 883/2013.

[1591] The EP considered the fact that several MSs have introduced CCL justifies the POI Directive's application to them. See also amendment 39.

Nevertheless, even if the Directive had covered legal persons, not all questions would have been answered: the aforementioned uncertainties would also apply to legal persons too.[1592] On the basis of the Directive's text, MSs could have granted legal persons a limited privilege by stipulating that only a small circle of corporate officials or agents can invoke it.[1593]

Recitals 14 and 15 of the Directive make it clear that legal persons can nevertheless rely on the POI,[1594] as incorporated in particular in the ECHR and in light of the case law of the ECtHR and the CJEU. Furthermore, recital 15 refers to existing legislative safeguards. One of the specific EU legal instruments in which the privilege is laid down is Articles 3(8) and 9(2) of the 2013 Regulation on OLAF investigations.[1595] Articles 2(5)–2(6), 3(8) and 9(2) of that Regulation, Article 5 of Council Regulation (Euratom, EC) 2185/96 of 11 November 1996 concerning on-the-spot checks and inspections carried out by the EC in order to protect the European Communities' financial interests against fraud and other irregularities and Article 7 of Council Regulation (EC, Euratom) 2988/95 of 18 December 1995 on the protection of the European Communities' financial interests imply that in OLAF investigations legal persons have access to the PSI. Article 41 of the EPPO Regulation confirms that in the EPPO's criminal proceedings any suspected or accused person[1596] benefits from the right to remain silent and the POI as provided for in the POI Directive. At the same time, the cross-reference in Article 41 to specific Directives has been criticised, as protection would be reliant on national implementation.[1597]

The privilege in E&W has been restricted over time, particularly in relation to documents and through the introduction of compulsory questioning provisions. These two issues are particularly relevant for corporate defendants. Compulsory questioning provisions are often found in the economic sphere, both in the context of non-punitive inquiries and in serious punitive fraud cases.

Triplex Safety Glass Company is a landmark case on the corporate PSI.[1598] A company and its director faced a claim for damages. The case raised the issue of the applicability of the privilege to corporations in relation to interrogations.[1599] Its director invoked the privilege, arguing that his answers could be self-incriminating. The company's secretary similarly objected to the interrogatories on that ground, on behalf of the corporation.[1600] The court accepted that corporations

[1592] Lamberigts, 'The Directive on the Presumption of Innocence' (n 1582) 38.

[1593] ibid.

[1594] This notion is understood broadly by the Directive and it seems that the reference in the recitals also refers to the privilege.

[1595] Regulation (EU, Euratom) 883/2013.

[1596] Persons includes, according to Art 2(2) of the Regulation, legal persons.

[1597] T Wahl, 'The European Public Prosecutor's Office and the Fragmentation of Defence Rights' in K Ligeti et al (eds), *The European Public Prosecutor's Office at Launch* (Wolters Kluwer, 2020) 99–100.

[1598] *Triplex Safety Glass Co Ltd v Lancegaye Safety Glass (1934) Ltd* [1939] 2 KB 395.

[1599] The facts of the case involved allegations of libel and slander.

[1600] The secretary thus acted in a representative capacity. He was not personally required to testify.

could rely on the privilege.[1601] It did not accept the distinction between legal and natural persons, as the elements of the offence could be proven against a corporation.[1602] In other words, if a corporation can be held liable for an offence, it should, in the court's view, be able to rely on the privilege the way a natural person can. It attached particular importance to the negative consequences of a conviction for a corporation's reputation, as well as to its members.[1603] This is an interesting approach, as it does not focus on some of the traditional justifications of the privilege, such as the protection against the cruel trilemma, or the protection of privacy. Instead, the focus is on the negative consequences of a possible conviction for the corporation and its members.[1604] In this sense, the CoA implicitly takes into account the compulsion that a corporation faces when it risks being prosecuted and convicted of a punitive offence. The court does not explicitly refer to it, yet one may also understand its approach of linking the privilege's applicability to the risk of facing a conviction in light of another justification of the privilege: the privilege has been justified by the argument that the prosecution is not to shift the burden of proof to the defendant. This idea is reflected in the court's finding that one should not be required to admit an offence. The CoA thus relied on a fair play argument.[1605] Nevertheless, the court's reasoning on its decision to apply the privilege to corporations is short.

Other courts have also accepted the privilege's applicability to corporations.[1606] Still, it remains unclear to what extent a person can refuse to cooperate by arguing that the corporation would be incriminated. Can a corporation refuse to cooperate by arguing that its corporate officials would be incriminated? Where both the corporation and the individuals can rely on their own privilege, the discussion is considered purely academic,[1607] as the privilege of the one is likely to benefit the other too.[1608] It has been argued that the privilege of a corporation would not provide much protection if the statements or documents could be obtained from its officials or employees through the back door.[1609] Yet, this argument has faced opposition, as the privilege is said to be a personal right that only protects the person claiming it.[1610] In other words, if a person is himself required to

[1601] *Triplex Safety* (n 1598) 408. Some other objections turned on more general issues, such as the improbability that a prosecution would be brought.

[1602] Critically on this judgment and on the acceptance of it by the UKHL, see Sedley (n 362) 122.

[1603] *Triplex Safety* (n 1598) 409.

[1604] Pinto and Evans (n 4) 223.

[1605] O'Neill (n 464) 131.

[1606] *Rio Tinto* (n 991); *Kensington International* (n 543) para 40; *Volaw Trust* (n 615) para 39; Gobert and Punch (n 248) 196; O'Neill (n 464) 130.

[1607] *Kensington International* (n 543) para 39.

[1608] Where grants of immunity can be given, this issue is not theoretical: one could imagine that immunity is given to an individual or the corporation. In such a case, the evidence could in principle still be used against the other one.

[1609] eg *Kensington International* (n 543) para 41. See also the opinion of Viscount Dilhorne in *Rio Tinto* (n 991) 632.

[1610] *Rio Tinto* (n 991) 637–38.

provide information and complying would not lead to self-incrimination, he can apparently[1611] not refuse to cooperate by claiming that he would incriminate the corporation.[1612] Thus, where the requirement is addressed to the corporation, one of its officials can in principle still appear and invoke the privilege on the corporation's behalf.[1613]

The second question was addressed in *Tate Access Floors*.[1614] The CoA refused to exempt a corporation, which, in the concrete case, could not claim the privilege,[1615] from the obligation to provide information. It argued that this would lead to the incrimination of senior officials or shareholders of the corporation, but that argument was not accepted.[1616] This finding relied on the argument that only the person who would tend to incriminate himself can rely on the privilege.[1617] If one conducts his business through a legal person, this implies a certain choice. One cannot claim that the corporation is a separate entity, for example for the purpose of liability, yet claim the contrary[1618] when evidence is sought. The CoA thus rejected the idea that the privilege of corporations has an additional justification: ensuring the effectiveness of the privilege of its individual employees or officers.[1619] It applied the argument that the privilege is a purely personal right in a very strict way.

In light of these restrictions, it is essential that when requests for information are addressed to a corporate officer or employee, or to the corporation itself, clear indications are given on that person's status.

Since the privilege applies to corporations in E&W,[1620] my analysis on the privilege of individuals is to be applied *mutatis mutandis* to corporations.[1621] Courts have generally tended to apply the privilege to corporations in the same way as to individuals. For example, in *R v Herts CC Ex p Green Environmental Industries*, the UKHL did not differentiate between individuals and corporations.

[1611] As there is no binding opinion on this issue, see *Kensington International Ltd v Republic of Congo (formerly People's Republic of Congo) (Vitol Services Ltd and others, third parties)* [2008] 1 WLR 114.

[1612] *Kensington International* (n 543) para 47; Keane and McKeown (n 535) 717. Since the individuals in *Rio Tinto* (n 991) were entitled to the privilege, this issue was not as such decided in the UKHL ruling in *Rio Tinto*. Lord Diplock was particularly critical of the idea that a corporation's PSI could be constructed as to allow its officers and employees to refuse to answer questions that could incriminate the corporation: *Rio Tinto* (n 991) 637–38. Where the corporation would be a one-man corporation, the answer might be different: *Kensington International* (n 543) para 47.

[1613] A certain formalism has been applied in order to determine whether one can be considered as the corporation's representative: *Walkers Snack Foods Ltd v Coventry City Council* [1998] 3 All ER 163.

[1614] *Tate Access* (n 1383).

[1615] As it could not claim that there was a tendency that it would expose itself to self-incrimination: ibid 530.

[1616] Keane and McKeown (n 535) 717.

[1617] *Tate Access* (n 1383) 531.

[1618] Namely, that it is his creature: ibid 531–32.

[1619] In contrast, see Roles (n 82) 33.

[1620] *Umbro Holdings Ltd and others v OFT* [2005] CAT 22, 61; *Volaw Trust* (n 615) para 39; Pinto and Evans (n 4) 222; Sime (n 541) 347; Veenbrink, *Criminal Law Principles* (n 386) 118–19.

[1621] Ormerod and Perry (n 540) 2800.

Belgium adopted an autonomous CCL model, strongly relying on an anthropomorphic approach to corporations. One may wonder whether that approach has impacted the availability of procedural rights such as the PSI to corporations. This issue is primarily addressed by case law and doctrine, rather than in legislation.[1622] The main legislative measure, the AHR, nevertheless shows that the legislator was aware of potential conflicts of interests and their impact on the corporation's effective defence in a *sensu stricto* criminal case. Before I analyse the current state of the corporation's privilege under Belgian law, I briefly examine that concept.

As conflicts of interest between individuals and the corporation can occur,[1623] the legislator attempted to put in place a mechanism to protect the corporation against a hidden agenda of one of its representatives and to ensure that it fully benefits from a possibility of effectively exercising its defence rights.[1624] To this aim, Article 2*bis* of the PT of the CCP introduced the position of the AHR. The *sensu stricto* criminal action needs to have been launched against the corporation and against the person competent to represent it.[1625] The AHR represents the corporation, but is not its lawyer that pleads on its behalf. It nevertheless has important tasks, such as choosing a lawyer and introducing legal remedies (or instructing an attorney to do so).[1626] To serve and act in the interests of the corporation, he has to consult with the directors and the partners of the corporation.[1627] This well-intended measure has from the start given rise to several questions and problems,[1628] which have led to calls for the abolition of Article 2*bis*.[1629] Even after the abolition of the *decumul* rule, a better drafted statutory provision on the AHR can still be relevant, as some possible conflicts of interest are still around.[1630] Whether the appointment of such a representative

[1622] Some CCP provisions pay specific attention to legal persons: Art 91 CCP addresses the provisional measures an investigating judge can adopt against corporations. Art 20 of the PT of the CCP addresses the effects of, for example, the winding up of a legal person on the possibility of successfully prosecuting it.

[1623] Though not in all cases: ConsC 5 December 2006, 190/2006, 7, B.2.1; P Helsen, 'Lasthebber ad hoc' in X, *Strafrecht en strafvordering. Artikelsgewijze commentaar met overzicht van rechtspraak en rechtsleer* (Kluwer, 2019) afl 92, 138.

[1624] CoA Liège 8 September 2008, [2009] JDSC 261, 262; CoC 15 June 2016, P.16.0254.F.

[1625] The capacity to represent the corporation has to be assessed at the time of the AHR's appointment: Helsen (n 1623) 158. Moreover, where one person cannot represent the corporation alone, but only together with a second person, the fact that one of these two persons is charged does not suffice to trigger the statutory provision.

[1626] On this point, see CoC 6 September 2016, P.16.0052.N; Waeterinckx, 'Strafrechtelijke verantwoordelijkheid' (n 1430) 215.

[1627] P Waeterinckx, 'Het aanwenden van rechtsmiddelen voor de rechtspersoon door de lasthebber ad hoc, een verdere verfijning van de rechtspraak van het Hof van Cassatie' [2017] *Nullum Crimen* 78, 80.

[1628] ibid 78.

[1629] F Deruyck, 'Het is lastig te pleiten zonder toga – Over het onhoudbare artikel 2bis V.T.Sv.' [2013] *Nullum Crimen* 89, 96. Critically, see Helsen (n 1623) 139. Even after the *decumul* rule's abolition, Art 2*bis* is still in place. Art 34 of the Bill on the CCP similarly includes a provision on the AHR: Wetsvoorstel houdende het Wetboek van Strafprocesrecht, *ParlSt* Kamer 2019–20, 1239/001, 367.

[1630] On that matter, see de Formanoir (n 22) 94; M Delvaux, 'L'intérêt du mandataire ad hoc depuis la reformulation de l'article 5 du Code pénal' [2020] *Recueil annuel de jurisprudence en droit des sociétés*

is mandatory[1631] has been extensively debated.[1632] A strict reading of the statute suggests it is,[1633] but case law is not unanimous on the issue. When different lawyers represent the individual and the corporation, there is a certain acceptance not to appoint an AHR.[1634] Waeterinckx suggests that if no appointment is asked, the court has an obligation to check whether an *ex officio* appointment is opportune.[1635] In light of the corporation's defence rights, blindly and automatically appointing an AHR is, in my view, neither needed nor desirable. An *ex officio* appointment can give rise to issues: the corporation should be free to choose who will represent it and how to set up its defence. The ConsC has considered that the AHR takes the position of the ordinary corporate representative. According to the Court, he does not have to seek instructions from the corporation's organs. He takes their place and he alone determines the defence strategy.[1636] Such a far-reaching role can be problematic. The ConsC has, in the same ruling, strongly nuanced the aforementioned considerations by holding that the AHR's role is not to provide extensive legal advice to the corporation, nor to assist it in the framework of the criminal proceedings. Instead, he substitutes the persons who are ordinarily competent to represent the corporation.[1637] As Waeterinckx rightly considers, a substitute does not have more rights than the person that he substitutes.[1638] If a lawyer without knowledge of the specifics of the corporation[1639] is appointed as an AHR, the defence may not take place in the most effective way.[1640] Therefore, the preferable approach is to let the corporation choose its AHR,[1641] provided that this person has no conflict of interest.[1642] A corporation can, in any case, to pre-empt conflicts of interests or the *ex officio* imposition of an AHR, appoint a special representative who is not burdened by a conflict of interest.[1643] Another issue which the current

commerciales 202, 203; P Waeterinckx, 'De strafrechtelijke verantwoordelijkheid van de rechtspersoon – Moet de regeling i.v.m. de lasthebber ad hoc onder artikel 2bis V.T.Sv. "op de schop" omwille van de afschaffing (?) van de decumulatieregel onder oud artikel 5, tweede lid Sw.?' [2019] *Tijdschrift voor Belgisch Handelsrecht* 949, 969–71; Werding (n 22) 127.

[1631] CoA Ghent considered it not to be mandatory: CoA Ghent 1 March 2002, [2002–03] RW 1548, 1549. CoA Liège considers that there is room to test whether the appointment of an AHR is opportune: CoA Liège 8 September 2008 (n 1624) 262.

[1632] On this issue, see Helsen (n 1623) 143–47; Van Gerven (n 1434) 968.

[1633] FiC Liège 4 March 2015, [2015] Dr pén entr 237. The use of 'appoints' instead of can appoint supports such reading. See also Deruyck, 'Het is lastig te pleiten' (n 1629) 90.

[1634] Waeterinckx, 'Strafrechtelijke verantwoordelijkheid' (n 1430) 210–11.

[1635] ibid 212.

[1636] ConsC 17 November 2016, 143/2016, B.2.3.

[1637] ibid B.7.

[1638] Waeterinckx, 'De strafrechtelijke verantwoordelijkheid' (n 1630) 957.

[1639] It is true that he can gather information on the corporation and on what has happened, but this is not the most effective solution.

[1640] CoA Ghent 1 March 2002 (n 1631) 1550.

[1641] The ConsC also stresses that the corporation can indeed propose its own AHR: ConsC 5 December 2006 (n 1623) B.7. See also Deruyck, 'Het is lastig te pleiten' (n 1629) 93–94.

[1642] CoA Liège 3 February 2011, [2011] Dr pén entr 97, 98; Waeterinckx, 'Strafrechtelijke verantwoordelijkheid' (n 1430) 216.

[1643] For example, a member of the legal department or another director.

legislation tackles poorly is the stage at which the representative is appointed. As the legislation currently stands, Article 2*bis* only applies once an investigative judge is in charge of the investigation and the corporation has been charged (in accordance with the CCP)[1644] or when the case is pending before a trial court. As the large majority of investigations are conducted by the prosecutor and not by an investigative judge,[1645] there is a clear gap in legal protection. By the time an AHR is appointed, major damage may already be done: if the representative that is charged has had a chance to scapegoat the corporation, putting in place an AHR will not necessarily remedy the problem.[1646] Similarly, an appointment of an AHR at the trial stage, often years after the investigation was started, may be too little, too late. Important evidence might have disappeared, as investigations regularly last an excessively long time. Another problem is that the statutory provision does not apply until the corporation itself is charged. In practice, the corporation itself is often only charged after the key individuals, who may have a conflict of interest, have been questioned.[1647]

Turning to the specific issue of the corporation's PSI, case law on the topic at the time of writing is rather limited, and more case law is needed to answer certain open questions. What is clear by now is that the privilege does indeed apply to corporations.[1648] In *Citibank*, the CoC confirmed that the privilege applies to corporations.[1649] As I outlined before, the issue at hand was that both the corporation and some of the individuals working for it had been threatened with penalties if they would not hand over the requested information. The Court did not distinguish between individuals and corporations for the purpose of the privilege, nor did the CoA of Brussels dealing with the case before it.[1650] In light of the anthropomorphic approach to CCL, this is not surprising, but the CoC's reasoning does not explicitly make this connection to the anthropomorphic CCL model. Neither did the Court apply the *Jalloh* criteria to this case. *Citibank* suggests that in relation to documentary evidence, the same privilege applies to corporations as to

[1644] CoC 8 February 2022 (n 1453).

[1645] Van den Wyngaert et al (n 35) 648.

[1646] Admittedly, the statement of such an individual is not the only piece of evidence. Interrogations of other persons or documents can cast another light on the statements of the individual that tried to scapegoat the corporation. Deruyck, 'Het is lastig te pleiten' (n 1629) 96–97; Helsen (n 1623) 143.

[1647] Waeterinckx, 'Strafrechtelijke verantwoordelijkheid' (n 1430) 222–23.

[1648] Beernaert et al (n 405) 32; M Faure and P Waeterinckx, 'De strafrechtelijke verantwoordelijkheid van de rechtspersoon: een blik op de rechtspraak en enkele knelpunten uit de praktijk' [2004] *Tijdschrift voor Strafrecht* 318, 338–39; S Lamberigts, 'Het zwijgrecht van rechtspersonen: aandachtspunten en (supra)nationale perspectieven' [2018] *Tijdschrift voor Strafrecht* 302, 311; D Van Gerven, 'Grondslagen van het rechtspersonenrecht' [2020] *Tijdschrift voor Privaatrecht* 887, 909. Critically, see Bloch (n 1050) 13.

[1649] CoC 19 June 2013 (n 1) 3–5. See also CoA Antwerp 16 June 2015 (n 1303); CoC 17 October 2017, P.16.0854.N.

[1650] CoA Brussels 21 May 2012 (n 1) 151. It explicitly held that the privilege is applicable regardless of the fact that the suspect is a legal person. It held that if a legal person can face CCL, it should be able to benefit from the same rights as an individual.

individuals. Several authors share the view of these courts.[1651] There are no reasons to believe that the courts would be more generous when applying the privilege to corporations, eg in relation to documentary evidence. This has been demonstrated by a critical 2015 judgment of the FiC of Liège.[1652] A company had been obliged to provide the authorities with information pursuant to applicable legislation, which stipulated sanctions in case the information was not submitted. The court critically recalled the privilege's historical origin and its connection to natural persons, without excluding the applicability to corporations.[1653] It concluded that the privilege had not been infringed, as by operating in a regulated industry the corporation had waived its privilege.[1654] Although it is accepted in Belgium that one can waive one's PSI, the argument made by the court is not in line with Belgian and ECtHR case law. It attaches excessive importance to *O'Halloran* and disregards other judgments, such as *Saunders* and *Marttinen*.[1655] *Saunders* shows that engaging in, for example, complex corporate activities does as such not constitute a waiver.

A crucial issue that remains unsettled in Belgium is the circle of employees and corporate officials that can invoke the corporation's PSI.[1656] At the outset, it should be stressed that a corporate privilege does not necessarily render corporate prosecutions impossible. Even if certain corporate employees or officials can exercise it, other investigative tools remain available, such as interviews of persons without a personal[1657] or corporate privilege, searches, seizures or requests for information from third parties. Similarly, by using tools such as settlements, corporations can be incentivised to cooperate. Whistleblowers too can provide useful information. Moreover, the privilege is often not invoked in the context of economic crime.[1658] Thus, the PSI's availability does not necessarily imply that it will be used.

Belgian doctrine has presented several models for the corporate privilege. Deruyck favours a broad privilege for corporations.[1659] If a corporation wants to make a statement at trial or during the investigation, it can, through its board of directors, decide who will make that statement. This can either be the person who according to its internal organisation is warranted to represent the corporation or a specifically appointed person. Where the authorities want to question 'the corporation itself', again the competent corporate organ should decide who can speak/stay silent on the corporation's behalf. Thus, the authorities who set

[1651] De Raedt (n 637) 434; Deruyck, 'De rechten van verdediging' (n 287) 34–35; Huybrechts and Rozie (n 1342) 120. See also Dewandeleer (n 969) 160; Waeterinckx, 'De (afgeleide) rechten van verdediging' (n 316) 84, who connects the privilege to CCL.

[1652] FiC Liège 12 February 2015 (n 1386).

[1653] ibid 1857.

[1654] ibid 1859.

[1655] *Saunders* (n 393); *O'Halloran* (n 483); *Marttinen* (n 385).

[1656] On the importance of this exercise, see R Verstraeten, 'Kritische beschouwingen bij het nieuwe strafrechtelijke aansprakelijkheidsregime voor de rechtspersonen' in Jan Ronse Instituut, *Nieuw vennootschaps- en financieel recht 1999* (Biblo, 2000) 242–43.

[1657] Because they do not qualify as suspects or because they are merely heard as witnesses and are at no real risk of self-incrimination.

[1658] Deruyck, 'De rechten van verdediging' (n 287) 38.

[1659] ibid 34–39.

up the interview should not be able to decide who speaks on the corporation's behalf. Once an AHR has been appointed, he is the only one who can represent the corporation. This stresses the importance of involving the corporation in the choice of AHR. Deruyck argues that if the authorities want to interview witnesses, and not the suspected corporation itself, they can in principle interrogate any suitable person.[1660] He goes on to nuance this general approach by adding that where these persons are employees or officials of the corporation, two sub-hypotheses should be distinguished: to the extent that these individuals would themselves be suspects, they are entitled to their own privilege; if they are not, Deruyck thinks they should be able to rely on the corporation's PSI. He believes that such a broad corporate privilege is justified: any corporate employee or official can trigger the corporation's criminal liability and thus they should all be able to exercise its privilege.[1661]

Deruyck's model is very broad and leads to a situation where any corporate employee can invoke the corporation's privilege. It raises several concerns. At first sight, such a system seems to be clearer than one that distinguishes between different types of employees or officials to decide who can invoke the corporation's privilege. In my view, it would be hard to realise that model in practice: it will require substantial training of the corporation's employees, specifically in bigger corporations.[1662] Employees, particularly those without a legal background, will need coaching to be prepared to invoke the corporation's privilege.[1663] Moreover, such a broad privilege will often include employees who are not involved in the corporate wrongdoing, so in this sense it seems overly broad.[1664] Moreover, by proposing such a broad privilege, a corporation would achieve something a business owner who does not operate under the form of a corporation cannot achieve: any employee can refuse to speak against the corporation, whereas in a situation where the business owner is an individual, none of his employees can exercise the businessman's PSI. Justifying this merely by reference to the fact that any employee can trigger the corporation's criminal liability does not convince everyone.[1665] Self-evidently, the corporation will need individuals in order to exercise its defence rights, but this does not imply that all employees can do so. A more correct assessment seems to be that those who can represent[1666] the corporation and thus speak

[1660] ibid 36.
[1661] ibid 38.
[1662] For example, they should know what to do when they receive an invitation for a police interview.
[1663] For example, for situations where pressure is exercised against them during interrogations.
[1664] A suspect's PSI not only allows him not to make incriminating statements, but to stay silent as such.
[1665] G Stessens, 'Procedurele aspecten van de opsporing en de vervolging bij strafbare feiten gepleegd door rechtspersonen' in X, *Bestendig Handboek Vennootschap & Aansprakelijkheid* (Kluwer, 2000) afl 1, 37–38. Stessens points out that where an employee can trigger the corporation's liability, he would be able to rely on his own privilege as he would be a suspect (at least of participating in the corporation's offence).
[1666] The use of the word 'represent' here should not be considered in the strict sense of those who are legally mandated to represent it.

or stay silent on its behalf can exercise its privilege as they do so.[1667] Moreover, a corporation-wide privilege can in practice only work if the individuals are well prepared and if the corporation can instruct them to some extent.[1668] As long as the corporation's instruction to stay silent or to refuse to hand over documents does not amount to an offence, this should as such be possible.[1669] As I explained before, several sectorial statutes include an obstruction of supervision offence. Just like exercising one's own privilege[1670] should not lead to a conviction for this offence, exercising the corporation's privilege should not do so either. In any case, where the employee or corporate official has to defend himself against an accusation, his first priority will be his own defence strategy, and in such cases the corporation's privilege is very vulnerable. Moreover, individuals may decide to become whistleblowers and apply for specific protection on this basis.

Waeterinckx proposes a privilege that is more restricted than the one pictured by Deruyck. He rightly points out the importance of clear information on the status someone has when questioned and in the context of the investigation as such:[1671] is the corporation in fact already a suspect?[1672] Is its legal representative being interviewed in his capacity of representative of the corporation? As a witness? Or is he himself a suspect?[1673] It is important for the corporation's privilege that the corporation and the individuals who can exercise its privilege are aware of its availability. Waeterinckx rightly points out that invoking the privilege can be helpful in acquiring a better insight into the situation at hand.[1674] He suggests that the corporation's privilege can be invoked by those who, according to applicable legislation, can represent the corporation,[1675] as well as possibly by the management.[1676] This extension is warranted by the fact that their behaviour is of crucial importance for the attribution of the offence to

[1667] Which distinguishes the situation of a business owner and his employee. The employee's declarations during an interrogation will not be made in a representative capacity.

[1668] Critically on the idea that the corporation would give instructions to its employees, see Bloch (n 1050) 13; Stessens, 'Procedurele aspecten' (n 1665) 38.

[1669] In *Savic* (n 410) the ECtHR addressed an employee's refusal to provide information to the authorities. She referred to her employer's instructions not to provide information to the authorities.

[1670] Admittedly, there is a fine line between obstruction and the PSI as far as documents are concerned.

[1671] Waeterinckx, 'De (afgeleide) rechten van verdediging' (n 316) 85. For a concrete, problematic example, see CoC 25 September 2012, P.12.0544.F [2013] RABG 23.

[1672] Critically on interviewing all the relevant individuals first and only formally charging the corporation afterwards, see Waeterinckx, 'De (afgeleide) rechten van verdediging' (n 316) 84–85.

[1673] In which case he has his own privilege. In this case they should not be questioned as the corporation's representative.

[1674] In this sense, the privilege should not be considered as an obstruction of the truth.

[1675] These individuals should not be interrogated as witnesses. Waeterinckx, 'De (afgeleide) rechten van verdediging' (n 316) 85. See also CoC 17 October 2017 (n 1649); FiC Ypres 22 October 2018, not published.

[1676] ibid 86. This would, for example, include the employee in charge on a construction site or the person in charge of a plant of the corporation.

the corporation.[1677] It remains to be seen how the right to access to a lawyer, as enshrined in Article 47*bis* CCP, will be applied to corporations.[1678]

As for (oral) testimony, the approach proposed by Waeterinckx seems to be more balanced than Deruyck's. The AHR, the legal representatives,[1679] as well as the members of the executive body and other managing individuals[1680] should all be able to invoke the corporation's privilege in such a view. Most IT specialists within the company will fall outside the aforementioned circle and can thus be compelled to cooperate.[1681] Self-evidently, the risk is that investigators would look for individuals outside this circle in order to question them. Nevertheless, lower employees will often only have access to parts of the relevant information.

Several issues come up when an official or employee does not respect the corporation's best defence interests: what if an employee steals corporate documents and hands them over to the authorities? What if an employee's own defence would benefit from handing over the documents, while the corporation would prefer the documents not to be disclosed?

As to the first question, the evidence may have to be excluded as it could constitute illegitimate evidence. Since the Antigone doctrine was established,[1682] illegitimate evidence will only be excluded where the law provides for nullity in case of non-respect of formal conditions, if the illegitimate act has impacted the evidence's reliability or where use of the evidence would violate the right to a fair trial.[1683] Since there is no specific article that foresees nullity for the use of such evidence,[1684] it will only be excluded if the reliability has been impacted or the right to a fair trial would be impacted. Provided that there would be no doubts about the reliability, which is a factual question,[1685] the third ground is to be relied on to get the evidence excluded. As the privilege lies at the heart of a fair trial, and as the CoC has shown willingness in *Citibank* to also protect the privilege

[1677] Verslag namens de commissie voor de justitie, *ParlSt* 1998–99, 1-1217/6, 9–10.

[1678] Succinctly: Guideline 08/2011 of College of Prosecutors General on the Directive on access to a lawyer, revised on 18 October 2018, www.om-mp.be/nl/meer-weten/omzendbrieven, 189. On the pre-2016 era, see Waeterinckx, 'De (afgeleide) rechten van verdediging' (n 316) 87–95.

[1679] That the AHR and the legal representatives should be able to do so seems to be the minimum. Similarly, see Stessens, 'Procedurele aspecten' (n 1665) 36; Verstraeten, 'Kritische beschouwingen' (n 1656) 243. On this point, see also H Van Bavel, 'De Wet van 4 mei 1999 tot invoering van de strafrechtelijke verantwoordelijkheid van de rechtspersonen' [1999–2000] *Algemeen Juridisch Tijdschrift* 209, 224. Where they are themselves suspects, they can rely on their own privilege.

[1680] Critically on the possibility for employees to rely on the corporation's PSI, see Stessens, 'Procedurele aspecten' (n 1665) 37–38. Stessens argues that as they do not represent the corporation, they are not eligible to invoke it.

[1681] Dewandeleer (n 969) 160.

[1682] P Monville and D Holzapfel, 'Antigone: les évolutions législative et jurisprudentielle en droit pénal … Un bilan navrant et sévère !!!' in S Scarna (ed), *L'évolution de la jurisprudence Antigone sous le triple axe, pénal, social et fiscal* (Larcier, 2016) 21–41. That doctrine has meanwhile been included in Art 32 of the PT to the CCP.

[1683] Declercq, *Beginselen van strafrechtspleging* (n 549) 887–88; Monville and Holzapfel (n 1682) 24.

[1684] Such articles are an endangered species.

[1685] ibid 33.

of corporations, one may foster some hope that this third ground can offer some protection. At the same time, the elements that the CoC takes into account when considering this third ground may diminish this hope.[1686] If, for example, an employee steals documents without being encouraged to do so by the authorities, the chance that the evidence is excluded becomes smaller. Where the employee would merely violate the corporate policy to direct requests for documents to specific persons within the corporation, the exclusion becomes even less likely. Nevertheless, these criteria are not necessarily decisive.[1687] In one of the landmark cases on stolen evidence taken by corporate employees, the *KB Lux* case, the *sensu stricto* criminal case was in the end held to be inadmissible.[1688] At the same time, the questionable evidence laundering acts of the authorities were so serious that it is difficult to draw general conclusions from it.

As to the second question, the employee should be able to choose his own defence strategy, which may not correspond with the corporation's defence strategy. In other words, if the employee so wishes, he should be able to speak or stay silent if he believes this to be the best way to structure his own defence.

Unlike courts in E&W and Belgium, SCOTUS has repeatedly ruled that corporations and other collective entities[1689] cannot invoke the Fifth Amendment PSI.[1690] The so-called CED goes back to the 1906 *Hale v Henkel* case.[1691] Tracing its justifications and scope shows its concrete implications for corporations, their officers and employees. As I explained in chapter three, not granting the PSI to corporations can seriously impact their officials and employees too. It can lead to situations where they face compulsion in their capacity of corporate pawns, and their own defence may be harmed if the corporation does not have access to the privilege: evidence can be gathered against them through the corporation.

SCOTUS decided *Hale* 20 years after *Boyd*.[1692] In *Boyd*, SCOTUS had accepted that the privilege includes documentary evidence and had accepted that a document such as an invoice enjoyed such protection. In order to reach that conclusion, the Court had relied on a strong nexus between the Fourth and Fifth Amendments.[1693] Had SCOTUS accepted that the privilege applied to corporations too, then this would have given them a broad protection.[1694] The restrictions imposed on the privilege through the introduction of the RRD and the *Fischer* doctrine[1695]

[1686] ibid 35–36. See CoC 28 February 2017, P.16.0261.N.
[1687] ibid 36.
[1688] CoA Brussels 10 December 2010, [2011] JT 54; CoC 31 May 2011, P.10.2037.N.
[1689] Such as partnerships and unincorporated labour unions: *United States v White* 322 US 694 (1944).
[1690] Comisky et al (n 370) 2 and 22. For a recent confirmation, see *Pieciak v Thandi* 2021 WL 6133897 (D Vt, 2021), 4–5.
[1691] *Hale* (n 247).
[1692] *Boyd* (n 1053).
[1693] An approach that was not followed in *Hale* (n 247) 72.
[1694] Unless SCOTUS would have construed the scope more narrowly in relation to corporations.
[1695] *Fischer* (n 472).

still had to develop at that time. In other words, the broad ruling in *Boyd* was an important incentive to refuse the protection of the PSI to corporations.[1696] CCL developed in the USA at around the time *Hale* was handed down. CCL was seen as a tool to enforce the law against corporations that were becoming increasingly powerful.

In *Hale*, the corporation's secretary-treasurer received a subpoena to provide records belonging to the corporation, including correspondence between several corporations, and to testify before a grand jury in an antitrust case. SCOTUS emphasised that the purely personal character of the PSI is not to be relied upon to claim that the testimony may incriminate a third person, even if he is an agent of that person.[1697] It stressed the importance of documents in fighting illegal corporate behaviour, and the detrimental impact of allowing corporate employees to refuse to produce such evidence on the ground that it would incriminate the corporation.[1698] Proving antitrust cases relies to a large extent on the help of those participating in them, including the corporation's employees or agents involved, and the Court found that by accepting that the PSI also applies where a third person would be incriminated, antitrust legislation would de facto be annulled.[1699]

SCOTUS did not rely only on an effective law enforcement argument and on the PSI's personal character to refuse its applicability to corporations. It also relied on one of the theories of corporate personhood considered in chapter three, the concession theory. It distinguished between individuals and corporations for the PSI's purpose, holding that the latter are not entitled to refuse to produce their documents for analysis by the state.[1700] It found that individuals can carry out their private business as they wish and that they are not obliged to show to the state how they conduct that business when this could lead to their incrimination. Corporations owe their existence to the state that allows their incorporation, and with the privileges of a corporation come obligations, one of which is to allow investigations into its contracts and checks on the use of the corporation's powers.[1701] This view clearly reflects a specific view on the rights, privileges and duties of corporations and individuals in relation to the state.[1702] At the time of *Hale*, the number of corporations was limited compared to our contemporary standards,

[1696] Cole (n 1483) 26.

[1697] *Hale* (n 247) 67 and 69–70. The individual personally benefited from immunity. The personal character is also relevant where an individual wants to avoid production of documents that would incriminate himself personally. In *Waymo LLC v Uber Technologies Inc, Ottomotto LLC, Otto Trucking LLC* 870 F3d 1350 (Fed Cir 2017), an appellate court ruled that the PSI is a personal privilege and that the individual was not personally compelled to produce a specific report. Two companies were ordered to do so.

[1698] *Hale* (n 247) 70 and 74.

[1699] ibid 70 and 73.

[1700] ibid 74.

[1701] ibid 75.

[1702] Baer, 'Law Enforcement's Lochner' (n 853) 1705; Cole (n 1483) 21; M Rochon et al, 'Is It Time to Revisit the Corporate Privilege Against Compelled Self-Incrimination?' [2019] *The Champion* 52.

they often had a restricted scope of business in which they could engage and they were often tasked with activities such as transport or utilities.[1703] Establishing a corporation was more cumbersome in the past.[1704]

Like E&W have suggested in *Saunders* that choosing to use a corporate form has a price,[1705] SCOTUS too considers that with the choice of adopting the corporate form come obligations.[1706] This reasoning can be linked to the American CCL model, which also refuses to consider corporations in an anthropomorphic way. Instead of looking for an own act and fault of the corporation, the model is very much a derivative liability model. Similarly, the visitorial power argument is part of the idea that corporations are creatures of law who owe their existence to the state, and it can be contrasted with the idea that corporations are 'real actors'. Even though the classic E&W CCL model is also derivative, it already shows slightly more willingness to try to find a corporate identity, a tendency strengthened in the CMCHA. The argument that the benefit of incorporation comes with obligations is not prominent in Belgium. This might be an indication that corporations are indeed considered in an anthropomorphic way.

The rather short reasoning in *Hale*, which focused on the importance of the state's investigative powers, faced criticism.[1707] The idea that individuals benefited from a broad freedom whereas corporations were severely restricted in their action was already subject to criticism at the time of *Hale*. Incorporating a company was becoming increasingly easy thanks to general incorporation statutes, while the regulatory state's rise in the first half of the twentieth century impacted the broad freedom of individuals.[1708] Yet, SCOTUS's focus on law enforcement interests as a justification for the exclusion of corporations from the scope of the PSI gained importance.[1709]

Interestingly, SCOTUS did accept that corporations could enjoy protection from unreasonable searches and seizures under the Fourth Amendment.[1710] Thus, although the Court opposed the PSI's applicability, it accepted that corporations are entitled under the Fourth Amendment to prevent an excessively broad number of documents being requested without showing the necessity of that broad range of documents.[1711] Accepting the Fourth Amendment's

[1703] PJ Henning, 'The Conundrum of Corporate Criminal Liability: Seeking a Consistent Approach to the Constitutional Rights of Corporations in Criminal Prosecutions' (1995–96) 63 *Tennessee Law Review* 793, 802–03.

[1704] Above 33–34.

[1705] *Saunders* (n 393) para 64.

[1706] Critically on this issue, see Beale et al (n 600) §6:14, 2–3.

[1707] WJ Stuntz, 'The Substantive Origins of Criminal Procedure' (1995–96) 105 *Yale Law Journal* 393, 429.

[1708] Cole (n 1483) 25. The RRD is such an evolution.

[1709] *White* (n 1689) 700; *Braswell* (n 301); SS Beale and JE Felman, 'The Fifth Amendment and the Grand Jury' (2007) 22 *Criminal Justice* 4, 6; Cole (n 1483) 31.

[1710] *Hale* (n 247) 76.

[1711] ibid 77.

applicability to corporations while refusing them Fifth Amendment protection is odd, as there seems to be no apparent reason for giving the term 'person' in the Fifth Amendment a narrower meaning than 'people' in the Fourth.[1712] Accepting a corporate PSI had a much higher potential to severely restrict punitive enforcement against corporations than accepting that they should be protected from unreasonable searches and seizures under the Fourth Amendment.[1713] The Fourth Amendment protection of corporations is limited: as long as a subpoena is not too indefinite and as long as it seeks reasonably relevant information within the scope of the activities of the authority that asks for the documents, making a successful Fourth Amendment claim is difficult.[1714] The Fifth Amendment, at least in those days, offered much stronger protection:[1715] it did not include the type of balancing exercise that the Fourth Amendment's reference to 'unreasonable' requires and overcoming the privilege was very costly as it required transactional immunity.

SCOTUS has generously applied the provisions of the Bill of Rights to corporate entities.[1716] In that sense, the evolution in the USA corresponds to the development of case law by European courts. These courts have similarly extended several constitutional rights to corporations. Although some authors claim that there is some reason to SCOTUS's corporate constitutional rights case law,[1717] it is confusing that corporations do not have a PSI yet have a right to political speech.[1718] This is particularly so if one considers SCOTUS's argument that restrictions of a corporation's political speech cannot be justified by relying on the argument that they are not natural persons.[1719] Unsurprisingly, calls have been made to reconsider the CED.[1720] Recent SCOTUS case law on personhood has laid out a roadmap to reopen issues such as the CED.[1721] The CED's primary foundations seem to be that extending the privilege to corporations would significantly impact on law enforcement, particularly in a white-collar context, and that the privilege is limited to personal protection.[1722]

[1712] Similarly the dissenting opinion in *Hale* (n 247) 84 et seq. See also Saltzburg (n 1061) 37.

[1713] Henning (n 1703) 797.

[1714] Garrett, *Too Big to Jail* (n 1476) 208.

[1715] On the erosion of the *Boyd* protection, see Comisky et al (n 370) 3–4; Beale and Felman (n 1709) §6:13–§6:16.

[1716] On this topic, see Tushnet (n 271).

[1717] Garrett argues that SCOTUS has considered the purpose of the different Amendments and has ensured that the exercising of corporate constitutional rights does not prejudice the rights of natural persons; nor does it allow corporations to conceal their conduct from the state: Garrett, *Too Big to Jail* (n 1476) 217. See also MI Steinberg, *Understanding Securities Law*, 5th edn (Lexis Nexis, 2009) 437.

[1718] On this matter, see C Slobogin, 'Citizens United and Corporate Human Crime' (2011) 41 *Stetson Law Review* 127, 134.

[1719] *Citizens United v Federal Election Commission* 130 S Ct 876, 903 (2010).

[1720] Rochon et al (n 1702) 50.

[1721] Baer, 'Law Enforcement's Lochner' (n 853) 1689.

[1722] Alschuler critically examined the CED and finds none of its justifications convincing: Alschuler (n 288) n 48.

Hale's impact quickly expanded when SCOTUS reconfirmed in *Wilson* that corporations do not have access to the PSI,[1723] affirmed the state's visitorial powers[1724] with regard to corporate documents and imposed further limitations on corporate employees and agents.[1725] SCOTUS found that a corporate officer cannot refuse to hand over corporate documents where they would tend to incriminate him personally[1726] and where he and not the corporation is targeted by the grand jury.[1727] The officer suggested that his own privilege protected him from providing oral testimony, as well as from providing his private books.[1728] The Court ruled that accepting that a person could refuse to produce corporate documents that incriminate him personally is not justified by his personal privilege.[1729] It would unnecessarily limit the state's visitation. In its reasoning, SCOTUS attached particular importance to the fact that the documents belonged to the company, thus the employee did not hold them in a personal capacity.[1730] The fact that the employee has them in his possession, or that he drafted them, does not change their status of corporate documents according to SCOTUS. At the same time, SCOTUS confirmed that corporate employees cannot be forced to provide self-incriminating oral testimony[1731] unless their testimony is immunised.[1732] One should not underestimate *Wilson*'s impact on the PSI of individuals: at the time the judgment was handed down, the personal privilege of individuals protected them from the compelled production of documents.[1733]

[1723] *Wilson* (n 247) 382–83.
[1724] ibid 383–84.
[1725] *Wilson* dealt with a subpoena in a grand jury case against corporate officers. The president was served with a subpoena to produce corporate documents.
[1726] Wilson also claimed that he needed them for the preparation of his defence: *Wilson* (n 247) 367–69.
[1727] ibid 384–85. In *Wilson*, other corporate officers wanted Wilson to comply with the subpoena.
[1728] *Wilson* is a pre-*Fischer* (n 472) and pre-*Shapiro* (n 1059) case.
[1729] Determining whether materials are corporate or personal records relies on a multi-factor analysis. The essential nature of a document is key. Questions such as the identification of the person who drafted the document, its contents, purpose or use, as well as the person(s) who had access to it and the fact that the document's existence was necessary for the corporate business, are all relevant: *In Re Grand Jury Proceedings* 55 F3d 1012 (5th Cir 1995); WR LaFave et al, *Criminal Procedure*, 4th edn (Thomson West, 2016) 8.13(d), 3. The PSI applies to a personal passcode of a smartphone provided to an employee by a corporation, according to a district court: *SEC v Huang* 2015 WL 5611644 (ED Pan, 2015). The production of the passwords was sought and the court concluded that this was not a CED case, as the passcode was not a corporate record and the act of production was considered testimonial in nature. The foregone conclusion doctrine was not applied as the SEC could not show with reasonable particularity the existence or location of the documents it sought.
[1730] *Wilson* (n 247) 386; *White* (n 1689) 699.
[1731] *Wilson* (n 247) 385. A district court (*Pieciak v Thandi*, n 1690) ruled against the backdrop of a corporate insolvency that the CED applies only to corporate documents and individuals can invoke their personal privilege in response to interrogatories. The individual could refuse to identify his email addresses and phone numbers, as well as the same details with regard to a corporate entity.
[1732] *Curcio v United States* 354 US 118, 123–24 (1957). The custodian's responsibility to produce the records typically encompasses a duty to testify for the limited purpose of identifying the produced materials: LaFave et al (n 1729) 8.13(d), 2–3.
[1733] *Wilson* (n 247).

The Court's focus on the fact that the documents belong to the corporation and not to the individual raises several difficulties: distinguishing private and corporate papers can be difficult, for example, in the context of a one-person corporation. The distinction can also be difficult in the context of larger corporations: if a person uses his office computer to send an email through his private email address, one may wonder whether this implies that the privilege no longer protects him. Similar issues arise when someone writes down personal notes on a notepad with the corporate logo on it or stores private documents on a laptop belonging to the corporation. In addition to the difficulties linked to distinguishing between different types of documents, *Wilson* raises another challenge: the focus on the corporate ownership precludes an individual from claiming protection against personal self-incrimination. Therefore, one may consider that granting the corporation a PSI may be warranted to avoid restrictions to the individual's personal PSI. The CED is criticised as it precludes a specific class of individuals from (part) of their PSI and its consistency with other case law is questioned.[1734]

The argument that the privilege is purely personal is repeatedly addressed in US[1735] and E&W case law.[1736] At the same time, it is accepted in both countries that corporations are persons for the purpose of the application of criminal law.[1737] Moreover, SCOTUS accepted that the Fourth Amendment, which refers to 'people', applies to corporations. Corporations essentially rely on individuals to operate. For example, corporations need an individual to sign contracts on their behalf or employees to produce the goods they sell. Corporations similarly rely on individuals to exercise other constitutional rights. SCOTUS has similarly stressed that where a person produces corporate books, this is not his personal act, but the corporation's act.[1738] Thus, in my view, it is quite peculiar that a corporate official or employee acts in a representative capacity when he complies with a subpoena, but that the corporation cannot face compulsion through these individuals. In my view, it is artificial to rely on the personal character of the privilege to exclude corporations from its scope, while for so many other purposes it is accepted that acts by individuals can be considered to be the corporation's acts. The argument has also influenced E&W case law: although E&W courts accept that corporations can rely on the privilege, they have done so in a restrictive way. Corporations cannot refuse to provide evidence where it would incriminate its officials: allowing this would run counter to the privilege's personal nature. Similarly, these courts have criticised the idea that the corporate PSI would allow corporate officials and employees to refuse to provide evidence by arguing that it would incriminate the corporation. In practice, this has resulted in narrow protection for corporations.

[1734] Maclin (n 707) 1588–1603.
[1735] *Hale* (n 247) 69–70.
[1736] See 190–191 above.
[1737] Moreover, SCOTUS accepts that any employee of a corporation can trigger its criminal liability.
[1738] *Braswell* (n 301) 110.

In Belgian case law, the personal character of the privilege has not received significant attention in the debate on the corporate PSI.[1739]

In *White*,[1740] SCOTUS further extended the CED by applying it to a labour union, an unincorporated body. It suggested that the test to check whether an organisation can claim the PSI requires an analysis according to the following guidelines: can one fairly say that the organisation has an impersonal character, in terms of activities and membership, so that it does not embody or represent the purely personal interests of the individuals constituting it but merely their group interests? Where this is the case, the CED applies.[1741]

In *Bellis*, SCOTUS admitted that the *White* test raises difficulties.[1742] It is not helpful when the interests embodied by the entity are not entirely personal but are not pure group interests either. In that case,[1743] SCOTUS refused to accept that a former partner in a partnership of three could rely on the privilege to refuse to hand over business records of the partnership. *Bellis*, like *Fischer*, indicates the reduced importance of the PSI's privacy rationale. The Court found that there is no substantial claim of privacy in relation to the entity's financial records, since others within the entity have access to them as well.[1744] The Court concluded that the partnership had a sufficiently well-organised institutional activity[1745] to refuse the PSI's application.[1746]

After *Hale*, SCOTUS thus systematically broadened the CED's scope, by including partnerships and labour unions in its scope. In *Braswell*,[1747] it applied it to a corporation that was fully owned by one individual.[1748] This post-*Fischer*[1749] and post-*Shapiro*[1750] case could have been an opportunity for SCOTUS to find that, in light of the restrictions imposed on the privilege in relation to documents, excluding corporations from the PSI was no longer needed. Major changes had taken place since 1906: the content of documents lost the *Boyd* protection,[1751] the RRD had been developed, CCL was established and the need to provide transactional immunity had been replaced by use and derivative use immunity.[1752]

[1739] The CoC has acknowledged the PSI's personal character in general: CoC 6 February 2018, P.17.0560.N.

[1740] *White* (n 1689).

[1741] *Wilson* (n 247) 701.

[1742] *Bellis* (n 1055).

[1743] *Bellis* is indicative of the changed reasoning of SCOTUS: in *Boyd* (n 1053), where there was also a partnership, it considered that an invoice could be a private document, whereas in *Bellis* it refused to accept the applicability of the PSI to a former partnership partner. See also Cole (n 1483) 37.

[1744] *Bellis* (n 1055) 92.

[1745] In *Fridman* (n 1124) 180, the 2nd Circuit referred to the presence of a separate institutional identity from those of the individual members. It considered a trust to qualify as a collective entity.

[1746] *Bellis* (n 1055) 93.

[1747] *Braswell* (n 301) 101.

[1748] Braswell had operated the same business as a sole proprietorship, before establishing a corporation.

[1749] *Fischer* (n 472). Braswell did claim that the act of producing the documents would incriminate him.

[1750] *Shapiro* (n 1059).

[1751] Saltzburg (n 1061) 41.

[1752] Until *Kastigar* (n 589), federal law required transactional immunity. Therefore, it was understandable that at the time of *Hale* (1906) SCOTUS was hesitant to apply the PSI to corporations. Similarly, see Cole (n 1483) 45.

These changes had reduced the PSI's impact on the powers of law enforcement to investigate and prosecute crime.[1753] Moreover, the visitorial powers argument did not resonate well with the fact that corporations were no longer created through an individual charter but, rather, through general incorporation laws. One could have hoped that SCOTUS would reconsider the CED. Instead, it held, by a 5–4 majority,[1754] that Mr Braswell could not rely on the privilege to refuse the production of corporate records. When a corporate employee produces the corporate documents required by the subpoena, this is not a personal act, but an act of the corporation.[1755] An enlisted custodian can reply to a subpoena against the corporation.[1756] *Braswell* clearly shows SCOTUS's concern that accepting a claim of a custodian of records to rely on the privilege would be detrimental to the prosecution of economic crime.[1757] SCOTUS refused to accept the remedies Mr Braswell proposed to minimise the adverse impact of the production of the corporate documents on his defence.[1758] It held that the prosecution cannot make any evidentiary use of the individual's production of the documents at trial: it may thus not argue at trial that the given individual was the one providing the documents.[1759] The Court left open the question

> whether the agency rationale supports compelling a custodian to produce corporate records when the custodian is able to establish, by showing for example that he is the sole employee and officer of the corporation, that the jury would inevitably conclude that he produced the records?[1760]

What remains unclear is whether *Hubbell*[1761] has an impact on *Braswell*, as the CED did not apply in *Hubbell* and the Court thus did not have to deal with its

[1753] Cole suggests that by the time *Braswell* was decided the argument according to which a corporate privilege would be detrimental for law enforcement was no longer justified: Cole (n 1483) 49.
[1754] The dissenting opinion claims that the ruling violated the PSI.
[1755] *Braswell* (n 301) 110. The 2nd Circuit CoA has, like some other appellate courts, ruled that a former employee can invoke the PSI (act of production privilege) when they are given a subpoena to produce corporate records: *In re Three Grand Jury Subpoenas Duces Tecum Dated January 29, 1999* 191 F3d 173 (2nd Cir 1999). Other appellate courts have come to the opposite conclusion. On this issue, see Beale and Felman (n 1709) 5–6.
[1756] *United States v Stein* 2021 WL 3129628 (SD Fla 2021) 5. Yet appointing a (*pro forma*) official custodian unaware of the existence and the location of critical records is unlikely to be successful: *In Re Sealed Case* 877 F2d 83 (DC Cir 1989).
[1757] *Braswell* (n 301) 115. The dissenting opinion shows that effective enforcement and protection of the PSI are not necessarily incompatible.
[1758] He suggested that he should receive immunity in relation to the act of production, or alternatively that another person could produce the documents. The Court rejected the suggestion to grant him immunity as this would render the prosecution of the custodian of records significantly more difficult: *Braswell* (n 301) 117.
[1759] This concession was not well received by the four dissenting judges, who argued that the only appropriate remedy would be to provide immunity: Dissenting Opinion in *Braswell* (n 301) 120 and 129. On possible inferences from a person's role in the corporation, see *In re twelve Grand Jury subpoenas* 908 F3d 525, 530 (9th Cir 2018). Beale et al (n 600) 5 point out the limited protection offered by this part of *Braswell*.
[1760] *Braswell* (n 301) 118, fn 11.
[1761] *Hubbell* (n 1121).

findings in *Braswell*. It seems that where the prosecution can show that the possession and existence of the documents are a foregone conclusion, no issue arises.[1762]

SCOTUS's emphasis on the detrimental effects of a corporate PSI on effective enforcement against corporations resembles the CJEU's and EC's arguments in the field of competition law. Excluding corporations from the scope of the privilege on that ground is not entirely convincing. Since *Hale*, the privilege has been restricted on several points. Those reforms have limited the Fifth Amendment's impact on effective law enforcement. Similar arguments have been made in E&W, but in a more general way, in order to justify sector-specific provisions that restrict the privilege in general and thus not only for corporations.[1763] Similarly to E&W case law, Belgian case law on the topic has relied on the effective law enforcement argument in a more general way. There, too, the focus was on regulating economic activities, which are often of high relevance for corporations, rather than on the PSI's applicability to corporations as such.[1764] It should be recalled that a corporate PSI does not take away the other tools available to law enforcement to gather evidence, including searches, cooperating witnesses or whistleblowers, nor does it prevent them from incentivising corporate cooperation. Moreover, corporations are vulnerable to the selective use of immunity or of compelled cooperation powers, which can help authorities gather evidence against the corporation by granting key individuals immunity.

Braswell's odd outcome is that if one exercises one's business through a sole proprietorship and not through a corporation, one may be able to rely on the privilege in order to refuse to produce incriminating documents.[1765] Merely by adopting the corporate form, the same individual loses that ability.[1766] Particularly in cases like *Braswell*, where the company is really the individual's alter ego, this is an odd outcome,[1767] and the choice to run a business through a legal entity is thus considered as a waiver of the constitutional privilege.[1768] This shows that extending the

[1762] Cole (n 1483) 58–59.

[1763] These provisions are often found in statutes dealing with economic activities, particularly relevant for corporations. For example, in *Green Industries*, the UKHL did not distinguish between corporations and individuals for the purpose of the restriction of the privilege.

[1764] FiC Liège 12 February 2015 (n 1386) 1859–60.

[1765] NG Karambelas, *Limited Liability Companies: Law, Practice, and Forms* (Clark Boardman Callaghan, 2022) § 7:2, 2. Admittedly, in light of *Fischer* (n 472), this possibility has become much narrower.

[1766] *In re Grand Jury Proceeding* 961 F3d 138 (2nd Cir 2020).

[1767] *In re Grand Jury Empaneled on May 9, 2014* 786 F3d 255 (3rd Cir 2015). That court concluded at 261 that the question, left open in *Braswell* by SCOTUS in a footnote, does not detract from its decision that a custodian cannot resist a subpoena for corporate records by arguing that the act of production would be personally incriminating. It added that where employees were working at the corporation when the relevant records were created, it is hard to imagine that jurors would inevitably conclude that the sole director produced them. Other courts too have, with regard to corporations with one principal, accepted that the CED applies: see *United States v Stein* (n 1756) 4 and the case law quoted by the district court.

[1768] Critically, see Cole (n 1483) 43.

scope of the privilege to corporations can have a role to play in providing individuals with protection against compelled self-incrimination.

Some arguments pertaining to the PSI's (in)applicability to corporations have received less attention in the examined legal systems than one could have expected: the argument that corporations cannot directly face physical or psychological compulsion and the difficulty of applying the privacy rationale to corporations have not been extensively addressed in case law.[1769] Although some of the leading E&W cases have at times critically referred to the absence of improper compulsion in the context of misbehaviour in an economic context,[1770] this has not led to the PSI's unavailability to corporations. The CoA accepted the argument that corporations cannot suffer all the pains an individual can suffer, but it pointed to the grave consequences if the corporation were to be convicted.[1771]

My argument that corporations can face a modified version of the cruel trilemma through their officials and employees has not been considered explicitly in case law. Even in situations where corporate employees or officials would not be at risk of personal self-incrimination, they could face that trilemma in the absence of a corporate privilege: if they refuse to testify against the corporation, they may face sanctions;[1772] they may similarly face sanctions if they try to protect the corporation by telling lies; and if they do speak the truth, they could contribute to the conviction of the corporation for which they work. The employee or corporate official who would provide incriminating evidence against the corporation could thus still face a harsh choice, as he might be required to bite the hand that feeds him. The cruelty of incriminating someone with whom one has close ties has at times been accepted as a reason for not testifying against that person. These cases are typically limited to relatives or spouses, and they do not include one's employer.[1773] Admittedly, the relationship between an individual and a corporation is typically not as close as the one with a spouse or family member.

Unlike in the USA and in the reasoning in the Preamble of the POI Directive, E&W and Belgian courts have connected the availability of a corporate PSI to CCL. In other words, such reasoning presupposes that if corporations can face criminal liability, like individuals, they too should be able to rely on the privilege.[1774] In both countries, the privilege is considered to play a role in guaranteeing that one can freely set up one's defence strategy, and it is similarly linked to the POI.

[1769] The privacy issue was addressed in *Bellis* (n 1055) 93, where SCOTUS refused to accept a corporate privilege, ruling that there cannot be a substantial claim of privacy in relation to financial records.

[1770] *AT & T* (n 413) 52.

[1771] *Triplex Safety* (n 1598) 409. The ConsC has ruled that, in the context of the offence of stalking, corporations cannot be the victim of stalking under the applicable provision of the CC as stalking requires that one's peace of mind is disturbed: ConsC 10 May 2007 (n 66) (2007) B.7.

[1772] For failure to testify.

[1773] S 14 CEA and Art 156 CCP.

[1774] *Triplex Safety* (n 1598) 409; CoA Brussels 21 May 2012 (n 1) 151.

III. Linking Models of Corporate Criminal Liability to the (Un)availability of a Corporate Privilege against Self-Incrimination

My hypothesis is that the model of CCL impacts whether and to what extent the PSI applies to corporations, for instance because it indicates whether a corporation can have its own will.

As for the CoE, no solid link can be established between CCL and the PSI, as there is no case law of the ECtHR that explicitly grants or denies corporations access to the privilege. An explicit link cannot be established at the EU level either. The CJEU has, in competition cases,[1775] given a very narrow scope to the PSI of undertakings. This restrictive approach relies on the argument that a broad privilege would harm the effective enforcement of competition law. The reasons to exclude corporations from the POI Directive's scope are not linked to the CCL model promoted by the EU.

The main difference between the national CCL models is that the US model and the classic E&W model derive the corporation's criminal liability from individuals, unlike the Belgian model, which was set up with an anthropomorphic approach in mind.

The main E&W CCL model for offences requiring *mens rea*, which developed a few decades after the US model, limits the circle of individuals whose behaviour may trigger CCL. According to the identification doctrine, only the acts and *mens rea* of high officers can be considered for the purpose of CCL.[1776] Meanwhile, new CCL models have been introduced.[1777]

This contrasts strongly with Belgium, where CCL was only introduced in 1999. The Belgian anthropomorphic model takes a different approach, as it was not set up as a vicarious liability system but as an autonomous liability model.[1778] A corporation can face liability even in the absence of an identified individual who committed an offence, which distinguishes Belgian law from US federal law and the classic E&W approach. Similarly to the US requirement that the offence committed by the employee can benefit the corporation, Belgian law sets in place connecting factors between the wrongdoing and the corporation's interests. An own fault of the corporation is necessary in Belgium. Unlike in the USA, one employee's guilty mind is typically not sufficient to trigger CCL.

The US model developed in the early twentieth century, at a time when the country was confronted with the power of rapidly developing corporations. The focus was therefore on a model that allowed for effective enforcement against

[1775] EU competition fines are traditionally not qualified as criminal in nature by the CJEU: Ligeti and Tosza, 'Challenges and Trends' (n 298) 30. On the classification of proceedings, see *bpost* (n 51).
[1776] See 168 above.
[1777] See 168 above.
[1778] See 170–173 above.

corporations, and a broad *respondeat superior* model was adopted.[1779] CCL in practice is said to differ from that theoretical model. It is argued that prosecutors pursue and seek DPAs from corporations because the entities somehow played a role in affirmatively encouraging or acquiescing in the offence or because of their responsibility in putting in place structures or policies that they knew/should have known would result in such behaviour.[1780]

Returning to my hypothesis, there are indications, in some of the national systems, that the CCL model is interconnected with the PSI's (un)availability to corporations. The American model relies on vicarious CCL. Instead of considering the corporation as a real actor with an independent will, it focuses on the wrong-doing of one or more employees. The corporation is thus not considered in an anthropomorphic way. Considering the concession theory, SCOTUS found that the state has a right to look into the corporation's documents, and allowing corporations to invoke the PSI would be detrimental to law enforcement efforts against corporate misconduct. As far as the visitorial argument is concerned, it shows that the corporation is not seen as an individual and it shows that burdensome obligations can more easily be accepted. Just like precluding them from relying on the privilege is such a burden, CCL is another burden imposed on corporations. In that sense, it should come as no surprise that SCOTUS has not accepted that corporations can rely on the privilege. Although there are several reasons for that decision, the personal character of the privilege has played a significant role: SCOTUS has stressed that the privilege only protects against compelled self-incrimination. According to SCOTUS, a person can thus not invoke it by arguing that it would incriminate a third person, even if he is an agent of that (legal) person.[1781] The Court does not accept that the privilege can apply to a corporate entity that needs an individual to exercise its privilege. The strong focus on the personal character of the privilege may explain other case law of the Court that has allowed corporations to rely on other safeguards, where the focus on the 'personal' character is less important. Moreover, the US model of CCL reflects a strong focus on effective law enforcement.[1782] That constitutes a second link with its exclusion of corporations from the scope of the privilege: both the CED and the CCL model rely on an effective law enforcement argument.[1783] The US approach contrasts strongly with the Belgian CCL model, framed in such a way that it should, to the extent possible, assimilate corporations to individuals for the purpose of criminal liability. That anthropomorphic focus presupposes a proper corporate *mens rea*.

[1779] See 173–176 above.
[1780] Baer, 'Corporate Criminal Law Unbounded' (n 1479) 485.
[1781] *Hale* (n 247) 69–70.
[1782] The low number of corporate convictions is not at odds with that approach: the threat of a broad model of CCL has been an invaluable tool in ensuring that corporations, for example, accept cooperating during investigations, accept corporate monitors or pay significant payments under settlement agreements.
[1783] On the link between the CED and *New York Central*, see Cole (n 1483) 61 et seq; Henning (n 1703) 797–98.

It goes in principle further than merely verifying whether an individual has the *mens rea* required for a given offence.[1784] Also on the level of the *actus reus*, Belgian law requires one to look for an own act or omission of the corporation. This is demonstrated by the fact that no specific individual needs to be identified. It follows from this assimilation of corporations and individuals that Belgian courts have ruled in favour of applying the privilege to corporations. The underlying reason seems to be that where corporations can face CCL, similarly to individuals, they are entitled to the privilege. A similar approach was taken in *Triplex Safety* in E&W.[1785] The focus on the senior management for the purpose of CCL is somehow paralleled by a corporate PSI that entitles senior management to claim the privilege of the corporation, provided they clearly appear on the corporation's behalf. In sum, there seem to be some links between the model of CCL and the willingness to accept a corporate privilege, but these links do not allow for a firm affirmation that the two issues are connected.

IV. The Cooperating Corporation

Regardless of their position on the corporate PSI, the different national systems all have tools that can incentivise corporations to cooperate. More specifically, they all have mechanisms of negotiated justice, which are often welcomed by corporations as they may be able to avoid the stigmatising effects of lengthy and uncertain punitive proceedings, a public trial and a possible conviction. Although there are several underlying reasons for the use of negotiated justice, its extensive use creates challenges, including the lack of transparency.[1786]

Even though, under E&W law, corporations can rely on the privilege, they are incentivised not to do so and instead cooperate with the authorities. Concluding a court-approved DPA can constitute such an incentive.[1787]

A guidance document of the SFO, the Director of Public Prosecutions and the Director of the Revenue and Customs Prosecutions exemplifies this.[1788] It establishes general principles for corporate prosecutions, including the public interest factors that advocate for or against prosecution of a corporation. It stresses the need to consider the legal person's possible liability when deciding on the prosecution

[1784] This may be difficult in smaller corporations.

[1785] *Triplex Safety* (n 1598).

[1786] Ligeti and Tosza, 'Challenges and Trends' (n 298) 24.

[1787] On the different steps towards the approval of a DPA, see SFO and CPS DPA Code of Practice, www.sfo.gov.uk/download/deferred-prosecution-agreements-code-practice/ and Part 11 CrimPR 2020. The SFO has entered into more than 10 DPAs since 2014; 50% discounts have been awarded in most of them. DPAs cannot be concluded with individuals. Corporations too can enter a guilty plea, which typically entails lower discounts. The extent of the reduction depends on the timing of the plea: Pinto and Evans (n 4) 120–21.

[1788] www.sfo.gov.uk/?wpdmdl=1457, released late 2009/early 2010.

of individuals.[1789] Several factors listed in the document clearly encourage corporate cooperation.[1790] Where a corporation fails to report wrongdoing within a reasonable period after the misbehaviour's discovery or fails to report fully on the wrongdoing's extent, prosecution of the corporation is looked upon favourably.[1791] Nevertheless, corporations should, in my view, ensure that they are aware of the extent of the wrongdoing when deciding on whether to disclose or not. Failure to get a full picture of the situation is risky: incomplete disclosure may be understood as an attempt to hide certain elements.[1792] These factors are, moreover, supplemented by a further factor that advocates against prosecuting the corporation:[1793] a proactive approach once the offence is discovered, including self-reporting.[1794] This entails that the corporation will not only disclose the details of internal investigations,[1795] but also that it will make witnesses available.[1796] Nevertheless, internal investigations should be conducted with care: they should not harm the evidence and they should be conducted in cooperation with the authorities.[1797] Yet, where the authorities launch an investigation, after they have obtained information from other sources, this should not mean that a corporation has missed its chance of getting a favourable outcome.[1798] The *Rolls-Royce* DPA shows that even without self-reporting, a DPA is still possible.[1799] Nevertheless, in such a case, the cooperation and disclosure should be particularly extensive.[1800] Cooperation is a key factor if one wants to avoid a public trial and enter into a DPA.[1801]

[1789] See para 8 of the guidance document.

[1790] See also the SFO Corporate Co-operation Guidance published in August 2019, www.sfo.gov.uk/publications/guidance-policy-and-protocols/guidance-for-corporates/corporate-co-operation-guidance/.

[1791] Criteria e and f of the factors in favour of prosecution, 7–8 of the guidance document.

[1792] 'Reporting the wrongdoing but failing to verify, or reporting it knowing or believing it to be inaccurate, misleading or incomplete' is a factor that weighs in favour of a prosecution: SFO and CPS, *Deferred Prosecution Agreements Code of Practice* (DSFO and CPS, 2014) 5, www.sfo.gov.uk/?wpdmdl=1447. It can similarly lead to a subsequent prosecution: M Bisgrove and M Weekes, 'Deferred Prosecution Agreements: A Practical Consideration' [2014] *Crim LR* 416, 434.

[1793] Criterion a of the guidance document at p 8.

[1794] Director of the SFO and Director of the DPP, 'Bribery Act 2010: Joint Prosecution Guidance of The Director of the Serious Fraud Office and The Director of Public Prosecutions' (30 March 2011) 7 and 9, www.sfo.gov.uk/?wpdmdl=1456; the CPS guidance on corporate prosecutions, www.cps.gov.uk/legal-guidance/corporate-prosecutions. For example, in *Standard Bank*, the corporation informed the SFO and the SOCA very speedily: *Serious Fraud Office v Standard Bank Plc (now ICBC Standard Bank Plc)* [2015] 11 WLUK 804, para 8.

[1795] *ICBC Standard Bank* (n 1794) 6, para 14.

[1796] Cooperation is typically an essential element of the negotiations: Bisgrove and Weekes (n 1792) 427.

[1797] D Hall and R Hyde, 'Deferred Prosecution Agreements and Internal Investigations: *SFO v Standard Bank*' (2016) 31 *Journal of International Banking Law and Regulation* 115, 115–16.

[1798] On the factors considered when assessing whether the interests of justice are served by a DPA, see *Serious Fraud Office v XYZ Limited* [2016] 7 WLUK 211, para 20.

[1799] Pinto and Evans (n 4) 138.

[1800] As demonstrated by *Rolls-Royce*: the information disclosed was far broader than what was already known by the SFO, the internal investigation was disclosed, regular reports were issued to the SFO and the DOJ, and legal professional privilege was waived: *Serious Fraud Office v Rolls-Royce Plc* [2017] 1 WLUK 189, paras 17–20. In another case, settled by DPA, the cooperation was less than full until what the court considered a relatively late stage: *Serious Fraud Office v G4S Care and Justice Services (UK) Ltd* [2020] 7 WLUK 303, para 26.

The different factors can clearly lead to conflicts of interest between the corporation and its officers or employees. The evidence given by individuals in internal investigations can provide the corporation with an interesting bargaining instrument in its attempts to reach a favourable outcome.[1802] Nevertheless, a corporation's decision to fully cooperate is not without risk. The factors that will be applied in any given case depend on the case's specific facts.[1803] The seriousness of the offence,[1804] the fact that the wrongdoing was part of the corporation's established business practice and a history of similar wrongdoing may tilt the balance towards prosecuting the corporation, regardless of its attempts to cooperate.[1805]

Interestingly, the Crown Court at Southwark specified that the judgment in the DPA only dealt with the company's culpability.[1806] That should be considered in light of the growing number of acquittals of individuals after a DPA was concluded.[1807]

Belgian criminal procedure has several types of formal instruments[1808] that could be used to incentivise a person to adopt a cooperative attitude, including a settlement where one does not have to plead guilty (Article 216*bis* CCP). Since legislative changes in 2016, a guilty plea (Article 216 CCP) can be proposed.[1809] Both instruments have a wide scope of application in terms of the offences that can be handled, and therefore many types of corporate misconduct can be addressed in this way.[1810] Contrary to E&W DPAs and US NPAs and DPAs,

[1801] Pinto and Evans (n 4) 138. See the section 'Co-Operation' of the SFO's guidance on DPAs: www.sfo.gov.uk/publications/guidance-policy-and-protocols/guidance-for-corporates/deferred-prosecution-agreements-2/; 2.8.2, I of the SFO and CPS DPA Code of Practice, www.sfo.gov.uk/download/deferred-prosecution-agreements-code-practice/.

[1802] For example, the requirement to cooperate with the authorities in Standard Bank's DPA; Bisgrove and Weekes (n 1792) 6, para 13.

[1803] See para 32 of the guidance document, as well as the CPS guidance on corporate prosecutions, www.cps.gov.uk/legal-guidance/corporate-prosecutions.

[1804] ibid para 4.12.

[1805] Director of the SFO and Director of the DPP (n 1794).

[1806] *Serious Fraud Office v Amec Foster Wheeler Energy Limited* 1 July 2021 (Crown Ct (Southwark)), www.sfo.gov.uk/download/amec-foster-wheeler-energy-limited-deferred-prosecution-agreement-judgment/.

[1807] R Lööf, 'DPAs – Judicial Oversight Restated' (2021) 7 *Archbold Review* 4, 4–6; Pinto and Evans (n 4) 140.

[1808] A crown witness regime has meanwhile been introduced. Reference can also be made to Art 216*ter* CCP, according to which criminal proceedings can be terminated due to the implementation of measures and compliance with a number of conditions.

[1809] On these instruments, see T Bauwens and L Cornelis, 'Settlement Agreements in Criminal Cases' in A-P André-Dumont et al, *The Increasing Impact of Human Rights Law on the Financial World* (Anthemis, 2016) 133; Beernaert et al (n 405) 273; JP Collin and S Rosenblatt, 'La transaction pénale' in X, *Droit pénal et procédure pénale* (Kluwer, 2020) 27; N De Nil, 'Het verval van de Strafvordering voor sommige misdrijven onder bepaalde voorwaarden' [2018] *Nullum Crimen* 439, 442; Spreutels et al (n 1300) 364; H Van Bavel and D Verwaerde, 'Enième réforme de la transaction pénale: la fin des controverses?' [2018] *Journal des Tribunaux* 765.

[1810] No closed list such as the one included in sch 17, paras 15–28 of the Crime and Courts Act 2013 is used in the CCP. Some limitations do, however, apply: Art 216*bis* (1) and Art 216(1) and (3) CCP. A settlement cannot be used where the offence involved a serious impairment of physical integrity. Annex III to Joint Guideline 8/2018 of the Minister of Justice and the College of Prosecutors General clarifies that in principle all financial, tax and social law violations can be settled by application of

Belgian settlements[1811] do not formally include provisions on measures that the corporation should undertake, such as improving its compliance procedures or cooperating in subsequent criminal proceedings against individuals.[1812] Clearly, the prosecution service could use these instruments to incentivise corporations into cooperating with the authorities, eg in order to bring charges against corporate officials or employees closely involved in the corporate wrongdoing.[1813] Particularly where the corporation can avoid information on its alleged wrongdoing becoming public, corporations are likely to adopt such a cooperative attitude.[1814] At the present time, the published prosecutorial guidelines suggest that settlements are not used to encourage corporations to provide evidence against corporate officials or employees.[1815] It does not refer to criteria such as self-reporting or providing cooperation in the prosecution of individuals as relevant criteria when considering a possible settlement.[1816] Several settlements in major corporate cases cover both the corporation and the individuals involved in the alleged wrongdoing. Including both groups offers several advantages: by closing the cases as such and not only with regard to some suspects, the resources of the criminal justice system can be used for other cases. At least with regard to settlements that require judicial approval, concluding a settlement with all suspects avoids having to justify why some suspects are prosecuted while others can conclude a settlement.[1817] Whether adopting the US approach to corporate enforcement generates more effective enforcement also depends on elements other than the model of CCL and the availability of DPA-style instruments, such as local legislation on the PSI, employment law and data protection.[1818]

Art 216*bis* CCP: www.om-mp.be/nl/meer-weten/omzendbrieven. Customs offences can be settled with the customs administration pursuant to Arts 263–64 GCEA.

[1811] Belgian prosecutors can dismiss a case unless a judicial investigation has been initiated or a citation has been issued. The prosecutor can, in accordance with Art 28*quater* CCP, decide to reopen the case after a dismissal. Such dismissal of charges can be linked to conditions agreed between the prosecutor and the person involved: Van den Wyngaert et al (n 35) 812; Verstraeten and Verbruggen, *Strafrecht en strafprocesrecht* (n 574) 118.

[1812] M Fernandez-Bertier and R Rolland, 'La transaction pénale élargie appliquée aux personnes morales: cap sur le modèle américain des N/DPA's' [2016] *Droit pénal de l'entreprise* 92, 105. At the same time, the Prosecutor's Office can take corporate reforms into account, eg www.om-mp.be/fr/article/communique-presse-procedure-transaction-penale-elargie-hsbc-private-bank-sa-suisse.

[1813] Art 216*bis* CCP applies both to natural and legal persons: Guideline 8/2018, 12. A settlement with one suspect does not put an end to the criminal case against other suspect according to Art 216*bis* (2)11 CCP. CoC 14 June 2022, P.22.0350.N.

[1814] The Prosecutor's office in a number of cases provides information to the public after it has concluded a settlement: www.om-mp.be/fr/article/communique-presse-procedure-transaction-penale-elargie-hsbc-private-bank-sa-suisse.

[1815] Guideline 8/2018, 14 provides that the total absence of a confession or the existence of serious reservations on the part of the person concerned, both as regards the materiality of the facts and the adverse consequences for the victims, may render proposing a settlement inappropriate.

[1816] In addition to publicly available guidelines, a number of guidelines of the College are secret.

[1817] After a 2016 ConsC ruling, judicial control has been strengthened in cases where a settlement is concluded at the trial stage or in cases where a judicial investigation was launched (as opposed to an investigation supervised by the Prosecutor's Office).

[1818] Arlen and Buell (n 305) 728.

Those rules impact the collection and use of evidence in internal and governmental investigations.

Based on their exclusion from the PSI and the easily triggered model of CCL,[1819] one may conclude that a US corporate wrongdoer's position is not particularly appealing. In practice, a corporation's situation is often less critical as the compelled cooperation approach between corporations and the government often allows corporations to avoid criminal conviction.[1820] Nevertheless, it comes at a great price both for the corporation and for its shareholders, officials and employees.[1821]

Even if a corporate PSI were available in the USA, it would not necessarily prevent the use of alternative enforcement mechanisms. Such mechanisms can have a big impact on corporations too. A withdrawal of its licence to operate in a regulated industry or debarment from offering services to publicly traded companies can destroy a corporation. The importance of such mechanisms is clearly shown by Arthur Andersen.[1822]

There are several reasons for the relatively low number of federal corporate convictions in the USA,[1823] as well as the eagerness of corporations and prosecutors to handle cases by means other than trials.[1824] First, prosecuting every single case that could trigger CCL would be impossible. Given the broad vicarious liability model, a great number of corporations could in principle face prosecution. Imposing CCL because of the wrongdoing of one or a few employees could have far-reaching effects and may not be a suitable solution.[1825] It would require significant efforts by the prosecutors and courts,[1826] but would also impact on the corporation's interests, as well as those of its employees and shareholders.[1827] Although it is a rather extreme example,[1828] Arthur Andersen provides a valuable

[1819] Baer, 'Corporate Criminal Law Unbounded' (n 1479) 479. Difficulties could theoretically arise where no individual wrongdoer(s) can be found or where only the individual's interests were intended to benefit from the wrongdoing. On that scenario, see Baer, 'Corporate Criminal Law Unbounded' (n 1479) 479.

[1820] On the combination of sticks and carrots, see Baer, 'Law Enforcement's Lochner' (n 853) 1694. Self-evidently there are other reasons for this fact, such as offences that are difficult to prove and limited resources of the prosecution service.

[1821] On this topic, see Baer, 'Corporate Criminal Law Unbounded' (n 1479) 488–89.

[1822] Before being charged with obstruction of justice, the LLP was very concerned with the SEC's power to prevent it from working for public corporations. That would indeed be a death penalty for an auditing firm. Prior to the *sensu stricto* criminal case, Arthur Andersen had civilly settled with the SEC in another case. As part of that settlement, it had to refrain from breaking securities law. The way in which Arthur Andersen had audited Enron had the potential to amount to such a breach of securities law. See Garrett, *Too Big to Jail* (n 1476) 22.

[1823] For concrete data on the number of corporate convictions, acquittals and different types of agreements, see https://corporate-prosecution-registry.com/browse/.

[1824] Baer, 'Corporate Criminal Law Unbounded' (n 1479) 479 et seq.

[1825] JM 9-28.500.

[1826] Arlen and Buell (n 305) 707.

[1827] JM 9-28.1100.

[1828] As Garrett, *Too Big to Jail* (n 1476) 42 points out, not every corporate prosecution ends as dramatically as Arthur Andersen. For example, the Siemens prosecution did not lead to its bankruptcy.

insight into the damaging effects of a prosecution. After being convicted on an obstruction of justice charge, Arthur Andersen could no longer work for public corporations and thousands of employees were put out of work. The fact that the 500,000 USD fine was reimbursed after SCOTUS overturned its conviction did little to resolve the damage that was already done. Around the time of the dramatic demise of Arthur Andersen, numerous cases of corporate wrongdoing, such as Enron, filled the headlines of major news outlets, which led to the use of a different approach to corporate crime. The focus of prosecutors shifted to shaping a better corporate culture with less crime.[1829] An important tool in this new approach was the use of NPAs and DPAs.[1830] As part of this approach, corporations are often required to adopt or improve their compliance systems and in certain cases hire a monitor,[1831] as well as cough up large sums of money. NPAs and DPAs do not trigger collateral consequences typically caused by a formal conviction, including debarment or delicensing.[1832] CCL is considered as a means towards achieving two goals: the possibility of prosecuting individuals and the increased regulation of companies.[1833]

A key role in the compelled cooperation approach is played by the Principles of Federal Prosecution of Business Organizations.[1834] They include 11 non-exhaustive factors that federal prosecutors should consider when they decide on whether to prosecute a corporation or instead opt for a plea or an agreement such as an NPA or a DPA.[1835]

Two specific factors are particularly relevant for the purposes of compelled cooperation:[1836] (i) the corporation's timely and voluntary disclosure of the corporate wrongdoing; and (ii) the corporate willingness to cooperate, including as to potential wrongdoing by its agents. Although corporations cannot rely on the PSI, gathering all relevant evidence and understanding the wrongdoing's scope can be difficult for prosecutors.[1837] The prosecution has extensive powers to

[1829] Garrett, *Too Big to Jail* (n 1476) 47.

[1830] In the case of an NPA, no formal charges are filed with a court, whereas under a DPA the charges are filed but not pursued, provided the party to the DPA respects its conditions. Those instruments are a middle ground between a declination and seeking a conviction of the corporation: JM 9-28.200. On declinations of charges for corporations that self-report, fully cooperate and remediate, see Arlen and Buell (n 305) 702; Baer, 'Three Conceptions of Corporate Crime' (n 1466) 1–2. Critically on the use of NPAs and DPAs, see DM Uhlmann, 'Deferred Prosecution and Non-Prosecution Agreements and the Erosion of Corporate Criminal Liability' (2013) 72 *Maryland Law Review* 1295.

[1831] The Monaco memorandum on monitors: www.justice.gov/dag/page/file/1445106/download.

[1832] Arlen and Buell (n 305) 700; R Lööf, 'The EPPO and the Corporate Suspect' [2020] *Eucrim* 310, 313.

[1833] Baer, 'Corporate Criminal Law Unbounded' (n 1479) 477 and 487–89.

[1834] www.justice.gov/jm/jm-9-28000-principles-federal-prosecution-business-organizations.

[1835] JM 9-28.300. Specific policy goals, eg in competition cases, need to be considered by prosecutors: JM 9-28.400.

[1836] Cooperating offers no guarantee as even the most cooperative corporations can be charged: JM 9-28.740.

[1837] Key employees may have been promoted or fired, or they may have retired. Corporate cooperation can be critical in this context: JM 9-28.700. Similarly, analysing massive amounts of documentary evidence is very labour-intensive if no help is provided to prosecutors: Arlen and Buell (n 305) 724–25.

gather evidence, including subpoenas for witnesses and documents; nevertheless, conducting a full-scale (multijurisdictional) investigation is resource-intensive. Other procedural safeguards can limit the evidence gathering: corporations do benefit from Fourth Amendment protection against unreasonable searches and seizures. Corporations can also benefit from the attorney–client privilege.[1838] This privilege can help shield a particularly relevant type of evidence from the prosecution: the findings of the corporate internal investigation.[1839] Corporations often conduct these investigations with the help of external lawyers. During such investigations, crucial evidence can come to light, including the involvement of high-level managers. Also during such investigations, corporate officials and employees cannot typically rely on the PSI; they face at least disciplinary action if they refuse to cooperate. It thus goes without saying that the prosecution will generally want to have access to such evidence, yet it needs to stay critical and review the evidence so provided.[1840] It is against this background that the two aforementioned factors should be seen.

The 2015 update of the guidelines, through the Yates Memo, indicated a renewed focus on the prosecution of individuals, rather than on the corporation itself, although it did not exclude corporate prosecutions.[1841] The update made it clear that in order to score points with the prosecution, the corporation's cooperation and disclosure should be complete as the corporation cannot choose to protect some specific individuals and the corporation should disclose *all* relevant facts about individuals involved in corporate misconduct.[1842] That all-or-nothing approach was loosened during the Trump Administration. The guidelines, updated in November 2018,[1843] focused at 9-28.700 on the identification of individuals who were *substantially* involved.[1844] The Monaco Memorandum, issued on 28 October 2021,[1845] rescinds that approach as it explicitly points out that, in order to obtain cooperation credit, 'companies cannot limit disclosure to those individuals believed to be only substantially involved in the criminal conduct'. Individuals who may be involved less than substantially can still have important information according to the Deputy Attorney General. That same Memorandum requires prosecutors to consider *all* prior corporate misconduct, domestic and foreign, including by the parent company or other entities within the corporate family.

[1838] *Upjohn Co* (n 850); JM 9-28.710 and 720; Arlen and Buell (n 305) 721.
[1839] JM 9-28.720; Arlen and Buell (n 305) 721.
[1840] JM 9-28.700.
[1841] JM 9-28.210.
[1842] JM 9-28.700; JF Anderson, 'Constitutional Dilemmas on the Corporate Regulatory and Fifth Amendment Arc' (2020) *Charleston Law Review* 375, 375.
[1843] JM 9-47.120, updated in November 2019, similarly refers to substantially involved individuals in relation to the FCPA.
[1844] RJ Rosenstein, 'Remarks as Prepared for Delivery – American Conference Institute's 35th International Conference on the Foreign Corrupt Practices Act', www.justice.gov/opa/speech/deputy-attorney-general-rod-j-rosenstein-delivers-remarks-american-conference-institute-0.
[1845] www.justice.gov/dag/page/file/1445106/download. At the time of writing, the Memorandum has not been integrated in the JM yet. Further modifications to the Principles of Federal Prosecution of Business Organizations may be made due to the creation of the Corporate Crime Advisory Group.

The situation of corporate officers and employees is thus particularly precarious: they face the difficult choice in internal investigations between cooperating and thus possibly incriminating themselves or refusing to cooperate and thus facing negative consequences, while finding guilty individuals can provide the corporation with a chance to get credit from the prosecution. Moreover, the CED precludes those individuals from relying on their PSI to refuse the production of corporate documents. In conclusion, the cooperating corporation model capitalises on possible conflicts of interests between individuals and corporations.

In sum, such incentives to cooperate with the authorities have achieved considerable sophistication in the USA.[1846] They include declinations, NPAs, DPAs and guilty pleas. Considering the low CCL threshold,[1847] the fact that corporations cannot invoke the PSI and some notorious examples of corporate downfalls, the widespread use of these tools is unsurprising. The various forms of negotiated justice usually rely on corporate cooperation and corporate disclosure.[1848] The cost of these mechanisms for (former) corporate officials and employees can be very high. I identified similar trends in E&W, where DPAs have been introduced. So far, the track record of these agreements shows that extensive corporate cooperation is a relevant factor for the prosecution when they decide whether to seek a corporate conviction. Nevertheless, the higher CCL threshold in E&W and, to a lesser extent, the corporate PSI are factors that can impact a corporation's decision on its defence strategy and thus on the choice of whether to cooperate or instead take a hard stance. Compared to E&W and in particular the USA, one can only conclude that in Belgium the use of different types of negotiated settlements and pleas is still at an earlier stage, regardless of the numerous reforms since 2011. Belgium's position is not unique, as negotiated justice continues to some extent to be a novelty in continental systems.[1849]

[1846] On the continuum of those options, see Baer, 'Corporate Criminal Law Unbounded' (n 1479) 480.

[1847] That model is considered as the starting point of the US enforcement model: Arlen and Buell (n 305) 707.

[1848] On this matter, see ibid 705 et seq.

[1849] K Ligeti and G Robinson, 'Overprosecution and Negotiated Justice in Europe' in PHPHMC van Kempen and M Jendly (eds), *Overuse in the Criminal Justice System: On Criminalization, Prosecution and Imprisonment* (Intersentia, 2019) 107.

11

A Proposal for a Balanced Corporate Privilege against Self-Incrimination

In chapter three, I concluded that it is not in line with the principle of equality to exclude corporations from the PSI's scope. That conclusion was based first on the finding that the specific features of corporations do not warrant the conclusion that they constitute different categories. I conceded that treating corporations and individuals differently for the purpose of the privilege can serve a legitimate aim. Ensuring effective access to evidence in order to combat misconduct by corporations and their officials and employees constitutes such an aim. I concluded that the criterion of distinction, having a legal personality that is not linked to a specific single human body, similarly meets the requirement of an objective criterion of distinction. Nevertheless, having accepted that the measure of excluding corporations is suitable to achieve the legitimate aim, I found that it is not necessary as less restrictive alternatives are available. These alternatives include the possibility of offering different types of cooperation credit to induce corporations to provide relevant evidence, offering them a restricted version of the PSI or providing them with immunity or limited use protection. In light of the possibility of using less restrictive measures, the lack of differentiation between less and more serious corporate crime, and the impact on the corporation's ability to define its defence strategy and on other fundamental safeguards such as the POI, I concluded that the principle of proportionality is not respected and that corporations cannot be excluded from the privilege.

The analysis in the previous chapters clarified the key issues, such as the material scope of the PSI. Chapter ten showed the extent to which European and national law did or did not accord a differentiated treatment to corporations and individuals in relation to the privilege. This chapter considers different models of a corporate PSI, then a balanced corporate PSI is proposed.

I. Different Models of a Corporate Privilege against Self-Incrimination

Corporations should be entitled to the privilege because the principle of equality requires that they can benefit from it if individuals can. Corporations as such are worthy of the PSI's protection. This does not preclude that their privilege may in practice benefit some individuals too.

In chapter three, section IV, I addressed models of a corporate PSI. Here, I focus on their suitability to protect the corporation from being compelled to provide self-incriminating evidence, while taking into account their impact on the legitimate aim of ensuring effective access to evidence in order to combat corporate misconduct.

A. A Narrow Corporate Privilege against Self-Incrimination

Pursuant to this approach, only one individual can exercise the corporate PSI.[1850]

This very narrow model has several deficiencies in terms of the effectiveness of the protection of the corporate PSI. It does not preclude authorities from compelling evidence from other individuals, including corporate officials or employees. Unless they can and do invoke their personal PSI, they can be required to provide evidence against the corporation. Considered strictly, these other individuals are witnesses, provided that they are themselves not suspects. Particularly in those cases where the person who is entitled to invoke the corporation's privilege is poorly informed of the underlying facts of the case,[1851] the likelihood that the authorities will quickly turn to employees and corporate officials for evidence is high.

Therefore, where only one person can exercise the corporate PSI, it suffices to compel other individuals to collect incriminating evidence against the corporation. This model seems under-inclusive *ratione personae*. At the same time, this narrow model does not excessively restrict the possibility of gathering evidence of the criminal misconduct by the corporation, its officials and employees.

B. Legal Representatives

A second, broader model allows legal representatives who, individually or jointly, can represent the corporation to invoke the corporation's PSI.[1852]

Even under this model, many individuals within the corporation cannot rely on the corporation's privilege. Unless they can rely on their personal PSI, they can be compelled to provide evidence against the corporation. An engineer who was in charge of a car model that faces safety failures would most likely still fall outside

[1850] This model is addressed at 41 above.

[1851] The practice in Belgium to appoint attorneys as AHRs creates the risk that these representatives will not necessarily be well-informed. As they come from outside the corporation, they will take time to gain insight into the facts of the case.

[1852] See 41 above.

the scope of this model.[1853] A similar result arises when a CEO and a member of the board are discussing some of the corporation's corrupt practices and the CEO's PA overhears their conversation. Under this second model, both the CEO and the board member can rely on the corporation's privilege,[1854] whereas the PA cannot. Law enforcement officials can thus require the PA to testify about this conversation unless the assistant is personally involved in the corrupt practices.

The advantage of this model is that it sets clear boundaries on the corporation's PSI *ratione personae*: by adopting a formal criterion, it is feasible to check whether someone falls within or outside the scope. This model still seems under-inclusive, as key individuals may still fall outside the PSI's scope. From the point of view of effective evidence gathering, it is more likely that it impacts the possibility of collecting evidence of corporate wrongdoing.

C. Legal Representatives *Plus*

Still broader is the model according to which not only can the legal representatives invoke the corporation's privilege, but so too can leading individuals.[1855]

Such an intermediate solution offers a slightly more extensive protection to the corporation, yet not in cases such as that involving the aforementioned overheard conversation.

This model's advantage is that individuals that play a key role in a specific activity of the corporation, without qualifying as a legal representative, can invoke the corporate privilege. This model can also be relevant for smaller corporations as a strict application of the previous model could also exclude individuals with a key role in those corporations. Although it restricts the possibility of the authorities gathering evidence of corporate wrongdoing, it is not overinclusive, as it does not allow all employees to invoke the corporation's privilege. Admittedly, the broader the circle of individuals becomes, the more fragile it is: it is only as strong as its weakest link.

D. A Corporation-Wide Privilege against Self-Incrimination

Finally, one could consider adopting a corporation-wide PSI. Such a model allows any corporate employee or official to refuse to provide evidence that tends to incriminate the corporation.[1856]

[1853] eg www.justice.gov/usao-sdny/pr/manhattan-us-attorney-announces-criminal-charges-against-general-motors-and-deferred.
[1854] And typically also on their own privilege.
[1855] See 41 and 196–197 above.
[1856] See 42 and 196–197 above.

This model is, in my view, too broad and severely restricts the ability to gather evidence of corporate wrongdoing. Also, from the point of view of the corporation's defence, it can raise difficulties: such a broad corporate privilege is particularly fragile as it presupposes that all officials and employees are willing to exercise it. Moreover, in order for such a wide privilege to be effective, the corporation should be able to give instructions to the individuals on how to exercise the corporate privilege. Nevertheless, these corporate instructions cannot prevent an individual from deciding for himself whether or not to exercise his own privilege or to set up his personal defence strategy, nor can they go as far as exposing him to liability. From a practical point of view, one can add that such a broad corporate privilege will require extensive training of employees and officials who may not have a legal background. In other words, a corporation will need to decide how much of its resources it wants to invest in such training. These considerations evidently depend on the size of the corporation.

II. A Proposal for a Balanced Corporate Privilege against Self-Incrimination

I consider that the legal representatives *plus* model strikes the best balance between ensuring an effective corporate privilege and the ability to gather evidence of corporate wrongdoing. Chapter three highlighted that an exclusion of corporations from the PSI's scope mainly fails the principle of equality due to its lack of proportionality. Therefore, I examine whether the legal representatives *plus* model strikes a better balance. First, I focus on the corporate PSI's scope *ratione personae*. Then I consider the practical modalities of that privilege.

Previously, I only demonstrated that a total exclusion of corporations from the privilege's scope does not comply with the principle of equality. Nevertheless, that analysis by itself does not explain why I propose the legal representatives *plus* model. One could wonder why a corporate PSI, limited to one person or to the legal representatives of the corporation, is not broad enough in light of the principle of equality. Several legal orders have recognised the PSI as an essential safeguard. In my view, limiting the corporate privilege to one person would not guarantee a sufficiently effective privilege: the authorities could turn to all employees and corporate officials, except for that one person, and compel them to provide incriminating evidence against the corporation.[1857] Particularly in those cases where someone from outside the corporation is appointed to represent the corporation, for instance an attorney appointed as an AHR in a Belgian case with little knowledge of the underlying issues, that risk would be particularly real. The result would be an empty shell corporate PSI. The legal representatives model partly remedies the flaw of that under-inclusive model. I acknowledge that

[1857] Except where those individuals would be able to rely on their personal privilege and in fact do so.

the legal representatives model offers a potentially[1858] broader personal scope. Nevertheless, in my view, its scope is still too narrow. The limitation to legal representatives has an important drawback: corporate employees that play a key role in the corporation can easily fall outside its scope where they do not have the status of legal representative. Therefore, the second model does not guarantee a sufficiently effective privilege. At the same time, some models appear too broad. This is the case when all employees, or even people who indirectly work for the corporation, can invoke the corporation's PSI. Such models severely restrict the possibility of gathering evidence against the corporation and thus go beyond what is necessary to ensure a corporate PSI.

Having defined who can invoke the corporation's privilege, I now turn to other practical issues. More particularly, the following issues, addressed in previous chapters, need consideration in the context of the corporate privilege: self-incrimination; compulsion and the selective use of immunity; protected evidence; waiver; and incentives to cooperate. These issues need to be considered against the backdrop of the PSI's rationales and the need to grant corporations a privilege that is sufficiently broad, yet respects the delicate balance between the protection offered by the privilege and the need to effectively gather evidence of corporate wrongdoing.

Self-incrimination in this context covers incrimination of the corporation that can lead to a punitive sanction. As chapter three highlighted, information can at the same time be incriminating for the corporation and for one or more individuals. As long as it is incriminating for the corporation, it suffices as a triggering factor for the corporate PSI. I previously highlighted the weakness of a privilege limited to national self-incrimination: one may be required to provide incriminating evidence, which exposes one to a punitive case abroad. Therefore, I find that one should also be able to invoke the privilege where the incrimination would be under foreign law.[1859] In order to avoid frivolous PSI claims in relation to foreign law, one could require that the person seeking to invoke it demonstrates prima facie the risk of self-incrimination under foreign law.

In my view, the privilege should only apply when compulsion is used.[1860] Compulsion in the corporate context can take several forms: corporate officials can be threatened with obstruction charges; fines can be imposed on the corporation for failure to provide the documents sought; or cooperation can be sought through penalty payments. In light of one of the PSI's rationales – the protection from cruel choices – the corporate PSI should preclude the corporation

[1858] This depends on the corporation's size and the number of legal representatives.

[1859] Art 24(5)(e) of the European Investigation Order Directive provides, with regard to hearing by videoconference or other audiovisual transmission, that information should be provided on the right not to testify under the law of the executing and issuing state.

[1860] Suspects can typically stay silent in interviews with police officers or equivalent officers. Corporations too should benefit from that right.

from indirectly facing compulsion through its officials or its employees that can exercise the corporate privilege. In other words, where such an individual is entitled to invoke the corporate privilege, he cannot be punished for his choice to do so. Several national systems nevertheless allow compulsion, provided that it is accompanied by immunity for the compelled person or is equipped with a limited use rule. If a prosecutor or judge creatively uses such mechanisms, the corporation's privilege could be easily reduced to an empty shell: by offering immunity to a key corporate official, that official could be required, even against his will[1861] to provide information that could still be used against the corporation. In order to avoid such circumvention, one could apply the corporate privilege in such a way that those individuals who come within its personal scope cannot be required to provide evidence that would incriminate the corporation when they are only granted personal immunity. Thus, according to this first interpretation, the immunity or the limited use provision should not only offer that individual a guarantee that the compelled evidence is not used against him personally, but also that it will not be used against the corporation. In the selected systems, I have not found examples in the case law that interpret the corporate privilege so broadly. The choice (not) to adopt this wide approach essentially depends on one's preference: if one focuses on effective enforcement of corporate wrongdoing, one may be less inclined to follow that approach. If the immunity is not extended to the corporation, corporations can still be confronted with the cruel trilemma through their officials or employees: these individuals would be required to choose between incriminating the corporation and facing perjury or contempt charges. In this sense, that solution would not be in line with one of the PSI's rationales.

The national systems, as well as the ECtHR, tend, to some extent, to allow the use of adverse inferences. In my view, one should be cautious when using adverse inferences, as broadly allowing them can amount to a form of indirect compulsion. Nevertheless, where there is strong evidence against the corporation and the corporation fails to give any reasonable explanation at trial, adverse inferences can be acceptable. Drawing adverse inferences during the investigation from corporate silence should be done with particular caution. The silence of one corporate official during a police interview, for example because he has not had the chance to look into the relevant corporate documents before the interview, does not warrant an adverse inference against the corporation.

Applying the corporate privilege to oral statements is relatively straightforward: the individuals who can exercise the corporate privilege should be informed of the capacity in which they are interviewed, the applicability of the privilege and the possibility of having access to a lawyer. More challenging is the issue of documentary evidence. It is clear that this issue significantly impacts the PSI's practical value. Throughout this book, I have highlighted the different

[1861] Where immunity is offered or a limited use provision applies, one can no longer refuse cooperation.

views on the PSI's applicability to documentary evidence. The protection offered to documents has been restricted over time, yet not to the same extent in all legal systems. An important element in that evolution is the changing view on what compelled self-incrimination means in the context of documentary evidence: originally the focus was on the compulsion linked to handing over documents. In the USA and E&W, that view has largely been abandoned. As long as the documents are created voluntarily, the privilege has only a limited role to play, even when persons are compelled to hand them over themselves. The US act of production doctrine still offers some limited protection if requiring documents amounts to a fishing expedition: where the authorities do not have sufficiently concrete knowledge of the documents' existence and possession, the privilege can still be relevant.

Some authors and one of the Court's Sections have suggested that this is also the ECtHR's approach, but that is a particularly restrictive interpretation of the Court's case law. This inevitably leads to discussions whether the authorities have a sufficiently precise knowledge of the documents and their whereabouts. Moreover, both the US RRD and certain lines of Belgian case law have restricted the privilege's role in relation to documents even further: documents whose creation is obligatory under a statutory duty fall outside the privilege's scope.

In my view, both of these evolutions can be criticised: focusing on the documents' voluntary creation to argue that their production does not amount to compelled self-incrimination misses the point. As long as the person's active cooperation is needed to gain access to the documents and provided that compulsion is used to obtain it, the PSI should apply, as the corporation is forced to furnish self-incriminating evidence. This is in line with the POI, and it ensures the corporation's freedom to set up its defence strategy. Secondly, the RRD and similar approaches restrict the privilege's scope excessively: although these records can serve legitimate aims, such as facilitating the calculation of someone's taxes or checking whether a factory complies with its licence, their admissibility in a punitive case against the corporation that created them has a significant effect on the corporation's ability to freely set up its defence. The risk of the RRD is that statutory provisions impose an ever-broadening list of documents that need to be kept, in a wide variety of fields, and that the privilege in relation to documents becomes meaningless.

In my view, the preferable solution is to allow compulsion in order to force the handing over of documents for non-punitive aims. At the same time, these documents, obtained under compulsion from the corporation or the individuals that can exercise its privilege, should be excluded from punitive cases against them. Nevertheless, where the corporation, through those individuals, intentionally provides documents containing incorrect information, the documents should be admissible in evidence. That exception is justified as it is needed to ensure the provision of truthful information and sanctions should be available if incorrect evidence is provided. Similarly, my proposal does not prevent the common practice of imposing penalties for failure to file, for example, a tax declaration.

Thus, requiring someone to hand over documents dealing with his foreign bank accounts in order to assess his tax situation should be acceptable, whereas using these documents for tax evasion proceedings is not.[1862] This solution finds support in several ECtHR cases, such as *Marttinen*, *Chambaz* and *Van Weerelt*,[1863] in which the Court considered whether the evidence gathered under compulsion, could be used in proceedings in which punitive sanctions could be imposed. Moreover, it does not seem to be at odds with the general reference made by the ECtHR in *A and B*, in the context of *ne bis in idem*, to the avoidance of duplication of evidence gathering. My solution does not in general prevent the use of elements coming from one set of proceedings in another set of proceedings.[1864] Only to the extent that self-incriminating evidence is obtained under compulsion would its use against the corporation or the individuals that can exercise its privilege not be permissible.[1865] The broad reference in *A and B* should be read together with the Court's more specific case law, in which it has struck down the use of compelled self-incriminating evidence in punitive proceedings.

The suggested rule would not apply to simple requests for documents that are not backed by the possibility of imposing sanctions for failure to comply, as there would not be a sufficient level of compulsion. Nor would it, as outlined before, apply to prosecutions for providing false or incomplete information in those documents. Nothing prevents the authorities from prosecuting that person for having made a fraudulent declaration. Since the person would be sure at the time of filing that he cannot be prosecuted on the basis of information that he handed over under compulsion, it is reasonable to require him to provide correct information.[1866]

The suggested approach would to a certain extent reconcile the different interests at stake: checks and required handing over of documents remain possible in order to verify whether different legal obligations, such as paying taxes, have been fulfilled, while corporations are at the same time not compelled to incriminate themselves. I concede that my proposal can impact law enforcement: if corporations can be required to hand over documents but those documents cannot be used in a punitive case against them, discharging the burden of proof is more difficult. Yet, the privilege does not preclude the authorities from gathering the documents through other channels, including searches.[1867] In order to safeguard the PSI's effectiveness, the authorities should not be allowed to use the knowledge they have gained through compelled evidence in order to indirectly build their case against the corporation. In other words, the authorities can use

[1862] Favourably, Kuty, 'Le droit au silence' (n 1324) 386–89.
[1863] *Marttinen* (n 385); *Chambaz* (n 491); *Van Weerelt* (n 669).
[1864] *A and B* (n 38) para 132.
[1865] So this rule does not interfere with evidence found during searches.
[1866] In jurisdictions where immunty can be granted, perjury charges are typically excluded from the immunity.
[1867] Deruyck, 'De rechten van verdediging' (n 287) 39.

a search warrant to gather incriminating documents, but they cannot compel a corporation first to provide it with documents and then use those documents to do further searches. Otherwise, this would constitute indirect use of the compelled evidence. It is clear that a broad privilege in relation to documents may lead to more searches, provided that persons decide to exercise the PSI.[1868] In order to safeguard the PSI's effectiveness, authorities should show that they have not used the knowledge that they gained through the compelled production of documents to subsequently gather them through a search.

In my view, corporations should put in place a policy in relation to documentary evidence in order to avoid their defence strategy being undercut. This should include a mechanism whereby a single or multiple persons are charged with handling requests for documents from the authorities. The corporation should train its employees so that if requests for documents are made to them, the employees know to whom those requests should be transferred. This way, the corporation ensures control over which documents are handed over to the authorities.

In light of the use of cloud storage, email servers and other services that can leave digital traces, the role of third parties is increasingly important. Those third parties will be crucial partners for law enforcement, at times even against their will.[1869] To the extent that such obligations are imposed on persons that can provide this information without incriminating themselves[1870] or the corporation that employs them,[1871] such obligations raise no particular concerns for the privilege.[1872] Thus, if a bank has customers that are suspected of criminal wrongdoing, providing the requested information will in principle not lead to self-incrimination of the bank. Yet, one may imagine that there can be rare cases where complying with such obligations to provide information could lead to self-incrimination on the side of the institution concerned, provided it is involved in its customers' wrongdoing, or where providing the requested information would otherwise incriminate them. In those cases, the privilege of these institutions can come into play.

Moreover, in practice, corporations from whom self-incriminating documents are sought may be inclined to cooperate as this may fit their strategy of trying to reach a settlement or otherwise be credited for cooperating. Similarly, once they are aware that the authorities can otherwise gain access to the documents, they may decide out of pragmatism to hand over the documents, rather than have their premises searched.

[1868] CoA Antwerp 13 February 2002 (n 1024) 1065.

[1869] On compelled cooperation of such services: C Conings and S Royer, 'Verzamelen en vastleggen van digitaal bewijs in strafzaken' [2017] *Nullum Crimen* 311, 320 et seq.

[1870] ConsC 14 February 2013 (n 1338) B.17.

[1871] To the extent these persons would fall within the scope of persons that can exercise the corporation's privilege. On this issue, see Dewandeleer (n 969) 160.

[1872] Yet other practical concerns can arise: service providers will not necessarily be enthusiastic to cooperate with law enforcement.

In addition to the challenges presented by documentary evidence, the issue of compelled decryption also raises complex questions: chiefly, can the corporation refuse to disclose the key to its encrypted, self-incriminating[1873] data? In light of the freedom to set up one's defence and the POI, I believe that requiring a corporation to decrypt its self-incriminating data is not compatible with the PSI. Nevertheless, if the authorities can gather the password or the key from an individual who falls outside the scope of the corporate privilege, this is as such not precluded by the model that I propose. For example, where a low-level IT engineer has access to the password, the authorities will not be obstructed by the corporate PSI. Self-evidently, the authorities are free to seek access to the encrypted data through other channels too.

Corporations often exercise highly regulated economic activities. These activities are typically subject to supervision by agencies or other public bodies. In order to carry out their tasks, these institutions often have the power to require information from corporations. Failure to provide such information may lead to sanctions. In addition to supervision, these services can also have the power to investigate offences related to the activity that they supervise. Therefore, it is at times difficult to assess the aim of their investigations. In light of the broad *Engel* criteria, one may quite quickly enter the sphere of punitive cases. Therefore, there is a tension between the need to gather information in order to monitor potentially risky activities and the PSI, at least where compelled evidence is used or can be used against the corporation in a punitive case. In order to reconcile these interests, I refer to my proposal in relation to documents: corporations can be required under compulsion to provide documents and statements to such agencies, upon the condition that this information is not used against them in the course of punitive proceedings. Were the authorities allowed to use compelled cooperation provisions to require evidence from a corporation, before or even after an investigation has become punitive, the PSI would be an empty shell. Where the investigation's aim is clearly punitive, for example where a criminal investigation *sensu stricto* is launched, the corporation (through the individuals that can exercise its privilege) should be informed of its privilege and it should thus be able to refuse active cooperation.

A corporation should be entitled to waive its privilege, for example because the lure of an incentive such as an NPA or another settlement has convinced it to do so. Such a waiver is only acceptable when it is made voluntarily. In my view, incentives such as NPAs provide a particularly valuable tool to authorities to combat corporate misconduct. They ensure corporate cooperation and are likely to lead to evidence to which the authorities would otherwise not have access, such as the findings of internal investigations. Moreover, corporations have strong incentives to look for a soft landing, to avoid the reputational and other damage and uncertainties that come with a fully fledged punitive case.

[1873] I do not address the issue of compelled cooperation, for example, by ISPs or banks, to combat crime.

12

Overall Conclusion

I started this book off with the question 'Does the PSI apply to corporations, should it apply to corporations, and if so, to what extent?' I conclude that the privilege applies to corporations, at least to a certain extent, in certain (supra)national legal systems. Not only does it apply to them in some legal systems, I conclude that it should.

That affirmative answer finds support in the different chapters of the book. Chapter two showed that the PSI's ancestor with roots in the *ius commune*, the *nemo tenetur* principle, often had a limited practical impact. That limited impact was due to coercive evidence-gathering practices such as the *ex officio* oath and the use of torture in investigations. The principle had strong links to the Christian confession doctrine and the duty of self-preservation. *Nemo tenetur*'s supporters and their opponents disagreed on the conditions under which the principle could be restricted for evidence-gathering purposes. Torture and the oath were more frequent in courts which followed an inquisitorial model. The strictly regulated law of evidence in courts applying an inquisitorial model was a triggering factor for the use of those practices, as (compelled) confessions were crucial to impose the heaviest sanctions. Ecclesiastical courts throughout Europe, several English prerogative courts and secular courts in several continental states used that model. Conversely, English common law courts did not rely on that oath. Although the historical chapter demonstrated that the PSI's development is intertwined with the protection of individuals, some of the historical rationales are relevant for corporations too, such as the fact that the privilege is justified by the POI and hence the authorities' obligation to carry the burden of proof. In that sense, the privilege helps ensure a suspect's liberty to choose his defence strategy. The protection offered by the privilege against compulsion can similarly be relevant for corporations, particularly in the context of statutory provisions that penalise refusals to provide oral statements or documents.

The application of the principle of equality test supports the affirmative answer to the second part of my research question. Excluding corporations from the PSI's scope can serve a legitimate aim, has an objective criterion of distinction and can contribute to the aim. I nevertheless find that the availability of less restrictive alternatives, such as the use of cooperation credit and the assessment of the proportionality *sensu stricto*, imply that corporations cannot be entirely excluded from the PSI.

Chapter four demonstrated that the analysed legal systems are familiar with a multitude of (challenged) rationales to ground the PSI. It protects a patchwork of different interests, some of which are relevant to corporations. Whereas certain restrictions may be defendable in light of one or more rationales, such restrictions can be at odds with other rationales. The protection against cruel choices rationale is not to be mistaken for an outdated relic from the past. It is relevant in the context of provisions that criminalise failure to provide evidence, at least where no limited use rule has been adopted. Corporations may face painful consequences: even if evidence could not be used against a specific individual, use against third parties such as the corporation is likely not excluded. That rationale is also relevant in the context of the modified trilemma corporations can face through their officials and employees. The PSI's connection to the protection of the innocent does not provide a strong foundation for a corporate PSI. The PSI has also been justified by connecting it to the POI. It would not amount to much protection if the government could compel any accused person to provide evidence against himself. The justification of the PSI by reference to the POI is relevant for corporations too. The privilege has quite some value as it allows suspects to determine which attitude they want to adopt in relation to the accusations against them and thus freely set up their defence. If one accepts that corporations can face punitive liability, accepting their freedom to choose their defence strategy is nothing but the reverse side of the coin. A recurring justification, the PSI as a protector of a private enclave, seems to have lost importance and has generally received little attention in Belgium and in the ECtHR's case law. That rationale has not provided us with strong arguments in favour of a corporate PSI.

Chapter five showed that the PSI typically requires a risk of self-incrimination.[1874] In light of the *Engel* criteria, the scope of 'punitive' is broad, and the three national systems (Belgium, E&W and USA) have all recognised this to a certain extent, by also including self-incrimination that could lead to sanctions that are not criminal *sensu stricto* within the privilege's scope. Indirectly incriminating evidence can suffice to meet that requirement. The ECtHR's case law shows that the privilege typically comes into play where there are pending or anticipated punitive proceedings or where compelled evidence is relied upon in a punitive trial, yet its case law depends on the specific facts of each case. In competition cases, the CJEU adopted a very restrictive view on self-incrimination. Outside that field, notably in *DB v Consob*,[1875] its approach is oriented towards the ECtHR's case law. E&W case law, similarly to the ECtHR's, adopted a broad notion of self-incrimination. Evidence that could provide a stepping stone in the evidence chain required for prosecution is relevant in that legal system too. Belgian courts typically refer to

[1874] The different analysed legal systems are familiar with a right for suspects to stay silent, eg during police interviews in the course of *sensu stricto* criminal proceedings. That right is not limited to (in)directly self-incriminating questions.

[1875] As well as in *FN* (n 17).

the aforementioned ECtHR approach, although some case law suggests a stricter, less defendant-friendly application of those standards. In the US federal system, information should be of such a nature that it might subject the person providing it to the possibility of a punitive prosecution or punitive penalty in the USA. US case law corresponds to the ECtHR's, as a risk of indirect self-incrimination too triggers the Fifth Amendment PSI. Unlike in the USA and E&W, the issue of transnational self-incrimination, highly relevant to corporations active in multiple countries, has received little attention in Belgium.

Chapter six tackled compulsion. The privilege does not preclude a person's voluntary cooperation. It protects a person against compelled cooperation. Compulsion comes in different forms, such as the threat of a sanction, including a fine or even imprisonment, or the threat of loss of government employment. The ECtHR requires compulsion in order for the privilege to apply. It has repeatedly addressed statutory provisions that sanction failure to provide oral statements or other evidence. The ECtHR was, for instance in *Saunders*, *Marttinen* and *Chambaz*, critical where such provisions do not include a limited use rule. The Court's *Jalloh* test is particularly relevant in assessing whether the PSI has been violated. In competition cases, the CJEU has focused on coercion as a key requirement for the privilege to apply. Outside that field, it has picked up on the ECtHR's concept of 'improper compulsion'. E&W and Belgium have both been influenced by the ECtHR's case law and both countries require compulsion as a trigger to the PSI. Yet, one may wonder whether national case law respects the ECtHR's. E&W statutes that restrict the privilege are often equipped with limited use rules, at least restricting the use of statements obtained under compulsion. Such rules are typically lacking in Belgium. Unsurprisingly, Belgian courts have repeatedly concluded that the privilege was violated where compelled evidence was used, so have excluded the impugned evidence and the fruit of the poisonous tree. SCOTUS requires that one checks whether the free will was overborne by compulsion and, like the ECtHR, some pressure is tolerated. US federal immunity statutes can counter a person's PSI claim and compel that person to provide evidence. Currently, use and derivative use immunity is to be offered. In E&W, immunity notices can be issued in some limited cases. In a corporate setting, the selective use of immunity poses a risk for the corporation, as well as for its employees: by offering immunity to key individuals, the authorities can gather information that is admissible in evidence against the corporation. At the same time, the authorities could immunise the corporation and use the evidence against its employees or officials.

The threat of fines or other financial compulsion has been considered as a trigger for the PSI. Even if one does not accept that compulsion on corporate officials or employees can amount to compulsion exercised on the corporations, (supra)national case law shows that financial compulsion is relevant. As corporations can be confronted with the threat of adverse financial consequences if they fail to cooperate, the case law on compulsion through financial sanctions is relevant for them too.

Adverse inferences constitute a particular type of compulsion. Under certain conditions, they are accepted in a number of legal systems, including the ones considered in this book. Understanding when inferences can be drawn is technical and challenging for suspects. The specific question of from whose silence an adverse inference can be drawn against the corporation has not been clearly answered in the legal systems examined.

I highlighted that private compulsion, for instance during an internal investigation, has received significant attention in the USA, unlike in E&W and Belgium. Successfully claiming the PSI during such investigations is difficult as the PSI focuses on public compulsion and showing a sufficiently close nexus between the internal investigators and the authorities is challenging. It is advisable to provide interviewees in such investigations with certain information, notably that the investigator acts on behalf of the corporation and that the corporation may decide to share its findings with the authorities. Employees can find themselves trapped in a tricky situation as providing evidence might prejudice their position in punitive proceedings, while staying silent could have disciplinary consequences. Corporations should take care when applying pressure as too much pressure can endanger the statement's voluntariness.

Chapter seven addressed the PSI's scope *ratione materiae*, with a particular focus on documentary evidence, a key issue for corporations. Oral statements come within the privilege's scope, according to the ECtHR. The POI Directive too covers oral statements, most likely with the exception of routine questions. The CJEU, in *DB v Consob*, relied strongly on the ECtHR's case law. Yet, in the field of competition law, the CJEU only protects undertakings against compulsion that would require them to give answers that might involve an admission of the existence of a competition law infringement. In the three national legal systems, too, oral statements are afforded protection under the PSI, yet one needs to take into account the compelled cooperation provisions and their impact on the PSI.

Compelling someone to create new documents that contain self-incriminating information would amount to compelled self-incrimination as it presupposes the use of one's mind. Unsurprisingly, reporting duties are in place in the analysed national legal orders which, in case of non-compliance, can result in sanctions, eg the filing of a tax declaration or documents related to a factory's waste water. Refusing to comply with reporting duties by relying on the privilege is unlikely to be successful, just like purposely providing false information. Nevertheless, refusing to fill out specific parts of a document where the person can convincingly argue that this specific point would incriminate him can come within the PSI's scope.

In relation to pre-existing documents, the national systems have taken different approaches. In essence, legal systems adopt one of the following two approaches in dealing with pre-existing documents: one approach is to argue that requiring someone to hand over self-incriminating documents is no different from requiring that person to make self-incriminating statements, since they both imply a risk of self-incrimination. Conversely, one may defend the position that as documents exist independently of the person's will, and as long as they do not come into existence due to compulsion, the person is not required to create self-incriminating evidence. Whereas the first approach focuses on the compulsion involved in the handing over of the documents to justify the PSI's applicability, the second one focuses on the absence of compulsion at the time of creation to argue against its application.

The ECtHR's case law on documentary evidence, like Article 7(3) POI Directive, is not crystal clear and one needs to be cautious when attempting to draw conclusions from it. What is clear is that *Saunders* did not overturn *Funke* completely. Post-*Saunders*, pre-existing documents can still benefit from some protection under the PSI. The scope of that protection is less clear. According to some, including the ECtHR's Fourth Section, the PSI only applies where authorities mount a fishing expedition and thus lack sufficiently concrete information on the documents. In my view, that reading is too narrow. In light of *Jalloh*, the focus seems to be more on the element of compulsion to defy the person's will than on the type of evidence. The ECtHR repeatedly paid attention to limitations on the use of compelled evidence to non-punitive purposes and its exclusion from punitive cases. The *Jalloh* test, moreover, does not exclude that the privilege can cover documentary evidence. Instead, it imposes a broad balancing test that can be applied in relation to a wide variety of self-incriminatory types of evidence. In *De Legé* the ECtHR referred to it in relation to documents. The CJEU does not offer protection to pre-existing documents in competition cases. In *Qualcomm*, the GC ruled that an undertaking cannot claim a PSI violation where it has to compile information into a document in response to questions considered as factual by the GC. The CJ also did not find that the privilege was infringed, as the undertakings did not have to admit an infringement of competition law.

In E&W, it was accepted for a long time that the PSI included protection from the compelled handing over of documents, yet that position has been criticised as such protection is not in line with the privilege's rationales and the authorities can gather them anyway through searches and seizures. In light of the reference in *Saunders* to evidence, which exists independently of the will of the suspect, E&W's case law, similarly to US case law, now accepts that pre-existing documents are already in existence and that compulsory powers thus merely allow for them to come to the attention of the authorities. Thus, the compulsory powers do not lead to the creation of compelled self-incriminating evidence. Case law accepts that trial courts can use their general power to exclude documents where the fairness of the proceedings would require this. In *Beghal*, the UKSC still accepted that the privilege covers pre-existing documents. In *Volaw Trust*, the Privy Council found that it is too categorical to state that Article 6 ECHR is not engaged by compulsion to produce pre-existing documents and it considered that the *Jalloh* test had to be applied.

Belgian courts too have been strongly influenced by the unclear ECtHR case law. Belgian courts, including the CoC, have in principle accepted the PSI's applicability to pre-existing documents. At the same time, part of the case law suggests a distinction between different categories of documents. Documents the existence of which the authorities have sufficient knowledge, due to the legal obligation to create and keep them, do not fall under the PSI's protection according to that case law, whereas other documents would. This approach, incorporated in some statutes, reflects a vision, too restrictive in my opinion, that cases such as *Funke* imply that documents are only covered by the privilege when authorities carry out a fishing expedition for documents of whose existence they are not certain or which they do not know how to get access to. The legal obligation to create documents is imperfect as a distinguishing criterion: broad record-keeping obligations may tend to strongly limit the PSI's scope. Moreover, one can imagine situations where the authorities would know about the existence of documents for which there is no statutory retention duty. The interaction between the offence of obstruction of supervision, an offence enshrined in some specific statutes and the PSI, is complex. The CoC's ruling in *Citibank* and its ruling of 6 November 2018 support the view that, provided that the conditions to invoke the privilege are met, simply refusing to hand over requested documents does not constitute that offence.

A parallel can be drawn between Belgian case law that excludes documents created pursuant to a statutory duty and the American RRD. The privilege has been restricted not only by SCOTUS's case law, which largely abandoned *Boyd* and its adherence to the first of the aforementioned views on documentary evidence, but also by its RRD. According to that doctrine, a person cannot invoke the PSI in relation to records that he is required to keep as a condition of voluntarily engaging in a highly regulated activity, even where this would expose a link in a chain of evidence. Over the years, this doctrine has been applied more broadly. The result of the RRD and the Belgian case law that distinguishes between documents for which there is a legal retention duty and other documents is the same: the privilege does not apply.

Currently, the focus in the USA is on the second theory on documentary evidence. According to that theory, documents exist independently of the person's will, and as long as they do not come into existence due to compulsion, the person is not required to create self-incriminating evidence. Even under this theory, some protection is still granted to the act of production of documents: according to the act of production doctrine, the privilege can still be relevant where the act of actually handing over the documents in itself, rather than the documents' content, has an incriminating testimonial value. This is the case where producing the documents would have testimonial value, namely through the admission of the existence and possession, as well as the authentication of the documents. Nevertheless, the act of production is not protected if the possession and existence of the documents is a foregone conclusion. This is the case where the authorities have sufficiently precise knowledge of the documents' existence and their possession by the person concerned, in which case the act of producing them no longer has an incriminating value. *Hubbell* has nevertheless indirectly increased the protection offered to the content of documents through a backdoor: where a person has received act of production immunity, the use of the documents' content to build a case against him is only possible where the prosecution can meet its

Kastigar burden to show that it had an independent source to show existence and possession of the documents. Failure to do so would amount to a violation of the derivative use immunity.

As far as encrypted evidence is concerned, E&W courts, like their US counterparts, consider that the protected data exists independently of the person's will, yet they both provide some limited PSI protection as they accept that knowledge of the decryption key can have some incriminating value. Case law of the CoC and the ConsC accepts that a suspect can be required to provide access to a protected device or data, yet not to operate and search for specific data. The CoC ruled that the key is considered to be neutral as such and should be distinguished from the possibly incriminating data that can be obtained through the IT system. E&W has foreseen a specific set of rules as to whom should provide the electronic key in a corporate context.

The PSI's effectiveness partly depends on the timing of its availability. Chapter eight showed that determining the stage of (non)-punitive proceedings as of which a person can invoke the privilege is crucial. The ECtHR considers that the PSI is available in punitive cases. It has, in relation to non-punitive cases, repeatedly addressed two issues. In the first type of cases, information obtained in non-punitive cases under the threat of sanctions is later admitted in a punitive case, while in the second line of cases a person is already implicated in a punitive case, or such a case is anticipated, while a non-punitive investigation is similarly pending. The ECtHR ruled that the PSI was violated by the use at a *sensu stricto* criminal trial stage of statements obtained under compulsion in a non-punitive investigation. In *Marttinen*, a parallel proceedings case, it found that the PSI applied also in the non-punitive case. The ECtHR pays particular attention to the (un)availability of limited use rules. The CJEU has accepted that the PSI applies in EU competition cases from the investigating stage onwards. In *DB v Consob*, it held that an individual can rely on it in an insider dealing investigation that can lead to punitive penalties. It added that the need to respect the privilege in an investigation by a supervisory authority which cannot lead to a punitive penalty could also stem from the possibility that evidence is later used in punitive proceedings against that person. The implications of the latter judgment for corporations are uncertain.

In E&W, the privilege applies at the pre-trial and trial stages of a punitive case, as well as in non-punitive proceedings. Should the defendant decide to testify at his *sensu stricto* criminal trial, he can be cross-examined. Yet, several statutory restrictions, including in the framework of SFO investigations, have been introduced. In investigations which can be non-punitive, individuals and corporations are often under a punishable duty to cooperate. Many of those should be considered in light of the argument that limited use provisions can be used to protect the interest of the person who would be required to self-incriminate, while at the same time, other parties still have access to evidence. Such a limited use rule does indeed tackle the ECtHR's criticism expressed in *Saunders*. In extrajudicial investigations, particularly if the authority involved is merely looking into facts without having the power to launch a punitive case, *R v Herts CC Ex p Green Environmental Industries* suggests a reduced willingness to allow one to invoke the PSI, at times even in the absence of a limited use rule. Case law has accepted that the use of such evidence at a punitive trial can be precluded. Meanwhile, *Volaw Trust* affirms that breaches of Article 6 ECHR can also take place where one is compelled to self-incriminate in the course of extrajudicial inquiries.

Determining the PSI's applicability *ratione temporis* is not self-evident in Belgium, particularly where the proceedings' aim, punitive or non-punitive, is not clear from the outset. Non-punitive investigations can easily turn into punitive ones. Often civil servants of special inspection services can check compliance with the specific legislation for which they are competent, such as social law or environmental law, while they can also detect and gather information on offences that they have come across. It may thus be difficult to decide in which capacity these inspectors are acting. Specific statutory instruments furthermore impose cooperation duties, without providing a limited use rule. Once there is a reasonable suspicion that an offence has been committed, there is a (punitive) investigation. The CoC considers the privilege to be available once a criminal investigation is pending or anticipated. It considers the PSI to be inapplicable in purely administrative investigations aimed at making material findings to ensure compliance with applicable regulations, while the person who faces such investigation is not accused of an infringement or faces the threat of prosecution. In order to avoid evidence being later deemed inadmissible due to a violation of a safeguard such as the PSI, guidelines from the College of Prosecutors General cautiously recommend applying these safeguards from an early stage, also where the choice is made for administrative enforcement rather than *sensu stricto* criminal enforcement. It is understood that the former type of enforcement would often be punitive in light of the *Engel* criteria. In *sensu stricto* criminal cases, the PSI's availability is widely accepted. Defendants can decide to answer only some of the questions at their trial, unlike in E&W and the USA.

In the USA, a person can invoke the privilege in any type of proceedings, provided that the evidence sought is within the PSI's material scope and is self-incriminating and that compulsion is present. SCOTUS has adopted this broad position essentially to avoid a person being compelled in a non-punitive case to provide self-incriminating evidence that can be used in a punitive case. In other words, when a person cannot face such a punitive case, the PSI does not apply. The *Miranda* rules, which include a notification of the PSI, are mandatory in the context of custodial police interviews. The PSI is available in grand jury proceedings, yet SCOTUS does not require that the questioned person be notified of the possibility of invoking it, though DOJ guidelines stipulate that this should be done. At his *sensu stricto* criminal trial, the defendant enjoys an unqualified right (not) to testify.

Chapter nine showed that the PSI can be waived, as one may decide to adopt a cooperative attitude. The ECtHR has accepted that one can validly waive the PSI, yet it has attached importance to the waiver's voluntary character. In order to be valid, it must be unequivocal and surrounded by minimum safeguards, and must not run counter to an important public interest.

The CJEU has accepted that in competition cases, one can voluntarily make self-incriminating statements and thus waive the privilege.

In E&W, it is accepted that the PSI can be waived, both pre-trial and at trial. Testifying at trial amounts to a waiver of the privilege as one exposes oneself to cross-examination. Whether agreeing to a contractual PSI waiver is possible is unclear. Case law in relation to persons acting as a fiduciary has rejected the suggestion that one implicitly agrees not to rely on the privilege, just like it has been rejected that an agent cannot rely on the privilege. Yet provisions on the membership of the Institute of Chartered Accountants that preclude relying on the privilege have passed judicial scrutiny.

Belgian case law and doctrine accept, similarly to the ECtHR, that the privilege can be waived. At least one Belgian FiC has applied the idea of voluntary waiver in a particularly broad way: by engaging in a regulated activity, one waives one's privilege. That approach seems to be at odds with *Saunders*. Signing a contractual PSI waiver seems difficult to reconcile with the required voluntary character of the waiver, as one lacks information of what might happen in the future. Moreover, one can wonder whether an employee can, in light of the corporation's power, really freely decide to waive the privilege.

Under US federal law, too, one can waive the privilege, yet any waiver is proceedings-specific. US case law has been tolerant toward poor Fifth Amendment protection of employees, at least in cases where an internal investigation is ongoing. Only in rare cases are US courts willing to strike down practices where a private sector employee risks losing his employment for failure to waive the privilege.

In order to determine whether a corporation can waive its PSI in those legal systems where such privilege is available, one needs to ascertain which individuals can invoke the corporation's PSI. Where multiple individuals can do so, one may wonder whether one can challenge the waiver's voluntariness if one individual has waived the privilege against the other individuals' will.

Chapter ten started with a brief consideration of the CCL models used or promoted by the different legal systems considered in this book, a necessary step in testing my hypothesis.

The CoE tackled corporate, criminal or alternative liability mechanisms that appeared in a Recommendation as long ago as in the late 1980s. According to that instrument, legal persons should enjoy rights and guarantees equivalent to those enjoyed by individuals suspected of crime. Later on, CoE conventions required the adoption of CCL or other mechanisms. The liability of legal persons is, under the approach taken in those instruments, either triggered when an individual with a leading position commits an offence covered by a Convention or the legal entity is liable where another individual commits the offence and relevant supervision or control is lacking. The offence should be committed for the corporation's benefit or on its behalf. The EU CCL model (or alternative liability) corresponds to the one adopted in the CoE Corruption Convention.

Traditionally, the USA and E&W have adopted a model that derives CCL from specific individuals, unlike the Belgian model, which takes an anthropomorphic approach.

The traditional English model of CCL[1876] limits the circle of individuals whose behaviour may trigger CCL. According to the identification doctrine, only the acts and *mens rea* of senior officers can be taken into account for the purpose of CCL, as these are considered to be the corporation's. In addition to that doctrine, qualified vicarious liability has been introduced more recently, through failure to prevent offences. The CMCHA has introduced a more 'realistic' approach to CCL.

The Belgian anthropomorphic CCL model, adopted in 1999, was set up not as a vicarious liability system, but as an autonomous liability model, assimilating legal persons with natural persons. A corporation can face liability even in the absence of an identified individual. Like the US requirement that the offence committed by the employee can benefit the corporation, Belgian law has set in place connecting factors between the wrongdoing and the corporation's interests. In order to establish *mens rea*, an intentional decision taken within the corporation is needed, or a corporate negligence that has a causal link with the offence. Even where the offence is imputed to a leading individual within the corporation, this does not by itself suffice, as an own fault of the corporation remains necessary. In single person corporations, finding a corporate *mens rea* distinct from the individual's one is typically difficult.

The US model was developed in the early twentieth century, at a time when the country was confronted with the power of rapidly developing corporations. The focus was therefore on a model that allowed for effective enforcement against corporations: the USA adopted a broad *respondeat superior* model. It assumes that the corporation is in the best position to supervise its employees and to prevent them from committing offences. The corporation can face vicarious liability for the acts of its officers, agents and employees in the course of their employment. These acts and omissions need to be within the scope and nature of the person's employment, provided that the act partly or wholly benefits the corporation. The broad approach differs from the E&W identification doctrine, as it does not focus on the leading individuals within the corporation. It stands in stark contrast with the anthropomorphic Belgian approach, where a corporation can face liability even in the absence of an identified individual. This particularly broadly construed liability model has been taken even further by some controversial case law, which has accepted the collective knowledge doctrine. Although it is not difficult to trigger, in practice the number of federal corporate convictions is low.

Some legal systems have made clear and explicit choices as to the PSI's (in)applicability to corporate entities, whereas others are less explicit on the matter.

[1876] At least for offences requiring a blameworthy mental state. Simple vicarious liability is typically used for regulatory offences.

The ECtHR's case law fits in the latter category. No explicit decision has been handed down in which corporations are granted or denied the PSI's protection. Its case law is nevertheless highly relevant.

Cases dealing with sanctions, including fines for failure to provide statements or other evidence, are particularly interesting. If one applies these cases *mutatis mutandis* to corporations, I think that the ECtHR could be willing to accept that corporations can face compulsion and thus be entitled to the PSI's protection. The level of fines will in this sense be a relevant factor. Case law on damages shows that the Court is willing to look beyond the paper entity, and psychological or physical pressure on corporate officers or employees may be relevant. The second rationale attributed to the PSI by the ECtHR focuses on the connection between the PSI and the POI. That rationale is relevant for corporations too. If the privilege is an essential feature that allows a party to freely set up its defence strategy, corporations should similarly benefit from it. Nevertheless, I pointed out that this rationale at times considers the privilege as a protection of the balance between the state and private parties. The state has significant power when it builds a case against someone. Critics may argue that the issue of finding a fair balance between the state and private parties applies differently where the state confronts a corporation as the latter can have great economic power and vast resources. That is an overly broad generalisation that overlooks significant differences between different types of corporations. Moreover, even a multinational corporation is impacted by an investigation by the authorities, for instance through searches at the corporate premises, arrests of key officials or an official decision to charge the corporation, combined with media coverage. Focusing on the wealth of corporations in order to set them apart from individuals is also misguided in the sense that it fails to acknowledge that as long as they can both face punitive liability, they face a similar risk, and the POI and the privilege are thus relevant for both categories.

Saunders, a case involving a chief executive, suggests that the ECtHR does not find that by accepting a position of corporate official one waives one's personal PSI in relation to those corporate activities. The refusal to accept the complexity of corporate fraud as an overriding reason to restrict the PSI suggests that the Court would accept including corporations within its scope. At the same time, one may wonder whether *O'Halloran* will have an impact. In that case, the ECtHR found that those who own and use cars accept certain responsibilities and obligations as part of the regulatory regime linked to motor vehicles. Could one say that by choosing to operate one's business through a corporation, a choice that entails advantages such as limited liability, one subjects oneself to a regulatory regime? That case law is only firmly established in relation to road traffic offences, and *Saunders* shows that corporate officers are not excluded from the PSI. Nevertheless, certain elements in the Court's case law may cast doubt on its willingness to apply the privilege to corporations. First, it cannot be excluded that some of the *Jalloh* criteria, such as the nature and degree of compulsion, are applied more leniently when the applicant is a corporation. This could result in a very restrictive approach to the privilege of corporations, or possibly even a refusal to apply it to them. One can wonder whether the ECtHR's finding that there are criminal cases that do not amount to the hard core of criminal law would have an impact on the PSI in a case that involves a corporation and charges which are not part of the hard core of criminal law. So far, the ECtHR has been critical of restrictions on the PSI, particularly where they harm its essence.

Also with regard to Article 6 ECHR rights, the Court has not systematically lowered its protection because the applicant was a corporation. Outside the PSI's context, the Court has held several procedural safeguards protected by Article 6, including the POI, to be applicable to corporations and it has accepted that corporations are entitled to a fair trial. In other cases dealing with legal aid and taxes that had an impact on corporations' access to a court, the Court has at times referred to the lack of a consensus in the MSs of the CoE on the topic of legal aid for corporations, without, however, attaching decisive value to this argument. The Court has repeatedly applied Article 6(1) ECHR broadly. In a case on the excessive delay of a national court to decide a case, the Court accepted that a corporation can be the victim of an Article 6 violation where such a delay occurs. Interestingly, the Court accepted that it cannot be excluded that commercial companies should receive compensation for non-pecuniary damage, referring to its reputation, uncertainty in decision-making or disruption in the company's management. The Court again stressed the need to interpret the Convention in such a way that it ensures practical and effective rights. The factors to which the Court has pointed are particularly relevant as they tend to overlap with some of the elements that come up in the context of the prosecution of corporations. The Court's willingness to consider these elements may indicate that it would be willing to do so too in cases where corporations claim the PSI. In relation to Article 8 ECHR cases, the Court accepted that with regard to legal persons, more far-reaching interferences may be accepted than in the case of a natural person.

The CJEU has, contrary to the ECtHR, expressly ruled on the PSI of corporations in competition cases. Undertakings can be required in such cases to provide answers to (some) factual questions and to hand over pre-existing documents, but not to produce an oral or written admission of a violation of EU competition law. In order for this privilege to be effective, it is imperative to critically assess whether a question does in fact, rather than in form, require an admission of a breach of competition law. The CJEU's case law in competition cases reflects the Court's concern that the acceptance of a broad privilege could be an obstacle for the effective enforcement of competition law. This approach is in general more restrictive than the CJEU's *DB v Consob* ruling, yet that case dealt with an individual facing insider trading proceedings. Although its case law shows the applicability of several rights enshrined in the CFR to corporations, case law addressing the PSI of corporations outside the sphere of competition cases is lacking. The exact implications of *DB v Consob* for corporations are somewhat unclear. Given the fact that the preliminary reference involved a natural person, the CJEU did not have to answer the thorny question of whether corporations can benefit from a broader PSI in punitive cases, other than competition ones. I recall that though the EP tried to include legal persons within the POI Directive's scope, the adopted text excludes them from its scope.

E&W courts have repeatedly held that corporations can benefit from the privilege. Case law on the issue is rather limited, taking into account that it had accepted the corporate PSI as long ago as 1939. Where a corporate official appears on behalf of the corporation, he can exercise its privilege. Nevertheless, the adopted approach is very formal: where a person is called to testify personally, he can apparently not refuse to testify by arguing that this would incriminate the corporation. Were the person at the same time to incriminate himself by testifying against the corporation, he could rely on his own privilege. The formal approach suggests that the corporate privilege is at risk of being circumvented by requiring a person to testify in his personal capacity. Meanwhile, courts have also held that a corporation cannot refuse to provide evidence by arguing that it would incriminate its shareholders or officials. Since the privilege applies to corporations in E&W, my analysis on the privilege of individuals is to be applied *mutatis mutandis* to corporations.

Belgian case law on the corporation's privilege is limited. The CoC accepted, as had one of the CoA's before it, that corporations can rely on the PSI and that it covers documents to a certain extent. In my view, this approach can be explained by the anthropomorphic treatment of corporations in Belgian criminal law and thus by their freedom to set up their defence. Many questions remain unanswered in Belgium, including which individuals within the corporation can rely on the privilege of the corporation. For that reason, several authors have presented models of the corporate privilege, but case law on the issue is lacking. What is particular to the Belgian setting is that a statutory regime has been put in place on the representation of the corporation where its legal representative is prosecuted along with the corporation.

Corporations cannot benefit from the PSI in the USA, unlike in E&W and Belgium. The longstanding restrictive US approach, the CED, precludes corporations from relying on the Fifth Amendment self-incrimination clause. Its impact is not limited to the corporations themselves as it also prohibits corporate officials and employees from refusing to hand over corporate documents both in situations where doing so would only incriminate the corporation and in cases where they would incriminate themselves personally. The CED developed gradually, and in *Hale*, SCOTUS did not accept that a corporate official could refuse to hand over documents by arguing that doing so would incriminate the corporation. In *Wilson*, it ruled that a corporate officer could not refuse to hand over corporate documents where they would tend to incriminate him personally and where he and not the corporation was targeted by the grand jury. The Court did not accept the suggestion that the officer's own privilege protected him. SCOTUS relied on the argument that the documents belonged to the company. The employee thus held them in his official, representative capacity, and the fact that an employee has them in his possession or that he drafted them does not change their status as corporate documents. At the same time, SCOTUS confirmed that corporate employees could not be forced to provide oral testimony that would incriminate them personally unless they are provided with immunity. The CED applies even to one-person corporations and SCOTUS held in those cases too that the production of the documents is not a personal act, but the corporation's.

The underlying justifications for the different approaches to corporations and the PSI are particularly interesting. The PSI's purely personal character was addressed extensively both in the USA and in E&W. This argument can be criticised on a number of counts. First of all, it is accepted that corporations are persons for the purpose of the application of criminal law. Moreover, SCOTUS even accepted that the Fourth Amendment, which refers to 'people', applies to corporations. Corporations essentially rely on individuals in order for the corporation to function or to exercise other constitutional rights. Moreover, SCOTUS accepts that any employee of a corporation can trigger the corporation's criminal liability. It has similarly stressed that where a person produces corporate books, this is not his personal act, but an act of the corporation. It is quite peculiar that a corporate official or employee acts in a representative capacity when he complies with a subpoena, but that the corporation cannot face compulsion through these individuals. It is quite inconsistent to rely on the PSI's personal character to exclude a corporation from its scope, while for so many other purposes it is accepted that acts by individuals can be considered to be the corporation's. The purely personal character of the PSI has also influenced E&W case law: although the courts accept that corporations can rely on the privilege, they have done so in a restrictive way. Corporations cannot refuse to provide evidence where it would incriminate its officials: allowing this would run counter to the PSI's personal nature. Similarly, E&W courts criticised the idea that the corporate PSI would allow corporate officials and employees to refuse to provide evidence by arguing that it would incriminate the corporation. In practice, this has resulted in narrow protection for corporations. In Belgian case law, the personal character of the privilege has not received significant attention in the debate on the corporate PSI.

Another reason invoked by US courts is that with the choice of adopting the corporate form come obligations. One of these obligations is that corporations, which owe their existence to the state, need to allow investigations into their contracts and checks on the use of their powers. This reasoning can be linked to the American derivative CCL model, which also refuses to consider corporations in an anthropomorphic way. Similarly, the visitorial power argument is part of the idea that corporations are creatures of law, who owe their existence to the state, and it can be contrasted with the idea that corporations are 'real actors'. A similar reasoning was relied upon by the government in *Saunders*, where it was suggested that choosing to use a corporate form has a price. Even though the classic E&W CCL model is also derivative, it shows slightly more willingness to try to find a corporate identity. That the argument that with the benefit of incorporation come obligations has not been prominent in Belgium might be an indication that corporations are indeed considered in an anthropomorphic way there.

A further reason to exclude corporations from the privilege in the USA is that it would render enforcement against corporations very difficult. This argument has come up in several SCOTUS rulings. Excluding corporations from the scope of the privilege on the basis of this argument is not entirely convincing, and the CJEU's case law in competition cases shows that less intrusive approaches can be taken. Suffice it to recall that since *Hale* the privilege has in general been restricted on several points: reduced protection of documentary evidence through the *Fischer* doctrine and the RRD, and a transition from transactional immunity to the less protective use and derivative use immunity. Nevertheless, SCOTUS continues to rely on the law enforcement argument. Similar arguments have been made in E&W, but in a more general way, in order to justify sector-specific provisions that restrict the privilege in general and thus not only for corporations. Similarly, Belgian case law on the topic has relied on the effective law enforcement argument in a more general way. There, too, the focus was on regulating economic activities, which are often of high relevance for corporations, rather than on the PSI's applicability to corporations as such. A corporate PSI does not take away the other tools available to law enforcement authorities to gather evidence, eg through searches, cooperating witnesses or whistleblowers. Even in countries where the privilege is available to corporations, they can have strong incentives to cooperate. Moreover, as I have pointed out, corporations are particularly vulnerable to the selective use of immunity or of compelled cooperation powers, which can help authorities gather evidence against the corporations by granting key individuals immunity.

Some other arguments have received less attention than one may have expected: the argument that corporations cannot directly face physical or psychological compulsion and the difficulty of applying the privacy rationale to corporations have not been extensively addressed in case law. Although some of the leading E&W cases have at times critically referred to the absence of improper compulsion in the context of misbehaviour in an economic context, this has not led to the PSI's unavailability to corporations. The CoA accepted the argument that corporations cannot suffer all the pains an individual can suffer, but it pointed to the grave consequences if it were to be convicted.

My argument that corporations can face a modified version of the cruel trilemma through their officials and employees has not been considered explicitly in case law. Even in situations where corporate employees or officials would not be at risk of self-incrimination, they could face that trilemma in the absence of a corporate privilege: if they refuse to testify against the corporation, they may face sanctions; they may similarly face sanctions if they try to protect it by telling lies; and if they do speak the truth, they can contribute to the conviction of the corporation for which they work. The employee or corporate official who would provide incriminating evidence against the corporation could thus still face a harsh choice as he might be required to bite the hand that feeds him. The cruelty of incriminating someone with whom one has close ties has at times been accepted as a reason for not testifying against that person. These cases are typically limited to relatives or spouses, and they do not include one's employer. Admittedly, the relationship between an individual and a corporation is typically not as close as those between spouses and between close family members.

E&W and Belgian courts have connected the availability of a corporate privilege to CCL. In other words, such reasoning presupposes that if corporations can face criminal liability, like individuals, they too should be able to rely on the privilege. In both countries, the privilege is thus seen as playing a role in guaranteeing that one can freely set up one's defence strategy, and it similarly has links with the POI.

In the introductory chapter, I launched the hypothesis that the model of CCL has an impact on whether and to what extent the privilege applies to corporations. My research has not provided conclusive evidence on the correctness of my hypothesis. I did, however, find several indications that the CCL model has an impact on the (un)willingness to accept a corporate privilege. For example, the Belgian anthropomorphic approach to CCL is matched by a willingness to accept a corporate PSI. The US CCL model focuses on the wrongdoing of one or more employees, instead of recognising the corporation as an independent actor. In E&W, too, a corporate PSI was accepted in a case where the CoA concluded that the elements of the offence could be proven against a corporation.

Regardless of their position on the corporate PSI, the different systems all have tools that can incentivise corporations to cooperate. Mechanisms of negotiated justice are often welcomed by corporations as they may be able to avoid the stigmatising effects of lengthy and uncertain punitive proceedings, a public trial and a possible conviction. Guidance documents of the prosecuting authorities in E&W as well as in the USA emphasise the importance of corporate cooperation when deciding whether to prosecute a corporation or not. At the present time, the published prosecutorial guidelines in Belgium suggest that settlements are not used to encourage corporations to provide evidence against corporate officials or employees.

Chapter eleven brought together the different pieces of the jigsaw puzzle that I found in the previous chapters in order to set up a balanced corporate PSI. Among the different models of the corporate PSI, the most balanced model is, in my view, a model which allows the corporation's legal representatives, as well as leading individuals, to exercise it. That model avoids the pitfall of being under- or overinclusive. The corporation's privilege applies where the corporation, through certain individuals, faces compulsion[1877] to provide self-incriminating evidence. The model I propose does not as such exclude the use of adverse inferences. The evidence in relation to which the PSI can be invoked can include oral statements,

[1877] Yet see n 1860.

as well as documentary evidence. In order to balance the privilege, compelled production of pre-existing self-incriminating documents would still be allowed, albeit only where it is used in non-punitive cases and not in a punitive case against the corporation, unless it provided wrongful information. Moreover, corporations can, like individuals, waive their privilege. In order to secure corporate cooperation, tools such as settlements are useful. They will often lead to evidence to which the authorities would otherwise not have access.

BIBLIOGRAPHY

Achilles JL et al, 'United States' in J Seddon et al (eds), *The Practitioner's Guide to Global Investigations – Volume II: Global Investigations around the World*, 4th edn (Law Business Research, 2019) 567–84

Adam S, Colette-Basecqz N and Nihoul M, *La responsabilité pénale des personnes morales en Europe* (die Keure, 2008)

Afschrift T, 'Le rôle du fisc dans la procédure pénale' [2006] *Revue générale du contentieux fiscal* 283

Agostino F and Sannicandro LA, 'Invoking the Fifth Amendment in Audits with Offshore Issues: Required Records under the Bank Secrecy Act, Greenfield and Continuation Penalties' (2016) 18 *Journal of Tax Practice & Procedure* 5

Albano J and Sanyshyn A, 'Corporate Criminal Liability' (2016) 53 *American Criminal Law Review* 1027

Alen A and Muylle K, *Handboek van het Belgisch Staatsrecht* (Kluwer, 2011)

Allegrezza S and Rodopoulos I, 'Enforcing Prudential Banking Regulations in the Eurozone: A Reading from the Viewpoint of Criminal Law' in K Ligeti and V Franssen (eds), *Challenges in the Field of Economic and Financial Crime in Europe and the US* (Hart Publishing, 2017) 233–64

Allen C, Taylor C and Nairns J, *Practical guide to evidence*, 5th edn (Routledge, 2016)

Allen RJ et al, *Criminal Procedure: Adjudication and the Right to Counsel* (Wolters Kluwer, 2020)

Alschuler AW, 'Two Ways to Think about the Punishment of Corporations' (2009) 46 *American Criminal Law Review* 1359

Amar AR and Lettow RB, 'Fifth Amendment First Principles: The Self-Incrimination Clause' (1994–95) 93 *Michigan Law Review* 857

Anderson JF, 'Constitutional Dilemmas on the Corporate Regulatory and Fifth Amendment Arc' (2020) *Charleston Law Review* 375

Andersson H, *Dawn Raids Under Challenge: Due Process Aspects on the European Commission's Dawn Raid Practices* (Hart Publishing, 2018)

Arlen J and Buell SW, 'The Law of Corporate Investigations and the Global Expansion of Corporate Criminal Enforcement' (2020) 93 *Southern California Law Review* 697

Ashworth A, 'Self-Incrimination in European Human Rights Law – a Pregnant Pragmatism?' (2008) 30 *Cardozo Law Review* 751

Babin A, 'Corporate Criminal Liability' (2021) 58 *American Criminal Law Review* 671

Baer M, 'Three Conceptions of Corporate Crime (and One Avenue for Reform)' (2020) 83 *Law and Contemporary Problems* 1

Baer M, 'Corporate Criminal Law Unbounded' in RF Wright, KL Levine and RM Gold (eds), *The Oxford Handbook of Prosecutors and Prosecution* (Oxford University Press, 2021) 475–96

Baer MH, 'Law Enforcement's Lochner' (2021) 105 *Minnesota Law Review* 1667

Baert A, *Douane en accijnzen* (Wolters Kluwer, 2021)

Bailleux A, 'The Fiftieth Shade of Grey Competition Law, "Criministrative Law" and "Fairly Fair Trials"' in F Galli and A Weyembergh (eds), *Do Labels Still Matter?* (Editions de l'Université de Bruxelles, 2014) 137–52

Barker L, Combs M, Lyles K, Perry HW Jr and Barker T Jr, *Civil Liberties and the Constitution – Cases and Commentaries*, 9th edn (Routledge, 2011)

Barnes W, 'Hadley v Baxendale and Other Common Law Borrowings from the Civil Law' (2005) 11 *Texas Wesleyan Law Review* 627

Bauwens T and Cornelis L, 'Settlement Agreements in Criminal Cases' in A-P André-Dumont, I De Meuleneere and AS Pijcke (eds), *The Increasing Impact of Human Rights Law on the Financial World* (Anthemis, 2016) 133

Bauwens T, Vandebeek M and Lamberigts S, 'Belgium' in S Lach, M Hamwi and N Lubojanski (eds), *European Investigations Guide 2018* (Hogan Lovells International LLP, 2018) 39–46

Beale SS, 'A Response to the Critics of Corporate Criminal Liability' (2009) 46 *American Criminal Law Review* 1481

Beale SS, 'The Development and Evolution of the US Law of Corporate Criminal Liability', http://scholarship.law.duke.edu/cgi/viewcontent.cgi?article=5910&context=faculty_scholarship

Beale SS, 'Die Entwicklung des US-amerikanischen Recht der strafrechtlichen Verantwortlichkeit von Unternehmen' (2014) 126 *Zeitschrift für die Gesamte Strafrechtswissenschaft* 27

Beale SS and Felman JE, 'The Fifth Amendment and the Grand Jury' (2007) 22 *Criminal Justice* 4

Beale SS et al, *Grand Jury Law and Practice* (Clark Boardman Callaghan, 2021)

Beccaria C, *An Essay on Crimes and Punishments (translation)* (Little and co, 1872)

Beccaria C, *Traité des délits et des peines- traduction française* (Edition Cujas, 1966)

Bechor G, *God in the Courtroom: The Transformation of Courtroom Oath and Perjury between Islamic and Franco-Egyptian Law* (Brill, 2012)

Beernaert M-A, 'La recevabilité des preuves en matière pénale dans la jurisprudence de la Cour européenne des droits de l'homme: nouvel état de la question' in I Bouiouklíev and P Dhaeyer (eds), *La théorie des nullités en droit pénal* (Anthemis, 2014) 69–90

Beernaert M-A, Bosly HD and Vandermeersch D, *Droit de la procedure pénale*, 9th edn (die Keure, 2021)

Bekaert P, 'De rechten van verdediging in strafzaken' in X, *De Praktijkjurist XX* (Story, 2013) 226–40

Benzidi S and Lefèvre F, *Gros plan sur la FSMA: Chronique de jurisprudence depuis la création de la Commission des sanctions à nos jours* (Larcier, 2021)

Berger M, *Taking the Fifth* (Lexington Books, 1980)

Berger M, 'Self-Incrimination and the European Court of Human Rights: procedural issues in the enforcement of the privilege' [2007] *European Human Rights Law Review* 514

Berkmoes H, 'Verhoor-Regelgeving-Consultatie en bijstand door een advocaat- Proces-verbaal- Rechten arrestanten (Salduz-wet)' in X, *Postal Memorialis. Lexicon strafrecht, strafvordering en bijzondere wetten* (Kluwer, 2014) V112

Bernard TJ, 'The Historical Development of Corporate Criminal Liability' (1984) 22 *Criminology* 3

Bharara P, 'Corporations Cry Uncle and Their Employees Cry Foul: Rethinking Prosecutorial Pressure on Corporate Defendants' (2007) 44 *American Criminal Law Review* 53

Billing FMW, *The Right to Silence in Transnational Criminal Proceedings* (Springer, 2016)

Bisgrove M and Weekes M, 'Deferred Prosecution Agreements: A Practical Consideration' [2014] *Crim LR* 416

Bleustein IK, Kelleher LJ and Zeitz-Winston D, 'Corporate Criminal Liability' (2015) 52 *American Criminal Law Review* 851

Bloch A, 'Ook de eenhoorn bestaat en hij kan spreken' [2019] No 382 *Juristenkrant* 13

Bogan P, 'Self-Incrimination, the Privilege, and the Reverse Burden of Proof' in M Colvin and J Cooper (eds), *Human Rights in the Investigation and Prosecution of Crime* (Oxford University Press, 2009) 347–75

Bonita Chatterjee B, 'New but Not Improved: A Critical Examination of Revisions to the Regulation of Investigatory Powers Act 2000 Encryption Provisions' (2011) 19 *International Journal of Law and Information Technology* 264

Böse M, 'Die verfassungsrechtlichen Grundlagen des Satzes "Nemo tenetur se ipsum accusare"' [2002] *Goltdammer's Archiv fur Strafrecht* 98

Böse M, 'Corporate Criminal Liability in Germany' in M Pieth and R Ivory (eds), *Corporate Criminal Liability – Emergence, Convergence and Risk* (Springer, 2011) 227–54

Bosly HD, 'Le droit au silence pendant la phase administrative de la surveillance du respect des lois sociales' in CE Clesse (ed), *L'auditorat du travail: compétences civiles et pénales (Liber amicorum Robert Blondiaux)* (Larcier, 2012) 417–43

Braeckmans H and Houben R, *Handboek vennootschapsrecht* (Intersentia, 2020)
Brown JA and Burlingame RA, 'USA' in D Kelly and C Black (eds), *Corporate Investigations 2021* (ICLG, 2021) 139
Bucy PH, 'Why Punish? Trends in Corporate Criminal Prosecutions' (2007) 44 *American Criminal Law Review* 1287
Buell SW, 'Criminal Procedure Within the Firm' (2007) 59 *Stanford Law Review* 1613
Buell SW, 'Is the White Collar Offender Privileged?' (2014) 63 *Duke Law Journal* 823
Bulteel C et al, 'Arbeidsveiligheid en aansprakelijkheid' in X, *Aanwerven. Tewerkstellen. Ontslaan* (Kluwer, 2019)
Byl T et al, *Financieel rechercheren* (Politeia, 2020)
Carbasse JM, 'Les origines de la torture judiciaire en France du XIIe au début du XIV siècle' in B Durand (ed), *La torture judiciaire – approches historiques et juridiques* (Centre d'histoire judiciaire éditeur, 2002) 381–419
Carpenter CJ, 'Federal Prosecution of Business Organizations: The Thompson Memorandum and its Aftermath' (2007) 59 *Alabama Law Review* 207
Chalus D, 'La dialectique "aveu-droit au silence" dans la manifestation de la vérité judiciaire en droit pénal comparé' (2009) 43 *La Revue Juridique Themis* 321
Choi BH, 'For Whom the Data Trolls: A Reunified Theory of Fourth and Fifth Amendment Jurisprudence' (2015–16) 37 *Cardozo Law Review* 185
Choo AL-T, *The Privilege against Self-Incrimination and Criminal Justice* (Hart Publishing, 2013)
Claes AL and Horseele M, 'Finding nemo (tenetur)? Een stand van zaken en de toepassing in het douanerecht' [2021] *Nullum Crimen* 384
Clesse CE, 'Aperçu de jurisprudence en droit pénal social (2013–2015)' [2016] *Droit pénal de l'entreprise* 121
Clesse CE and Heirman JC, *Procédure pénale sociale* (Larcier, 2020)
Coffee JC, '"No Soul to Damn: No Body to Kick": An Unscandalized Inquiry into the Problem of Corporate Punishment' (1980–81) 79 *Michigan Law Review* 386
Cole L, 'Reexamining the Collective Entity Doctrine in the New Era of Limited Liability Entities – Should Business Entities Have a Fifth Amendment Privilege?' (2005) *Columbia Business Law Review* 1
Collin JP and Rosenblatt S, 'La transaction pénale' in X, *Droit pénal et procédure pénale* (Kluwer, 2020) 27–55
Comisky I, Feld L and Harris S, *Tax Fraud and Evasion: Offenses, Trials, Civil Penalties* (Thomson Reuters, 2021)
Conings C, 'Statusupdate: Belgische opsporing- voelt zich #verward bij het speuren in sociale media' in E Lievens, E Wauters and P Valcke (eds), *Sociale media anno 2015: Actuele juridische aspecten* (Intersentia, 2015) 267–304
Conings C, 'De medewerkingsplicht van houders van kennis (art. 88quater en 90quater, §4 Sv)' in J Kerkhofs and P Van Linthout (eds), *Cybercrime 3.0* (Politeia, 2019) 533–69
Conings C and De Keersmaecker R, 'To Save but Not Too Safe: hoogste Belgische rechters zien geen graten in het decryptiebevel voor de verdachte' [2020] *Tijdschrift voor Strafrecht* 163
Conings C and Royer S, 'Verzamelen en vastleggen van digitaal bewijs in strafzaken' [2017] *Nullum Crimen* 311
Cras S and Erbežnik A, 'The Directive on the Presumption of Innocence and the Right to Be Present at Trial' [2016] *Eucrim* 25
Daube M, 'Nouvelles obligations de déclaration fiscale: exigence légitime ou auto-incrimination prohibée?' [2013] *Revue générale du contentieux fiscal* 249
Dauchy S, 'La torture judiciaire dans les anciens Pays-Bas' in B Durand (ed), *La torture judiciaire – approches historiques et juridiques* (Centre d'histoire judiciaire éditeur, 2002) 507–38
Davis FT, *American Criminal Justice* (Cambridge University Press, 2019)
Day C and Hodges L, 'Witness Interviews in Internal Investigations: The UK Perspective' in J Seddon et al (eds), *The Practitioner's Guide to Global Investigations – Volume I: Global Investigations in the United Kingdom and the United States, 4th* edn (Law Business Research, 2019) 122–50

Declercq R, 'Le droit au silence' in Centre interuniversitaire de droit comparé, *Rapports belges au IXe Congrès de l'Académie internationale de droit comparé* (CIDC, 1974) 611–26

Declercq R, *Beginselen van strafrechtspleging*, 6th edn (Kluwer, 2014)

de Formanoir E, 'La nouvelle loi sur la responsabilité pénale des personnes morales' in C De Valkeneer and HD Bosly (eds), *Actualités en droit pénal 2019* (Larcier, 2019) 66–96

Delanote M, 'Het zwijgrecht van een tot medewerking gehouden belastingplichtige' in B Peeters et al (eds), *Liber Amicorum Stefaan van Crombrugge* (RMG, 2020) 269–84

Delanote M, 'Hof van Justitie erkent ruime draagwijdte van het zwijgrecht' [2021] No 7 *Fiscale Actualiteit* 5

de la Serna I, 'Discours prononcé par Monsieur le Procureur général I de la Serna – Le droit au silence', www.om-mp.be/om_mp/files/en-savoir-plus/mercuriales/parquets%20generaux/Mons/PG%20Mons%20mercuriale%202014.pdf

de la Serna I, 'Le droit au silence' [2015] *Le Pli juridique* 3

Delvaux M, 'L'intérêt du mandataire ad hoc depuis la reformulation de l'article 5 du Code pénal' [2020] *Recueil annuel de jurisprudence en droit des sociétés commerciales* 202

De Meyer GM and Van Den Elzen EWF, 'Tortura incognita – Het pijnlijk verhoor in de Zuidelijke en Noordelijke Nederlanden tijdens de middeleeuwen' (1986) 54 *Legal History Review* 307

De Nauw A, 'De rechten van de mens, stuwende kracht van een nieuwe golf van penalisering in het social en fiscaal strafrecht' [2001] *Tijdschrift voor Strafrecht* 216

De Nauw A, 'Het zwijgrecht in het strafrecht van het bedrijfsleven' in F Moeykens et al (eds), *De Praktijkjurist XVI* (Story Publishers, 2010) 249–69

De Nil N, 'Het verval van de Strafvordering voor sommige misdrijven onder bepaalde voorwaarden' [2018] *Nullum Crimen* 439

Dennis I, 'Instrumental Protection, Human Right or Functional Necessity? Reassessing the Privilege Against Self-Incrimination' (1995) 54 *CLJ* 342

Dennis I, *The Law of Evidence*, 5th edn (Sweet & Maxwell, 2013)

De Raedt S, *De draagwijdte van het recht op privéleven bij de informatie-inzameling door de fiscale administratie* (Larcier, 2017)

Deruyck F, 'Het is lastig te pleiten zonder toga – Over het onhoudbare artikel 2bis VTSv' [2013] *Nullum Crimen* 89

Deruyck F, 'De rechten van verdediging van de rechtspersoon in de Belgische strafprocedure: van verre evident, maar verre van evident' [2016] *Nullum Crimen* 17

Deruyck F, *Overzicht van het Belgisch algemeen strafrecht* (die Keure, 2021)

De Schepper K and Verbruggen F, 'Ontsnappen space invaders aan onze pacmannen? De materiële en formele strafrechtsmacht van België bij strafbare weigering van medewerking door elektronische dienstverleners' [2013] *Tijdschrift voor Strafrecht* 143

De Smet B, 'Het beginpunt van de redelijke termijn in zaken van sociaal strafrecht' [2000–01] *RW* 623

De Smet B, 'De regelmatigheid van bewijs afkomstig uit het buitenland, de eed van de verdachte en te laat neergelegde conclusies' [2015–16] *Rechtskundig Weekblad* 1104

De Troyer I and Vandenberghe L, *Fiscale procedure inkomstenbelasting* (Intersentia, 2020)

De Valkeneer C, *Handboek Strafonderzoek* (Politeia, 2018)

De Vel G, 'La responsabilité pénale des personnes morales dans les instruments juridiques du Conseil de l'Europe' in S Adam, N Colette-Basecqz and M Nihoul (eds), *Corporate Criminal Liability in Europe* (La Charte, 2008) 343

Dewandeleer D, 'Misdrijven en strafonderzoek in de IT-context' in R Verstraeten and F Verbruggen (eds), *Themis Straf- en strafprocesrecht* (die Keure, 2010) 125–63

Dewey J, 'The Historic Background of Corporate Legal Personality' (1926) 35 *Yale Law Journal* 655

De Wolf D, 'Recente ontwikkelingen in het bewijsrecht (2013–2019)' in F Deruyck (ed), *Strafrecht – In/uit balans* (die Keure, 2020) 1–77

Diamantis M, 'The Body Corporate' (2020) 83 *Law and Contemporary Problems* 133

Diamond PS, *Federal Grand Jury Practice and Procedure* (Juris Publishing, 2014)

Dine J, 'Criminal Law and the Privilege Against Self-Incrimination' in S Peers and A Ward (eds), *The European Union Charter of Fundamental Rights* (Hart Publishing, 2004) 269–86

Doak J, McGourlay C and Thomas M, *Evidence: Law and Context*, 5th edn (Routledge, 2018)
Dressler J and Michaels AC, *Understanding Criminal Procedure – Volume 2: Adjudication* (Lexis Nexis, 2006)
Dressler J and Michaels AC, *Criminal Procedure – Investigation* (Lexis Nexis, 2013)
Duane JJ, 'The Extraordinary Trajectory of Griffin v California: The Aftermath of Playing Fifty Years of Scrabble with the Fifth Amendment' (2015) 3 *Stanford Journal of Criminal Law and Policy* 1
Dubuis OF and Ostorero M, 'La torture en Suisse occidentale (XIVe–XVIIIe siècles)' in B Durand (ed), *La torture judiciaire – approches historiques et juridiques* (Centre d'histoire judiciaire éditeur, 2002) 539–98
Durand B, 'Réflexion préliminaire: Une histoire juridique de la torture est-elle possible?' in B Durand (ed), *La torture judiciaire – approches historiques et juridiques* (Centre d'histoire judiciaire éditeur, 2002) 1–37
Edward D and Lane R, *Edward and Lane on European Union Law* (Edward Elgar, 2013)
Eerens F, 'De vraag om inlichtingen: vraag maar raak?' [2015] *Tijdschrift voor Fiscaal Recht* 386
Eichbauer MH, 'Medieval Inquisitorial Procedure: Procedural Rights and the Question of Due Process in the 13th Century' (2014) 12 *History Compass* 72
Elias B and Van de Perre S, *Sociale inspectie* (Intersentia, 2021)
Emmerson B, Ashworth A and Macdonald A, *Human Rights and Criminal Justice*, 3rd edn (Sweet & Maxwell, 2012)
Engelhart M, 'Corporate Criminal Liability from a Comparative Perspective' in D Brodowski et al (eds), *Regulating Corporate Criminal Liability* (Springer, 2014) 53–76
Esmein E, *History of Continental Criminal Procedure* (Little, Brown and Company, 1913)
Faure M and Waeterinckx P, 'De strafrechtelijke verantwoordelijkheid van de rechtspersoon: een blik op de rechtspraak en enkele knelpunten uit de praktijk' [2004] *Tijdschrift voor Strafrecht* 318
Feldman D, 'Corporate Rights and the Privilege Against Self-Incrimination', in D Feldman and F Meisel (eds), *Corporate and Commercial Law* (LLP, 1996) 361–93
Ferguson CM, 'The Required Records Doctrine, the Fifth Amendment Privilege Under Attack' (2011) 115 *Journal of Taxation* 218
Fernandez-Bertier M and Rolland R, 'La transaction pénale élargie appliquée aux personnes morales: cap sur le modèle américain des N/DPAs' [2016] *Droit pénal de l'entreprise* 92
Fisch JE, 'Criminalization of Corporate Law: the Impact on Shareholders and Other Constituents' (2007) 2 *Journal of Business and Technology Law* 91
Fischer J and Clifford A, *The Criminal Finances Act 2017* (Informa Law from Routledge, 2019)
Flore D, *Droit pénal européen*, 2nd edn (Larcier, 2014)
Foyer D, 'Régards théologiques sur la torture (période scolastique)' in B Durand (ed), *La torture judiciaire – approches historiques et juridiques* (Centre d'histoire judiciaire éditeur, 2002) 361–79
Franssen C and Litannie T, *Manuel de procédure fiscale* (Anthemis, 2019)
Franssen C and Traversa E, 'La demande de renseignements adressée au contribuable à l'impôt sur les revenus et le droit de se taire' [2012] *Revue générale du contentieux fiscal* 3
Franssen V, 'Daderschap en toerekening bij de rechtspersoon' [2009] *Nullum Crimen* 227
Franssen V, 'European Sentencing Principles for Corporations' (DPhil Thesis, KU Leuven, 2013)
Franssen V and Verstraeten R, 'La volonté et la faute de la personne morale' [2010] *Journal des Tribunaux* 65
Garrett BL, 'Corporate Confessions' (2008) 30 *Cardozo Law Review* 917
Garrett BL, 'The Constitutional Standing of Corporations' (2014) 163 *University of Pennsylvania Law Review* 95
Garrett BL, *Too Big to Jail* (Harvard University Press, 2014)
Gerstein RS, 'Privacy and Self-Incrimination' (1970) 80 *Ethics* 87
Giacometti M and Grisard L, 'Salduz à la lumière de la jurisprudence: passé, présent et … futur ?' in V Pirson (ed), *Actualités en procédure pénale: de l'audition à l'exécution* (Anthemis, 2020) 29–57
Gilliaux P, Droit(s) européen(s) à un procès équitable (Bruylant, 2012)
Glover R, *Murphy on Evidence*, 14th edn (Oxford University Press, 2015)
Gnedasj S, 'Wat zijn de gevolgen op fiscaal vlak als speurders het zwijgrecht miskennen?' [2014] *Fiscale Actualiteit*, nr 18, 4

Gobert J and Pascal AM, *European Developments in Corporate Criminal Liability* (Routledge, 2011)
Gobert J and Punch M, *Rethinking Corporate Crime* (Cambridge University Press, 2003)
Goldstein H and Witzel SM, *Grand Jury Practice* (Law Journal Press, 2015)
Grano JD, 'Miranda v Arizona and the Legal Mind: Formalism's Triumph over Substance and Reason' (1986–87) 24 *American Law Review* 243
Gray A, 'The Privilege: Using American and European Law to Protect a Fundamental Right' (2013) 16 *New Criminal Law Review* 527
Green BA and Podgor ES, 'Unregulated Internal Investigations: Achieving Fairness for Corporate Constituents' (2013) 54 *Boston College Law Review* 73
Greer S, 'The Privilege, Defence Disclosure, and Confession Evidence' (1994) 21 *Journal of Law & Society* 102
Griffin LK, 'Compelled Cooperation and the New Corporate Criminal Procedure' (2007) 82 *New York University Law Review* 312
Hall D and Hyde R, 'Deferred Prosecution Agreements and Internal Investigations: SFO v Standard Bank' (2016) 31 *Journal of International Banking Law and Regulation* 115
Harris DJ, O'Boyle M, Bates EP and Buckley CM, *Law of the European Convention on Human Rights*, 3rd edn (Oxford University Press, 2014)
Harvey T, 'United Kingdom' in JT Wells (ed), *International Fraud Handbook* (Wiley, 2018) 368–71
Haverkort-Speekenbrink S, *European Non-Discrimination Law – A Comparison of EU Law and the ECHR in the Field of Non-Discrimination and Freedom of Religion in Public Employment with an Emphasis on the Islamic Headscarf Issue* (Intersentia, 2012)
Helmholz RH, 'Origins of the Privilege against Self-Incrimination: The Role of the European Ius Commune' (1990) 65 *New York University Law Review* 962
Helmholz RH, 'The Privilege and the Ius Commune: The Middle Ages to the Seventeenth Century' in RH Helmholz, CM Gray, J Langbein, E Moglen, HE Smith and AW Alschuler (eds), *The Privilege against Self-Incrimination* (University of Chicago Press, 1997) 17–46
Helsen P, 'Lasthebber *ad hoc*' in X, *Strafrecht en strafvordering. Artikelsgewijze commentaar met overzicht van rechtspraak en rechtsleer* (Kluwer, 2019) afl 92, 1–30
Henning PJ, 'The Conundrum of Corporate Criminal Liability: Seeking a Consistent Approach to the Constitutional Rights of Corporations in Criminal Prosecutions' (1995–96) 63 *Tennessee Law Review* 793
Herring J, *Criminal Law*, 9th edn (Oxford University Press, 2020)
Hödlmayr C and Ortiz Blanco L, 'Investigation of Cases (I)' in L Ortiz Blanco (ed), *EU Competition Procedure*, 4th edn (Oxford University Press, 2021) 337–74
Hofkens J and Lenders Y, 'Belgium' in D Kelly and C Black (eds), *Corporate Investigations, 2021* (ICLG, 2021) 37–43
Horowitz DM and Wirth SK, 'The Dead and Resurrection of the Required-Records Doctrine' (2017) 86 *Mississippi Law Journal* 513
Horseele MJ and Verbruggen F, 'Zelfkastijding met een slapstick. Strafrechtelijke aansprakelijkheid van politieke publiekrechtelijke rechtspersonen met eenvoudige schuldigverklaring als enige straf' [2019] *Nullum Crimen* 195
Horseele MJ, Van Dyck S and Franssen V, 'Requiem voor de decumulregel (oud artikel 5, lid 2 Strafwetboek)' [2020] *Tijdschrift voor Strafrecht* 3
Hubert E, *La torture aux Pays-Bas autrichiens pendant le XVIIIe siècle* (Office de publicité J Lebège et Cie, 1897)
Huybrechts L, 'Het niet meewerken aan zijn eigen beschuldiging in belastingzaken' [2014] *Nullum Crimen* 394
Huybrechts L and Rozie M, 'De rechten van de verdediging bij de behandeling ten gronde' [2008] *Nullum Crimen* 106
Huysmans J, *Legitieme verdediging* (Intersentia, 2017)
Huysmans J, 'Het recht op bijstand van een advocaat bij het verhoor: een ruim maar relatief recht' [2020] *Politie & Recht* 40

Inghelram J, *Legal and Institutional Aspects of the European Anti-Fraud Office (OLAF)* (Europa Law Publishing, 2011)

Israel J and LaFave W, *Criminal Procedure, Constitutional Limitations in a Nutshell* (West Academic, 2014)

Jackson JD, 'Re-conceptualizing the Right of Silence as an Effective Fair Trial Standard' (2009) 58 *ICLQ* 835

Jackson JD and Summers SJ, *The Internalisation of Criminal Evidence* (Cambridge University Press, 2012)

Jacobs A and Dister J-F, 'Responsabilité pénale des personnes morales' in X, *Postal Mémorialis. Lexique du droit pénal et des lois spéciales* (Kluwer, 2019), R 130/01–25

Joncheray N, 'De l'usage de l'article 6 CEDH face aux autorités administratives indépendantes dotées d'un pouvoir de sanction' in L Fromont and A Van Waeyenberge (eds), *Actualités de la protection juridictionnelle dans et par l'Union européenne* (Larcier, 2017) 231–57

Jones A and Sufrin B, *EU Competition Law*, 6th edn (Oxford University Press, 2016)

Jones CA, 'Into the parallel universe: procedural fairness in private litigation after the Damages Directive' in P Nihoul and T Skoczny (eds), *Procedural Fairness in Competition Proceedings* (Edward Elgar, 2015) 209–30

Jörgens K and Ortiz Blanco L, 'Opening of the File' in L Ortiz Blanco (ed), *EU Competition Procedure*, 4th edn (Oxford University Press, 2021) 311–36

Kalintiri A, *Evidence Standards in EU Competition Enforcement – The EU Approach* (Hart Publishing, 2019)

Karambelas NG, *Limited Liability Companies: Law, Practice, and Forms* (Clark Boardman Callaghan, 2021)

Keane A and McKeown P, *The Modern Law of Evidence* (13th edn, Oxford University Press, 2020)

Kéfer F, 'L'employeur est-il tenu d'être présent et actif lors d'un contrôle social?' [2013] *Revue de Jurisprudence de Liège, Mons et Bruxelles* 1861

Kelly HA, *Inquisitions and Other Trial Procedures in the Medieval West* (Ashgate, 2001)

Kent R and Thomas J, 'United States of America' in S Spehl and T Gruetzner (eds), *Corporate Internal Investigation: A Systematic Overview of 13 Jurisdictions* (Hart Publishing, 2013) 401–36

Kerkhofs J and Van Linthout P, *Cybercrime* (Politeia, 2013)

Kerr OS, 'Compelled Decryption and the Privilege Against Self-Incrimination' (2019) 97 *Texas Law Review* 767

Kestler JL, *Questioning Techniques and Tactics*, 3rd edn (Clark Boardman Callaghan, 2021)

Khanna VS, 'Corporate Defendants and the Protections of Criminal Procedure: An Economic Analysis' (2004) Law & Economics Working Papers No 04-015 http://repository.law.umich.edu/cgi/viewcontent.cgi?article=1029&context=law_econ_archive

Klip A, *European Criminal Law*, 4th edn (Intersentia, 2021)

Kloeber R, '"Between the Rock and the Whirlpool": Corporate Cooperation Credit and Issues of Compelled Self-Incrimination' (2018) 32 *Notre Dame Journal of Law, Ethics and Public Policy* 635

Koning F, 'Cour. Eur. DH, Chambaz contre Suisse, 5 avril 2012 Prohibition de l'auto-incrimination' [2012] *Revue générale du contentieux fiscal* 403

Koning F, 'Reconnaissance du droit du citoyen de refuser de donner accès à un système informatique nonobstant l'ordre de la loi, et reconnaissance d'un droit de recours contre un refus du parquet de laisser consulter son dossier d'information' [2016] *Revue de Jurisprudence de Liège, Mons et Bruxelles* 733

Koning F, 'Droit au silence et à ne pas s'incriminer: quo vadis?' [2020] *Journal des Tribunaux* 204

Koops EJ and Stevens L, 'JB versus Saunders. De groeiende duisternis rond nemo tenetur' [2003] *Delikt en Delinkwent* 281

Koops EJ, Conings, C and Verbruggen F, *Zoeken in computers naar Nederlands en Belgisch recht* (Wolf Legal Publishers, 2016)

MJ Kranacher and R Riley, *Forensic Accounting and Fraud Examination*, 2nd edn (Wiley, 2019)

Kuty F, 'L'étendue du droit au silence en procédure pénale' [2000] *Revue de droit pénal et de criminologie* 309

Kuty F, 'Le droit au silence, les investigations de l'administration fiscale et l'enquête pénale' [2008] *Journal des Tribunaux* 386
Kuty F, *Principes généraux du droit pénal belge Tome III: l'auteur de l'infraction pénale*, 2nd edn (Larcier, 2020)
LaFave WR *et al*, *Criminal Procedure*, 4th edn (Thomson West, 2016)
Laird K, 'Fair Trial: Volaw Trust and Corporate Services Ltd v Office of the Controller of Taxes; Volaw Trust and Corporate Services Ltd v HM Attorney General for Jersey Privy Council: Lords Reed, Kerr, Sumption, Carnwath, Hodge, Kitching and Lady Arden: 17 June 2019; [2019] UKPC 29' [2020] *Crim LR* 75
Lamadrid de Pablo A and Kellerbauer M, 'Investigation of cases (II)' in L Ortiz Blanco (ed), *EU Competition Procedure*, 4th edn (Oxford University Press, 2021) 375–415
Lamberigts S, 'The Directive on the Presumption of Innocence. A Missed Opportunity for Legal Persons?' [2016] *Eucrim* 36
Lamberigts S, 'The Privilege against Self-Incrimination: A Chameleon of Criminal Procedure' (2016) 7 *New Journal of European Criminal Law* 418
Lamberigts S, 'Het zwijgrecht van rechtspersonen: aandachtspunten en (supra)nationale perspectieven' [2018] *Tijdschrift voor Strafrecht* 302
Langbein JH, *Torture and the Law of Proof – Europe and England in the Ancien Régime* (University of Chicago Press, 1977)
Langbein JH, 'The Historical Origin of the Privilege against Self-Incrimination at Common Law' (1994) 92 *Michigan Law Review* 1047
Langbein JH, *The Origins of Adversary Criminal Trial* (Oxford University Press, 2003)
Lasagni G, *Banking Supervision and Criminal Investigation – Comparing the EU and US Experiences* (G Giappichelli Editore/Springer, 2019)
Lasagni G, 'Investigatory, Supervisory and Sanctioning Powers within the SSM' in S Allegrezza (ed), *The Enforcement Dimension of the Single Supervisory Mechanism* (Wolters Kluwer, 2020) 49–91
Le Marc'hadour T, 'La question préparatoire dans les Pays-Bas français (1679–1790)' in B Durand (ed), *La torture judiciaire – approches historiques et juridiques* (Centre d'histoire judiciaire éditeur, 2002) 743–800
Lenaerts K, 'Procedural Rights of Private Parties in the Community Administrative Process' (1997) 34 *CML Rev* 531
Lenaerts K, 'How the ECJ Thinks: A Study on Judicial Legitimacy' (2013) 36 *Fordham International Law Journal* 1302
Lenaerts K, 'The Principle of Equal Treatment and the European Court of Justice' [2013] *Il Diritto dell'Unione Europea* 461
Lenaerts K and Van Nuffel P, *EU Constitutional Law* (Oxford University Press, 2021)
Levy LW, *Origins of the Fifth Amendment* (Oxford University Press, 1968)
Levy LW, 'Origins of the Fifth Amendment and Its Critics' (1997) 19 *Cardozo Law Review* 821
Liégeois Y and Bockstaele M, 'Over "toezicht" en "opsporing" door bijzondere inspectiediensten' [2016] *Nullum Crimen* 406
Liégeois Y and De Smet B, 'Twintig jaar zuivering van nietigheden tijdens het gerechtelijk onderzoek. Tijd voor verandering of opfrissing van het systeem?' [2019–20] *Rechtskundig Weekblad* 3
Ligeti K and Robinson G, 'Overprosecution and Negotiated Justice in Europe' in PHPHMC van Kempen and M Jendly (eds), *Overuse in the Criminal Justice System: On Criminalization, Prosecution and Imprisonment* (Intersentia, 2019) 101–28
Ligeti K and Tosza S, 'Challenges and Trends in Enforcing Economic and Financial Crime: Criminal Law and Alternatives in Europe and the US' in K Ligeti and S Tosza (eds), *White Collar Crime – A Comparative Perspective* (Hart Publishing, 2019) 1–34
Lööf R, 'The EPPO and the Corporate Suspect' [2020] *Eucrim* 310
Lööf R, 'DPAs – Judicial Oversight Restated' (2021) 7 *Archbold Review* 4
Lowell AD and Man CD, 'Federalizing Corporate Internal Investigations and the Erosion of Employees' Fifth Amendment Rights' (2011) 40 *Geo LJ Ann Rev Crim Proc* iii
Lowell AL, 'The Judicial Use of Torture' (1897) 11 *Harvard Law Review* 220

Lucraft M (ed), *Criminal Pleading, Evidence and Practice 2021* (Sweet & Maxwell, 2020)
Ludlam J and Garfield H, 'England and Wales' in S Spehl and T Gruetzner (eds), *Corporate Internal Investigation: A Systematic Overview of 13 Jurisdictions* (Hart Publishing, 2013) 105–40
Macculloch A, 'The Privilege against Self-Incrimination in Competition Investigations: Theoretical Foundations and Practical Implications' (2006) 26 *Legal Studies* 211
Macgregor L, Peacey C and Ridsdale G, *Civil Litigation 2020–2021* (Oxford University Press, 2020)
Maclin T, 'Long Overdue: Fifth Amendment Protection for Corporate Officers' (2021) *Boston University Law Review* 1523, 1602
Macnair MRT, 'The Early Development of the Privilege against Self-Incrimination' (1990) 10 *OJLS* 66
Mason S, 'Electronic Evidence: Dealing with Encrypted Data and Understanding Software, Logic and Proof' [2014] *ERA Forum* 25
Masset A, 'La responsabilité pénale des personnes morales' [2011] *Droit pénal de l'entreprise* 3
Matthews P and Malek HM, *Disclosure*, 4th edn (Sweet & Maxwell, 2012)
Maus M, *Handboek fiscale sanctionering* (die Keure, 2017)
Meese J, 'The Sound of Silence. Het zwijgrecht en het nemo tenetur-beginsel in strafzaken. Een historisch en rechtsgevergelijkend overzicht' in A Van Oevelen, S Rutten and J Rozie (eds), *Zwijgrecht versus spreekplicht* (Intersentia, 2013) 37–72
Meese J, 'Recht om te zwijgen maar toch verplicht om te spreken?' [2019–20] *Rechtskundig Weekblad* 1322
Meese J, 'Onrechtmatig verkregen bewijs in strafzaken' in J Rozie, S Rutten and B Vanlerberghe (eds), *Bewijsnood na het vernieuwde bewijsrecht* (Intersentia, 2020) 61–97
Meganck B, 'Strafrechtelijke verantwoordelijkheid van een eenmansvennootschap: het eigen schuldpatroon van de rechtspersoon' [2015] *Tijdschrift voor Strafrecht* 81
Michiels O and Falcque G, 'L'infraction d'obstacle à la surveillance sous le spectre du droit au silence et du droit de ne pas s'auto-incriminer' [2016] *Orientations* 2
Michiels O and Falcque G, *Principes de procédure pénale* (Larcier, 2019)
Minnaert M, 'De Salduz-wet' [2011] *Nullum Crimen* 273
Mitsilegas V, *Money-Laundering Counter-Measures in the European Union* (Kluwer, 2003)
Moglen E, 'The Privilege in British North America: The Colonial Period to the Fifth Amendment' in RH Helmholz et al (eds), *The Privilege against Self-Incrimination* (University of Chicago Press, 1997)
Monballyu J, 'De Raad van Vlaanderen en de hervorming van het Strafrecht (1756–1787)' (1996) 64 *Legal History Review* 48
Monballyu J, *Zes eeuwen strafrecht- de geschiedenis van het Belgische strafrecht (1400–2000)* (Acco, 2010)
Monville P and Holzapfel D, 'Antigone: les évolutions législative et jurisprudentielle en droit pénal … Un bilan navrant et sévère !!!' in S Scarna (ed), *L'évolution de la jurisprudence Antigone sous le triple axe, pénal, social et fiscal* (Larcier, 2016) 21–41
Mulholland M, 'Introduction' in M Mulholland and B Pullan (eds), *Judicial Tribunals in England and Europe, 1200–1700* (Manchester University Press, 2003) 1–17
Munday R, *Evidence*, 10th edn (Oxford University Press, 2019)
Muyshondt N, 'Zwijgrecht in fiscale zaken: wat zijn wilsafhankelijke gegevens?' [2012] No 1302 *Fiscoloog* 7
Naidoo L and Vandercruyssen R, 'United Kingdom' in S Lach, M Hamwi and N Lubojanski (eds), *European Investigations Guide 2018* (Hogan Lovells International LLP, 2018) 264–70
Nanda VP, 'Corporate Criminal Liability in the United States: Is a New Approach Warranted?' (2010) 58 *American Journal of Comparative Law* 605
Nijboer JF, 'A Plea for a Systematic Approach in Developing Criminal Procedural Law Concerning the Investigation, Prosecution and Adjudication of Corporate Entities' in A Esser, G Heine and B Huber (eds), *Criminal Responsibility of Legal and Collective Entities* (MPI, 1999) 303–20
Oliver P, 'Companies and Their Fundamental Rights: A Comparative Perspective' (2015) 64 *ICLQ* 661
O'Neill A, 'The Privilege and the Company' (2004) 39 *Irish Jurist (New Series)* 111
Ormerod D and Laird K, *Smith, Hogan, and Ormerod's Criminal Law* 13th edn (Oxford University Press, 2020)
Ormerod D and Perry D (eds), *Blackstone Criminal Practice 2021* (Oxford University Press, 2020)

Ortiz Blanco L, *EU Competition Procedure*, 4th edn (Oxford University Press, 2021)
Ortiz Blanco L and Jörgens K, 'The Institutional Framework' in L Ortiz Blanco (ed), *EU Competition Procedure*, 4th edn (Oxford University Press, 2021) 4–88
Palmer JG, 'The Fifth Amendment Act of Production Doctrine and the Collective Entity Rule: A Primer' (2018–19) 33 *Criminal Justice* 22
Pattenden R, 'Self-Incrimination and the Threat of Prosecution under Foreign Law: Brannigan v Davison' (1998) 2 *International Journal of Evidence & Proof* 44
Pech L et al, 'Right to an Effective Remedy and to a Fair Trial' in S Peers, T Hervey, J Kenner and A Ward (eds), *The EU Charter of Fundamental Rights: A Commentary* (Hart Publishing, 2014) 1197–1276
Peers S, *EU Justice and Home Affairs Law – Volume II: EU Criminal Law, Policing and Civil Law*, 4th edn (Oxford University Press, 2016)
Pieck M, 'The Accused's Privilege against Self-Incrimination in the Civil Law' (1962) 11 *American Journal of Comparative Law* 585
Pieth M and Ivory R, 'Emergence and Convergence: Corporate Criminal Liability Principles in Overview' in M Pieth and R Ivory (eds), *Corporate Criminal Liability – Emergence, Convergence, and Risk* (Springer, 2011) 3–60
Pihlajamäki H, 'Swimming the Witch, Pricking for the Devil's Mark: Ordeals in the Early Modern Witchcraft Trials' (2000) 21 *Journal of Legal History* 35
Pinto A and Evans M, *Corporate Criminal Liability*, 4th edn (Sweet & Maxwell, 2021)
Pivaty A *et al*, 'Opening Pandora's Box: The Right to Silence in Police Interrogations and the Directive 2016/343/EU' (2021) 12 *New Journal of European Criminal Law* 328
Polaschek M, 'The History of Torture in Austria' in B Durand (ed), *La torture judiciaire – approches historiques et juridiques* (Centre d'histoire judiciaire éditeur, 2002) 599–612
Quirk H, *The Rise and Fall of the Right of Silence* (Routledge, 2017)
Rainey B, McCormick P and Ovey C, *The European Convention on Human Rights*, 8th edn (Oxford University Press, 2021)
Rangaviz DR, 'Compelled Decryption & State Constitutional Protection' (2020) 57 *American Criminal Law Review* 157
Redmayne, M, 'Rethinking the Privilege Against Self-Incrimination' (2006) 27 *OJLS* 209
Roberts P and Zuckerman A, *Criminal evidence*, 2nd edn (Oxford University Press, 2010)
Rochon M *et al*, 'Is It Time to Revisit the Corporate Privilege Against Compelled Self-Incrimination?' [2019] *The Champion* 50
Roef D, 'Corporate Criminal Liability' in J Keiler and D Roef (eds), *Comparative Concepts of Criminal Law*, 3rd edn (Intersentia, 2019) 333–73
Roggen F, 'La responsabilité pénale des personnes morales' in X, *Droit pénal et procédure pénale* (Kluwer, 2015) 97–165
Roles PJ, *The Privilege Against Self-Incrimination* (Lambert Academic Publishing, 2010)
Rose AM, 'Public Enforcement: Criminal versus Civil' in J Gordon and W-G Ringe (eds), *The Oxford Handbook of Corporate Law and Governance* (Oxford University Press, 2015) 946–59
Royer S and Yperman W, 'Wankele argumenten van hoogste Belgische hoven in uitspraken over decryptiebevel' [2020] *Nullum Crimen* 441
Rozie J and Vandermeersch D, *Commissie voor de hervorming van het strafrecht. Voorstel van voorontwerp van boek 1 van het strafwetboek* (die Keure, 2017)
Rozie J, Vanderhallen M and Tersago P, 'Het zwijgrecht als tweesnijdend zwaard: een fundamenteel recht van verdediging of een katalysator voor schuldigverklaring?' [2021] *Nullum Crimen* 461
Rule C, 'United States v Greenfield: A Triumph of the Fifth Amendment's Act of Production Privilege; or Confirmation that the Privilege Can Be Entirely Abrogated by Any Act of Congress, or Even by a Treasury Regulation' 71 (2018) *Tax Law* 335
Sacharoff L, 'Unlocking the Fifth Amendment: Passwords and Encrypted Devices' (2018) 87 *Fordham Law Review* 203
Salky SM, *The Privilege of Silence – Fifth Amendment Protections Against Self-Incrimination*, 3rd edn (American Bar Association, 2019)

Saltzburg SA, 'The Required Records Doctrine: Its Lessons for the Privilege Against Self-Incrimination' (1986) 53 *University of Chicago Law Review* 6

Sanchez Graells A and Marcos F, '"Human Rights" Protection for Corporate Antitrust Defendants: Are We Not Going Overbroad?' in P Nihoul and T Skoczny (eds), *Procedural Fairness in Competition Proceedings* (Edward Elgar, 2015) 84–107

Santucci MR, 'L'exception anglaise' in B Durand (ed), *La torture judiciaire – approches historiques et juridiques* (Centre d'histoire judiciaire éditeur, 2002) 209–40

Sayers D et al, 'Right to an Effective Remedy and to a Fair Trial' in S Peers et al (eds), *The EU Charter of Fundamental Rights: A Commentary* (Hart Publishing, 2014) 1197–1276

Sayers D, 'Presumption of Innocence and Right of Defence (Criminal Law)' in S Peers et al (eds), *The EU Charter of Fundamental Rights: A Commentary* (Hart Publishing, 2014) 1303–50

Schabas WA, *The European Convention on Human Rights – A Commentary* (Oxford University Press, 2015)

Schmoeckel M, 'La survivance de la torture après la chute de l'Empire romain' in B Durand (ed), *La torture judiciaire – approches historiques et juridiques* (Centre d'histoire judiciaire éditeur, 2002) 315–29

Sedley S, 'Wringing Out the Fault: Self-Incrimination in the 21st Century' (2001) 52 *Northern Ireland Legal Quarterly* 107

Signorelli WP, *Criminal Law, Procedure and Evidence* (CRC Press, 2011)

Silving H, 'The Oath: I' (1959) 68 *Yale Law Journal* 1329

Sime S, *A Practical Approach to Civil Procedure*, 23rd edn (Oxford University Press, 2020)

Skarlatos NC, 'The Fifth Amendment Privilege Against Self-Incrimination and Tax Returns: Oil and Water or Peanut Butter and Jelly?' (2016) 18 *Journal of Tax Practice & Procedure* 15

Slobogin C, 'Citizens United and Corporate Human Crime' (2011) 41 *Stetson Law Review* 127

Smith KJ and Colvin Stone LR, 'Conducting Effective Internal Investigations' (2017) 44 *Employment Relations* 91

Soetens E and De Cock S, 'Verslagen studienamiddag van 23 november 2017 – Vereniging voor de Studie van het Mededingingsrecht – Mededingingsrecht met een arbeidsrechtelijk staartje' [2018] *Competitio* 219

Sottiaux S, 'Het gelijkheidsbeginsel: langs oude paden en nieuwe wegen' [2008–09] *Rechtskundig Weekblad* 690

Sottiaux S, *Grondwettelijk recht*, 2nd edn (Intersentia, 2021)

Spagnoli K, 'De ongewenste getuige en het zwijgrecht' [1999] *Tijdschrift voor Fiscaal Recht* 64

Speecke J, *Fiscaal strafrecht en strafprocesrecht* (Kluwer, 2021)

Spencer JR, *La procédure pénale anglaise* (Presses Universitaires de France, 1998)

Spencer JR, 'Introduction' in M Delmas-Marty and J R Spencer (eds), *European Criminal Procedures* (Cambridge University Press, 2002) 1–80

Spencer JR, 'Curbing Speed and Limiting the Privilege' (2007) 66 *CLJ* 531

Spreutels J et al, *Droit pénal des affaires* (Larcier, 2021)

Steinberg MI, *Understanding Securities Law*, 5th edn (LexisNexis, 2009)

Stephens B, 'Are Corporations People? Corporate Personhood under the Constitution and International Law' (2013) 44 *Rutgers Law Journal* 1

Sterkens M, 'Hormonen: de misdrijven' in X, *Postal Memorialis. Lexicon strafrecht, strafvordering en bijzondere wetten* (Kluwer, 2014) H122/1–32

Stessens G, *De nationale en internationale bestrijding van het witwassen* (Intersentia, 1997)

Stessens G, 'The Obligation to Produce Documents versus the Privilege against Self-Incrimination: Human Rights Protection Extended Too Far?' [1997] *EL Rev*, 22 Suppl, 45

Stessens G, 'Procedurele aspecten van de opsporing en de vervolging bij strafbare feiten gepleegd door rechtspersonen' in X, *Bestendig Handboek Vennootschap & Aansprakelijkheid* (Kluwer, 2000) afl 1, 32–47

Stessens G, 'Buitenlandse geheimhoudingsplichten en de spreekplicht voor de Belgische onderzoeksrechter' [2003] *Tijdschrift voor Strafrecht* 193

Stocker T et al, 'United Kingdom' in J Seddon et al (eds), *The Practitioner's Guide to Global Investigations – Volume II: Global Investigations around the World*, 4th edn (Law Business Research, 2019) 528–66
Stoitchkova D, *Towards Corporate Liability in International Criminal Law* (Intersentia, 2010)
Stuntz, WJ, 'The Substantive Origins of Criminal Procedure' (1995–96) 105 *Yale Law Journal* 393
Summers SJ, *Fair Trials – The European Criminal Procedural Tradition and the European Court of Human Rights* (Hart Publishing, 2007)
Tarvin TR, 'The Privilege Against Self-Incrimination in Bankruptcy and the Plight of the Debtor' (2014) 44 *Seton Hall Law Review* 47
Tersago P, 'De voorlichting van verdachten over hun procedurele rechten als fundamentele waarborg voor het recht op een eerlijk proces' [2018] *Politie & Recht* 183
Tersago P, Verklaringen van verdachten in het strafproces (Intersentia, 2020)
Thomas W, 'Corporate Criminal Law Is Too Broad – Worse, It's Too Narrow' (2021) 53 *Arizona State Law Journal* 199
Tilleman B and Van Damme N, *Proceshandelingen van en tegen rechtspersonen* (die Keure, 2020)
Tompkins AM, Avergun J and Duncan JR, 'Witness Interviews in Internal Investigations: The US Perspective' in J Seddon et al (eds), *The Practitioner's Guide to Global Investigations – Volume II: Global Investigations around the World*, 4th edn (Law Business Research, 2019) 151–58
Trainor SA, 'A Comparative Analysis of a Corporation's Right Against Self-Incrimination' (1994) 18 *Fordham International Law Journal* 2139
Tran TP et al, 'Managing Cross Border Internal Investigations' (2020) 24 *Currents: Journal of International Economic Law* 52
Treschel S, *Human Rights in Criminal Proceedings* (Oxford University Press, 2006)
Tushnet M, 'Do For-Profit Corporations Have Rights of Religious Conscience?' (2013) 99 *Cornell Law Review* 70
Uhlmann DM, 'Deferred Prosecution and Non-Prosecution Agreements and the Erosion of Corporate Criminal Liability' (2013) 72 *Maryland Law Review* 1295
Van Bavel H, 'De Wet van 4 mei 1999 tot invoering van de strafrechtelijke verantwoordelijkheid van de rechtspersonen' [1999–2000] *Algemeen Juridisch Tijdschrift* 209
Van Bavel H, 'De strafrechtelijke aansprakelijkheid van vennootschappen en leidinggevenden – De lege lata, de lege ferenda' [2017] *Tijdschrift voor Strafrecht* 3
Van Bavel H and Verwaerde D, 'Enième réforme de la transaction pénale: la fin des controverses?' [2018] *Journal des Tribunaux* 765
Vanbiervliet F and Visschers A, *Taxatie- en geschillenprocedure* (Gompel & Svacina, 2020)
Van Caenegem RC, *Geschiedenis van het Strafprocesrecht in Vlaanderen van de XIe tot de XIVe Eeuw* (Koninklijke Vlaamse Academie voor Wetenschappen, Letteren en Schone Kunsten van België, 1956)
Van Caenegem RC, 'Reflexions on Rational and Irrational Modes of Proof in Medieval Europe' (1990) 58 *Legal History Review* 263
Van Caenegem RC, *European Law in the Past and Future* (Cambridge University Press, 2002)
Van de Heyning C and Coppens J, 'Het bevel tot medewerking van artikel 88quater Sv, het zwijgrecht en het verbod op zelfincriminatie' [2016] *Tijdschrift voor Strafrecht* 260
Van de Heyning C, 'Het zwijgrecht in digitale tijden: de strijd om decryptiesleutels naar het Grondwettelijk Hof' [2019] *Tijdschrift voor Strafrecht* 307
Van de Heyning C and Tersago P, 'Onderzoeksrechter kan code smartphone afdwingen van verdachte' [2020] *Juristenkrant* 1
Van de Heyning C, 'Presumption of Innocence: Procedural Rights in Criminal Proceedings – Social Fieldwork Research (FRANET)', https://fra.europa.eu/sites/default/files/fra_uploads/belgium-2021-country-research-presumption-innocence_en.pdf
Van De Mosselaer G, 'Sociaal strafrecht- aansprakelijkheid van de rechtspersoon' [2014] *Oriëntatie* 58
Van den Wyngaert C, Vandromme S and Traest P, *Strafrecht en strafprocesrecht in hoofdlijnen*, 11th edn (Gompel & Svacina, 2019)
Vandeplas A, 'Over het verhoor' [2002–03] *Rechtskundig Weekblad* 1095
Vanderkerken C, 'Dwangmaatregelen in het fiscaal onderzoeksrecht: de zaak VW en het actueel belang ervan' [2020] *Tijdschrift voor Fiscaal Recht* 35

Van Dyck, S and Franssen V, 'De strafrechtelijke verantwoordelijkheid van vennootschappen: wie, wanneer en hoe?' in Departement Permanente Vorming van de Orde van Advocaten van de Balie van Kortrijk, *De vennootschap in de verschillende takken van het recht* (Larcier, 2013) 15–55

Van Eeckhoutte W, *Sociaal Compendium 2016–2017* (Kluwer, 2016)

Van Gerven D, 'Grondslagen van het rechtspersonenrecht' [2020] *Tijdschrift voor Privaatrecht* 887

Van Gerven D, *Handboek vennootschappen – Algemeen deel* (Larcier, 2020)

van Kempen PHPHMC, 'The Recognition of Legal Persons in International Human Rights Instruments: Protection Against, and Through, Criminal Justice?' in M Pieth and R Ivory (eds), *Corporate Criminal Liability. Emergence, Convergence, and Risk* (Springer, 2011) 355–89

Vanlerberghe B and Verbist J, 'Le droit de l'avocat de se taire en matière disciplinaire enfin reconnu par la Cour de cassation' [2012] *Revue de Jurisprudence de Liège, Mons et Bruxelles* 342

van Toor DAG, *Het schuldige geheugen? Een onderzoek naar het gebruik van hersenonderzoek als opsporingsmethode in het licht van eisen van instrumentaliteit en rechtsbescherming* (Kluwer, 2017)

Veenbrink M, 'The Privilege against Self-Incrimination in EU Competition Law: A Deafening Silence?' (2015) 42 *Legal Issues of Economic Integration* 119

Veenbrink M, *Criminal Law Principles and the Enforcement of EU and National Competition Law: A Silent Takeover?* (Kluwer Law International, 2019)

Vercauteren V et al, 'De controle' in A Tiberghien (ed), *Tiberghien. Handboek voor Fiscaal Recht* 40th edn (Kluwer, 2021) 1062–1108

Vermeulen G, De Bondt W and Ryckman C, *Liability of Legal Persons for Offences in the EU* (Maklu, 2012)

Verstraeten R, 'Kritische beschouwingen bij het nieuwe strafrechtelijke aansprakelijkheidsregime voor de rechtspersonen' in Jan Ronse Instituut, *Nieuw vennootschaps- en financieel recht 1999* (Biblo, 2000) 231–48

Verstraeten R, *Handboek strafvordering*, 5th edn (Maklu, 2012)

Verstraeten R and Traest P, 'Het recht van verdediging in de onderzoeksfase' [2008] *Nullum Crimen* 85

Verstraeten R and Verbruggen F, *Strafrecht en strafprocesrecht voor bachelors*, 13th edn (Intersentia, 2020)

Vested-Hansen J, 'Respect for Private and Family Life (Private Life, Home and Communications)' in S Peers, T Hervey, J Kenner and A Ward (eds), *The EU Charter of Fundamental Rights: A Commentary* (Hart Publishing, 2014) 153–82

Voordeckers O and Lamberigts S, 'Belgium' in S Allegrezza (ed), *The Enforcement Dimension of the Single Supervisory Mechanism* (Wolters Kluwer, 2020) 181–233

Waeterinckx P, 'De (afgeleide) rechten van verdediging van de rechtspersoon. Heeft een rechtspersoon het recht te zwijgen, eventueel met of zonder bijstand van een raadsman?' [2015] *Nullum Crimen* 73

Waeterinckx P, *De strafrechtelijke verantwoordelijkheid van de rechtspersoon en zijn leidinggevenden* (Intersentia, 2015)

Waeterinckx P, 'De eenpersoonsvennootschap en de grenzen van het antropomorfisme. Botst de autonome strafrechtelijke verantwoordelijkheid van de rechtspersoon werkelijk op haar grenzen bij de eenpersoonsvennootschap, of is dit het gevolg van rechtspraak die het antropomorfisme niet volledig doortrekt?' [2016] *Nullum Crimen* 58

Waeterinckx P, 'Strafrechtelijke verantwoordelijkheid van en binnen de onderneming (bestuurders, bedrijfsleiders en rechtspersonen)' in P Waeterinckx et al (eds), *Strafrecht in de onderneming*, 3rd edn (Intersentia, 2016) 171–248

Waeterinckx P, Deruyck F and Van Volsem F (eds), *Strafrecht in de onderneming*, 3rd edn (Intersentia, 2016)

Waeterinckx P, 'Het aanwenden van rechtsmiddelen voor de rechtspersoon door de lasthebber ad hoc, een verdere verfijning van de rechtspraak van het Hof van Cassatie' [2017] *Nullum Crimen* 78

Waeterinckx P, 'De strafrechtelijke verantwoordelijkheid van de rechtspersoon – Moet de regeling i.v.m. de lasthebber ad hoc onder artikel 2bis VTSv. "op de schop" omwille van de afschaffing (?) van de decumulatieregel onder oud artikel 5, tweede lid Sw.?' [2019] *Tijdschrift voor Belgisch Handelsrecht* 949

Waeterinckx P and Van Herpe R, 'De wettelijke regeling i.v.m. de strafrechtelijke verantwoordelijkheid van de rechtspersoon ontdoet zich na 19 jaar van twee groeipijnen' [2018] *Nullum Crimen* 541
Wahl T, 'The European Public Prosecutor's Office and the Fragmentation of Defence Rights' in K Ligeti et al (eds), *The European Public Prosecutor's Office at Launch* (Wolters Kluwer, 2020) 85–113
Walden I, *Computer Crimes and Digital Investigations*, 2nd edn (Oxford University Press, 2016)
Ward T and Gardner P, 'The Privilege against Self-Incrimination: In Search of Legal Certainty' [2003] *European Human Rights Law Review* 388
Ward T et al, '13. Enforcement and Procedure' in D Bailey and LE John (eds), *Bellamy & Child European Union Law of Competition*, 8th edn (Oxford University Press, 2019) 1123–1249
Wells C, 'Corporate Manslaughter: Why Does Reform Matter?' (2006) 123 *African Law Journal* 648
Wells C, 'Corporate Criminal Liability in England and Wales: Past, Present and Future' in M Pieth and R Ivory (eds), *Corporate Criminal Liability – Emergence, Convergence and Risk* (Springer, 2011) 91–112
Wells C, 'Economic Crime in the UK' in K Ligeti and S Tosza (eds), *White Collar Crime – A Comparative Perspective* (Hart Publishing, 2019) 253–75
Wells JT, *International Fraud Handbook* (Wiley, 2018)
Werding A, 'La responsabilité des personnes morales: au revoir décumul, bienvenue responsabilité pénale de l'état?' in V Franssen and A Masset (eds), *Actualités de droit pénal et de procédure pénale* (Anthemis, 2019) 73–130
Werquin T, 'Droit pénal social: le droit de ne pas contribuer à sa propre incrimination, le droit au silence et l'obstacle à la surveillance' [2000] *Journal des Tribunaux* 81
Weyembergh A and Joncheray N, 'Punitive Administrative Sanctions and Procedural Safeguards – a Blurred Picture that Needs to be Addressed' (2016) 7 *New Journal of European Criminal Law* 190
Whelan P, *The Criminalization of European Cartel Enforcement – Theoretical, Legal and Practical Challenges* (Oxford University Press, 2014)
Whitman JQ, 'The Transition to Modernity' in MD Hubber and T Hörnle (eds), *The Oxford Handbook of Criminal Law* (Oxford University Press, 2014) 84–110
Wigmore JH, *A Treatise on the System of Evidence in Trials at Common Law Including the Statutes and Decisions of All Jurisdictions of the United States* (Little, Brown & Co, 1905)
Wijsman LCA and Delanote M, 'Het zwijgrecht en niet-meewerkrecht in de rechtspraak van het EHRM met enkele reflecties vanuit het Belgisch fiscaal (sanctie)recht' in M Delanote et al (eds), *Fiscaal en sociaal strafrecht – wegwijzer doorheen het labyrint* (Story Publishers, 2021) 387–429
Williams ML, Patel AP and Gardener J, 'Employee Rights: The US Perspective' in J Seddon et al (eds), *The Practitioner's Guide to Global Investigations – Volume I: Global Investigations in the United Kingdom and the United States*, 4th edn (Law Business Research, 2019) 256–68
Wissink L, *Effective Legal Protection in Banking Supervision* (European Law Publishing, 2021)
Wood SG and Scharffs BG, 'Applicability of Human Rights Standards to Private Corporations: An American Perspective' (2002) 50 *American Journal of Comparative Law* Suppl 531
Zeeman A, *Dulden of meewerken? – een onderzoek naar de toepassing van het nemo tenetur-beginsel bij de sfeerovergang van controle naar opsporing* (Gompel & Svacina, 2019)
Zuckerman A, 'The Privilege against Self-Incrimination May Not Confer a Right to Refuse Disclosure of Incriminating Documents that Came into Existence Independently of the Disclosure Order' [2007] *Civil Justice Quarterly* 395

INDEX

www.ingramcontent.com/pod-product-compliance
Ingram Content Group UK Ltd.
Pitfield, Milton Keynes, MK11 3LW, UK
UKHW020905190926
475560UK00010B/275

9 781509 953318